POETICA 30

The Divine Comedy

Poetica *is a series of texts, translations and
miscellaneous works relating to poetry*

Poetry by Peter Dale

WALK FROM THE HOUSE

THE STORMS

MORTAL FIRE

MORTAL FIRE: SELECTED POEMS

CROSS CHANNEL

ONE ANOTHER

TOO MUCH OF WATER

A SET OF DARTS: EPIGRAMS
(with W.S. Milne and Robert Richardson)

EARTH LIGHT

EDGE TO EDGE: NEW AND SELECTED POEMS

In translation

FRANÇOIS VILLON: SELECTED POEMS

THE SEASONS OF CANKAM
(with Kokilam Subbiah)

NARROW STRAITS

POEMS OF JULES LAFORGUE

Dante

THE DIVINE COMEDY

HELL · PURGATORY · HEAVEN

*A Terza Rima Version
by Peter Dale*

ANVIL PRESS POETRY

Published in 1996
by Anvil Press Poetry Ltd
Neptune House 70 Royal Hill London SE10 8RF
Reprinted with corrections 1998

ISBN 0 85646 287 X (hb)
ISBN 0 85646 280 2 (pb)

A catalogue record for this book
is available from the British Library

Peter Dale has asserted his right under the Copyright, Designs and
Patents Act, 1988 to be identified as the author of this book

This book is published with financial assistance from
The Arts Council of England

Designed and typeset in Monotype Dante at
Libanus Press, Marlborough, Wiltshire
Printed in Great Britain at
Alden Press Limited
Oxford and Northampton

CONTENTS

Dante: A Brief Life   VII

Introduction   IX

A Short Bibliography   XXIII

HELL   I

PURGATORY   139

HEAVEN   279

The Illustrations   416

Index of Proper Names   417

ACKNOWLEDGEMENTS

Thanks and gratitude are due to many people. First and foremost my gratitude goes out to all those scholars and translators of Dante whose researches and enthusiasms have encouraged and enabled the making of this version – a short bibliography appears at the end of the Introduction.

I am grateful to the editors of the following publications in which parts of this version have appeared: *Acumen*; *Agenda*; *Antigonish Review* (Canada); *Outposts*; *The Swansea Review*; *Words International*.

More personally, I should like to record my thanks, for their help, improvements and encouragement, to the following people: my wife, Pauline, who is now justifiably tired of the name of Dante and all his works; William Cookson who lent me many texts and made many suggestions up to the penultimate text; Kenneth Crowhurst for his support and critical comments; Humphrey Clucas for his prosodic vigilance; Roland John for his reading of versions and enthusiastic support. I am also grateful to Peter Jay and to Bill Swainson for the patience with which they offered valuable suggestions for improvements while seeing the book through the press and tolerated last-minute changes of mind. Lastly, I should like to thank Antonio D'Alfonso who first believed in this version and kept alive my hopes of seeing it in print.

P. D.

JULY 1996

DANTE: A BRIEF LIFE

DANTE ALIGHIERI was born in 1265 into the lesser nobility of Florence, traditionally of the Guelf faction in the politics of the time. His mother died in his childhood; his father had children by a second marriage. In 1274 an incident occurred that shaped Dante's life and work, his meeting with Beatrice – to judge by its results, one of the most astonishing encounters in history, if factually true. But, in 1277, his father arranged a marriage for him with Gemma Donati, daughter of a leading noble family. In 1283 his father died; on May Day Dante encountered Beatrice for the second and last time.

Detailed knowledge of Dante's life is sparse but it is known that on 11 June 1289 he was among the Guelf horsemen at the battle of Campaldino where the Ghibellines were defeated. In December, Beatrice's father died, as did Beatrice herself six months later. In 1290, he wrote *La Vita Nuova* (The New Life) which shows how his idealized love for her inspired most of his work.

It is assumed that Dante married Gemma around 1291. They had two sons and probably two daughters. He is recorded among the knights who welcomed Charles Martel, the Anjou prince, to Florence in 1294. He joined the Guild of Apothecaries and Physicians on 6 June 1295 in order to qualify to enter public and political life. From November to April 1295–6 he was a member of the People's Council of Florence. In 1300 he was sent as a special envoy to San Gemignano; on 15 June he was elected as a Prior of the Guilds, one of the six chief magistrates in Florence. Pope Boniface excommunicated these men in the September. Dante fortunately escaped this penalty as he was no longer in office. However, he was sent with two others to negotiate with Boniface in Rome where he was left largely kicking his heels. The rival faction within his party, the Neri or Blacks, seized power and Dante was faced with either a heavy fine or banishment. As an innocent man he refused to pay and was forced into exile – which was later made perpetual on pain of being burned alive. In 1303 his sons were also banished. His wife never accompanied him into exile.

Despite, or because of, these troubles, he worked on *Il Convivio* (The Banquet) and *De Vulgari Eloquentia* (Concerning Common Speech) during 1304–7. In 1310 his political hopes were raised when Henry VII entered Italy with his army, though the subsequent amnesty towards Dante's faction, the Bianchi, or Whites, did not include him. In 1313 his hopes finally faded with the collapse of the invasion when Henry unexpectedly died. However, still active, Dante wrote urgently to the cardinals begging them to return the papal see from Avignon to Rome. Then, with all real political hope gone, he communicated his ideals in his book *Monarchia* (Monarchy) which he probably wrote during 1312–14. On 6 November 1315, the sentence of exile and the penalty of death were confirmed against Dante and his sons. Between 1315 and 1321 he worked on his masterpiece, *La Divina Commedia* (The Divine Comedy) – though the imagined date of the recording of events within it was 1300. He died in Ravenna on 14 September 1321.

INTRODUCTION

'The reader who comes freshly to Dante will see very quickly that
no other secular author is so absolutely convinced that his own work
is the truth, all of the truth that matters most.'

HAROLD BLOOM, 'The Strangeness of Dante: Ulysses and Beatrice' in
The Western Canon (1994)

I

THE DIVINE COMEDY is probably, in theme and execution, the greatest
epic of the western world, certainly outside of the classical languages.
Dante himself never applied that term to his poem since in its happy
ending, episodic sequence and vernacular language, he felt he was not
aiming for the sublime and tragic qualities associated with the true epic.
Yet his chosen form gave him a freedom to include material that has made
his work more comprehensive and thus more epic in its dimensions than
others of more rigid definition.

Where Homer and Vergil were much concerned with wars leading to
the founding of nations and empires, Dante's subject was no less than the
war between good and evil in and for the soul, the conflict of darkness and
light, the foundations of the eternal. The poem's closest parallel in all but
style is Milton's *Paradise Lost*, a poem many consider by comparison to set
in high relief the excellences of Dante's work.

Dante and Milton were 'Not sedulous by Nature to indite / Warrs,
hitherto the onely Argument / Heroic deem'd' (*Paradise Lost* 9.27), though
humankind, and angels, being what they are, wars come into both poems –
Milton's ludicrous war in Heaven directly, and the Guelf-Ghibelline
conflicts by report in Dante. The extraordinary quality of Dante's imagina-
tion is his ability to give his vast subject a concrete realization: the reader
assents to his assertion about his experience in the poem, that 'I was there'.
In so presenting his picture of the after-life almost as the topography of his
own mind Dante has internalized the exterior struggles of earlier epic as
has Milton in his study of the psychology of Satan. Indeed, in the ambience
of the two poems, Dante's Satan is a token figure beside Milton's ruined
angel of light – one of the few areas of the subject where Milton shows a
clear superiority.

In parallel with its epic dimensions, Dante's work also contains – in its
formal skills, its imagery, and the inclusion within it of dramatic and lyrical
modes – a microcosm of European poetry in essence.

In structure, as the protagonist in the poem, Dante, accompanied by Vergil through Hell, Vergil and Statius through Purgatory, and Beatrice through Heaven, journeys from sinful internecine Italy towards reconciliation with Beatrice and with Edenic nature. Beatrice then guides him into the empyrean and the light of God. Through meetings in the course of this journey / pilgrimage with sinners, penitents and saints, Dante as a poet presents us with a cross-section of human thought and history; through encounters with heroes, poets and factionists from his own day, he also provides a contemporary view. Add to this his skill in using the liturgy and services of the church as framing devices and the sheer range of content in the poem becomes amazing yet never burdensome.

Both Milton and Dante were more original and tangential in religious sensibility than many Christian exegetes allow. Dante found his salvation in the poem emotionally through Beatrice; Milton places the redemption of mankind with Christ in the wilderness of temptation rather than in Christ crucified. Uncommitted modern sensibilities may find Milton's concept of the fortunate fall of man more manageable than Dante's Catholic certainties. One could say that an understanding of both poems is needed to comprehend the history of modern Europe. The insights they offer may be found by diligent research elsewhere but these two poems, for all their bulk, give them succinctly and with the added pleasure of poetry.

In speaking next of Dante's influence I concentrate on its effects in the English-speaking communities but his influence is world-wide as is shown for example in the work of writers such as Anna Akhmatova and Osip Mandelstam in Russia. His influence because of his genius for visualization has been wide in the fine arts; one thinks of artists as various as Doré, Botticelli and Blake. It is said that Modigliani could recite the *Inferno* from memory and when drunk was unstoppable. But it is a two-way process and modern scholarship is revealing the influence made on Dante from beyond Europe by the Arabic world and Islamic mysticism.

II

Dante's *Comedy* – the label 'Divine' was added at a later period – became almost immediately popular and influential. His two sons and Boccaccio wrote commentaries upon it as it was almost instantly observed to deal with Catholic truth in open and covert ways, not to mention its methods of handling contemporary events. Six hundred scribal and other copies were produced. Considering the limited means of text-reproduction and communication in the period, Chaucer's knowledge of Dante, only a couple of generations later, is somewhat surprising, even when considering his Italian visits. It is extensive as well as deep. He seems first to know him by reputation, spelling his name Englished as 'Dant' in the early poems but in his mature work shows increased familiarity, using 'Dante'. He must have had texts. (He adapts Bernard's Prayer to Mary (*Heaven* 33) in the '*Invocacio ad Mariam*' in *The Second Nun's Prologue* and the Ugolino episode from *Hell* 32, for *The Monk's Tale*; he cites him in *The Wife of Bath's Tale*, lines 1125–30. There are many other references and reminiscences.) Robinson, in his *The Works of Geoffrey Chaucer*, comments on *The House of Fame*: 'the poem has been regarded – unjustifiably, to be sure – as an imitation of the Divine Comedy.'

From the outset, Dante's pervasive influence was twofold. As a master technician his work had far-reaching effects on poetic form and techniques. As an author committed uncompromisingly to his truth he has had an influence on the world-views of all sorts of unlikely poets, both sympathetic and, like Milton, antipathetic to his religion and philosophy.

Boccaccio, in *Amorosa Visione*, and Petrarch, in his *I Trionfi*, both imitated Dante's terza rima and Chaucer followed suit in England in a short passage in the fragmentary 'A Complaint to his Lady'. But it was Wyatt who first really developed the form to any degree in his 'Satires' and his 'Psalms'. But as he fell foul of Henry VIII so did the Catholic Church, and Dante's influence went largely underground and unacknowledged in England. Indeed, Harold Bloom remarks, in his essay from which the epigraph above is drawn, 'Dante vanished until the nineteenth century; he was scarcely esteemed during the Renaissance and the Enlightenment'. In Italy, also, few poets, it seems, continued the terza rima tradition because of its intrinsic difficulty. If Italians were hesitant it is not surprising that English poets, more restricted in choice of rhyme, were unenthusiastic.

With the stirrings of Romanticism, Dante's vision and technique attracted more interest, a change which may have been helped in the early part of the nineteenth century by the Act of Catholic Emancipation. Blake in his poems and art was the first, most visionary enthusiast but, somewhat surprisingly, Byron was influenced to write his *The Prophecy of Dante* and to use Dante's form:

Many are poets who have never penn'd	*a*
Their inspiration, and perchance the best:	*b*
They felt, and loved, and died, but would not lend	*a*
Their thoughts to meaner beings; they compress'd	*b*
The god within them, and rejoin'd the stars	*c*
Unlaurell'd upon earth, but far more bless'd	*b*
Than those who are degraded by the jars	*c*
Of passion, and the frailties link'd to fame,	*d*
Conquerors of high renown, but full of scars . . .	*c*

(Opening lines of Canto 4)

It captures the onward fluent movement of Dante fairly well. Keats also felt the influence in drafting his second version of *Hyperion* in a more direct Dantescan rather than Miltonic style. But Shelley was the poet most akin to the fluent movement of Dante's verse and form. Ezra Pound, in *The Spirit of Romance*, shows the extent of that influence clearly: 'Few men have honoured Dante more than did Shelley.' He remarks that 'the best of Shelley is filled with memories of Dante' and gives examples. But the influence is clear for all to see. The 'Ode to the West Wind', in using terza rima with couplets every twelve lines to create a sonnet stanza for the ode, shows the influence of the form and incorporates adaptations of Dantescan images. It is in Shelley's unfinished poem 'The Triumph of Life', in title and matter reminiscent of Petrarch, that we find the best, up to that time, reproduction of Dante's impetus and address in English terza rima. Shelley was deeply influenced by Dante's lyrical approach to nature and his portrayal of muse-type women like Matilda in the closing cantos of *Purgatory*. His poem 'Epipsychidion' clearly shows something of his deep response to Dante. Later in the century even Browning, cavalier as a formalist, turned his hand to terza rima, for example in his single canto tale, 'The Statue and the Bust'.

The nineteenth century began the task of translating Dante completely into English. Cary's blank verse translation was the staple for years. He published in this the first Italian text to be printed in England. His *Inferno* appeared in 1805 and the whole *Comedy* in 1814. Coleridge praised its severity and simplicity. Curiously, Cary worked at the British Museum, as did the later translator of Dante, Laurence Binyon, whose terza rima version Pound praised and helped to revise. But few other translators have been keen to reproduce Dante's form, least of all those doing the whole of the *Comedy*. Within certain stylistic limits imposed by the literary expectations of his period, Dante Gabriel Rossetti did a workmanlike and sometimes better job, in *The Early Italian Poets*, of naturalizing Dante's minor poems and those of his contemporaries. The translation that has so far probably done the most to spread Dante's influence in the English-speaking world is the Temple Classics version of the *Comedy* first published by Dent in 1900, using translations by J. A. Carlyle, Thomas Okey, and P. H. Wicksteed respectively for *Inferno*, *Purgatorio* and *Paradiso*. A literal prose translation with a facing Italian text in handy little volumes, it enabled anyone with Latin to puzzle out much of Dante for themselves. Indeed, Eliot, with his usual false modesty, remarks that he could 'read Dante only with a prose translation beside the text'. It was this version.

With Eliot and Pound at the opening of our century the combined influence of Dante as thinker and poet comes together. Eliot, in acknowledgement of Pound's editing of *The Waste Land*, quoted Dante, applying to his friend a phrase concerning Arnaut Daniel (see *Purgatory* 26), 'il miglior fabbro' – the better craftsman. Thus Pound tends always to be considered the master technician whereas, in fact, he was less interested than Eliot in the problems and advantages of terza rima. His interest was in Dante's style and organizational skill in giving fluency and impetus to images and complex ideas. More important, he was influenced by Dante's vision of the world, his concern with justice and good government. He was envious of Dante's possession of what Pound regarded as a complete world-view, of the intellectual, spiritual and civic philosophy with which he could comprehend and contain his contemporary world. *The Cantos* are filled with echoes and reminiscences of Dante and the structure hankers after the tripartite certainties of Dante's three after-worlds that give such a vital vision of this world. But, after a second world war in one's lifetime and being charged as a traitor, it would be difficult for anyone to conceive of a Heaven; a contemporary Hell might come easier. Nor had Pound's Odysseus a handy mentor like Vergil to help him through the journey. As late as the 1940s, Pound was making remarks, like those in the opening of his *Introduction to the Economic Nature of the United States*, that he had schooled himself for forty years to write an epic that began in the dark forest, crossed a purgatory of human error to end in the light. Undeniably the *Cantos* are filled with citations and reminiscences of Dante. The Italian-language Cantos, written before *The Pisan Cantos* but published only fugitively in Pound's lifetime because of their political content, include the closest imitations of Dante in the whole work. One of the most powerful attractions of Dante for Pound was his resolute opposition to usury and the depth to which he consigned the perpetrators in Hell. In *Hell* 11.49–51 and 94–111, Dante, referring to the sin of usury as 'Cahors' (a locality in southern France notorious for usurers) consigns such sinners – because they were contrary to nature and God – to the last group in the seventh circle (*Hell* 17).

Nevertheless, it is easy to agree with Michael Alexander, one of the more commonsensical Pound enthusiasts, when he remarks in *The Poetic Achievement of Ezra Pound* (1979): 'Dante indeed provided an *intermittent* [my italics] model for the structure of the *Cantos*.' Though, in fairness to Pound, one should probably consider also a remark he made in a letter during 1937: 'When I get to the end, pattern ought to be discoverable. Stage set à la Dante is *not* modern truth.' (Quoted in *A Guide to the Cantos of Ezra Pound*, William Cookson, 1985.) Nevertheless, Pound lacked Dante's architectonic skills and frequently got stuck in fragments of luminous detail when it came to developing image and symbol.

Finally, it has to be admitted that Pound's Dante is as eccentric as many of Pound's other enthusiasms in that he conceives of a Dante virtually without Dante's religion. In fact, then, Pound's conception of Dante is almost as astounding as Dante's conception of Beatrice. But, on this point, let Alexander have the last word on the *Cantos*: 'the objective ambitions represented by the "real" history and the moral authority aspired to in emulation of Dante or Confucius are not attained. . . . the Odyssean analogy was more natural and useful to Pound, and accommodated his chaotic Ovidian mythopoeia better than the deep symmetries of Dante.' Still, the *Cantos* are difficult enough to read already, so a knowledge of Dante does help.

On the other hand Eliot, in his remarks on Dante's influence upon him, while he echoes points made by Pound, seems to be concerned chiefly with the terza rima problem.

'Twenty years after writing *The Waste Land*, I wrote, in *Little Gidding*, a passage which is intended to be the nearest equivalent to a canto of the Inferno or the Purgatorio, in style as well as content, that I could achieve.'

'What Dante Means to Me', *To Criticize the Critic*, 1965

Instead of alternating the rhyme in the pattern *aba, bcb, cdc* and so forth, his method was to alternate stressed and unstressed syllables in the same scheme. In the same essay, though, he remarks: 'Nor do I wish to speak now of any debt which one may owe to the thought of Dante, to his view of life, or the philosophy and theology which give shape and content to the Divine Comedy.' Eliot was always chary of addressing deeply personal concerns openly in prose but it is clear from the quotations and appropriations in his work, from the lines adapted in *The Waste Land*, through the pervasive influence in the *Ash Wednesday* poems to the concerns of *Four Quartets*, that Dante had a profound spiritual influence on Eliot's religion, psychology and poetry. But before passing to other points it is worth repeating his opinion in the closing remarks from his essay quoted above: 'No one is more local [than Dante] . . . but I think the foreigner is less aware of any residuum that must for ever escape him . . . than in reading any other master of a language that is not his own.'

The difference between Pound's and Eliot's Dante, then, is that for Eliot Dante, the matchless poet, is also a vital living force in his spiritual quest for order. The complex use of the epigraph from Dante (*Hell* 27.61–6) for 'The Love Song of J. Alfred Prufrock' shows how deeply Dante's thoughts and imagery had invaded Eliot's thinking. Further adaptations occur in *The Waste Land*:

> I had not thought death had undone so many.
> Sighs, short and infrequent, were exhaled, . . .

Their source is in *Hell* 3.55–7.

It is known that Eliot had been deep in Dante before he wrote the

Ash Wednesday poems. In his 'Shakespeare and the Stoicism of Seneca', published the same year as these poems, he was reflecting on Dante's attempt in *La Vita Nuova* (The New Life) to construct something 'permanent and holy' out of 'private failures and disappointments'. In early drafts of the poems he had used citations from Dante for the titles of all except one. These clues, he rightly decided, seemed hardly necessary. The poems themselves clearly show how much he had felt and absorbed of Dante's purgatorial imagery, particularly the three steps into Purgatory proper (*Purgatory* 9.94–108) which he uses in poem III. His poem 'Animula' opens with a line from *Purgatory* 16, and reflects on lines 85–93.

By the time of writing *Four Quartets*, he was using terza rima not as an interesting technical experiment but as a form capable of controlling complex and disturbing experience. The basic source canto for 'Little Gidding' is *Hell* 15 but Eliot is not merely citing, as Pound so often does; he is adapting the form and content to his own deepest feelings.

Yet Eliot's Dante, like Pound's though in a different way, is only another partial Dante. Eliot's view of Dante concentrates on his concern for sin and wickedness and the need for the purgatorial pain of penitence. Eliot responds very little to the almost unconscious fascination that Dante has for life, for men of action, thought and power. Dante wanted to order the heavens and earth; Eliot seems to be struggling to order a single psychology. Eliot has little of Dante's appreciation of detail in nature and in close observation; he has little of Dante's lyrical intensity in producing responses to the larger aspects of nature. Eliot has more sense than Pound of Dante's architectonics, but the structuring of *Four Quartets* is rather laboured and overt compared to the subtlety of Dante; in juxtaposition, they seem a tessellation of formal variations unequally handled.

The obsession with Dante's form reappears in some strange places. Somewhat surprisingly, Edward Thomas, in 'The Ash Grove', and Robert Frost, in 'Stopping by Woods on a Snowy Evening', both adapt terza rima to a quatrain system by doubling up the first *a* rhyme to a couplet. Frost was always interested in the strict form and used it impressively in his terza rima sonnet 'Acquainted with the Night'. Even Allen Tate has tried his hand at terza rima, in slight lyrics, and more extensively and interestingly throughout section three of *The Swimmers and Other Selected Poems* (1970).

A commitment to the form even more large-scale than Eliot's is to be found in Archibald MacLeish's long poem, *Conquistador* (1932), where he uses modern oblique and half-rhymes to accommodate the rhyme and tries to capture the Italian double-rhyme effect by frequently allowing his rhymes a light unrhyming last syllable. To give a more recent example, Dante has had a powerful influence on Seamus Heaney, notably in his poem 'Ugolino' (*Field Work*, 1979).

But their Dante is not my Dante nor your Dante, just as my Hamlet is not your Hamlet. What Arnold said of Shakespeare is true of Dante:

> Others abide our question – thou art free!
> We ask and ask – Thou smilest and art still,
> Out-topping knowledge!

Though a different smile and a different kind of knowledge from Shakespeare's.

III

Important though Dante's influence is, it is Dante the poet that matters most – the poem as poem. Dante is a world poet and there is something in his work for everyone; he is not just a poet's poet, nor even a theologian's poet.

This is not the place to go into the poem's significance on the linguistic level as one of the first works of vernacular literature to compete with the great classics, nor the proper place to indicate its part in the development of the Italian language. Yet something may be said briefly. Dante's skill was to draw on the work of immediate predecessors and contemporaries in the attempt to create a unified Italian language for the highest literary purposes. He puts his case for this in his book *De Vulgari Eloquentia* (Of Common Speech) where he argues that the poets who use Italian are using colloquial forms identifiable with their own cities and regions; that none of them is writing the language identifiable as the whole nation's. He points out failings in the dialect of each city and the use poets make of it and concludes: 'Having, thus, found what we were seeking, we declare that in Italy the Illustrious, Cardinal and Curial Vulgar Tongue is that which belongs to all the towns of Italy but does not appear to belong to any one of them and it is the one by which all the local dialects are measured, assessed and compared.' From his remarks on the Tuscan dialect it is clear which poets have led him to these conclusions: 'Yet stubborn as are almost all Tuscans in keeping to their degraded dialect, we have observed that some have recognized the Vulgar Italian Tongue, namely Guido, Lapo, and another, all Florentines, and Cino of Pistoja . . .'. He refers here to Guido Cavalcanti (*Hell* 10, *Purgatory* 11.97–9), Lapo Gianni, translated in Rossetti's *The Early Italian Poets*, as also the third, Cino of Pistoia. The phrase 'and another' is the way Dante often refers to himself – compare *Purgatory* 11.99. On this point it is interesting to note that in his journey through the after-life, Dante presents himself as frequently recognized by his Tuscan accent while he distinguishes others also by indications of dialect. (But he still resorts to Latin vocabulary in tight spots in the poem.)

There is little room here to discuss his poem as an influence on religious developments or as part of the history of religious sensibility – even if I were qualified or tempted, if that is the right word, to do so. But I cannot leave this issue without referring, once more, to Harold Bloom: 'Perhaps Dante really was both pious and orthodox, but Beatrice is his figure and not the church's; she is part of a private gnosis, a poet's alteration of the scheme of salvation.' And he concludes from this: Dante 'imposed his vision on Eternity, and he has little in common with the flock of his piously learned exegetes.'

But, setting aside these considerations, it is the poem as poem which has the widest appeal. A primary quality in its appeal as a universal work lies in the many levels on which it may be read. At the simplest and most attractive level is the skilfulness of the story-telling: such episodes as the love of Paolo and Francesca (*Hell* 5); Ulysses' journey (*Hell* 26); Ugolino's incarceration (*Hell* 33); the death of Manfred (*Purgatory* 3); the life of St Francis (*Heaven* 11). Equally appealing are the dramatic encounters with comrades and enemies: with Farinata (*Hell* 10); with his old mentor Ser Brunetto (*Hell* 15); the encounter with Beatrice (*Purgatory* 30). To these must be added the lyrical power of the laments over Florence (*Purgatory* 6; *Heaven* 15, 16) and over exile (*Heaven* 17); not to mention the beauty of the descriptions of Matilda and the Garden of Eden (*Purgatory* 28), and the river of Heaven – as an illusion of the senses, turning to a circle of spiritual light (*Heaven* 30). Even for the non-religious there is something powerfully moving in St Bernard's prayer to the Virgin (*Heaven* 33). Many other passages of immediate appeal, not least the metaphors and similes, could be cited; no other epic covers such a range.

Like any long poem the *Comedy* has in some respects suffered from its success in these areas, becoming known to many people only in episodes and parts rather than as a whole of immensely architectonic skill. The poets have not helped much here, with their penchant for confining their translation skills to such episodes.

However much Bloom dislikes it and Pound chooses to ignore its cause, few would dispute that another area of the poem's success, as Eliot evidences, is its skill and lucidity in formalizing in its allegory the main tenets and ideas of the Catholic faith. This too has had the frequent result of distracting interest from the poem as a whole. Many exegetes and pedagogues in their love of this admittedly large dimension of the poem have focused on this aspect at the expense of the poetry.

Yet it is in this guise that the poem presents the multivalency that makes its appeal to so many different readers. First, it appears to be an exposition of the Aristotelian/Thomist organization of Catholic belief. Second, it is an allegory of the Christian's life on earth, the journey from darkness to light. (A protestant equivalent, though much less sophisticated, would be Bunyan's *The Pilgrim's Progress*.) Third, it celebrates the liturgy and rituals of the church in the way in which the structure is framed with references to and citations from the daily services and worship of the church and its orders. Fourth, it is Dante's spiritual biography as well as Everyman's – his testimony to what he sees as the truth. Most astonishingly, interwoven through all these strands, runs the world's most intriguing love-poem in his journey to reconciliation with Beatrice who, in the poem, is the immediate cause of his salvation in many senses. Indeed, *Purgatory* 30, which deals with his reconciliation with her, is in many respects the emotional centre of the poem.

In fact, although some scholars cast doubt upon the authenticity of its authorship, Dante's *Epistle X*, to his great patron Can Grande, presents these aspects very clearly. It is still a most useful piece of succinct background reading. On the simplest level the author claims that his basic aim is 'to remove those living in this life from a state of misery and bring them into a state of happiness'. He asserts that the main purpose of the work was not to create speculation but a practical result. Nevertheless, the letter goes on to explain that the poem operates on four levels of meaning roughly consonant with those mentioned above: the literal level of the actual journey; the allegorical level; the moral level, and the anagogic, or mystic level beyond the senses. This last level Dante explains with a text he used more than once. In *Purgatory* 2.46, the new entrants arrive singing the psalm, 'When Israel went up out of Egypt'. On the anagogic level this may refer to the sinner's turning away from sin and becoming free, master of his soul. Dante's own word for this approach to levels is 'polysemous'. Frequently in the course of the poem Dante alerts the reader to one or other level beyond the first. The boldness of Dante's mind lies in the use he makes of the anagogic, which until then had been reserved for harmonizing the literal detail of the scriptures, and was regarded as more or less sacrosanct by theologians. Dante, however, applies it to the fictive literality of poetry.

There are two other levels or strands that result from this layering. In his choice of character and event Dante inevitably gives a finely detailed portrait of the Italy of his day with all its political and religious problems. On the level of mystical meanings, he has also included a level, in many areas of the work, which might be called hermetic. This is a subject so complex that here I will only touch upon it to alert those readers who wish to go deeper. It seems quite clear that running through the poem is a sympathy for the Knights Templars who were tortured and suppressed on trumped-up charges to suit the purposes of Philip the Fair, Dante's arch-enemy. The most accessible clue is probably *Purgatory* 20.93, where Capet refers to his descendant Philip as a new Pilate desecrating the Temple. In this text he is called 'lawless' for this action, but the Italian *sanza decreto* means literally 'without papal decree' – a greater sin than mere lawlessness, though Philip had engineered papal connivance in this persecution. Dante's remarks on the Templars and other topics had to be veiled if he was to avoid similar persecution.

This awareness of layered meaning has led to all sorts of hermetic readings such as those that find a level of Sufism or gnosticism as the powerhouse behind the poem. Readers of this particular bent are also encouraged by the symbolic and hermetic uses that Dante would be able to employ with the colours and crests from the heraldry of the time. He certainly indicates many families and identities by these devices. (In English an example might be J. L. Hotson's explication of *The Nun's Priest's Tale* of Chaucer as a veiled account of the confrontation between Bolingbroke and Mowbray/Richard.)

Dante also had an intention, it seems, to be encyclopedic: in his discussions of embryology and spirit bodies, among other things, and in his explanations of philosophy and theology – linked then through the influence of astrology into the medieval Ptolemaic cosmology – he comes close to his aim.

What holds all this together is the most astonishing quality of the poem which can only be truly appreciated by a close familiarity with the whole. This is the shaping spirit of Dante's imagination. I have already referred to his architectonic skill but it needs to be emphasized into what fine detail that skill penetrates. The poem is the most balanced and symmetrical of epics, topographically, sequentially, imagistically and prosodically. On the level of numbers alone the poem is extraordinarily tightly organized, as Anderson, among others, shows in his critical biography with the following figures concerning Beatrice. The number nine is the sacred number. Dante encountered Beatrice in life at the ages of nine and eighteen and that number dominates her appearances in the poem. Her name occurs 63 times in the poem, a multiple of nine whose digits add to nine; she reappears in *Purgatory* 30, canto 64 of the whole poem, preceded by 63 cantos and succeeded by 36, both multiples of nine, adding to nine in their digits. Her canto, 64, adds to ten, the perfect number that dominates the *Comedy*. She appears at line 73 whose digits add to the perfect ten. Her canto contains 145 lines whose digits also add to ten. Her name appears as a rhyme nine times.

On the prosodic level he invented terza rima in honour of the Trinity and each canto ends with a quatrain, the number four signifying wholeness. With an author as skilful in small detail as Dante, it is easy for experts to over-sophisticate their response and to find imaginary felicities. For example, some commentators, noticing that Dante changes from the formal *voi* to informal *tu* in addressing Beatrice in *Heaven* 31, also observe that her name consistently in this canto is scanned with 'ea' as a single syllable which distinguishes the Italian Christian name from the dissyllabic pronunciation used in religious, conventual names. This, with the pronoun, is said to indicate the risen Italian woman Beatrice Portinari as opposed to her allegorical and spiritual significance. With Dante, this seems plausible. But the distinction does not seem to be consistent in *Heaven*. Moreover, in *Purgatory* 30.73, and 31.114 the name is again pronounced with a monosyllabic 'ea' but becomes dissyllabic again at *Purgatory* 32.36. It would be clear, with most other poets, that the distinctions are metrical conveniences rather than meaningful subtleties. It is out of such sophistications that some of the weirder hermetic interpretations arise. But it is almost indisputable, if anything in this world is, that Dante employs acrostics in *Purgatory* 11 and *Heaven* 19.

Such detail, added to the knowledge of levels and numerology, has, as might be expected, unleashed all sorts of cryptographers on the poem to chase their own wild geese – so there really is something for everyone in this epic.

Binding all this together is the wonder of Dante's style, 'the sweet new style' (*Purgatory* 24.57), a fluent and supple style that sweeps the reader almost unconsciously along.

IV

Having said all this, I have clearly indicated the inadequacy of any version to comprehend and represent so much. I had better say what I can in my own defence.

In 'The Poet as Translator', the sixteenth Jackson Knight Memorial Lecture, delivered at the University of Exeter, November 8, 1984, C. H. Sisson, himself a translator of the *Comedy*, with his typically succinct good sense remarked: 'What we call a translation is no more than a reading, in one time and place, of a text from another time and place. It siphons off something from the original, but as much only as we in our different world are able to take.'

That is precisely where this version began: as a reading, as a thwarted reading – which arose in a curious way. In writing a short book on rhyme-technique, having criticized the opening rhymes of several versions of the first canto of the *Comedy*, I felt obliged to risk my neck in a footnote with an attempt of my own out of a sense of fairness. But terza rima is a running rhyme and you haven't really achieved it until at least the end of the canto. So, this version is perhaps one of the longest footnotes in history. Every version I had tried to read and had looked at for my book on rhyme had irritated me in similar ways. I had no Italian but, in reading these versions,

I felt four basic reservations. First, they did not make me feel, as Sisson suggests they should, that they were readings from my time and place. Secondly, many made Dante sound post-Authorized Version whereas he predates nearly all vernacular versions of the Bible, citing the Vulgate himself. Or, if not like the Authorized Version, then the versions made him sound post-Milton in style and prosody – translation into too 'protestant' and 'literary' a tradition. Moreover, these faults mysteriously affected prose versions also. Thirdly, in metrical versions, the authors had done fracturing contortions with syntax to get rhymes or blank verse more or less right. Fourth, the sum total of this was, it seemed to me, to make versions that were far too distant from the 'sweet new style' with its ease and fluency, its echoes of the colloquial. A Latinate non-Italian speaker can puzzle out, with the aid of a good literal crib, the impetus and flow of Dante, even at his most allusive and oblique. His style, it seemed, was generally straightforward, difficult though his thought and mind might be.

My initial impressions and poetic intuition told me that his style, to use an inadequate English comparison, was frequently closer to the openness and freshness of Chaucer than most versions led one to believe. After all, he chose Italian – a selection of spoken forms – as his vehicle, when there were precious few Italian texts to offer him an ongoing written literary tradition to follow. Later, when Milton dithered over whether to use Latin, English had already developed a considerable body of literary texts and traditions, so it was not quite the same sort of choice as Dante faced. C. H. Grandgent remarks of Dante's situation in his introduction to his edition of the *Commedia* : 'His literary medium was virtually his own handiwork.'

So I wanted a version that could be read naturally without having to stop to puzzle over the word order or diction, without being distracted by awkward and archaic rhymes. In short, a version that presented a poem, not a sacred text or quasi-scripture. Also important was to give an impression of the fluency and impetus of the terza rima – in which endeavour I have avoided all modern oblique rhymes as anachronistic in effect. The driving force of my effort was the desire to read Dante for myself without let or hindrance.

The difficulty in English of terza rima has been somewhat exaggerated. The lack of handy rhymes compared with Italian is offset by the vaster vocabulary of English. In fact, Dante himself was not without problems. Again, as Grandgent observes in his introduction: 'The foreign and unusual words and those employed in a strange sense occur for the most part in the rhyme. Dante was generally averse to periphrasis or deviation from his idea and was loath to end a verse with an insignificant word; so he was sometimes forced to do violence to usage in his rhymes.'

In English, rhyming custom is the reverse of the Italian where the line is largely eleven-syllabled because of the prevalence of double-syllable rhymes similar to our 'holy/lowly' – or sometimes even triple like 'mystery/history'. It is the monosyllabically rhymed final stress that is the rarity. In English, it is the other way round and so I have used double rhyme only sparingly as a special effect or when all else fails.

As for the metre, it seems fairly clear that Dante keeps a more or less staple rhythm of alternating light and heavy syllable, closer to English custom than the theoretical requirements of Italian metric would demand. I have therefore used the English pentameter – with a Shakespearean licence in some dramatic and spoken passages, not to say also in some of the more intransigent philosophical or theological parts.

Only in the course of the preparation of my version did it become apparent to me how skilfully layered the poem was. No translation can convey all the subtlety of this, but I have tried not to disrupt too much by maintaining, as closely as possible, the literal meaning, the integrity of line and tercet in the same manner as the original. I hope that these endeavours will provide a good first introduction in a contemporary English of my time and place to Dante the poet who should not be left like Ariel, trapped from English-speakers, in the trunk of an Italian tree nor entangled in the thickets of Milton and the Authorized Version. Nor should the modern reader be misled or distracted from the poem by the personal, and some-times wilful way, in which Pound and Eliot have used him as a kind of intellectual's defensive palisade.

An important element in the poem is Dante's commitment to define an area for free will and moral responsibility within the theological tenet of predestination and the astrological/astronomical determinism of the geo-centric Ptolemaic universe (see, principally, *Heaven* 8.97–148). Dante's earth was in a sense the lowest sublunary part of actual Heaven whereas in most modern conceptions Heaven is supranatural. The crystalline spheres of his universe influenced human conduct and the earth directly through the individual angelic intelligence that was their indwelling motive force. Each angel in its sphere took its influence from the sphere above in a chain of command that hung directly down from God himself (see, mainly, *Heaven* 2.127–44).

Dante does not always clearly distinguish between the operation of the angel in its sphere and its planet. In the thought of his day it was scarcely necessary to do so since the planets and stars in their circles were the appearance of the divine in this world. The difference might be indicated in modern usage by using 'heavens' for the firmament in its material form and 'Heaven' for its spiritual manifestations. I found this distinction impos-sible to maintain without risk of confusion or over-interpretation. I have therefore used capital initial letters in either case and trusted to the reader's good sense to make any distinction.

Wherever possible I have included background details in the headnotes if I thought they might help in responding to the poetry. Rarely, under the exigencies of versification – and because of Dante's superior succinctness – a little background help has slipped into the text. My excuse is that obliqueness in using allusion becomes increasing obscure through time and change over the course of history and may bear a little clarifying of its address and aim. Finally, I again quote from Pound's letter cited above: 'Binyon has shown that Dante needs *fewer* notes than are usually given the student.'

PETER DALE

A Short Bibliography

Dante's *Inferno*, *Purgatorio*, *Paradiso* (three volumes), revised by H. Oelsner: Temple Classics, J.M. Dent, 1970

La Divina Commedia, edited, annotated by C.H. Grandgent, revised by Charles S. Singleton: Harvard University Press, 1972

The Divine Comedy, translated by Laurence Binyon, with *La Vita Nuova* translated by D.G. Rossetti: Agenda Editions, 1979

The Divine Comedy, translated by C.H. Sisson: Carcanet Press, 1980; Oxford, World's Classics, 1993

The Divine Comedy (three volumes), translated with commentary by John D. Sinclair: Oxford University Press, 1982

Hell, translated by Steve Ellis: Chatto and Windus, 1994

The Divine Comedy, translated by Allen Mandelbaum: Everyman's Library, 1995

The Inferno of Dante, A New Verse Translation by Robert Pinsky: J.M. Dent, 1995

Dante, *La Vita Nuova*, translated with an introduction by Barbara Reynolds: Penguin Classics, 1971

Dante, *De Vulgari Eloquentia*, translated by A.G. Ferrers Howell, introduction by Ronald Duncan: Rebel Press, 1973

The Early Italian Poets, translated by Dante Gabriel Rossetti, edited by Sally Purcell with an introduction by John Wain: Anvil Press Poetry, 1981

William Anderson, *Dante the Maker*: Routledge & Kegan Paul, 1980

HELL

INTRODUCTION

Dante's Inferno is conceived as a conical funnel with its vertical axis running through Jerusalem, the midpoint of earth. Around the inner surface of the funnel run the rings of Hell in which sinners are punished. The wider rings at the top are for the less heinous sinners and the tight, deep rings at the bottom for the worst of all – Satan. The sinners are thus arranged on the following levels:

PRIOR TO THE FIRST CIRCLE
Those who were neither for nor against God

THE FIRST CIRCLE
The Pagans who were virtuous within their lights

SECOND CIRCLE
The Incontinent
The Lascivious

THIRD CIRCLE
The Gluttons

FOURTH CIRCLE
The Avaricious and Spendthrift

FIFTH CIRCLE
Those given to Anger

SIXTH CIRCLE
The Heretics

SEVENTH CIRCLE
The Violent
Those violent against others
Those violent against self
Those violent against art, nature, and God

EIGHTH CIRCLE
The Deceitful
Panders and Seducers
Flatterers

Simonists, those who buy, sell or use spiritual offices
for secular and material gain
Diviners
Barrators, swindlers in public office
Hypocrites
Thieves
Deceitful Counsellors
Sowers of Discord
Falsifiers: alchemists, forgers

NINTH CIRCLE
The Treacherous
False to kindred
False to country or cause
False to guests
False to lords and benefactors

The cone of Hell is a kind of inverted mockery of the mountain of
Purgatory which Dante conceives as rising out of the ocean that covers
the obverse hemisphere opposite Jerusalem. The mountain has the same
vertical axis as Hell.

CANTO 1

Good Friday, 1300; Dante, thirty-five years old, finds himself lost in a dark wood, wondering how he strayed from the straight way. He spends a fearful night. Dawn lights on a hill toward which he heads, encouraged by the sun's light. He finds his way barred by various wild animals: the leopard of lust, the lion of pride, the she-wolf of avarice. Retreating, he is met by the spirit of Vergil who explains that there is no way past the she-wolf – though one is destined to come to drive her back to Hell. He offers to conduct Dante another way to safety through Hell, Purgatory and Heaven. Dante agrees to go.

Along the journey of our life half way,
    I found myself again in a dark wood
    Wherein the straight road no longer lay.
Ah, tongue can never make it understood:
    So harsh and dense and savage to traverse
    That fear returns in thinking on that wood.   6
It is so bitter death is hardly worse.
    But, for the good it was my chance to gain,
    The other things I saw there I'll rehearse.
– Yet still I cannot readily explain
    How I had entered it, so near to sleep
    I was, on losing that true way and plain.   12
But, when I trod the rising of a steep,
    Toward the ending of that fearful vale
    Whose terror pierced into my heart so deep,
I looked and saw the shoulder I'd to scale
    Arrayed already in that planet's light
    Which leads men straight on every road they trail.   18
And then my fear lulled somewhat from its height
    That on my heart's sea gathered more and more
    Where I so piteously had passed the night.
As one who has escaped from sea to shore
    With panting breath turns round to catch the sight
    Again of all the dangerous waves that roar,   24
Exactly so, my mind, though still in flight,
    Turned itself round to see that defile where
    None had passed through alive before this night.
And, when my weary frame had rested there,
    I took my way along the barren strand,
    The firmer foot the lower of the pair.   30

Then, see, near to the start of rising land,
    A leopard stood, of swift and nimble grace,
    With mottled coat, opposing on the sand.
It would not give its ground before my face;
    No, but impeded me so that I turned
36   Often away, and faltered in my pace.
The time was earliest morning. I discerned
    The sun mount with those stars that ever climb
    Beside him, since first God's Love had yearned
And moved those lovely things; so that the prime
    Of day, and the sweetness of the season's air,
42   Inspired good hopes in me at the same time
Towards this beast of the bright fur; but there
    Were none to quell my fear of the next sight:
    A lion that appeared with ravenous stare,
And head erect, before me, in its might
    So that the air itself began to quake,
48   It seemed, with fear, and trembled in the light.
And, with it, came a she-wolf that seemed to ache
    With craving in her leanness; she has compelled
    Many to live in sorrow for her sake.
The terror of that visage I beheld
    Brought so much heaviness I felt hope drain
54   Of ever rising till that brute were quelled.
And, as a person keen to make some gain,
    When comes a time he sees what loss he'll meet,
    His thoughts all turn to sadness, tears and pain,
Like that, the restless beast made me, and beat
    Me backward step by step, till its defiance,
60   Down where the sun is silent, forced my retreat.
And, as I rushed back downward in compliance,
    It seemed, before my eyes someone drew near
    Whose voice was hoarse out of a long silence.
Seeing him in that barren tract appear,
    I cried, 'Have pity on me; pity me,
66   Whether a spirit or truly man out here.'
He answered: 'No man; I used to be.
    My parents were both Lombards and their state
    Was Mantua from their nativity.
And I was born *sub Julio*, though late;
    In good Augustus' Rome my life was run,
72   When false and lying gods still carried weight.

I was a poet; I sang Anchises' son,
 The just one, who embarked from Trojan ground
 When haughty Ilium was burned and done.
But you, why panicked now and turning round?
 Why not ascend to that Delectable Height,
 The source and cause where every joy is found?' 78
'Are you that Vergil, then, the spring so bright
 That pours abroad so rich a stream of speech?'
 I answered him, my face abashed and white.
'Glory and Light of poets, may my long zeal teach
 Me, and the deep love that made me pore
 Upon your volume stead me well, I now beseech. 84
You are my origin and master. You're
 The one alone from whom I take my style,
 The good style that I'm so honoured for.
Ah, famous seer, look on that beast awhile
 From which I ran away, and rescue me.
 It makes my pulses tremble at the trial.' 90
'You ought to go another way,' said he,
 When he had seen my tearful eyes, 'if you
 Expect to flee this place of savagery.
The beast you cry out at lets no one through;
 Lets no one pass this way at all, unless
 To tangle with her. She kills them as her due. 96
She has a nature steeped in viciousness,
 And satiates her appetite in vain,
 For, having fed, she's hungry to excess.
She mates with many brutes and then again
 With many more until the hound shall rise
 And kill her in an agony of pain. 102
Lucre and land he will not gourmandize;
 But valour, wisdom, love shall be his fare.
 His land between a Feltro and Feltro lies.
He'll save that Italy of lowly air,
 For which the virgin Camilla has died –
 A death Euryalus, Turnus, Nisus, share. 108
Through every town he'll chase her, far and wide,
 Until he turn her back to Hell, the base
 From which pure envy let her take her stride.
Therefore, I think this course the best you face:
 That I should be your guide; you, follow me.
 I'll lead you out through an eternal place, 114

Where you will hear the hopeless cry, and see
    The ancient spirits in such pain they quest
    A second time for death's mortality.
And you will also see, among the rest,
    Others, contented with the fire, aspire
120   To dwell, when they are due, among the blest.
If scaling to those Heights is your desire,
    There shall arrive a worthier than I,
    When I depart, and she will lead you higher.
That Emperor who holds his reign on high,
    Because his law I never could obey,
126   Wills that his city never greet my eye.
He rules all parts and there he holds his sway.
    There is his city, there is his high throne.
    O blessèd ones whom he elects to stay.'
And I replied: 'Poet, by the God unknown
    To you, I beg: so that I obviate
132   This trial, or worse, lead me through that zone
That you have mentioned, so I see the Gate
    St Peter guards and, in the interim,
    Those who are so saddened with your state.'
    Then he moved onward and I followed him.

CANTO 2

However, Dante suddenly has doubts when he considers the few occasions when people have been allowed by grace to make the journey Vergil proposes. Vergil gives great detail of the concern shown for Dante by Heaven, particularly by Beatrice. Encouraged, Dante decides to continue the enterprise.

Day was departing and the dusky air
    Freeing the earthly creatures from their toil
    And labours; I, the only being there,
Prepared myself to bear the brunt and broil
    Of both the journey and the pity spent –
    Of which memory, unerring, tells without recoil.   6
Muses, High Genius, help in my intent;
    And memory that writes down all I met
    Display, in this, your true and noble bent.
I started, 'Poet, guide, look deeper yet;
    Consider if I have sufficient worth
    To trust to the arduous journey we are set.   12
Sylvius' father, while of corruptible birth,
    You say, had travelled the immortal zone,
    Fully aware in flesh and blood of earth.
Yet, if the Enemy to Sin has shown
    Such favour, knowing the high consequence,
    And what, and who, should spring from him alone,   18
To one that understands, that makes good sense
    Since he was chosen, in the Empyrean air,
    Father of Rome and all her realm immense.
Both these were destined for the Holy Chair,
    To speak rightly, that place of sanctity
    Where sits the great St Peter's lineal heir.   24
And from his journey through that territory
    For which you honoured him he learned what led
    To victory and prepared the Papacy.
Later, the Chosen Vessel there would tread
    For confirmation of the Faith to lead
    The way to our salvation. Why should I head   30
That way? And who allows it? No Paul, indeed,
    Nor am I an Aeneas, so there's no
    One thinks me – nor do I – fit to proceed.

It may be foolishness to undergo –
    If I resign myself to going there.
36   You're wise, and better than I speak you know.'
As one who now unwills what will would dare,
    And, thinking further, changes purpose more
    Till from his first intention he forbear,
So did I falter then on that dim shore
    In second thoughts, halting the enterprise
42   That hastily I'd entered in before.
'If I have clearly followed your replies,'
    Answered the shade of that magnanimous one,
    'It is some coward fear your soul now sighs,
Which often hinders men and makes them shun
    An honourable enterprise, as a false glance
48   Will start a timorous animal to run.
To free you from this terror to advance,
    I'll tell you why I came, and what I heard,
    When first I pitied you in your mischance.
I was with those in long suspense deferred;
    Then spoke a Lady, oh so fair and blest
54   I begged her to command me with her word.
Her eyes shone more than stars and her request
    In an angelic voice at once began,
    Softly and gently, in her tongue expressed:
"Courteous Mantuan Soul, whose fame as man
    Lives on within the world, and will survive
60   As long as time continues in its span,
My friend – and not fortune's – who is still alive,
    Is so opposed, on the barren tract astray,
    He turns wherever terror seems to drive.
I fear he may be so far off his way
    That I have come to his relief too late –
66   From what I've heard those in the Heavens say.
Now go. Both with your ornate speech debate
    And give all help to strengthen his physique
    So I may be consoled about his fate.
Beatrice, it is, that sends you. Now I seek
    To go back to the place from which I've sped.
72   Love moved me. Love has made me speak.
And when I come before my Lord and Head
    I'll voice your praises often." Then ceased that tone,
    And I began to answer what she'd said.

"Lady, through whose virtuousness alone
    Mankind excels all that is limited
    Beneath the sky of the least circle's zone,   78
Your wish so pleases me that if I'd sped
    And finished it already my obedience
    Were much too slow; enough, what you have said,
But say the reason and the exigence
    You never shrank from the inmost centre here
    While burning for return to Heaven immense."   84
"Since into such deep things you wish to peer,"
    She said, "I'll briefly tell you why this place
    Holds nothing that my coming needs to fear.
The only fear in things we have to face
    Lies in their power to harm. All others, not;
    Which, not for fearing, leave for fear no base.   90
And, by his grace, God made me such, your lot
    In misery has no effect. What burns
    Here, not a single flame to me feels hot.
There's a gentle Lady in Heaven who yearns
    So much, in pity at the hindrance I send
    You to, that the stern law she overturns.   96
She summoned Lucia to her: 'I commend
    Your faithful one; he is in need of you,
    And I commend him to you to that end.'
Then Lucia, opposed to every cruelty, flew
    And came towards the place where I was seated,
    Near ancient Rachel I was talking to.   102
'Beatrice, true Praise of God,' she then entreated,
    'Why don't you help him since he left the taint,
    For your sake, of the vulgar and conceited?
Why can't you hear his miserable complaint?
    Can you not see what death claws him adrift
    On the river where the sea has no constraint?'   108
Never on earth was anyone more swift
    To find their good, or flee away from harm,
    Than, since those words were spoken, I made shift
To come down from my seat at this alarm,
    Confident in your noble speech that draws
    For you, and those that hear you, honour's palm."   114
She turned aside her weeping eyes; a pause
    That, after she had said all this to me,
    Impelled me all the swifter in her cause.

And here I rushed to end your jeopardy,
    Drew you from the wild beast blocking your way –
120   To those Delectable Heights – by savagery.
What is the matter then? Why linger, stay?
    Why harbour in your heart such coward fear?
    Why aren't you brave, free, as at break of day,
When three such blessèd Ladies in the sphere
    Of Heaven care for you, and words of mine
126   Have made you promises so good and clear?'
As tiny flowers, when closed and in decline
    From chills of night, erect their heads again
    When, lighting on them, sun begins to shine,
So I, with failing courage; and such a vein
    Of daring pulsed into my heart that I
132   Began to speak as one released from strain:
'Ah, Lady of Compassion, who heard my cry;
    And courteous of you so swiftly to obey
    Her words and tell me all of her reply.
You have disposed my heart, by what you say,
    To such an eagerness that I revert
138   To that first purpose, and to go your way.
Lead on; both have one will, I dare assert.
    You guide, my lord and master.' Thus I said,
And he began to move, and I, alert,
    Entered on the harsh and savage tract ahead.

CANTO 3

They pass through the portals of Hell, meeting a rabble immediately of those displeasing both to God and his enemies since they pursued neither good nor evil. Dante recognizes Pope Celestine V who made the great refusal and resigned in favour of Boniface VIII – Dante's great enemy. When they reach the River of Acheron that encircles Hell, Charon refuses to ferry Dante. Waiting on the bank, Dante is stunned by an earthquake.

'THROUGH ME YOU GO TO SORROW'S CITADEL:
   THROUGH ME YOU GO TO THE ETERNAL PAIN:
   THROUGH ME YOU GO WHERE THE LOST ONES DWELL.
THE JUSTICE OF MY HIGH CREATOR'S REIGN
   MADE PRIMAL LOVE AND SUPREME WISDOM REAR
   ME UP IN POWER DIVINE. HERE I REMAIN.   6
NO THINGS THAT ARE CREATED ARE MY PEER,
   ONLY ETERNAL; AND ETERNAL I ENDURE.
   ABANDON ALL HOPE YOU WHO ENTER HERE.'

These words, in colour dark, the entablature
   Above a portal showed. 'Master,' said I,
   'Their meaning leaves me fearful, insecure.'   12
As one experienced he offered this reply:
   'All distrust must be left. All cowardice
   Must here be given up and left to fly.
We have arrived, I told before of this,
   Where you will see those wretched people lie
   Who could the Good of Intellect dismiss.'   18
Placing his hand on mine, with cheerful eye
   That gave me comfort then, he led me on
   To knowledge of the secret things near by.
Here, sighs and groans, and suffering undergone,
   Resounded through the dark and starless air.
   At first I watched it tearfully and wan.   24
Strange tongues, cries horrible to bear,
   Outbursts from pain, angered tones and spurned,
   Deep voices hoarse – and sounds of hands were there,
Whirling a tumult everywhere that turned
   In air forever dyed like sands that stain
   The whirlwinds in some barren desert churned.   30

And I, with terror leaguered round my brain,
    Spoke out: 'Master, what is this I hear?
    And who are these so overcome with pain?'
He answered me: 'This is the wretched sphere
    Of dreary souls who lived without all blame
36   And without praise, and they are gathered here
With all the spineless angels, much the same,
    Who neither kept their faith nor yet rebelled
    Against their God; themselves their only aim.
To keep its beauty clear, they were expelled
    From Heaven. Hell – since wickedness might gain
42   Some glory next to them – has been withheld.'
I asked: 'What is so grievous? Master, explain
    Why they lament so bitterly.' He, replying:
    'I'll tell you briefly their chief pain.
They do not have the slightest hope of dying.
    Their blind life is so mean they always feel
48   Envy of other fates, and hence this sighing.
With no report of them will the world deal.
    Justice and Mercy both disdain their fate.
    Don't speak but look and pass and turn the heel.'
I saw an ensign rush at such a rate
    It seemed in flight from all that might encumber –
54   Whirling, never to make a stand and wait.
Behind, I saw a crowd of people lumber;
    So long a retinue came after this
    I never thought death had undone that number.
And some I recognized; one could not miss:
    I saw and knew one shadow: he that made
60   The great refusal out of cowardice.
At once I knew it was that dire parade,
    That rabblement of wretches who never strive,
    Hateful to God, and to his foes no aid.
These wretched ones who never were alive
    Went bare, by wasps and hornets stung,
66   That all around, and on them, seemed to thrive.
These made their faces stream with blood among
    The tears which, flowing to their feet,
    Were gathered up by loathsome worms that clung.
I looked ahead and saw a mob that beat
    Towards the brink of some great river's flow.
72   'Master,' I asked, 'explain why these retreat.

Who are they then? What custom makes them go
    And press so fast to reach the other side?
    Or so I gather in the faint light's glow.'
'These things will be quite obvious,' he replied,
    'When, on those joyless banks of Acheron, we wait
    And find its waters hindering our stride.'   78
And then with eyes ashamed and downcast state,
    Fearing my words offensive to his care,
    I held my peace until we reached that strait.
And there, an ancient, white with agèd hair,
    Bringing his boat towards us, shouted: 'Woe,
    Woe to you, souls depraved that linger there.   84
Hold out no hope of seeing Heaven so.
    I come to lead you to the other shore,
    Eternal darkness, fire and ice below.
And that one, you! What are you waiting for,
    Alive among the dead? Now move away.'
    But when he saw I moved not from that shore: 90
'A lighter boat is needed to convey
    You and elsewhere; you cannot cross it here.
    Some other ferry, or another way.'
And then my guide replied: 'Now have no fear,
    Charon. It is the will of That whose will
    Can be performed. No more expect to hear.'   96
The unkempt cheeks that huffed were dumb and still,
    As was the steersman of that livid fen,
    Around whose eyes were whirls of fire that mill.
But those close spirits, stark and wasted, when
    They heard these words of such a bitter edge,
    Changed in complexion with much gnashing then.   102
They blasphemed God and damned their parentage;
    The human race; birthplace and period;
    Their seed in origin and lineage.
Then, all together, weeping wildly, trod
    Towards the dark, accursèd shore that lies
    In wait for all who hold no fear of God.   108
Charon, demonic spirit, with his eyes
    Of burning coal, collects them with a sign,
    Clubs with his oar the ones who temporize.
And, as the leaves, when autumn brings decline,
    Fall, one by one, until the branch can see
    All of its spoils upon the ground repine,   114

So did the wicked seed of Adam flee
    Down to the shore by signal, one by one,
    As does a hawk recalled in falconry.
And so they leave on the water brown and dun,
    And yet, before they reach the further side,
120   Again, on this a fresh crowd has begun.
'My son,' the courteous master spoke, aside,
    'All those who died beneath God's wrath meet here,
    Coming from every country, far and wide.
And, for this crossing, they are prompt and near,
    For Divine Justice spurs them across the flow,
126   And quickly changes to desire their fear.
But by this route good spirits never go.
    So now you see the reason for his word,
    If Charon queries why you linger so.'
Just as he stopped, the darkling country stirred
    With so much violence I am bathed in sweat
132   Whenever I recall what then occurred.
The tearful ground exhaled a wind and jet
    That flashed a crimson light that, in its sweep,
Numbed all my senses till I felt beset
    Like someone overcome with sudden sleep.

CANTO 4

Waking, Dante finds he is over Acheron on the brink of a great Abyss. Vergil takes
him down to the first circle, Limbo, filled with the unbaptized and the virtuous
heathen. Vergil tells him of Christ's visit there. They meet Homer and the chief
poets of Classical times. Vergil's place is here. Together they enter a noble castle
where stay the heroes and heroines of those times, its philosophers and thinkers.

A heavy thunder broke through my deep sleep.
    I started up, as someone rudely raised
    By threat of violence might wildly leap;
And, having got upright, I turned and gazed
    With rested eyes to peer about and see
    Where I had woken while in sleep so hazed.   6
Impressions left were true: I proved to be
    Upon the valley brink of woe's abyss
    Reverberating endless wails to me.
So dark, profound and clouded was all this
    That, though I stared and stared towards the base,
    I fixed on nothing from that precipice.   12
'Now let's descend into this stoneblind place,'
    Began the poet, pale. 'Here, I will lead
    And you, the second, follow in my pace.'
I, noting his lost colour, disagreed:
    'You can't expect me to descend with you,
    When you, my strength, lack courage that I need.'   18
He answered, 'The anguish of the people who
    Are here below has drawn into my face
    The pity which you think is fear shown through.
So let us go; the way is slow to trace.'
    Thus he went down; I followed at his word
    To the first circle round the abysmal place.   24
Here were no cries, or none that could be heard,
    Except the sound of sighs which made the air,
    That was eternal, tremble where they stirred.
No torment there, but sorrow was the share
    Borne by the multitudes, which were so vast,
    Of women, children, men, all gathered there.   30
The good master said: 'Your glance you cast
    Yet do not ask who are these crowds that sigh.
    I wish that you should know before we've passed.

These never sinned; yet all their merit, why,
   It mounts to little for they were not shown
36   The Baptism, door to the Faith that you live by.
They lived before Christianity was known,
   And could not worship God in truth and right.
   And I belong with them in this sad zone.
For such a lack, and for no other slight,
   We're lost; our only suffering's to yearn
42   And, without hope, to feel desire outright.'
Great sadness was it in my heart to learn,
   Because I knew a good worth of men
   The long suspense in Limbo must intern.
'Tell me, good master,' I began, since then
   I wished for surety of the Faith, defeat
48   Of every error, 'tell me if, and when,
Has any, by his own or other's feat,
   Gone from this place to be among the blest?'
He, noting my intent, veiled and discreet,
Answered: 'I was new among the rest.
   I saw the entry of a Mighty One,
54   Crowned with signs of his victorious quest.
The shade of our first parent, and his son
   Abel, Noah, and the obedient
   Lawgiver Moses, their stay with us was done.
The Patriarch Abraham, King David went;
   And Israël, his father and his sons,
60   Rachel – for whom he did so much – were sent;
And others, and He made them blessèd ones.
   No human souls, I'd have you understand,
   Were ever saved before these paragons.'
While talking we moved onward through the land,
   Continuing through the forest, I would say,
66   Forest of crowded souls on either hand.
From where I'd slept we weren't far on the way
   When I beheld a blaze which had erected
   A hemisphere in darkness from its ray.
While still some distance off, I yet detected,
   To some extent, what honourable folk
72   In that one crowded place were all collected.
'O you who honour art and science, evoke
   Who these are here whose claims to honour stand
   To shield them from the rest that sigh.' He spoke:

'The honour of their names in their earthly land –
   Which echoes still – has earned for them this state
   That Heaven's grace endorses for their band.'   78
And then I heard a voice communicate:
   'Honour the lofty poet. He's returned,
   The shade that travelled out from us of late.'
And when the voice was silent, I discerned
   These four great shades in our direction made.
   They had no joyful look, nor one that yearned.   84
My good lord said: 'The one who bears the blade,
   That sword, d'you notice how he comes before
   The other three as lord to be obeyed?
The sovereign poet, Homer. Furthermore,
   Horace, the satirist, next, and Ovid third,
   Then, lastly, that is Lucan, of the four.   90
Because each of them share with me that word
   And name the voice extolled, they welcome me
   Honourably, and it is well conferred.'
And so assembled to my scrutiny
   That goodly school, the lords of highest song,
   Soaring above the rest, like eagles, free.   96
After exchanging words, they were not long
   Before they turned to me and gave a sign –
   My master smiled – of welcome to their throng.
And then they made a greater honour mine
   In choosing me one of their number few;
   In those intelligences, sixth in line.   102
So we moved onward to the light that grew,
   Speaking of things not proper now to sound,
   As it was proper then we should pursue.
We reached a noble castle's base and mound,
   With lofty walls encircled sevenfold,
   Defending which a lovely river wound.   108
We passed across as solid ground would hold,
   And, with those sages, seven gates I passed,
   And to the fresh verdure of a meadow strolled.
People with slow eyes, and gravely cast,
   Were there, and great authority they bore.
   They seldom spoke, their voices mild at last.   114
Then we withdrew, towards one side the more,
   Into a vantage point, open and high
   And luminous, and watched them from that tor.

And there, directly stood before my eye,
  Were clear to me upon that gloss of green,
120   Great spirits I glory to have seen close by.
I saw Electra; her many friends I've seen;
  Among them, recognized Aeneas, Hector,
  Caesar in arms, his falcon eye still keen.
Camilla, Penthesilea, in one sector;
  I saw the Latian King and by his side
126   Lavinia, his daughter; saw the ejector
Of the Tarquin, Brutus. I descried
  Lucretia, Julia, Marcia, Cornelia; and where
  Saladin sat alone and to one side.
I raised my eyes a little in the air
  And saw the master of all those that know
132   Amid his philosophic kindred there.
All look on him; all honour they bestow.
  Plato and Socrates I saw keep stance
  Nearest to him, while others hung back so.
Democritus who gave the world to chance;
  Diogenes, Anaxagoras, Thales, lean;
138   Empedocles, Heraclitus, Zeno, my glance
Revealed; the culler of qualities, I mean
  Dioscorides; Orpheus and Tully, there were,
  With Linus, Seneca, the Moralist, in between.
Ptolemy, Euclid, the geometer,
  Galen and Avicenna, Hippocrates;
144   Averroës, of the *Great Comment*, in the stir.
I may not paint in detail all of these
  For the great theme so drives me on and on
  Words fail of the reality they would seize.
The company of six has come and gone.
  And to another road the sage inclines,
150   Out of the quiet which a little shone,
  Into the trembling air where nothing shines.

CANTO 5

Here, the second circle is the true beginning of Hell. It is reserved for the carnal sinners. Minos presides over the entry as Judge, and assigns the damned to their appropriate circles. He forbids entry to Dante, but Vergil quells his objection. The sinners here are tossed on never-ending winds. Dante wishes fervently to speak with one pair of lovers: Francesca da Rimini and Paolo Malatesta, brother of her husband – to whom she was married for reasons of state. Dante is so overcome he faints in pity for their plight.

Thus I descended from the first and came
    Into the second ring, of lesser space
    And greater pain, that goads to wailing shame.
There Minos sits, horrific, grinning face,
    Examines every crime upon descent,
    And as he girds himself judges each case.   6
I mean that when the ill-born soul is bent
    Before him it confesses all its crime;
    That expert on sin decides the punishment
And where in Hell to place it all its time.
    Then with his tail he circumscribes the rings
    And shows the culprit's circle in such mime.   12
Always before him is a crowd. He brings
    Them all to judgement. They confess and hear,
    And next are whirling down to sufferings.
'You, who come to this abode of pain and fear,'
    Said Minos at me when he saw me leave
    His great office in session, 'beware how near   18
You enter, for the width of entrance may deceive.'
    And then my guide replied and answered so:
    'Why do you cry out here, and seem to grieve?
Don't hinder. It is determined he shall go.
    It is the Will where what is willed to be
    Can be performed. No further seek to know.'   24
And now the sounds of sorrow reach to me;
    Now am I come where many agonies
    Rise and strike my spirit chillingly.
I'd come into a place where no light is;
    Where outcries like tempestuous waters soar
    When warring gales attack insurgencies.   30

The Hellish storm, that never ends its roar,
    Drives round the spirits in its ceaseless sweep,
    Churning and goading them for evermore.
When they arrive before its rage, they weep
    There, shrieks and moans and lamentations cry;
36   The Power Divine they blaspheme loud and deep.
I learnt this tortuous torment was to try
    The sensual sinners who subject the reason
    Beneath their lusts; their doom is in this sky.
And, as the starlings, in the colder season,
    Take to the wing in large and crowded flocks,
42   So with that blast the troop of evil flees on:
Hither and thither, over and under it knocks.
    No hope will ever comfort them of rest;
    Much less the thought of pain ending its shocks.
As cranes go chanting their lays, the slenderest
    Long line in stretching themselves airborne,
48   So could I see these shadows stream, oppressed
With wails, upon that strife of winds gale-torn.
    And so I asked: 'Master, who are these
    Whom the black air so lashes in its scorn?'
'The first of those of whom you question, she's
    Empress of many tongues,' he then replied,
54   'And so undone with lechery that her decrees
Mingled her lust into her law and tried
    To shift away from her own acts the blame
    Which to her own loose conduct had applied.
Queen Semiramis was her earthly name;
    We read she was to Ninus wife and heir.
60   She held the land which is the Sultan's claim.
The next had killed herself in love's despair,
    And broke her faith to dead Sichaeus' will.
    The third is wanton Cleopatra there.
And Helen, look, from whom those years of ill
    Wound on and on. The great Achilles, behold,
66   Who fought with love at last – and was the kill.
Look, Paris, Tristan.' More than a thousandfold
    He showed to me; and, pointing with his finger,
    Of those love parted from our life he told.
After I'd heard my master dwell and linger
    On naming these, this lady and that knight,
72   Pity dismayed me; I was bewildered. 'Singer,'

I started, 'willingly would I come in sight
 And speak with that pair there who seem to be
 Always together, on the wind so light.'
He said: 'When you are nearer you shall see.
 And, if you then entreat them, by the love
 That leads them, to approach they will agree.'   78
Once winds had brought them near us from above:
 'If One does not object to it,' I cried,
 'Oh weary souls, come, talk with us.' As dove
And dove in yearning, wings spread open wide,
 Borne on their will towards their gentle nest,
 So those two spirits came from Dido's side,   84
Leaving her band, and, still together, pressed
 Across to us through that malignant air;
 Such power had my loving cry's request.
'O living creature, gracious and kind to bear
 The black fumes, and visit us who stained
 The earth with blood when we were living there,   90
If the King of all the universe remained
 A friend to us, our prayer would be your peace,
 Because you pity our fate perverse and pained.
We'll talk and listen, if the winds should cease,
 On anything you'd like to ask or give.
 And here their silence gives us this release.   96
The town where I was born, and used to live,
 Lies where the river Po sweeps coastal parts
 In peace, no chasing torrents' fugitive.
Love, that is swiftly caught in gentle hearts,
 Seized him for the fair form snatched from me –
 The manner of it still inflicts and smarts.   102
Love, that for lover lets no reason be
 For curbing love, gave me such strong delight
 In him it has not left me, as you see.
Love led us to one death. Caina's spite
 Awaits for him who quenched our life in cloud.'
 These words were borne to us out of their plight.   108
And when I heard those wounded souls, I bowed
 My face, and bowed so long the poet spoke
 To ask: 'What thoughts are these that have so cowed?'
When I replied I started to invoke:
 'Ah, love, what sweet thoughts, what longing led
 Them on to undergo this fearful stroke!'   114

And then I turned to them again and said:
    'Francesca, how your torment makes me weep;
    In grief and pity for you these tears I shed.
But tell me, in the time when sweet sighs sweep,
    In what way, how was it that love chose
120   To let you know desires so dubious and deep?'
She said: 'There is no greater pain than flows
    From memory of a time of happiness
    In misery. And this your teacher knows.
But if you yearn as much as you express
    To know our love's initial root, I'll be,
126   In telling, one who weeps and tells no less.
One day, to pass the time, we read to see
    How love constrained Sir Lancelot; alone,
    We were together, from misgiving free.
Several times the reading changed our tone
    And colour, drove our eyes to meet; just one
132   Defeated us, one moment on its own.
When we were reading how the kiss was won
    From such a lover with the longed-for smile,
    What he who'll never part from me had done
Was tremblingly to kiss my mouth. – Book, style,
    Was Galeotto, and he that wrote it. That day
138   We read no further in it.' And all the while
One spirit spoke about it in this way,
    The other wept, so that, in pitying it all,
I fainted as if dying and I lay
    Fallen just as a dead body would fall.

CANTO 6

*Recovering, Dante finds himself transported to the third circle made for gluttons
and epicures who have lusted after the lowest of sensual pleasures. Storms of hail
and foul water perpetually assail them. They are kept prostrate in the foul water
by Cerberus. Ciacco sits up and prophesies the outcome between the feuding parties
of Florence.*

My consciousness returned that closed on me
    Before the piteousness and sorrowing
    Of those two kinsfolk; then all about I see
New sights of further torture, suffering
    Of souls in torment; everywhere in view,
    Or where I moved, I saw a painful thing.   6
Into the third circle I had come through
    To the eternal, cursed and freezing rain
    Whose quality and measure's never new,
Huge hailstones, turbid water, snows that stain
    And burst through dark and pestilential air.
    The ground stinks putrid with it, sluiced in vain.   12
The monster Cerberus defends this lair;
    From three throats, wild and weird, he howls,
    Doglike, to keep them in the welter there.
His eyes are red, and greasy black his jowls,
    His paunch is wide, and talons are his hands.
    He bites and flays them piecemeal as he prowls.   18
The deluge makes them yelp like dogs it strands.
    They shield one with the other side and pause
    And turn, impious wretches, spits over brands.
The dragon opened all three sets of jaws
    And showed his fangs when he clapped eyes on us.
    In every limb he quivered with his cause.   24
My guide spread out his hands, not timorous,
    And quickly snatched up fistfuls of the dirt
    And threw them in the gullets, gaping ravenous.
Then, as a mastiff barking, ears alert,
    Goes quiet as it scoffs away its food,
    Straining and struggling to gulp it, not to hurt,   30
So these foul faces of Cerberus changed mood –
    That otherwise would thunder on the damned,
    And they on benefits of deafness brood.

And so we passed upon the shadows lammed
    With driving rain, as if on stepping stones
36   Of hollowness which seemed real bodies shrammed.
All lay outstretched on ground, men, maidens, crones,
    Save one who sat bolt upright as we came,
    And, as we passed, addressed us in these tones:
'You, guided there, across this Hell, now name
    And recognize me, if you can down here:
42   You, jointed before I was disjointed, the same!'
I answered him: 'Your agonies appear
    To blur my memory. I can't recall
    I ever saw you. Let me get things clear.
Remind me who you are, and why you sprawl
    In such a grievous place, and punitive;
48   More loathsome nowhere, if a worse at all.'
And he replied: 'The city where you live,
    So crammed with envy that it fills the sack,
    Was mine in the bright life it had to give.
You fellows called me Ciacco in days back.
    Here for the fault of gluttony I soak,
54   Broken by rain, you see, from clouds that crack.
But, in this misery, not alone: these folk
    All suffer, for like sin, like penalty.'
    And, saying that, he nothing further spoke,
Till I replied: 'Ciacco, your misery
    So weighs me down I need to weep a space.
60   But tell me, if you can, what destiny
Awaits the citizens of our factious place?
    And are there any left still just and true?
    And why division splits it to the base?'
He said: 'And it will come to bloodshed, too,
    From long contentions. The faction from the land
66   Will drive the others out; offence ensue.
And then, through one of temporizing hand,
    That sect in three years tumble from on high,
    And these prevail because he takes his stand,
And long hold up their heads while those will sigh
    Under the heavy burden, harsh and hard,
72   In shame and grievances to raise their cry.
Two men are just, but held in disregard;
    Smouldering envy, pride and avarice
    Spark in the rest till all their hearts are charred.'

At that he stopped. 'I would hear more of this,
    And further information, were I to choose.
    Your gift of further words I would not miss.   78
Farinata, Tegghiaio, of such worth and views,
    Rusticucci, Arrigo, Mosca, the rest,
    Who put their mind to doing good? What news?
Where are they now? Ah, answer this request.
    I greatly yearn to know if Heaven fold
    Or Hell envenom them in all its zest.'   84
And he replied: 'Among the blackest told,
    But worse their crimes, and lower they are hurled.
    Further descend; you'll see where they are shoaled.
But when you are returned to the sweet world,
    I ask you to remember me to men;
    I'll say no more, nor answer more.' He swirled   90
His straight look in a squint, gazed at me then,
    And beat his head and fell down with its weight
    And lay like his blind fellows in that fen.
My guide explained: 'He'll waken from that state
    Never again until the Trumpet sounds
    When the opposing Power comes. Then each inmate   96
Shall visit his sad grave, and to the bounds
    Of flesh and blood return; then shall they hear
    A thing that everlastingly resounds.'
Thus we traversed the filthy mix of sheer
    Rain and the shadows, and our walk was slow,
    Touching the future life a little here.   102
I asked him: 'Master, will these torments grow
    Or dwindle after the Last Judgement? Or Hell
    Persist in this intensity they know?'
And he retorted: 'Knowledge you have should tell:
    The greater perfection, the greater is the sense
    Of pleasure or of pain, as you know well.   108
Though these poor people, in accursed offence,
    Will never reach the truly perfect state,
    They hope for some approach as consequence.'
We went round on that road with much debate,
    Which I shall not repeat, and came to be
Where the next descent begins, and found in wait   114
    Plutus, confronting us, the great enemy.

CANTO 7

In this fourth circle of Hell – along with that of the usurers, identified armorially (canto 17) – Dante names no individuals, for their sin is so anonymously widespread and undeserving of note in its selfishness. The punishment is an adaptation of the torment of Sisyphus. The hoarders and misers on the left roll their burden of an immense boulder until it collides with that of the spendthrifts rolling theirs from the right. Thus both have to return and start the process over again. Dante in his hatred of the avarice of the contemporary church particularly emphasizes the clergy. The description of Fortune as a Goddess is justly renowned; Dante, the exile, has cause to refer to this concept many times in the course of his journey to Heaven.

'Pape Satan, Pape Satan aleppe,' blurted
    Plutus, in clucking voice. My gentle sage,
    The all-knowing, to comfort me, asserted:
'Don't let your fear disarm you at this stage.
    Whatever power he has cannot prevent
6   Our going down this rock; so let him rage.'
He turned to the bloated features of dissent:
    'Silence, accursèd wolf. Your own guts gnaw
    Internally with raging discontent.
Not without cause our journey here must draw
    In to the depths. It is the Will on high
12   Where Michael bent proud spirits under law.'
As sails, billowed with wind across the sky,
    Fall in a heap when the mainmast cracks,
    So that foul beast collapsed and let things lie.
Thus we descended to the fourth vale's tracks,
    Along the dismal bank whose gaping neck
18   Retains the world's evil like a sack's.
– Ah, why does our guilt bring our own wreck?
    Ah, justice of God, that shapes so many woes
    And penalties, I see, to give us check!
As wave meets wave and breaks itself in throes
    Over Charybdis, so must these souls dance
24   Their round, collide and counterpose.
There were more people here, I saw at a glance,
    Some left, some right, who yelled out as they rolled
    These great weights with their chests to make advance.

They crashed together, turned, and slowly bowled
    Their weights back round, and then they boom:
      'Why niggard gold?' to hear: 'Why squander gold?'   30
So they return along their circuit's gloom,
    In their first tracks towards the other side,
      And, turning there, the same reproach resume.
And, having done so, then again divide,
    Return along the same half-circle's curve
      Until the next joust comes and they collide.   36
'Master,' I said, heart wrung with every nerve,
    'Explain to me who are these people here?
      And did those tonsured, left, as clerics serve?'
Then he replied to me: 'Each in this sphere
    Was so squint-eyed of mind in the first life
      They spared of no expense, found nothing dear.   42
Most clearly do they show this in the strife
    When next they meet and bark their charges out,
      Where ends meet and faults divide like a knife.
These who are bald were clerics without doubt,
    And cardinals and popes in whom the sin
      Of avarice brings its worst excess about.'   48
And I replied: 'Then, surely, master, in
    This ring are some I know amid the throng
      Who were defiled by this vice or its kin?'
'You've added two and two together wrong.
    Their lack of judgement, all their sordid days,
      Gives them this obscurity where they belong.   54
Forever will they butt each other's ways,'
    He said. 'These, from their graves, will rise, fists tight;
      And these with hair shorn off and heads like glaze.
They have deprived themselves of the world so bright
    In niggarding or waste, and joined this feud,
      And what a feud! My words won't gild the sight.   60
But you, my son, can see, by all you've viewed,
    Fortune's trick with worldly goods comes soon,
      Though man may strive with man in deadly mood.
For all the gold there is beneath the moon,
    Or ever was, could never offer rest
      To one of these drawn souls who sought that boon.'   66
'Master,' I said, 'this Fortune you suggest,
    What sort is she that holds the world's good things
      So tightly in her grasp which none can wrest?'

And he replied: 'Oh, foolish underlings,
　　　How deep the ignorance in which you wade.
72　　　Now learn that judgement of her which mine brings:
He whose wisdom transcends all that he made
　　　Created all the Heavens, and gave them guides,
　　　So part lights part and every part is rayed
With equal distribution from all sides.
　　　Likewise with earthly splendours he did ordain:
78　　　One general minister, singled from his guides,
To shift, at times, from man to man, the vain
　　　Possessions, kin to kin, and clan to clan,
　　　Beyond prevention of the human brain,
So, in obedience to her doom and plan
　　　That is hidden like a serpent in the grass,
84　　　Some people languish, others rule a span.
Your knowledge cannot fathom her dark glass;
　　　She gives, she judges and maintains her state;
　　　As other powers rule theirs, she brings to pass.
Her permutations have no truce, no date.
　　　Necessity makes her exactions swift;
90　　　Men come to take their turn at such a rate.
She is the much reviled one. Men cannot sift;
　　　They blame her wrongfully, who ought to bless.
　　　With evil words they have reviled her gift.
But she, in bliss, hears nothing they express;
　　　With all the primal ones, and joyously,
96　　　She turns her sphere, enjoys her blessedness.
– We must descend to deeper misery.
　　　Each star that rose when I came out has set,
　　　And longer stay is not permitted me.'
We crossed the circle to the bank's silhouette,
　　　Toward a spring that boils and fumes away
102　　　Into a fissure cut by its own fret.
Darker than perse that water was, blue-grey,
　　　And we accompanied the dreary flow,
　　　And so descended by this eerie way.
The dreary rine exudes in marsh below,
　　　Called Styx when it has reached across the floor
108　　　Of grey malignant shores where it must go.
And I who concentrated to explore
　　　Glimpsed miry people wading in that fen,
　　　All naked, furious, and in a roar.

They fought each other with their fists and then
    With head and chest and feet they kick and heave
    And next, with teeth they maim opposing men.   14
My kindly master said: 'Now you perceive
    Those souls whose anger overcame control,
    And I would have you assuredly believe
That, underneath this marsh, more of them shoal
    Whose sobs come boiling to the surface. Gaze,
    Your eyes will tell you: everywhere they roll.   120
Fixed in the slime, they say: "Sullen our days
    In the sweet air so gladdened by the sun,
    Bearing, within, the sluggish fumes that haze.
Now we lie sullen as we've always done
    In this black mire." This is the hymn
    They gurgitate for clear speech have they none.'   126
Thus, between the dry bank and marsh's brim,
    Along an arc of the foul morass we passed,
And watched them gulping filth in which they swim.
    We reached the groundwork of a tower at last.

CANTO 8

The two companions are ferried by Phlegyas across the fifth circle towards the city of Dis. In an episode many find distasteful, Dante requests that Filippo Argenti be soused deeper in the stinking fen for his outrage in trying to sink their boat. Dante is panic-stricken when the guardian-furies of the city announce that only Vergil may enter. They have crossed the fifth circle and appear to have reached an impasse.

I say, continuing, long before we'd pressed
    Close to the groundwork of that tower's height,
    Our eyes looked up, by chance, toward the crest
Because of two small flames we saw ignite,
    And then, afar, another signal burned,
6   So distant that it almost thwarted sight.
Toward my fount of knowledge there I turned
    And asked: 'What is this sign? What answer's made?
    And who are these whose lights we have discerned?'
He answered, 'On the waters is displayed
    What is expected. If the vapour hadn't scarfed
12   Your vision, you'd have seen without my aid.'
And never did a bow-string flight a shaft
    More swiftly through the air than, to the strand,
    I saw a small boat come, of shallow draught,
Across those waters, guided by the hand
    Of a lone steersman who now raised a howl:
18   'Now you are caught, dire spirit, in this land.'
'Phlegyas, Phlegyas, this time vainly growl.
    You'll have a measure of our company
    No longer than we cross your marsh so foul!'
As someone, hearing some great trickery
    That has been played against him, feels a great
24   Resentment, so, in his wrath, he seemed to be.
My guide stepped down into the boat whose weight
    Did not increase until he made me get
    On board, and then it lowered in the strait.
As soon as both my guide and I were set,
    Its ancient prow, that was long past its prime,
30   Cut deeper than with others it would fret.
We ran the dead channel, when, draped in grime,
    A figure rose before us, crying, 'Say
    Just who you are that come before your time.'

And I replied: 'Yes, come, but not to stay.
　　But who are you, so filthy in your sty?'
　　'The weeping's mine,' he managed to convey.   36
And I retorted: 'Stick with tears and sigh,
　　Accursèd spirit; I recognize you now
　　In all your filth. Back down where you should lie.'
At which he reached both hands upon the prow.
　　My wary master cast him on the polder,
　　Saying: 'Off, dog, rejoin those in the slough.'   42
And then he cast his arm around my shoulder,
　　Embraced me, as he said: 'Indignant soul,
　　Blest be the womb that bore you, blest your moulder.
He was all arrogance when live and whole;
　　No trace of good to grace his memory,
　　And so his shade here's furious, out of control.   48
How many in your world there still may be,
　　Thinking themselves great kings, will yet lie there,
　　Like swine in mire, and leave but obloquy.'
And I replied: 'I should be glad, while near,
　　To see this furious wretch dunked to the heel
　　In all the swill that slabs this noxious mere.'   54
He answered me: 'Before the shores reveal
　　Their lines to you, your wish shall be fulfilled.
　　And right it is to gratify your zeal.'
And quickly then I saw that miry guild
　　Tear at him so much that, to this very day,
　　I thank and praise our God that he so willed.   60
All bellowed: 'Get Filippo Argenti! Flay!'
　　And the irascible Florentine just spent
　　His teeth upon himself and gnawed away.
I say no more of this; and on we went.
　　But, in my ears, an uproar dinned ahead,
　　So that I turned my eyes that way, intent.   66
My kind guide spoke: 'The City of the Dead,
　　Named after Dis, approaches. There it lies
　　With its great guard, grave citizens outspread.'
I said: 'Its mosques already catch my eyes;
　　Distinctly, in the Valley there, they swell –
　　And red, as if from out of fire they rise.'   72
He said: 'As you observe, this deeper Hell
　　Burns with eternal fire that makes them red
　　And underlies the reeking citadel.'

We now approached those deep fosses spread
    To moat that joyless city in. Its walls
78   Were forged of iron, I would have said.
And then, when we had ended a long haul's
    Circuit of them, we reached a landing-place.
    The boatman snapped: 'Out. The entrance calls.'
More than a thousand spirits, gone from Grace,
    I saw above the gates – who roared and said:
84   'Who is that one which without a trace
Of death goes through the kingdom of the dead?'
    My wise master made it clear and plain
    He wished to speak in secret on that head.
Then they desisted in their great disdain
    And muttered: 'You move forward on your own.
90   Leave him who dares to enter this domain.
Let him retrace his foolish steps alone,
    As if he could, for here you surely stay,
    For giving him your escort through this zone.'
– Judge if my courage did not drain away
    To hear accursèd words like that. I thought
96   I never would again see light of day.
'Oh, my dear guide, now seven times you've brought
    Me safely through, and rescued me from deep
    Dangers where I was close to being caught.
Do not desert me now,' I pleaded, 'keep
    Together if we can no further go,
102   And let's retrace our steps before they leap.'
That gracious lord who'd led me there below
    Replied: 'Calm down. None can waylay us long.
    The One who promised us can fear no foe.
Wait here for me; take comfort and be strong,
    And feed your weary spirit with good hope.
108   I never will forsake you in this throng.'
And so the gentle guide went up the slope
    And left me there in gnawing, shifty doubt;
    And true and false, in mind, had all the scope.
I couldn't hear what the offer was about,
    But little time it took to be explored.
114   They rushed like rivals back to their redoubt.
The foe barred up the gates against my lord
    And he remained outside, then slowly turned
    And came to me with lagging steps, ignored.

He looked upon the ground with gaze concerned;
    His brow devoid of vigour, he said in sighs:
    'Who bans me from this house of sorrows earned?'   120
He said: 'Don't fret to see my anger rise,
    For I will overcome them all in this,
    Whatever hindrances they may devise.
This insolence of theirs is not amiss,
    Or new for them. At one less secret gate,
    And still unbarred, they once thought they should hiss.   126
You saw its deadly words, and what they state.
    – Already this side, and coming down the steep,
Crossing the circles with no escort, straight,
    Nears one who opens up this city's keep.'

CANTO 9

The city of Dis represents the beginning of the Hell reserved for deliberate and intentional sinners. Dante is here at the most fearful part of all his journey, except for its beginning where he first met Vergil. Even Vergil himself shows hesitation and doubt until he hears the coming of the angelic assistance. Dante again adapts classical myth to create the guardians of the gate to this circle.

The colour cowardice painted in my face
    When I could see my guide turn back, repressed,
    Dispelled from his the slightest troubled trace.
He stopped, all ears, as one would listen best,
    For sight could only reach about a span
6   In that black air and fog, unless he guessed.
'We have to win this skirmish,' he began;
    'If not – well, help was offered us, indeed.
    How long they take to come and end this ban!'
I noticed start and finish disagreed,
    And that he veiled with second thoughts his first,
12   Which I was never meant to note or heed.
But nonetheless from that I feared the worst,
    Though maybe drawing from the broken thread
    More fearful meaning than it had rehearsed.
'Do any from the first degree descend
    Into the depths of this vile shell – of those
18   Whose punishment is lack of hope without end?'
I put this question: this reply arose:
    'On such a trek as mine across this plain
    It's rare that any of us ever goes.
But, yes, I've entered once this place of pain,
    Conjured by foul Erichtho who revoked
24   The shadows to their bodies once again.
From flesh my shade had not long been uncloaked,
    When she enforced me here beyond this wall
    To raise a spirit in that Judas-circle yoked.
This is the deepest place, darkest of all,
    The furthest from the Heaven that surrounds
30   Them all. I know the way. Your fear forestall.
The marsh that reeks these stenches bounds
    The woeful city which we may not see
    Without some stroke of anger which astounds.'

He said much more that slipped the memory
    Because my eye was caught to concentrate
    On the high tower with its burning turretry,   36
Where instantly there rose, in gory state,
    Three Hell-bent Furies with the life and limb
    Of women, with their bearing and their gait,
Girdled with greenest hydras; hair the whim
    Of serpents which cerastes bound in spleen
    About their loathsome brows in vicious trim.   42
My guide, who knew these handmaids of the Queen
    Of everlasting lamentation, said,
    'Watch. The fierce Erinyes: that, seen
Upon the left, Megaera: the weeping head,
    Upon the right, Alecto. Between the two,
    Tisiphone.' With that his speech was fled.   48
Each tore her breasts with claws; and then they flew
    Against themselves with open palms; each crone
    Howled out so loud I clasped the poet, fear all through.
'Medusa, come; let's turn him into stone!'
    They glared down on us, launching furious cries.
    'Our vengeance failed on Theseus in this zone.'   54
'Turn your back and firmly shut your eyes,
    For, if the Gorgon show, and you should look,
    There would be no revisiting the skies.'
And, saying so, he spun me round and took
    No chances with my hands, blindfolding me
    With his as well where tremblingly I shook.   60
– And you who have the healthy minds may see
    The doctrine which is hidden and concealed
    In these strange verses and their symmetry! –
Now came upon the water's scum congealed
    A crash of fearful noise in which the shores
    Began to quaver as its fury pealed;   66
A noise as of a wind that keenly roars,
    Seeking the adverse heat, shaking the height
    Of forests with a force that nothing floors;
It breaks the branches, drives them in its might,
    A cloud of dust ahead, it travels proud,
    Stirring wild beasts and shepherds all to flight.   72
He took his hands away and murmured loud:
    'Turn your vision on that ancient scum,
    There, where the smoke is harshest in its cloud.'

As frogs disperse, seeing a serpent come,
    And leap in all directions till they land
78   And squat upon the bottom, still and dumb,
Likewise a thousand ruined spirits fanned
    In flight in front of one who made across
    The Styx with soles untouched with wet or sand.
He brushed the noxious airs out of the fosse
    Away before his face with his left hand;
84   Only that nuisance left him at a loss.
The messenger of Heaven in this land
    I well could see; toward my lord I turned,
    Who signalled me to bow and, silent, stand.
With indignation crammed, it seemed, he burned.
    He reached the gates which open to his wand,
90   For there was no resistance I discerned.
'Outcasts of Heaven, race despised and bond,'
    He said, upon that loathsome sill, 'Why, why
    This insolence with which you fixedly respond?
This baulking at the Will that is so High
    Its purpose never can be thwarted here?
96   It has before increased these pains you sigh.
Why butt your heads against the fates? A dear
    Gain, that! Recall what Cerberus displays:
    Flayed, throat to muzzle, for his snarl and sneer!'
Then he returned by the same filthy ways,
    And spoke no word to us, but seemed a man
102   With other worries to command his gaze,
Much more than theirs who stand before him can.
    Towards that city then we turned our pace,
    After these sacred words, secure from ban.
Unchallenged there we entered in the place.
    In my anxiety to note the state
108   Which such a fortress hems within its space,
I looked around as soon as in the gate,
    And saw, to right and left, a vast plateau,
    Full of all sorrow, evil torment, hate.
And, as at Arles with Rhone stagnant and slow,
    Or Pola where the Quarnero gulf confines
114   Italy, bathing its borders in her flow,
The sepulchres disjoint the level lines –
    So here, on every side, the graveyard looms,
    But with more bitterness among the signs,

For scattered flames disgorge between the tombs,
    And turn them all to such a reddened glare
    No hotter iron came from smithy fumes.   120
Their covers all were raised, and in despair
    Exuded groans, so grievously they stirred,
    It seemed, from sad and wounded spirits there.
I asked: 'Now who are these that lie interred
    In sepulchres, and only by their groans
    And painful outcries can be known and heard?'   126
He said: 'Here, beneath these lifted stones,
    Are the Heresiarchs, sects and followers.
    These tombs are laden with much more than moans.
Like is buried with like; the sepulchres
    Vary in heat.' Then, turning to the right,
He passed along between the sufferers   132
    And battlements in all their louring height.

CANTO 10

The companions pass between the city wall and the sepulchres of the heretics into the sixth circle. The soul of Farinata, the great leader of the Ghibellines, rises up and speaks to them. He was father-in-law to Dante's great friend, the poet Guido Cavalcanti. Hearing their conversation, Cavalcante de' Cavalcanti, Guido's father, enquires why his son is not with Dante. Farinata forecasts Dante's exile and explains the ability of souls in Hell to know remote aspects of past and future. This embarrasses Dante over his misunderstanding that dictated his attitude to Cavalcante's enquiry.

It was a secret path my master knew
    Between the torments and the city wall;
    I followed as he led me safely through.
'Supreme in virtue, winding me through all
    The wicked circles, tell me this one thing,
6   And satisfy these wishes that befall.
Might I not see those shades who're suffering
    Inside these sepulchres? No guards are posed;
    The slabs are raised which were their covering.'
He said: 'All will be sealed, forever closed,
    When from Jehoshaphat they redescend,
12   Bringing their bodies now in earth reposed.
Here all those who followed Epicurus' trend
    Are tombed with him because he held and taught
    The soul dies when the body meets its end.
But now the question that you had and brought
    Shall soon find satisfaction inside here –
18   As, also, will that wish you don't report.'
I said, 'Kind guide, if ever I appear
    To hide my heart from you, it is from need
    Of brevity in which your mastery's clear.'
'Ah, you, who walk alive, of Tuscan breed,
    Across this fiery city, speaking well,
24   Please linger here awhile, and pay some heed.
And from the way you speak I clearly tell
    You are a native of that noble land
    I too much troubled in my living spell.'
Suddenly, from a sepulchre near at hand,
    Issued this sound so that, in very fear,
30   I edged to where my guide had taken stand.

He said: 'Turn round. What are you doing? Look here,
    It's Farinata risen up. How well
    You'll see him, from the waist above quite clear.'
Already I'd fixed my eyes on his to dwell
    Upon that figure – head and chest in pride
    Thrown back, as if in mighty scorn of Hell.   36
The firm and eager handling of my guide
    Pushed me among the tombs to him. He said,
    'Be brief. Don't waste your words!' in an aside.
When to the foot of his tomb I had been led,
    He looked almost contemptuous of me,
    And asked: 'From what long line, then, were you bred?'   42
I hushed up nothing, told my ancestry
    In eagerness to answer his request.
    He raised his brows a little, I could see,
And snorted out: 'Fiercely did they contest
    With me and with my family and party.
    But twice I scattered them and had the best.'   48
'If they were driven off,' I answered tartly,
    'They certainly returned from every point.
    But yours have not acquired that skill so smartly.'
Then up beside him rose, on a knee-joint,
    I think, another shadow clearly seen
    From chin upward, staring, at this point.   54
It looked around me, baffled, as if keen
    To know if some companion came with me.
    But deep the disappointment must have been.
It said, in tears: 'If height of genius be
    Your guarantee through this blind house of woe,
    Why's my son not with you? And where is he?'   60
'I have not come by my own worth below.
    That one waiting there's my guide through here,
    Perhaps to her your Guido scorned to know.'
Already, in his words, and by his sphere
    Of punishment, I knew his name and so
    The answers that I gave were full and clear.   66
Rising erect, he cried: 'What? How d'you know?
    "Scorned"? Is he dead, then? What did you say?
    Sweetness of light in his eye not glow?'
When he perceived I faltered in delay,
    He fell down on his back at once again,
    Unable to support a longer stay.   72

The first, that mighty spirit, could detain
   Me with his wishes, and did not look to see,
   Nor leant to hear, but carried on again:
'It is a greater torment here to me,
   If my supporters poorly learnt that art,
78   Than all the tortures of this bed may be.
The features of the Queen who rules this part
   Shall not light fifty times when you'll have cause
   To learn yourself the harshness of that art.
That in the sweet world you may once more pause,
   Now tell me why your kin are cavillers
84   So fierce against my kindred in your laws.'
'The havoc and the widespread massacres,'
   I then replied, 'which dyed the Arbia red
   Produced that litany of our ministers.'
Shaking his head, he sighed, but then he said:
   'I was not alone in that; nor without cause,
90   Assuredly, would I have joined that head.
But I alone, it was, that made them pause
   When all planned razing Florence to the ground,
   And I stood up for her with all her flaws.'
'Ah, so your seed some day have rest,' I found
   My prayer, 'now free my baffled judgement here
96   Out of the tangled knot in which it's wound.
It seems that you foresee what will appear
   In time, and yet you have a different view
   Of present detail – if I've seen things clear.'
'Like one who has his sight impaired, we do
   See things remote and far, for so much light
102   The Supreme King permits to filter through.
When things are closer, or immediate to sight,
   Our intellect draws nothing peeringly,
   And knows but what is heard of human plight.
And all our knowledge here, and what we see,
   D'you follow?, at that point must surely die
108   Which shuts the doorway on futurity.'
Then, sorry for my fault, I made reply:
   'In that case, would you tell the shade I felled
   His son is still alive beneath the sky?
Please let him know the silence that I held
   Was made by this same error in my thought
114   Which your remarks to me have now dispelled.'

And in the greatest hurry then I sought –
    Because I saw my master called and beckoned –
    Of his companions there some brief report.
He answered: 'There is Frederick, the second;
    The Cardinal. I say nothing of the rest.
    More than a thousand of them may be reckoned.'   120
At that he hid himself, and so I pressed
    My pace to where the ancient had delayed,
    Turning in mind the hostile words addressed.
He moved along, and as our way we made,
    He asked: 'What's given you this distraught air?'
    I answered him, the troubling words conveyed.   126
'What you have heard against you always bear
    In mind,' the sage advised me. 'Note what I say!'
    And, saying this, he raised his finger there:
'When you are standing before the sweet ray
    Of that Lady whose bright eye sees the whole,
    You'll learn the journey of your life and way.'   132
Then, to the left, he turned on heel and sole.
    We left the wall and, to the centre, walked
A path toward a valley, our next goal.
    Even from there its stench annoyed and baulked.

CANTO 11

Vergil and Dante now reach a precipice which divides the sixth circle from those beneath it. On the edge of this they find a great mausoleum to a heretical pope. They shelter behind it to accustom themselves to the stench rising from the lower circles. Vergil takes the opportunity to explain what types of sin are punished in the remaining circles. Dante wants to know why usury offends God so much.

On the brink of a high cliff, underlaid
    By a cirque of broken stones, we saw the welter,
    Below, a still more cruel pen had made.
And here, what with the loathsome stench and swelter
    That rose and reeked from that profound abyss,
6   We sought to make approach behind the shelter
Of a massive mausoleum which said this:
    'Pope Anastasius I hold. From the straight way
    Photinus drew him till he went amiss.'
'Further descent we must a time delay,
    Until our senses find this stench less grim,
12   And then we shall not heed it on the way.'
So said my master, and I answered him:
    'Find compensation for the time that's lost.'
    He said, 'You know I'll use this interim.
My son, down there, three circles will accost
    You, set within these stones, arranged in grades,
18   In system similar to those we've crossed.
They all are crammed full of accursèd shades;
    Now learn of why and how they're penned in here,
    So that the sight may tell without more aids.
Most abhorred by Heaven is the sheer
    Malice which means to injure. Such an end,
24   By fraud or violence inflicts on others fear.
Fraud most displeases God, and must offend,
    Since it is found in man alone confined;
    So, in the worst pain, fraudulence is penned.
To violence the first ring is assigned.
    But violence is done to one of three,
30   So it divides in three, one to each kind.
Violence may be done to God, or be
    Imposed on fellow man or self, in this sense:
    Either direct to person, or to property.

First, to one's neighbour, bringing death, intense
    Wounding, or else against his goods directed,
    By arson, ruin, extortion, comes the offence.   36
So, in the first ring, murderers are subjected,
    And all who wound in malice, those that steal
    And plunder, are in separate groups collected.
Then violence to self a man might deal
    Or to his substance; in the second ring,
    Therefore, a vain repentance must those feel   42
Who cast your world away or those who fling
    Their wealth away on gambling or the spree,
    Weeping where they should rejoice in everything.
Then, violence is done the Deity,
    Denying him within the heart of hearts;
    Despising Nature's bounty, or in blasphemy.   48
Therefore, the strictest ring seals in its parts
    Both Sodom and Cahors, and all who name
    God with disparagement within their hearts.
Then, conscience-gnawing fraud a man may frame
    Against all those who trust him, or those beyond
    Who credit nothing such a man might claim.   54
The latter seems to break only the bond
    Which Nature builds, so, in the next ring,
    Are those of hypocrisy and lying fond;
Sorcerers, flatterers, tricksters, panders cling;
    Thieves, simonists, barrators despond,
    And all such filth lie there in suffering.   60
The former fraud denies both Nature's bond
    And nurture's strengthening which adds to this
    A special trust with which we should respond.
Thus, in the strictest circle, seat of Dis,
    And very centre of the universe,
    All traitors are consumed in that abyss.'   66
I intervened: 'Your guidance is clear and terse,
    And well delineates the whole ravine,
    And all the inmates, both the worst and worse.
But tell me one thing: those that we have seen
    In the gross marsh; those that the wind drifts
    Or rain lashes; those that clash with tongues so keen –   72
If God is angry with them, what is it lifts
    Them from the flame-red city and its pain?
    If God's not angry, why put them to such shifts?'

He said: 'Why are you off the track again,
        And worse than usual? Or have you let your mind
78   Wander away along some other lane?
Don't you recall the dispositions, defined
        According to your *Ethics*, where one reads
        Of three unwilled of Heaven in mankind?
Incontinence, malice, mad bestial deeds?
        And, also, how incontinence offends God less,
84   And, therefore, slighter punishment it needs?
Now, if you think through clearly and address
        Your memory to consider who they are,
        Punished outside and higher, you will confess
What they may be, why separated far
        From those fell spirits, not to mention why
90   God's anger strikes at them with lesser jar.'
'O Sun, healer of the troubled eye,
        You gladden me so much, in settling doubt,
        Asking's no less a pleasure than knowing why.
But would you please retrace those words about
        Usury which you asserted an offence
96   To divine Goodness, unravelling all out?'
He said: 'Philosophy, for those with sense
        To hear, distinguishes in not one part
        But everywhere how Nature is a consequence
Of the divine Intelligence and Art.
        And, if you note your *Physics*, you may find –
102   Not many pages from the very start –
That your art follows her as a scholar's mind,
        The master's; so that your art, or so to speak,
        Is grandchild of the Deity's in kind.
By these two – if your memory will seek
        The start of Genesis – you'll see a man
108   Must earn his bread to prosper week by week.
Usurers go a different way; that clan
        Despises Nature in herself and in
        Her follower, hoping in a different plan.
But follow me; I wish now to begin.
        The Fishes quiver on the skyline; the Wain
114   Lies over Caurus; and there's the origin
        Of the descent, just further, to the plain.'

CANTO 12

The descent is perilous by way of fallen rocks; more perilous the Minotaur who challenges them before they reach it. He is soon quelled by Vergil. They clamber down to the River of Blood that encircles the seventh circle, first of the triple divisions distinguishing the violent. Those violent against others are punished here, their depth in the flow according to their guilt. The banks are patrolled by Centaurs who enforce the punishment. Their chief, Chiron, appoints Nessus to be a guide for the poets.

The place of the descent was alpine steep,
    And from the very look of that ravine
    Every eye would shun that ruinous heap.
For, like the fall of rock that can be seen
    This side of Trent, in the Adige's shoulder –
    Earthquake or subsidence it must have been –   6
From peak to base, and boulder after boulder,
    Had tumbled down so that a passageway
    Was seen as possible, to any beholder.
Likewise, down this chasm, descent must stray;
    But, on the crumbled brink, that infamy
    Of Crete, conceived in the false cow, lay.   12
And, when he saw us coming to the scree,
    He gnashed himself; like one whose furies fume
    Inwardly against himself he seemed to be.
'The Duke of Athens you perhaps assume,'
    My guide exclaimed, 'returned again alive,
    Who, in the upper world, dealt you your doom!   18
Vanish, beast; this man does not arrive
    Trained by your sister, but he travels here
    To see the punishment in which you strive.'
As a bull, mortally wounded, lunges clear
    But cannot charge, yet plunges here and there,
    I saw the minotaur react and rear.   24
My guide, alert, cried, 'Quickly, run to where
    The passage starts; while he still runs amok
    It's best that you descend the rocky stair.'
And so we took our way down stacks of rock,
    Over the loose boulders which sometimes fell
    Beneath my feet with the strange weight's shock.   30

I went down, thinking. – 'Ah, perhaps you dwell
    Upon this ruin by that bestial wrath
    Guarded,' my guide supposed, 'that I'd to quell.
I'll tell you this: the last time I came forth
    Into this Underworld, the precipice
36   Had not yet fallen in this tumbled swathe.
Not long before the highest ring of Dis
    Was seized as spoil by One, come from above,
    A shudder thrilled throughout this foul abyss,
So that I thought the Universe felt love,
    By which, as many think, the world was tossed
42   Often in chaos; with that quake, that shove,
This ancient rock was, in that moment, lost
    And fell in ruins here – the same as those
    Elsewhere, in other parts we have not crossed.
But look into the chasm. Just there flows
    The river of blood where all of those must seethe
48   Who injure others with the violence of blows.'
– Ah, blind greed, mad rage, goading while we breathe
    Our brief life, and, in eternity,
    Steep us in bitterness they must bequeath! –
I saw, just as my guide explained to me,
    A wide fosse curving to enclose a plain,
54   And sweeping on to circularity.
And, in the area between that massive drain
    And broken cliff, were Centaurs, armed with bows,
    Hunting in line, as if on earth again.
Perceiving us, they stood stock-still as foes,
    And three came from the band with javelin
60   And bow, whom, seemingly, the others chose.
And from a distance: 'Come no further in
    Or else I draw this bow. Now tell me why
    And for what torments you descend. Begin!'
'Our answer is for Chiron,' came his reply,
    'Just over there. Unhappily, your will
66   Was always just as rash in days gone by.'
He nudged me, saying, 'That's old Nessus still.
    He died for fair Deianira, and when
    He sought revenge, on self avenged that ill.
And there, stood in the middle of his men,
    Is the great Chiron; he it was who nursed
72   Achilles. That's Pholus, furious now, as then.

Around the fosse, and following the cursed
    They go in thousands, piercing with a shaft
    Those who try changing depth where they're immersed.'
We neared the speedy beasts. He took a haft,
    Chiron, and pushed his beard back with the nock
    To clear his massive jaws, said, with some craft,   78
To his companions, 'Have you kept good stock
    Of that one there who stays toward the rear?
    Whatever he touches moves beneath the shock.
Feet of the dead have never done that here.'
    My guide, the good, was face to face with him
    Whose compound natures in one form appear.   84
He answered, 'Live he is, unique in this dim
    Valley I am commanded he should see.
    Not sport, necessity brings him to this brim.
From singing alleluia she appeared to me
    With this new office. He's no thief, I say,
    Nor I, a spirit given to thievery.   90
But, by that virtue guiding me this way
    In such a wild terrain, give us your aid,
    A man of yours to find the ford, convey
My friend across upon his back. No shade,
    He cannot travel on the yielding air.'
    So asked my good guide as Chiron stayed.   96
He turned toward his right, to Nessus there,
    And said, 'Turn and guide them to the ford.
    If other groups approach, defend the pair.'
We moved on with our trusty guide; the gored
    And seethed in blood were shrieking in the sweep
    As we followed where the boiling purple roared.   102
I saw how some of them were eyebrow-deep.
    The Centaur said, 'Tyrants, who took to sword
    And pillaging, and here lament and weep
Their merciless offences in this ford.
    There's Alexander. Dionysius, who set
    Sicily on years of woe, finds his reward.   108
And that head, there, so black and jet,
    Is Azzolino. The other, who is blond,
    Obizzo of Este whose blood his step-son let
Within the upper world.' And, to respond,
    I turned toward the poet who said, 'He's guide
    To you for now. I'm second till beyond.'   114

A little further round he paused beside
   A group that, from the throat, emerged, head
   Free of that seething stream in which they ride.
He showed me a spirit left apart instead:
   'That one pierced, in God's bosom, the heart
120   That bleeds, revered, beside the Thames,' he said.
I saw some, passing next, whose upper part,
   From waist to head, emerged and floated clear.
   Many I recognized, too many to chart.
The depth grew shallower till it could sear
   Only the feet. We found the crossing-place
126   Where we might safely ford the fosse just here.
'The seething current which you watch and trace
   Grows shallow here,' the Centaur said,
   'But realize that, opposite, its race
Wears deeper and deeper down into its bed
   Until it reaches round again to surge
132   Where tyranny is doomed to mourn its dead.
Divine Justice torments Attila, scourge
   Of all the earth; Pyrrhus and Sextus grieve,
   And, to eternity, its seethings urge,
Milking the tears it drags from those who thieve,
   Like Rinier of Corneto and his confrère,
138   Rinier Pazzo, highwaymen.' He took his leave
   And crossed the ford again, quitting us there.

CANTO 13

The second division of the seventh circle is the miserable Wood of those violent against themselves. Turned into trees, they are savaged by the Harpies. Pietro delle Vigne, the poet of the Sicilian school, notary, and chancellor to Emperor Frederick II, tells his tragic life-story to Dante. They are interrupted by a noisy chase: Lano of Siena and Jacomo da Sant' Andrea pursued by hounds. These had squandered their gifts and brought on their own ruin. A suicide countryman of Dante's – believed by some to be the prior Lotto degli Agli – forecasts calamities to befall Florence.

Nessus had not yet made the further shore
    Before we'd reached a wood in which there lay
    No clearly marked out pathway any more.
Not green in foliage but a dusky grey;
    Not smooth the branches – warped and gnarled like roots;
    No apples there but poisoned stuntings sway.   6
Between Cecina and Corneto the wild brutes
    That hate the cultivated land infest
    No brakes as harsh and dense in barbs and shoots.
Here the loathsome Harpies roost and nest.
    They drove the Trojans from the Strophades
    With dire omens of coming woes oppressed.   12
They perch with mournful cries in the weird trees.
    Their necks and visages are human, though;
    Paunch feathered, wings huge, feet clawed to seize.
My kind master said: 'Before much further, know
    You're in the second circuit which will last
    Until we come eventually below   18
Upon the ghastly sand. Therefore cast
    Your eyes about you well, and see such things
    That, put in speech, would strain faith very fast.'
Already I had heard pained utterings,
    On every side, but still saw nothing there,
    So stood stock-still, in doubts confusion brings.   24
I think he thought I thought cries tore the air
    From people hiding in among the trees,
    Disturbed by our approach toward their lair.
'Break off a shoot of any one of these,'
    The master said, 'and those thoughts in your head
    Will be defective the instant that you seize.'   30

I stretched my hand a little as he said,
    And plucked a branch down from a massive thorn.
    The trunk cried: 'Why d'you tear me?' And it bled.
And, dark with blood, it started again to mourn,
    'Why do you tear at me? Have you no feeling?

36   We may seem trees but men we all were born.
You ought to show more mercy in your dealing,
    Even with serpent souls, than you extend
    To me, with all your savagery and stealing.'
As a green log, burning at one end,
    Lets fall the drops and hisses with the air

42   Expelled, so did that torn and split wood send
Out words and blood together from that tear,
    So that in shock I dropped it to the ground,
    And stood, as one afraid, with vacant stare.
'O injured soul,' the poet answered the sound,
    'If he had but believed what he had read,

48   Though only in my verses to be found,
He never would have moved against your head;
    But this incredible thing had prompted me
    To make him try what grieves me to have said.
But tell him who you are, and used to be,
    So that, as some amends to you, he may

54   Refresh your fame in the world he will re-see.'
The trunk replied: 'With those sweet words you say,
    You lure me to break silence. So, if I snare
    Myself to talk a bit, don't weary on the way.
Both keys to Frederick's heart were in my care;
    Locking, unlocking, I softly slid the wards:

60   His secrets almost no one else could share.
Such great fidelity I brought my lord's
    Glorious office that, in its good care,
    I lost both sleep and health. That curse of hordes,
That palace vice, the whore that cannot tear
    Her shameless eyes from Caesar's retinue,

66   Inflamed all minds against me then and there;
And these, inflamed, inflamed Augustus, too,
    So that my happy honours by distrust
    Were changed, and wretched misery my due.
My soul in its disdain, thinking the thrust
    Of death itself would free me from disdain,

72   Made me unjust against myself the just.

By the new roots of this tree, I swear again,
    I never did break faith against my lord,
    So worthy of all honour. Ah, make it plain,
If either of you ever are restored
    Into the world, and save my faithful name
    Which lies outstretched from envy's vicious sword.'   78
The poet listened, and, when no more came,
    Said: 'Now that he has stopped don't lose your chance,
    But say if you need more about his claim.'
I answered then: 'You speak for me, advance
    The points I ought to ask, and need to know.
    I can't, for pity, either speak or glance.'   84
Then he continued: 'So that he may go
    And do what you desire, now, more than all,
    Imprisoned soul, say how your soul came so
Entangled in these knots and, further, tell
    Us whether any spirit is released
    From all these boughs in which it seems to dwell.'   90
The exhalations of the trunk increased,
    And changed the gusts to these words in reply:
    'You shall be answered, briefly, at the least.
When fierce spirits tear themselves to die
    And leave the body, Minos sends them straight
    Into the seventh circle where they lie   96
Within the wood, no chosen place, where fate
    Or chance has flung them; they spring up there
    And bud, like grains of spelt, and reach the state
Of sapling, then to wild trees flourish, where
    The Harpies eat the leaves, and give the pain,
    And, to that pain, an outlet in each tear.   102
We'll fetch our spoils, like others, but in vain,
    Since we shall never put them on to wear,
    For what a man rejects he ought not regain.
We'll drag them here; the mournful wood shall bear
    Them each suspended from the thorny tree
    That is its own guilt-laden spirit there.'   108
We stood there listening for the trunk, to see
    If it would tell us more. A sudden crash
    Disturbed us – noises as of those who flee.
Like one who thinks the boar and hunters thrash
    Towards his post, who hears the boar's mad charge,
    Hears branches, all around him, crash and lash,   114

We saw, on the left, two spirits barge,
    Naked and torn, in such a violent flight
    They splintered all the branches, thin or large.
'Come now, death; now,' the first cried out in fright;
    The second, furious that he was so slow,
120   Cried, 'Lano, your legs were not so fleet, in fight
At Toppo, in those jousts.' – He seemed to know
    His wind was gone, and therefore took to hide,
    And so into a bush he seemed to grow.
The wood behind them filled, from every side,
    With ravenous black bitches, swift in pursuit
126   As greyhounds racing from the leash untied,
And in the man who hid there every brute
    Buried its fangs, and tore him piece from piece,
    And carried off his wretched limbs as loot.
Towards the bush whose groanings would not cease,
    Though vain, in all its savage wounds, my guide
132   Led me by the hand, and we heard this release:
'O Jacomo da Sant' Andrea,' it cried,
    'What profit was there making me your screen?
    Your sinful life was not my fault,' it sighed.
My master, when drawn near enough to lean
    Over it, asked: 'But who were you that sigh
138   Such words of woe through blood and wounds so green?'
And he to us: 'You spirits passing by,
    That saw the havoc in its violent shame
    Which stripped my leaves from me and let them fly,
Gather them round my roots again. I came
    From that city which changed its patron, Mars,
144   For John the Baptist; and, for his ousted claim,
His arts prolong its sorrows and its scars;
    And were there not some semblance of his might
    Upon the bridgework that the Arno jars,
Those men, who raised it on the ruined site
    Attila left in ashes, had toiled in vain.
150   But, as for me, from my own dwelling's height
    I made myself a gibbet, straight and plain.'

CANTO 14

In fellow feeling for his countryman, Dante gathers the torn shreds as requested. Vergil leads him through the remainder of the wood to the edge of the third division of the seventh circle, a barren plain of fiery sand where those who have done violence against God, Nature and Art are punished. The first, pinioned down, are represented by Capaneus. A slow fire descending in an eternal rain adds to their punishment. The poets proceed between wood and sand till they reach a crimson rivulet that leaves the wood and crosses the desert.

Love of my native place constraining me,
    I gathered all the twigs and scattered leaves
    And heaped them all around the now-hoarse tree.
The limits where the second circuit cleaves
    From the third we reached, and there we found
    The fearful form that Justice here conceives.   6
To make this clear: I saw we'd reached a ground
    Which was so desert-like that from such bed
    No hint of vegetation could abound.
And, all around its rim, is garlanded
    The mournful wood, as round the wood there flows
    The dreary moat; and here we stayed our tread.   12
The soil was dry thick sands, and quite like those
    In texture which were trodden by the feet
    Of Cato, joining Juba, to attack his foes.
God's Vengeance! How men should go in fear to meet
    What was revealed before my human eyes,
    When they have read this record I complete.   18
I saw great herds of naked souls whose cries
    Were wretched wails. They seemed to undergo
    A sentence suited to the crime it tries,
For some were supine on the ground below;
    Some squatting on their haunches; others ploughed
    Incessantly back and forth, and to and fro.   24
These wanderers were the most numerous crowd;
    Those lying in their torment were but few –
    Yet not their cries of pain which were most loud.
And, falling slowly across that desert-view,
    Dilated flakes of fire drifted, like snow
    Falling upon the Alps when no wind blew.   30

As flames which Alexander watched fall low
   Upon his army in the Indian heat,
   Entire pieces on the ground aglow,
Which he extinguished with his stamping feet,
   Mimicked by all his legions, since the fire
36   Was easier to douse while still discrete,
So fell the eternal heat by which the dire
   Sands were enkindled, like tinder under steel
   And flint, to double pain and raise it higher.
Ceaseless the flap of wretched hands to deal,
   Now here, now there, with every spot of flame,
42   To quench its life before it raised a weal.
'Master, Victor of all save those who came
   Against us at the entrance to the gate,
   Those stubborn demons,' I began, 'just name
That great spirit seeming not to rate
   The fire as much; disdain twists on his bed
48   So that the rains don't ripen up his state.'
But he himself exclaimed, and this he said,
   Because I'd asked my guide concerning him:
   'What I was living, so am I being dead.
Though Jove exhaust his smith whose bolt so grim
   He snatched in anger, and, on my last day,
54   Transfixed me with it; though his angry whim
Weary the others, one by one away,
   At the black forge in Mongibello, crying:
   "Help me, help, good Vulcan; help, I say!"
Just as he did at Phlegra, and send them flying
   Against me with his utmost strength again,
60   He never would enjoy revenge and hear me sighing.'
Then my guide spoke forcefully and plain,
   In such a way I had not heard before:
   'Capaneus, the more your quenchless pride remain
So will your punishment increase the more.
   No torture, except your raving, would be pain
66   Proportioned to your fury and its roar.'
And, gentler toned, he faced me to explain:
   'He was one of the Seven Kings that laid
   The siege of Thebes; he held, and holds again,
God in defiance, it seems; but, as I made
   Quite clear, his denunciations ornament
72   His own breast, befittingly displayed.

Now follow me, and make sure you prevent
    Your feet from treading in the burning sand.
    Keep close in under the wood, and bent.'
In silence then we reached a point where land
    Gave way to rivulet that crimson gushes.
    Its gore still makes me shudder out of hand.   78
Just as from Bulicame there rushes
    A little rill the sinful women share,
    So this runs down, and over sands it flushes.
I gathered that our crossing would be there,
    For bed and banks and sides were petrified;
    Along its way was always stone, and bare.   84
'Of all that I have shown you, as a guide,
    Since first we entered through the fearful gate,
    That threshold where no one has been denied,
You've seen no sight as notable as this strait
    Which quenches all the fire along its course.'
    These were my guide's words; they did not sate   90
My hunger so I begged for more discourse
    To feed the appetite his words created,
    And nourishment to break that hunger's force.
'In mid sea is a waste country,' he stated,
    'Its name is Crete, under whose king the earth
    Was once a chaste place; and situated   96
There is a mountain, Ida, once glad with mirth
    Of waters and of leaves – deserted now,
    Like something antiquated and no worth.
Rhea, of old, made a nursery on its brow
    To hide her son and, to conceal his cries,
    Filled it with all the Corybantics' row.   102
Inside the mountain, and of massive size,
    Stands an old man erect who turns away
    From Damietta; Rome mirrors his eyes.
His head is pure gold, his arms and chest display
    Pure silverwork; brass goes to the cleft;
    From there choice iron to right foot of clay,   108
Baked clay, on which, more than upon the left,
    He seems to distribute most of his weight.
    All, save the gold, is split, and, as bereft,
Each fissure wells with tears which perforate
    The grotto as they gather to a head;
    From rock to rock they drop into this strait.   114

They form the Acheron, the Styx; they shed
    Phlegethon and, by a conduit, sink
    Down where they may cut no deeper bed.
There they form Cocytus, and what that rink
    Of water is you yet shall see, and so
120   I give no picture here, but let you think.'
I answered him: 'If this rill then must flow
    Out of the world above, why now appear
    Only at this bank first, I'd like to know.'
He answered me: 'You know this is a sphere.
    You've come a distance, but left we always go,
126   And now to the lowest depths of all we steer.
You have not turned full circle here below,
    So, if a new sight sometimes comes around,
    Scant wonder on your face you ought to show.'
I asked, 'Where's Phlegethon; where's Lethe found?
    You haven't mentioned one, and say the other
132   Is fed from all this rain that burns the ground.'
'Your questions please me; but you might discover
    One issues from the seething of red water,'
    He answered me. 'But Lethe in another
Place you will later see, not in this quarter,
    But where the spirits go to wash themselves
138   When penitence has made their guilt much shorter.'
Next he said, 'Now where this wood shelves
    We have to leave. Make sure you follow me.
The margins next to where the torrent delves
    Don't burn, and leave a path from fire free.'

CANTO 15

The rivulet, or canal, has raised banks on which Dante may walk safely, protected by the murky exhalation that quenches the fiery rain. They encounter a group of spirits coming along beside the bank. Dante is recognized by the withered figure of Brunetto Latini. Addressing him in the customary mode of address to notaries, Dante has much respect for his old mentor and they talk with great feeling.

Now one of the hard banks directs our feet,
    And smoke from that torrent makes a shade,
    Sheltering banks and flow from fiery sleet.
In dread of flood that threatens to invade,
    Flemings, from Wissant to Bruges, prepare
    A bulwark to repel the billow's raid;   6
Paduans, likewise, by the Brenta there,
    Defend their forts and hamlets from the heat
    Of Carentana so the spate will spare.
These banks were formed by somewhat similar feat;
    Though not so high nor wide were they designed
    By whichever master planned what was our street.   12
The wood already we had left behind
    So far that, had I turned my head anew,
    It would have been impossible to find.
When we approached a troop of shades that drew
    Towards us by the bank and, coming by,
    Each one gave us a stare as men will do   18
Under a new moon in the evening sky –
    Look at each other with brows creased to see,
    As an old tailor peers at his needle's eye.
That family so focused onto me
    One of them recognized me, pulled my sleeve
    And called out loudly, 'What a prodigy!'   24
And when he stretched his hand to stop me leave,
    I fixed my eyes upon his fire-seared look
    So that the scorched features did not deceive
My mind from knowing who: and, leaning to crook
    My face to his, I answered, 'What, you here, too,
    Ser Brunetto?' He said, 'If I forsook   30
My band a little and walked back with you,
    Would Brunetto Latini disturb your walk?'
    And I replied, 'With all my heart, please do.

And if you'd like to sit awhile and talk
    I'll gladly sit with you, if this one here,
36   Who I am with, does not object or baulk.'
'Ah, son,' he said, 'not sit. Whenever we're
    An instant still a hundred years succeed
    When we can't brush away these flakes that sear.
Therefore go on. I'll follow where you lead,
    And, later, join again my little band,
42   Lamenting their eternal loss decreed.'
I dared not leave the raised stones to stand
    Upon his level but I walked, head bowed,
    Like one with reverence; he, on the sand.
He asked, 'What chance or destiny allowed
    You here before you've suffered your last day?
48   And who is this that guides you through the crowd?'
'Above, in the clear life, I lost my way,'
    I answered him; 'before the fullness of years,
    In a dark valley I seemed to be astray.
Only yesterday morning, it appears,
    I turned my back on it, and he arrived
54   As I back-tracked, to guide me where he steers.'
He answered me: 'You cannot be deprived
    Of glorious haven, if you follow your star;
    If what I see my eyes truly derived.
And, if I had not died too young by far,
    I would have cheered you in your work, to find
60   Heaven so favourable to what you are.
But that ungrateful and malignant kind
    That comes of old from Fiesole, and who
    Still savour of the stone and mountain, mind,
Will turn your foe for all the good you do –
    And with good cause; for it is never done,
66   In tart sorbs, for sweet fig to fruit, like you.
Ancient tradition names that race as one
    That's avaricious, envious, proud and blind.
    So wash your hands of them; their customs shun.
Your fortune holds such honour, you will find
    Both parties hunger in pursuit of you,
72   But grass is far from them; each goat is pined.
Let those wild beasts of Fiesole chew
    And raven up themselves but let them leave
    The plant – if any in their filth break through –

In which the holy seeds may re-conceive
    Of Romans, who remained within the place
    When malice nested there to hiss and weave.'   78
'If my wish had its way,' I said, 'your face
    Would not be banished yet into this night
    From human nature, for in memory's space
Is fixed and goes now to my heart, the sight
    Of you on earth those times you taught me how –
    Dear, kind and fatherly – a man might   84
Immortalize himself. I must allow,
    As long as I may live and have the force,
    My tongue to voice how grateful I am now.
What you have said about my future course,
    Along with one more text, I write to show
    A Lady for comment should I reach that source.   90
And this much I should like you now to know,
    So that my conscience in this point be clear:
    What Fortune wills I'm schooled to undergo.
Such forecast is not new upon my ear,
    So let her turn her wheel just as she may,
    As yokel with his mattock, year by year.'   96
At which the master turned his head to say,
    Giving me a straight look, 'He listens well
    Who hears and takes a thorough note away.'
Nevertheless, I begged Brunetto to tell
    Who were most notable among his friends
    And who were of the noblest as it fell.   102
'Of some it's good to know,' he said, 'but spends
    The precious time to speak about the rest.
    More laudable is silence on their ends.
Briefly, all clerks and scholars, worthiest,
    And of a great renown, and all made vile
    By one identical crime – even the best.   108
Priscian tags along that wretched file.
    Francesco d'Accorso: if you like such dross,
    You'd recognize amongst them, in a while,
One whom the Servant of servants brought across
    From Arno to Bacchiglione where
    He left his ill-strained sinews to their fosse.   114
I would say more; but now I cannot spare
    More time in talk or going on this way.
    Look, new smoke reeks from sand into the air.

People arrive with whom I may not stay.
    Let me commend that *Treasure* where I live

    To you, and more I do not ask or pray.'
He turned back then. The picture it would give
    Is of a man who raced through open fields
For the green cloth at Verona, competitive,
    And more like one who wins than one who yields.

CANTO 16

Dante can already hear the stream cascading to the next depth when he encounters three spirits who hurry to him, having recognized his style of dress. Tegghiaio and Rusticucci, mentioned earlier, are two of these patriots. Dante gives them firmly an indication of the present evils besetting Florence. Virgil brings him where the rivulet cascades, borrows his girdle and throws it to the depths – which brings forth a monstrous form that comes towards them on the cliff-edge.

Already I had come to where the dive
    Of waters, falling to the lower ring,
    Was sounding like the humming of a hive,
When these three shades, together hurrying,
    Ran from their troop beneath the burning rain
    And its sharp torment; each was clamouring   6
And calling: 'Stop! Your garments make it plain
    That you must be a traveller that hails
    From our perverse land. A little while remain!'
– Ah me, what wounds I saw on their limbs, scales
    Of previous and recent weals the rain had burned.
    It hurts me still to think, and my heart fails. –   12
My teacher listened to their cries, and turned
    His face to me and said, 'Now *you* must wait,
    For signs of courtesy all these have earned.
But for the fire that's natural in this state,
    The proper thing would be for you to run
    To meet them, and for them to hesitate.'   18
And they renewed their pace, the former one.
    We waited till, when they had reached our place,
    They formed a little wheel in front and spun.
As wrestlers, naked and anointed, face
    Each other, looking for the hold they need,
    And feint before they lock in strong embrace,   24
So, wheeling round, each turned to take good heed
    Of me, and feet moved counter to the neck,
    Till one of them began, and took this lead:
'If the misery of this loose place we trek,
    Our stained and scorched-up countenances here,
    Bring us and all our prayers contemptuous check,   30

Then let our fame persuade you to make clear
   Who you may be that so securely pace
   On living feet across Hell's sands that sear.
That one, there, whose footsteps now I trace,
   Flayed and naked as he is in shame,
36   Was higher in rank than you would think the case.
Grandson he was to good Gualdrada, his name
   Guido Guerra; he did a deed or so;
   By counsel and the sword he built his fame.
The next who treads the sand behind me, know:
   Tegghiaio Aldobrandi, whose voice on earth
42   Should have been listened to some time ago.
Myself, in torment with them here, by birth
   Jacopo Rusticucci; and, most to blame,
   My savage wife has ruined all my worth.'
If there had been some shelter from the flame,
   I should have leapt right down and joined their band –
48   I think my guide would have allowed that aim.
Yet, since I would have burnt upon the sand,
   Fear overcame the goodwill of that urge
   That made me want to take them by the hand.
I answered: 'Not contempt, but sorrows surge
   In me for your condition, and so immense
54   They will not leave me soon but re-emerge,
Since what my lord has said to make me sense
   That men such as yourselves might well approach.
   Your city's mine; and with benevolence
I've heard, and with affection, heard men broach
   The honour of your names and of your deeds.
60   Leaving the bitterness and the reproach,
I'm going for the sweet apples from seeds
   My truthful master promised; but first I must
   Descend to that centre where he leads.'
'Long may your spirit give your body thrust,'
   He then replied, 'and may your honour there
66   Shine afterwards when it has come to dust.
Tell me, do courtesy and courage fare
   As once they did within the city's bounds,
   Or do they fade and vanish in thin air?
Guglielmo Borsiere who's traipsed these grounds
   Of pain a time – there with our comrades – strains
72   And tortures us with all that he propounds.'

'Oh Florence! Upstarts and their sudden gains
    Have bred so much excess and so much pride
    That she already weeps for all her stains.'
With face uplifted, loudly had I cried;
    And each, then, taking this as my reply,
    As men revealed the truth, the others eyed.   78
'If it always costs no more to satisfy
    Others, than this,' they answered in this vein,
    'How happy you, to speak your mind unshy!
Therefore, if you escape this dark terrain,
    And can return to see the lovely stars,
    When glad to say "I once was there!" again,   84
Make sure you speak of us to men.' The spars
    That held their wheel were broken; as they fled
    Their swift legs winged across the sand that chars.
'Amen!' could not so quickly have been said
    As they had vanished, so my master thought
    The time had come for us to move ahead.   90
I followed him; but not much further brought
    The sound of water close; when we conversed
    What we were saying hardly could be caught.
As that river – the first whose waters burst
    From Monte Veso eastwards, on the left flanks
    Of the Apennines, and whose course is first   96
Named Acquacheta on the higher banks,
    But, at the lower, leaves that name behind
    At Forli – resounds against the mountain ranks,
Above San Benedetto, where its currents find
    One fall to their descent, when there was space
    For a thousand cataracts to plunge and wind –   102
Like that, we found the crimson water race
    Over the precipice, so that the din
    Would stun the ears, if long beside the place.
I had a cord about my waist, and, although thin,
    It seemed the thing once, in my mind, to noose
    And trap the Leopard with the Painted Skin.   108
After I'd undone it for my master's use,
    As he commanded me I gave it him,
    Coiled and knotted up, not trailing loose.
Swinging it right and back, beside the brim,
    He threw it far out from the very brink,
    Down into the abyss so deep and grim.   114

'Surely,' to myself I chanced to think,
   'Something strange must answer this new sign,
   Which now my master notes without a blink.'
– Ah, cautious one should be where those divine
   Not only deed but, with their sense, see through
120   Into the inner thoughts and their design! –
He said, 'What I expect to swim in view
   Will soon emerge, and what in thought you dream
   Will then be quite revealed and plain to you.'
– A man should not narrate those truths that seem
   Like lies, as far as he controls the affair;
   Though blameless, reproach will come to his esteem.
126 But here I cannot hold my peace. I swear,
   Reader, by the notes of this my Comedy
   (If they should find a lasting favour anywhere)
I saw, through gross dark air, as if through sea,
   Come swimming up a figure of a sort
   Marvellous to every steadfast heart, as he
132 Returns who dives to free an anchor caught
   Against a rock – or other sunken thing
The water hides – and spreads his arms athwart
   And pulls his legs up ready for a spring.

CANTO 17

Still in the third area of the seventh circle, Dante here describes the monstrous beast Geryon, representing the evil of fraud. He is granted time to observe the usurers and shows his contempt for them in two ways: none are named except armorially; Dante himself is remarkably silent and addresses none while eaves-dropping their inane conversation. His guide meanwhile has been negotiating with the fearful monster.

'Behold the savage beast with pointed tail
    That crosses mountains, breaks through arms and walls.
    Behold the world's corrupter in its stale.'
These words my guide began to say, with calls
    Beckoning him to come upon the shore
    Where our rock path concluded by the falls.   6
Fraud's filthy image came on more and more
    Yet landed with but head and chest in view,
    Leaving his tail where all the waters roar.
His face was that of a just man and true,
    So mild in aspect outwardly; the rest
    Akin to some reptilian body grew.   12
Two paws he had, hairy to the chest;
    Painted in knots and circles were the thighs,
    As was the back, and all around the breast.
Never did Turk or Tartar use such dyes
    To make their groundwork and embroidery;
    Nor Arachne on her loom such webs devise.   18
He lay just like those boats you often see
    Half in, half out, of water; and, as there,
    Among those guzzlers up in Germany,
The beaver dips his tail to catch his share
    Of fish, so lay that worst of savage brutes
    Where stone retains the sand around his lair.   24
His tail thrashed in the void the water shoots,
    Twisting its venomed fork that, scorpion-like,
    Armed its barb to pierce in fierce disputes.
My guide informed me: 'Now from our safe dyke
    We must descend a little to that beast
    That crouches there, armed with its vicious spike.'   30

So down we went on the right, taking at least
    Ten paces on the edge so that we might
    Avoid the sand and flames that never ceased.
And, when we came to him, I caught the sight
    Of people, sitting further on, beside
36   The brink that looked upon that vacuous height.
My master said, 'To carry far and wide
    The full experience of this ring, now go
    And see the state of those by that divide.
But let your talk be brief there, even so.
    And, while you're there, I'll speak with this brute here
42   To ferry us upon his shoulders down below.'
So, on the utmost edge, abrupt and sheer,
    Ending the seventh circle, alone I went
    To that lamenting group, and waited near.
Grief poured out through their eyes; they were bent
    Now here, now there, to brush away the flame
48   Or searing of the sand with hands intent.
The mongrels of the summer act the same,
    And frantic, now with snout, and now with paw,
    After the fleas, the flies and gadflies aim.
I studied many faces but I saw
    None that I recognized on whom the fire
54   Descended – noticing beneath each jaw
Hung down a pouch their eyes bent to admire
    And feast upon; each was a certain shade,
    And bore some impress that never seemed to tire.
And, as I moved among them there, I made
    Out one which was a yellow purse that bore
60   An azure lion's shape and stance inlaid.
Continuing to look, I saw one more
    On which was shown the image of a goose
    Whiter than butter on a ground like gore.
Then one (whose whitened pouch upon its noose
    Revealed a sow, pregnant, azure) hectored me:
66   'What are you doing here? What is the use?
Go! Yet, since you're still alive, just see
    How Vitaliano, here, shall always sit
    On my left side, and there will always be.
I'm Paduan, stuck here, in the thick of it,
    With all these Florentines who din my ears
72   With yelling: "The Sovereign Cavalier admit.

Who brings the pouch of three goats."'' Like a steer's,
    He writhed his mouth, and thrust his tongue out long
    To lick his nose to shift the flame that sears.
And I, afraid that more delay were wrong
    And might offend my guide who bade me stay
    But briefly, turned from that exhausted throng.   78
I found my guide already climbed half way
    Upon the dreadful haunches, and he said:
    'Be brave, bring all your courage into play.
By such a stair as this we must be led
    Below. You ride in front, with me behind,
    To shield you from the tail that's overhead.'   84
Like one to quartan fever now resigned,
    With nails turned blue, and shivering at the mere
    Appearance of some shade that seems outlined,
That was myself, when such words struck my ear;
    But sign of fright for shame I dared not show.
    A worthy master quells a servant's fear.   90
I climbed the huge shoulders, set to go.
    I wished to ask but could not voice the thought:
    'Support me as we journey down below.'
But he, who elsewhere helped and gave support,
    As soon as I had mounted held me tight,
    And in his arms I was clasped round and caught.   96
And then he said: 'Geryon, on your flight;
    And make your spirals large; slow the descent.
    Remember this strange weight and stay upright.'
Then, as a barque, stern first from hawser sent,
    Stern first the monster inched himself from shore,
    And, when he felt himself quite clear, he bent   102
His tail around where chest had been before,
    And, stretching it, he moved it like an eel,
    And pawed the air towards him more and more.
It was no greater fear, I think, to feel
    When Phaëthon dropped reins and scorched the sky –
    As still appears the course of that ordeal,   108
Nor when poor Icarus, in soaring high,
    Felt molten wax and wings unfeathering,
    His father calling: 'An evil course you fly!',
Than this of mine to see myself on wing
    With air on every side, and not a sight
    To fix on, but the beast was everything.   114

He swims on slowly, slowly, motion slight,
   Wheels and descends. I noticed just the wind
   In front and underneath as we lost height.
Already to the right a whirlpool dinned
   With hideous roaring, under, in the dark.
120   I stretched my neck and peered – and courage thinned.
I was more fearful then to disembark
   Than I had been to mount; for groans and fire
   Made me cling closer as we swung our arc.
I was aware – though not when we were higher –
   Of circling down through evils there that group
126   On every side of us, terrible and dire.
And as a falcon, tired of flight, will swoop
   – After a long time without lure or prey,
   So that the falconer cries, 'At last you stoop!' –
But then in weariness descends away
   From where he waits, with many circlings round,
132   And, sullen and disdainful, there will stay –
So, at the base, Geryon reached the ground
   And set us close beside the jagged rock;
And, from our weight relieved, with sudden bound,
   He soared, an arrow from the bow-string's shock.

CANTO 18

Malebolge – the 'purses of evil' – is the deepest region of Hell, divided into ten concentric ravines or chasms, each lower and deeper and smaller than the previous until they centre on the precipitous pit of Hell where Satan is confined. These ravines are spanned by cliff bridges from which the two travellers may observe the sinners allotted to each chasm. Vergil turns left along the outer wall and right on to the first bridge from which they see the dwellers in the first chasm, the panders and seducers; in the second that they observe are the flatterers. This is the eighth circle of Hell.

There's a place called Malebolge in Hell,
    All stone, and iron-coloured like the wall
    That braces round it, guard and sentinel.
And, in the inmost centre of it all,
    There gapes a shaft immensely wide and deep
    Whose structure, further on, I will recall.   6
Between this shaft and the towering rocky steep
    The belt of stone is subdivided more
    In ten chasms which all round it sweep.
And, as the land appears that lies before
    A castle wall, where moat on moat surround
    Each other as defence in case of war,   12
They made the selfsame pattern on this ground;
    And just as bridges reach out from the walls
    Toward the outer banks, so here, we found.
From the ring of rocks, we saw, at intervals,
    Proceeded cliffs that crossed embankment, moat,
    And reached the shaft centring these pens and stalls.   18
Shaken impatiently off Geryon's coat,
    We found ourselves within this place; my guide
    Turned to the left and I, behind, take note.
Upon the right, fresh misery spread wide:
    New torments, new tormentors which now filled
    The first chasm seen upon this side.   24
And, at its bottom, naked sinners milled:
    Our side the cliff they came toward our face;
    The other, with us, with greater paces drilled.
Likewise, when the Jubilee took place,
    The Romans organized the milling throng
    Upon the bridge so that one side would trace   30

Their route toward St Peter's all along,
   While those upon the other side could walk
   Toward the Mount, and nothing could go wrong.
On this side and that, beside the hideous baulk,
   I saw horned demons with their scourges thrash
36   Them fiercely from behind, and stragglers, stalk.
Ah, how they raised their pace at that first lash!
   None ever waited for a second there,
   But picked their feet up fast and made a dash.
As I advanced my eyes met with a stare
   And instantly I said, 'This is one face
42   I've seen before, would notice anywhere.'
So, to acknowledge him, I eased my pace
   And my kind guide drew back to wait for me,
   And a few steps allowed me to retrace.
There, that scourged shade to avoid discovery
   Lowered his face, but he was much too late.
48   I said, 'You, looking on the ground, must be
Venedico Caccianemico, if gait
   And face aren't in disguise. What have you done
   To get in this sharp pickle of a state?'
He answered, 'The clearness of your speech has won
   And, though I speak reluctantly, compels,
54   Reminding of the world up in the sun.
The tale is nasty, never mind who tells:
   I lured Ghisolabella to the Marquis' will;
   No unique Bolognese this scourging quells.
The place is full of them; they don't instil
   Our 'yep' into so many tongues between
60   Savena and Reno; if, of such a skill,
You want a further proof, recall the keen
   Avarice in our hearts and, in a flash,
   You'll know the truth of what we've been.'
And, as he spoke, a demon swung a lash
   And said, 'Move on, pander, move away.
66   There are no women here for you to cash.'
I joined my escort with no more delay;
   A few steps further on, we reached a place
   Where, leading from the bank, a cliff-top lay.
We climbed on this with ease and turned our pace
   Upon the right, along its jagged back,
72   And left these eternal circles. When a space

Yawned underneath to leave a sort of track
    For all the scourged, my guide said, 'Stop, and let
    The abject looks of these low spirits smack.
You have not really seen their faces yet,
    Since they've been scurrying round without a halt
    Heading the same direction as we're set.'   78
Upon our ancient bridge we watched the vault:
    A column driven to us, just the same
    As were the others, by the whip's assault.
My kind master, before I could exclaim,
    Said, 'Just you look at this great soul here
    Who seems to shed no tears of pain. His name   84
Is Jason. How kingly still his looks appear!
    By courage and by counsel he deprived
    The Colchians of the Fleece they held so dear.
Upon the Isle of Lemnos he arrived,
    After the bold and ruthless women sent
    All of their males to death. There he contrived   90
To deceive, by words and gifts, of his intent
    The young Hypsipyle who deceived the rest.
    He left her pregnant, deserted, when he went.
Such guilt condemns him to this torture's test,
    As does his treatment of Medea as well.
    In further vengeance then he is oppressed.   96
And all who have deceived are in this hell;
    So let this be enough to understand
    The first chasm, and those it seeks to quell.'
We had arrived where now the pathway spanned
    The second bank which, as a buttress, serves
    To raise another arch across the land.   102
Now we could hear, within the chasm's curves
    A people whining, puffing mouth and nose,
    And with their hands they beat at all their nerves.
The banks were crusted with a mould that grows
    From all the rising vapours which congealed.
    It stings the eyes and nostrils where it flows.   108
The base was dug too deep to be revealed,
    Except when we had reached the arch's crest,
    Where the cliff rises high and unconcealed.
We rose on it, and, in the gulf suppressed,
    We saw a people dipped in filth that seeped,
    It seemed, from human privies to infest.   114

And, while I searched, I saw one head so heaped
   In filth, I could not gather whether clerk
   Or layman in such excrement was steeped.
He bawled: 'Why is it that you stare and mark
   Me out more than the others in their mess?'
120   I said, 'If I remember rightly you that bark
I've seen once when your hair was dry. And, yes,
   Alessio Interminei of Lucca you are.
   So more than these I know you, more or less.'
He started banging his own head. 'Thus far
   Those flatteries of which I never tired
126   Have sunk me – and with this my visage mar.'
'Crane your face forward,' my guide required
   At that, 'until your vision well retails
   Of that obnoxious strumpet, mired,
Dishevelled in this ordure, with filthy nails
   Scratching herself; now standing in it still,
132   Now cowering on her calves in all the stales –
Thaïs, the Harlot, that is. Asked, of a slave:
   "D'you thank me much for it?" by her paramour,
   "A million thanks," the answer that she gave.
   But we have seen enough. The rest ignore.'

CANTO 19

In the third chasm of the eighth circle are the simonists – buyers and sellers of spiritual office – buried head-first in apertures in the solid rock. (Burial head-first, alive, was a punishment in Dante's time for hired assassins.) Dante makes an impassioned speech against the simoniacs and earns Vergil's full approval.

O Simon Magus, and your wretched following,
   Robbers, who prostitute the things of God
   That should be one with righteousness, to bring
In gold and silver for your thieving squad,
   The trumpet sounds the justness of your doom
   Within the third chasm, with flame well shod.   6
Already we had mounted to the next tomb
   Upon the crest of the flinty cliff that lies
   Immediately above the middle of the coomb.
– Supreme in Wisdom, shown amid the skies,
   On earth, and in the evil world below!
   The justice you dispense, how good and wise! –   12
I saw the livid stone, and row on row
   Of holes in sides and base; all seemed to be
   Of equal size and rounded to an O.
No narrower did they appear to me
   Nor wider than the ones that are inside
   My lovely San Giovanni's baptistry –   18
Where, some time back, I broke one as I tried
   To save a man from drowning. (This reveals
   The truth to clear men's minds, my seal applied.)
Out of the mouth of each emerged the heels
   And calves of sinners; all the rest remained
   Within the hole which face and form conceals.   24
The feet of all were flaming up, and pained
   The joints to shake so strongly they would break
   Haywire or withes – if they'd been so restrained.
And as with things immersed in oil, flames take
   Along the surface only, so, on toes
   And heels of all, the flames would play and rake.   30
'Master,' I said, 'who's this that writhes in throes
   Much worse than all the others seem to do,
   Who's licked by redder flames than all of those?'

He said: 'If you would like a closer view,
 Down by the lower bank, I'll bear you there,
36 And you may ask his wrongs and of him, too.'
I said, 'What pleases you I'm pleased to share.
 You are my lord, and know I will obey.
  You also know the thoughts I do not air.'
We then approached the fourth bulwark's way,
 Turned and descended next on the left hand
42 Which to that hole-filled narrows would convey.
My good master never set me down to stand
 Till he had brought me to the very hole
  Where he I'd noticed wailed, and shanks most fanned.
I said, 'Whoever you are, O wretched soul,
 Planted, like some stake, your upper plumb
48 Beneath, speak – if you still have such control.'
I stood there like a friar confessing some
 Assassin-traitor who, when fixed, takes care
  To call him back so death delays to come.
'Are you there already, standing there
 Already, Boniface? By several years
54 The writ has lied to me of your affair.
And have you tired as quickly as appears
 Of all the wealth for which you felt no shame
  To seize the lovely Bride in outrage and tears?'
Like one made ill at ease then I became,
 Not following the answer he is made,
60 And, as if mocked, his words he cannot frame.
Then Vergil helped, 'Quickly must be conveyed:
 I'm not the one you think, not who you seek.'
  And what he ordered me, I then obeyed.
At which the spirit kicked his heels in pique,
 And, sighing in a tearful voice, he said:
66 'What is it then you wish for me to speak?
But, if the need to know me vexed your head
 So much that you have clambered down the bank,
  Know that the Great Mantle I wore – and shed.
And son of that she-bear, to be truly frank;
 So eager to advance the cubs, I pursed
72 Up wealth above, and, here, myself to the shank.
Beneath my head are thrust those who precursed
 Me in their simony; they cower deep,
  In fissures of the stone wholly immersed.

I too shall sink down further where they keep,
     When he arrives whom I mistook you for
     Just now, and made my sudden question leap.   78
But I've already baked my heels much more,
     And stood up-ended here, than he will stand
     With burning feet upon this wretched floor.
For after him shall come, from western land,
     A lawless Shepherd of far uglier deeds,
     One fit to plug us both, and burn his brand.   84
The new Jason to be, of which one reads
     In Maccabees; and, as to that high priest
     His king was pliant, so France where this one leads.'
I might have been foolhardy when he ceased
     Because I answered him: 'How much treasure
     Did the Lord ask Peter to have pieced   90
Together for the Keys? Surely the measure
     He asked of him was only "Follow me!"
     Nor did St Peter, or the others, pressure
Matthias for gold and silver as a fee
     When he was chosen for that holy work
     The guilty soul had lost deservedly.   96
Therefore stay just where you are and jerk;
     You're justly punished; guard those ill-gained fees
     That made you bold against all Charles's work.
But for my reverence of the Great Keys
     You held in the glad life – that hinders me –
     I should have spoken heavier words than these,   102
Because your avarice grieves the world to see
     You trampling down the good, and raising high
     The wicked by the sin of simony.
The Evangelist had such shepherds in his eye
     When she that sits beside the waters he saw
     In fornication with the kings to lie –   108
She that was born with seven heads to draw
     Her strength from ten horns while her groom extolled
     And took delight in virtue and its law.
You made your god of silver and of gold;
     So what's the difference from idolaters
     When they had one, and you a hundredfold?   114
Ah, Constantine, what wickedness occurs,
     Not from your conversion, but all the estate
     You gave the first rich Father still confers.'

And while I sang this air, either irate,
    He flailed his feet more wildly in his rage,
120   Or conscience gnawed him with his own self-hate.
Indeed, it seemed to please my guide, the sage;
    He was so satisfied to hear the sound
    Of true words spoken out just at this stage.
In both his arms I was clasped up and wound,
    And, when he had me raised against his breast,
126   He climbed the same path back to higher ground.
Nor did he weary or require a rest
    From bearing me till on the arch's top
    That crossed from fourth to fifth along our quest.
Here, he gently let his burden drop,
    Gently because that rough sheer ridge would be
132   So hard to pass that even a goat might stop.
    From there a further chasm I could see.

CANTO 20

In this fourth chasm of the eighth circle, Dante observes the sorcerers and diviners who wickedly claimed to foretell the future will of God which the Almighty alone can perceive. Principal among them is Manto, which gives Vergil the opportunity to tell of the origins of Mantua, his own city. This narrative enables Dante to distance Vergil from his medieval reputation as a necromancer.

Verse of new punishment I now evoke,
    Material of the twentieth canto write
    For the first canzone on the sunken folk.
Now I was all absorbed to strain my sight
    Into the gulf that was revealed to lie
    Bathed in the tears of anguish from their plight.   6
And weeping, silent people struck my eye,
    Coming at what would be a litany's pace,
    Along the curving valley plodding by.
I looked all down the column to its base.
    Each seemed amazingly deformed in stance,
    From chin to start of chest, with lowered face   12
That bent towards the loins with downcast glance.
    They had to travel backward as they came.
    They were denied to see where they advance.
Perhaps some kind of palsy was to blame
    For this deformity: I've never seen
    It quite like that, and don't think it's the same.   18
– Reader, as God may grant that you should glean
    Some profit from your reading, consider how
    I could have kept from tears before that scene,
Where, close at hand, I saw our form so bow
    And twist that as they wept the tears that fell
    Must down the parting of the buttocks plough.   24
Indeed I wept, leant on the rock a spell,
    Against the stern cliff, till my escort said:
    'What, are you one of the fools, as well?
Here, pity lives when it is utterly dead.
    What could be more faithless and less worth
    Than mourning at God's judgement? Raise your head.   30
Raise it and see the one for whom the earth
    Gaped in front of all the Thebans' sight.
    They cried out: "Where d'you dash across the turf,

Amphiaraus? Why desert the war in flight?"
    He never ceased to plummet down below
36   To Minos who lays hold of sinners as his right.
See how he's made a breast of shoulders, though;
    Because he wished to see too far ahead
    He now must look behind and backward go.
There, that's Tiresias who changed and shed
    His male appearance to a woman's outer view,
42   Transforming all his limbs, and every shred.
Later he had to strike again the two
    Intertwisted serpents with his rod
    Just to assume his manly plumes anew.
There, back to belly, after Tiresias' plod,
    Is Aruns who, in the range of Luni, stayed
48   Where, lower, Carrarese must hoe the clod.
Amid the white marble there he made
    A cave his dwelling, and from that could see
    The stars and seas in boundless view displayed.
And she who hides her breasts in modesty –
    So you can't see – with her dishevelled hair,
54   Above her other hairiness – now she
Was Manto who searched through many lands, and where
    I happened to be born she chose to dwell.
    It pleases me to tell you the affair.
When her father's life had closed, the citadel
    Of Bacchus into servitude then came,
60   And she to roam the world for a long spell.
There lies a lovely lake the mountains frame
    In Italy and set their bounds on the Hun,
    Above the Tyrol; Benaco, is its name.
I think a thousand springs that have begun
    From there bathe Garda and throughout the space
66   From Val Camonica to Pennino run.
And, in the middle of it, there's a place
    The Trentine Pastor, Brescian and Veronese,
    Might bless, if there they ever show their face:
Peschiera, a castle good and strong, one sees,
    There where the shores are lowest round the lake,
72   To front the Brescians and the Bergamese.
And there the overspills of Benaco make
    All their escapes a river, taking its course
    Through green pastures which its waters slake;

And, this achieved, it leaves that name at source
    And now becomes the Mincio that flows
    To Governolo and falls to the Po's force.   78
And not much further on, it levels, slows
    And spreads into a marsh of swampy ground,
    At times in summer noxious to the nose.
The vicious virgin, coming that way, found
    A land amidst those fens and swamps, untilled,
    And uninhabited for miles around.   84
There, to avoid all human contact, she filled
    It with the ministrants that worked her arts;
    There, lived and laid her body, void and chilled.
Afterwards, men scattered in all parts,
    Gathered together in that very place
    The ring of marsh makes safe when conflict starts.   90
They built above the bones in that dead space
    A city now called Mantua from her name,
    Without a further augury in the case.
Most populous as a city it became
    Till Casalodi's folly was expelled
    By Pinamonte with the people's claim.   96
If you should hear some other source upheld
    For my own city, let no falsehood hinder,
    Nor yet your faith in this be crushed or quelled.'
'Your words are sure to me; they fire the tinder
    Of belief so any others that I'd find
    Would be to me just so much ash and cinder.   102
But tell me of the people as they wind,
    If any seen are worthy of remark,
    Because this topic dominates my mind.'
'That one who spreads his beard over his dark
    And swarthy shoulders was indeed a seer
    When Greece of males was barren and so stark   108
That there were scarcely any left to rear.
    Calchas and he it was who told the time
    To cut the first cable in Aulis clear.
His name's Eurypylus; in my sublime
    Tragedy I sing of him at one stage.
    You know that well and knew it since your prime.   114
There, lean about the flanks, follows the mage
    Michael Scott; he certainly had the knack
    Of all the magic frauds of any age.

Look, Guido Bonatti; Asdente who'd go back
To stitching leather still, within his mind,
120   But now repents too late around this track.
Look at that group of wretched womankind
Who dropped the needle, spindle, shuttle; cast
Oracles, spells with dolls and herbs to bind.
Come: Cain with his thorns already holds fast
The confines of both hemispheres, his touch
126   Beyond Seville upon the waves so vast.
Last night, already, you should recall as much,
The moon was full; she never hurt you there,
On no occasion in the dark wood's clutch.'
So he spoke and we journeyed from that lair.

CANTO 21

*The fifth chasm of the eighth circle which they observe contains the barrators –
buyers and sellers of public office. They are kept submerged in boiling tar by a
patrol of demons that guard the banks. Dante probably intended this and the
next canto as something like light relief. Some commentators have compared them
with the miracle plays with their farcical devils. The names of his demons, such as
Dragon-nose, would support this suggestion. The travellers after some altercation
are given an unwholesome detachment of these demons as a safe-conduct. Dante
does not trust them.*

My Comedy prefers not to repeat the talk
    We had in walking arc to bridging arc,
    Until we reached the summit of one baulk
In Malebolge where we paused to remark
    Its next chasm and heard vain mournings jar,
    And I found that it was marvellously dark.   6
As, in the Venetian arsenal, the clammy tar
    Is boiled in winter to caulk the damaged ships,
    When they can't be navigated as things are,
So they're rebuilt instead, and, on the slips,
    One plugs the ribs of those much travel-worn;
    Some make new oars, or twist ropes in their grips;   12
Some hammer at the prow; some, stern that's torn,
    While others mend the jib, another one
    Repairs the mainsail where it has been shorn.
So, not by fire, but by divine art done,
    A dense pitch boiled down there and drenched like glue
    The banks on every side where it had run.   18
All that I saw, but nothing came to view
    But bubbles which the boiling seethed and raised,
    Subsidings, heavings that compressed and grew.
And, while on this sight fixedly I gazed,
    My guide, exclaiming: 'Now beware, beware!'
    Hauled me to him from where I stood amazed.   24
And, turning round like one who wants to stare
    On what he needs must shun, and, dashed with fear,
    Cannot delay his flight by peering there,
Behind us then, I saw a black demon rear,
    Running headlong up the rock divide
    Towards us. Ah, how savage did he peer!   30

How fierce his gestures were, with his wings wide
    And stiff, as he approached before my eye,
    And yet how nimble were his feet and stride.
He bore, on shoulders that were sharp and high,
    A sinner, thigh and thigh each side his head.
36   The tendons of the heels he held him by.
'You, Evil-Claws,' from on our bridge he said,
    'One of Santa Zita's elders, look!
    Plunge him down; I'm off for more instead.
That city's crammed with them in every nook.
    All but Bonturo's a barrator in that place.
42   And yes is no for money in their book.'
He hurled him over, wheeling round to race
    Along the cliff; no mastiff was set free
    With such a rush to catch a thief in chase.
The sinner plunged and surfaced writhingly,
    And twisted, rump first; but demons, concealed
48   Beneath the bridge, cried, 'No Sacred Face, quite, see!
A different swim than in the Serchio. Yield,
    And never surface from the pitch except
    To test and try the grapnels which we wield.'
They struck him with a hundred prongs, and swept
    Him, yelling: 'Covered you must dance down here
54   So you can filch in private where you're kept.'
Not unlike that, cooks make scullions spear
    The flesh and dip it in the boiler to stop
    It rising to the surface, floating clear.
My kind master said: 'Behind this outcrop,
    So that they cannot see that you are here;
60   And keep some shield, behind which you can drop.
Whatever outrage meets me, do not fear
    Or fret. I understand the whole affair.
    I've had a previous fray along this tier.'
And then he passed the bridge's arching there,
    And, when he had arrived on the sixth bank,
66   He had to show a steadfast front and air.
With all the rage in which the dogs will yank
    A poor wretch who has knocked to ask for food,
    So rushed the demons at my master's flank,
Out from the bridge, with forks in selfsame mood.
    But he cried out to them: 'Stop; no affray!
72   Before those tridents touch me yet, conclude

Who should come forth to hear what I must say.
    And then go back and all consider well
    Whether to grapple me out of your way.'
All cried, 'Let Malacoda go, and tell.'
    At which one shifted forward, the rest stayed.
    He murmured, 'What's he hoping to dispel?'   78
'Do you expect then, Malacoda,' conveyed
    My master, 'that I've come so safe and straight,
    And facing all the hindrances you've made,
Without the Will Divine, propitious Fate?
    Let me pass on. For it is willed on High
    I show another this savage country's state.'   84
His pride then drooping, this was his reply:
    'Don't strike at him!' He called back, as his hook
    Fell by his feet, and there he let it lie.
My guide looked back to me: 'You, in that nook
    Of boulders splintered from the bridge, who quake
    And quake! You now may join me safely. Look!'   90
At which I moved, and no time did I take.
    The devils launched themselves at once at me
    So that I thought our compact was to break.
I saw the same fear once in infantry –
    After the treaty, leaving Caprona's fort –
    Who had to march out through the enemy.   96
I crept right in against my guide's support,
    And could not draw my eyes away from theirs;
    The way they glared was not so good, I thought.
They lowered their draghooks, not their stares,
    And talked among themselves: 'Now, shall I prick
    His rump?' 'Yes, give it some rents and tears.'   102
The demon talking with my guide was quick
    To turn and say at once: 'Peace, now; peace,
    Scarmilione.' To us he said, 'But pick
Another way. This cliff will shortly cease
    And so you cannot cross it. The sixth span
    Lies in fragments at the bottom, piece by piece,   108
But, if you must go on, then your best plan
    Is now to go along this ridge some way
    And join the next cliff, crossing where you can.
Five hours after this one yesterday,
    One-thousand two-hundred and sixty-six years
    Have been completed since our span's decay.   114

A party's off to catch whoever appears
  Out of the pitch to snatch a breath of air.
   Go along. They'll not hurt, so end those fears.
Step forward, Alichino, Calcabrina, and there,
  Cagnazzo,' he ordered them. 'The one to lead
120 Is Barbariccia. Take charge, and take good care.
And Libicocco, too, it is agreed:
  Draghignazzo, tusked Ciriatto, the pair;
  Graffiacane, Farfarello, Rubicante, proceed.
Search around the boiling tar; don't spare.
  Keep these safe to the next bridge of stone
126 Which spans unbroken straight across this lair.'
'Ah, master, what's all this? Let's go alone,
  And unescorted, if you know the way.
   It's not a path I'd choose, I needs must own.
If you're as wary as before today,
  Look how they grind their teeth and feint our harm
132 In all these frowning looks that they convey.'
And he replied, 'Don't be in such alarm.
  And let them grind away, and as they will.
  It's for these boiling wretches. Cease this qualm.'
By the left-hand bank they turned, but not until
  They each had pressed their tongues between their teeth,
138 Towards their captain as a signal-drill,
  And he'd blown the arse-trumpet underneath.

CANTO 22

The demons hook up a sinner to torment but Vergil, prevailed on by Dante, steps in to find out his life story. Having told it, the sinner tricks the demons and escapes, leaving a furious argument behind him.

I'd seen before how cavalry move camp,
    Or mount a charge, and muster ranks again,
    Sometimes retreating at a rush, or tramp.
Coursers have I seen upon your plain,
    O Aretines, and seen the march of those
    That forage, race of lists, the tourney's strain;   6
Now with the trumpets, now with bells, the blows
    Of drums, and castle signals, now the thing
    Is native, now the gear of foreign foes;
But never to such uncouth trumpeting
    Had I yet seen the horse or foot to group,
    Nor ship, by star or landmark, voyaging.   12
We went with the ten demons, hideous troop;
    But, as the saying goes: 'with saintly share
    The church, with guzzlers share the inn and stoup.'
My full intent was in the pitch to stare,
    And learn the habits of the deep abyss,
    And of the people who were burning there.   18
As dolphins arch their backs, adopting this
    To signal mariners they should make shift
    To save the ship as billows roar and hiss,
So, now and then, some sinner there would lift
    His back to ease the searing of the pitch,
    And hide again – more than the lightning, swift.   24
As, at the water's edge of some dull ditch,
    The frogs show only nostrils, hiding all
    Their feet and bulk in the thick stream, mud rich,
So, everywhere, we saw the sinners stall,
    But soon as Barbariccia came, away
    Beneath the seething pitch they sink and crawl.   30
I saw – and still I quake – one sinner stay
    Too long as sometimes happens a frog is slow,
    While others spout off down without delay.

And Graffiacane, nearest, with a blow
    Hooked him by the tarry hair and hauled
36   Him, as it seemed, an otter from below.
As I had learned the names that they were called
    Already at their choosing, when they cried
    To one another I listened in, appalled.
'Rubicante, claw into his hide
    And flay him now,' as one voice was roared
42   By that accurst detachment at our side.
'Master, if you can learn,' I then implored,
    'Inquire who that wretch is, his place on earth,
    On whose arrest his foes now gloat and lord.'
My guide drew closer to that wretched serf,
    And asked him where he used to live and fare.
48   'In the kingdom of Navarre I had my birth,'
Answered that man. 'My mother made me there
    A servant to a lord, being in line
    A spendthrift, and a wastrel's son and heir.
Good King Thibault's service next was mine,
    Within his household, where I started out
54   On barratry; this burning pays the fine.'
Then Ciriatto, fanged like a hog's snout,
    Soon made him realize how that might feel,
    And ripped it in him with a savage clout.
Circled with wicked cats the mouse must wheel.
    In Barbariccia's lock he soon was grasped.
60   He yelled: 'Mind out, my fork will make him squeal.'
And, turning round to face my master, rasped:
    'Ask on, if you require more answers still.
    These will unseam him when my grip's unclasped.'
My guide complied, 'Tell me, if you will,
    Under this pitch, now, have you seen or met
66   A Latian or two?' He answered, 'In that swill,
I've just left a neighbour of their set
    On the far side: I wish I still were there,
    Covered by no claws and no hook's threat.'
And Libicocco yelled: 'Too much you dare.'
    And with his hook seized on his arm and gashed
72   A part away as brawn into the air.
Draghignazzo wished to try and slashed
    His legs till their Decurion wheeled around,
    Around; with evil looks and glares he dashed.

When they were pacified and ceased to hound,
   My guide, without delay, inquired of him
   While he still stared upon the wound and frowned: 78
'Who was it then you say it felt so grim
   To leave, and end on shore?' And he replied:
   'Friar Gomita, of every fraud the limb,
Galluran-born, and, in his hands, he plied
   His master's enemies, and did so well
   At it that he was lauded far and wide.   84
Money he gathered for himself to tell
   Them smoothly their dismissal, so he brags.
   No minor, but a sovereign barrator in Hell.
Don Michel Zanche of Logodoro tags
   Along with him; talk of Sardinian lore!
   The tongue of neither of them ever flags.   90
Ah no, I see that grin. I would say more
   But fear that he is sizing up to claw
   At me again, my scurf to rake and score.'
But their great marshal, turning on them, saw
   Farfarello roll his eyes to strike, and boomed:
   'Off, villainous bird, off; away, withdraw!'   96
'But if it's Lombards, Tuscans,' the sinner resumed,
   Still frightened, 'that you really want to hear,
   I'll get them from the pitch to which they're doomed.
But make these wicked claws desist so fear
   Of vengeance shall not hinder them, and I,
   One sitting here, for my poor self stuck here,   102
Will make full seven of them come out, by
   This whistle, usual signal that we make
   Should any of us clamber in the dry.'
Cagnazzo raised his snout and, with a shake
   Of head, complained: 'The cunning of the man!
   Hear how he plans to dive off down, the fake.'   108
At which the victim, well stocked with tricks, began:
   'Cunning I am, indeed, to plot such pain
   And torment for my comrades as a plan.'
No more could Alichino then contain
   Himself, and, differing from all the group,
   Burst out: 'You plunge and I'll not sprint again   114
Along the side, but fly right out and swoop
   Above the tar. Let's leave the top; its height
   Will hide us. Now see if you foil the troop.'

– Oh, Reader, now more sport for your delight! –
   All turned to watch the further side, and first,
120   The one who least approved most fixed his sight.
His chance the Navarrese had well rehearsed;
   He slapped his soles upon the bank and leapt
   At once, and from their purpose freely burst.
At which they all were stung by guilt that swept
   The one that caused the fault; it made him start
126   And shout out, 'Caught you, caught you!' – but inept.
It was no good: wings could not outsmart
   That terror; underneath, the sinner went.
   He only just pulled from his diving dart.
Not otherwise is the duck's sudden descent
   When swoops the falcon which must, thwarted, rise
132   Again, in anger and in discontent.
Calcabrina, maddened by the ruse, now flies
   At him in hopes the wretch may flee and cause
   A quarrel over all his enterprise.
And once the barrator had gone, he claws
   His fellow demon, and they grapple there,
138   And, hovering off the fosse, they briefly pause.
His foe, a sparrow-hawk, could claw and tear,
   And both of them together dropped and rolled
   Into the seething pitch, a tangled pair.
At once the heat made them release their hold,
   But they could not take off from all that pitch
144   With wings too glutinous to be controlled.
Barbariccia, lamenting at this hitch,
   Then detailed four to fly to the far side
   And take their hooks with them across the ditch.
Swiftly to posts on either bank they glide,
   And stretch their hooks toward the limed pair,
150   Though both were cooked into a crusted hide
   By then. And, so embroiled, we left them there.

CANTO 23

Dante, still uneasy about the demons, finds himself of one mind with Vergil who devises an escape. They arrive in the chasm of the hypocrites, chief of whom is the high priest who passed Christ on to the Romans. It is the fifth chasm of the eighth circle. They reach the sixth chasm by desperate measures.

Silent, apart, unescorted, we went;
    One leading, one behind, we forward pressed
    Like Minor Friars on their journey bent.
My thought, by all this conflict, was addressed
    To Aesop's fable telling the affair
    Of mouse and frog that caught my interest.   6
For Yet and But are not a better pair
    Than one case with the other, if, with mind
    Alert, the start and close of both you air.
And, as one thought leads to a further kind,
    So rose, from that, another one to me
    Which made my first fear more than doubly bind.   12
And to myself I thought, 'What mockery
    And scorn we've heaped on them, and injured pride
    Of such a kind that will enrage them – free.
If malice such as theirs were multiplied
    By rage, they will pursue us and will rend
    More fiercely than a dog the leveret's hide.'   18
Already I could feel my hair on end,
    And I was looking back with intent peer.
    I said: 'Master, if you do not intend
To hide yourself and me, too, fast, I fear
    The Taloned Demons after us. They hold
    Imagination so, I think I hear.'   24
And he: 'If I were leaded glass, your mould
    I never could have drawn so swiftly in,
    As I impress that inner image told.
Your thoughts have mingled into mine with twin
    Act and twin face, so I have made
    Of both one resolution how to win.   30
The right bank slopes, so we may soon evade
    The chase, imagined, by a gradual descent
    Into the next chasm without further aid.'

He'd hardly finished voicing this intent
 When I could see them coming, wings outspread,
36 To seize us, not far off, upon the scent.
My guide snatched me up at once and fled,
 As would a mother, wakened by a noise,
  To see beside her flames igniting red,
And grabs her child and runs, and, since the boy's
 Survival matters most, will never waste
42 The time that putting on a gown employs.
So, down that ridge of the hard bank, in haste,
 Upon his back, against that tilted steep
  Which dams up one side of the gulf, he raced.
Never did water from the chute so leap
 To load a mill-wheel's ladles to the brim,
48 Just where they rise to start the downward sweep,
As did my master down that bank now skim,
 Bearing myself away upon his chest;
  More as a son than friend I was to him.
And scarcely had his feet come down to rest
 Upon the chasm bed, than, on the bank,
54 They stood above; but small fear he expressed.
For Providence that willed on them the rank
 Of ministers in the fifth gulf allowed
  To none the power to leave that duty blank.
And, there below, we found a painted crowd
 Who walked their round with slowest of slow pace,
60 Weeping, their looks exhausted, overbowed.
And cloaks they wore with deep cowls on the face,
 Made in the selfsame pattern as those capes
  The monks of Cluny wear about the place.
They are so gilded in their glittering drapes,
 But inside they are loaded down with lead;
66 Frederick's would seem like straw upon their napes.
– Oh weary mantle for eternity ahead! –
 We turned again to left and went along
  With those intent on dreary tears they shed.
So tired of their burden was that throng
 That every movement of our hips we passed
72 Fresh company whose walk was not as strong.
So I suggested to my guide: 'Now cast
 Your eyes about to find some person here
  Whom we may know by deed or name at last.'

And one who knew the Tuscan in his ear
    Cried after us: 'You, running at such speed
    Through this swart air, linger and come near.   78
Perhaps you will obtain the one you need.'
    And, hearing this, my guide turned slowly round
    And told me, 'Wait, then by his side proceed.'
I waited there and saw a pair I found,
    By all appearance, in great haste of mind
    To join me, slowed by cloaks, the narrow bound.   84
When they'd arrived, at first they did not find
    A word, but merely looked with eye askance;
    Then, turning to each other next, they whined:
'This one seems alive, at the first glance,
    The way his throat works. And, if they're dead,
    By whose boon wear no cloaks in their advance?'   90
'O Tuscan,' then they turned to me and said,
    'Don't scorn to say who comes so lightly clad
    To see the college of hypocrites in lead.'
I answered: 'I was born and grew a lad
    In the great city on lovely Arno's shores,
    And have the body I have always had.   96
But who are you from whom such sorrow pours
    As I can see run down your face and cheek?
    What glinting punishment is this of yours?'
And one of them replied, 'Our poor physique
    Must bear these orange cloaks of lead so thick
    That weights like these have made the balance creak.   102
Jovial Friars and Bolognese when quick,
    My name's Catalano; Loderingo, his.
    Your city chose us both, that used to pick
But one alone to keep the peace, that is;
    And we were such that it is very plain,
    Around Gardingo, what our infamies.'   108
I started, 'Friars, your wicked –' but stopped again,
    For, there before my eyes, I saw a man
    On three stakes crucified beneath the train
Of feet. He writhed all over on that span,
    And sighed into his beard, on seeing me.
    Friar Catalano saw this and began: 114
'That cross-fixed one you are amazed to see
    Counselled the Pharisees that it was meet
    One man should die to leave the people free.

Across the path, and naked to all feet,
   Just as you see, he feels the heavy weight
120   Of all who pass along this narrow street.
In the same way, his father-in-law's prostrate,
   Racked in this trench, with many others pent –
   The counsellors who brought the Jews such hate.'
I noticed Vergil, how he gazed intent
   Upon this man, extended on that cross
126   So shamefully, in eternal banishment.
And then he asked the friar in his gloss,
   'If you're allowed, don't fret or feel dislike,
   But say if, on the right-hand of the fosse,
There lies a gap through which we yet may strike,
   Without requiring the black angels here
132   To come and extricate us from this dyke.'
He answered, 'Nearer, ah, much more near
   Than you had hoped, a stonework bridge extends
   From circuit wall, with each stern ridge its pier,
Except that, here, it's broken down and ends;
   But you can clamber up the rubble spread
138   Against this side, that, piled up here, ascends.'
My guide stood still awhile, head bowed, then said:
   'That one who hooks the sinners if they rise,
   Falsely he told us of the way ahead.'
The friar said: 'At Bologna they put you wise
   On many of the Devil's vices. I heard
144   He is a liar and father of all lies.'
Then, with long strides my guide was moving, stirred
   To anger in his looks at such deceit.
I left the burdened spirits without a word,
   Following the print of his belovèd feet.

CANTO 24

They climb out of the chasm of hypocrites on the ruins of the fallen bridge, Dante
requiring much encouragement. They come to the chasm of thieves, the seventh in
the eighth circle. Vanni Fucci, ashamed to be found in such company by Dante, tries
to upset him with forecasts of his future banishment from Florence.

In the youthful time of year just when the sun
    Tempers his locks beneath Aquarius' sign,
    And nights decrease to match the day that's done;
When hoar-frost traces a similar design
    To its white sister on the ground, though brief,
    Before the fading of his pen and line,   6
The peasant, whose fodder fails, looks for relief
    But sees the fields still white, at which he whacks
    His hand upon his thigh to show his grief,
And goes indoors, and back and forth he tacks,
    Just like a man not knowing what to do;
    Then, back out, grousing, finds the hope he lacks,   12
Observing how the world has changed its view
    In such a little time, and takes his crook
    And leads his lambs outside to feed anew.
The master made me despair like that to look
    Upon his troubled brow, and, in the same way,
    The plaster to the chafing place he took.   18
For, when we came to where the wrecked bridge lay,
    My guide turned to me with that pleasant face
    I first saw at the foot of the mountain-way.
He spread his arms, first having planned the base
    To work from in his mind, and, checking well
    The ruins, lifted me in his embrace.   24
As one who calculates and can foretell,
    Always providing beforehand, so, while he'd lift
    My weight up one great rock, collapsed pell-mell,
He'd look out for a further crag or rift
    Amid the ruins. 'Climb on that,' he said,
    'Test with your weight to see it will not shift.'   30
It was no route for people cloaked in lead.
    For we, he light, myself assisted, groped
    Only with great pains from jag to jag ahead.

Except that in this dyke the incline sloped
   Less far than down the next, after the rise,
36   Although he might, I never could have coped.
The rings of Malebolge drop in size
   Towards the deepest shaft; each chasm's drop
   Leaves outer higher, while the inner deeper lies.
At last, however, we had reached the top
   Where the last stone breaks off in the air,
42   At which I came, exhausted, to a stop.
The breath was gone out of my lungs just there,
   And I could go no further, so I sat
   As soon as I had climbed on that top stair.
'Now,' said my master, 'rid yourself of that,
   It's sloth; for men may never make their fame
48   By sitting on down or coverlet or mat.
Whoever spends his life without that aim
   Leaves such a vestige of himself on earth
   As smoke in air and foam on water claim.
So, up! End those gasps with your soul's worth
   That wins the battle, if it does not sink
54   Beneath the heavy body of its birth.
A longer ladder must be climbed; don't think
   That beating these is quite enough. But act
   And prosper, if you follow me; don't shrink.'
I rose, pretending to the breath I lacked,
   As well I knew, but said, 'Let us proceed
60   For I am strong, my resolution intact.'
We headed up the ridge which was, indeed,
   Rugged, narrow and hard, and steeper here
   Than was the last, and, while he took the lead,
I talked as on I went to make it clear
   I was not fainting; from the next deep fosse,
66   A voice launched sounds not sense to human ear.
I don't know what it said, although across
   The high-point of the baulk that bridged the rift,
   But, by its tone, the anger I could gloss.
I had looked down to see what I could sift;
   But never could my eyes have plumbed that dark.
72   So then I said, 'Master, let us be swift
To reach the other belt, and leave this arc;
   For, as I hear no sense that can be tracked,
   So I look down and nothing can remark.'

'No other answer shall I give, in fact,'
    He said, 'but deeds. Sensible requests
    Should be succeeded by the silent act.'   78
We went down from the bridgework where it rests
    On the eighth bank, and then I could behold
    The depth itself and all it manifests.
I saw a fearful horde of snakes untold,
    And some of such strange kinds that, even now,
    Remembrance of it makes my blood run cold.   84
Let sand-spread Libya boast no more: allow
    Her chelydri, jaculi, phareae; then add
    The cenchris, amphisbaena's hissing row.
So many malignant plagues it never had,
    Not with all Ethiopia could rear,
    Nor land beside the Red Sea, monster-clad.   90
Amid this vicious, dismal swarm appear
    Stark naked people, running, terrified;
    No hope of heliotrope nor hide-out near.
Their hands were forced behind their back and tied
    With snakes which, through the loins, thrust tail and head
    That knotted in the front of the divide.   96
Suddenly, one who past our bank had sped
    Was transfixed by a serpent which had bitten
    The point where shoulder to the neck is led.
No I nor O could be so quickly written
    As he took instant fire and burnt away,
    Sifting to ash and cinder soon as smitten.   102
And, once he was dissolved like this and lay
    Upon the soil, the silt resumed its mould
    And made its former shape of flesh and clay.
So with the Phoenix, mighty sages hold,
    It dies, and then is born again from flame
    When it's about five-hundred summers old.   108
Alive, it eats no leaf or grain, they claim;
    But tears of incense and amomum; nard
    And myrrh its shroud and winding-sheet they name.
Now, just like one who tumbles very hard
    And can't tell why – either some demon's force
    Which floors him, or some other hindrance barred –   114
And, when he rises, looks round for its source,
    Bewildered by the anguish of the pain
    Undergone, sighs and moves off in due course –

So was this sinner when he rose again.
    – The Power of God! Oh, how severe its Doom
120   That makes such blows of vengeance rain and rain. –
My guide then asked him who he was. To whom
    He answered: 'I rained down from Tuscany,
    Not long since, to this savage gullet's room.
The life of beasts, not human, pleasing me,
    Mule that I was; I am that savage brute
126   Vanni Fucci; Pistoia my den used to be.'
And I said to my guide, 'Don't let him scoot,
    But ask him what crime was it brought him here.
    I've seen him, blood up, raging absolute.'
That sinner, hearing, without pretence or fear,
    Directed on to me his mind and face,
132   And, with a look of dismal shame, made clear:
'It's much more painful that you find my place
    Within this misery than was the agony
    Which took away my life in the first case.
I can't deny you what you ask of me:
    I'm here in this great depth because I stole
138   The goodly furnishings of the sacristy,
And others falsely bore the blame on their soul;
    But so you may not gloat upon my plight,
    If ever you escape this gloom's control,
Open your ears to hear of my foresight:
    Pistoia weeds the Blacks out very thin;
144   Florence renews people and laws outright;
And, next, from Val di Magra, Mars shall spin,
    Out of its turbid cloud, a mist to wield
    And, with impetuous angry storm, begin
A battle to be fought on Piceno's field
    Where suddenly the fire shall split the mist
150   And strike down every White. I have revealed
    All this to grieve you.' So he had hissed.

CANTO 25

Vanni Fucci signals his total defiance of God and is punished by the surrounding serpents, as is the furious centaur Cacus who comes in pursuit of him. Still in the seventh chasm of the eighth circle, Dante encounters five thieving notabilities from Florence – which prepares for the sorrowful condemnation he gives his native city in the next canto.

As his words ended, so the robber threw
    Both hands and both their figs up and he roared:
    'Take that, God, for they are aimed at you.'
And from that instant all the serpent horde
    Became my friends, for one of them had coiled
    Around his neck to stop his vocal chord;   6
Another wound around his arms and foiled
    His chance of using them, it held so fast
    In front of him, no matter how he toiled.
– Ah, Pistoia, Pistoia, why not decree to blast
    Yourself to ash, since you outdo your seed
    In wickedness, and should no longer last. –   12
I saw, throughout all Hell's dark rings, indeed,
    No spirit of more arrogance to God;
    Nor he that fell from Thebes' wall a prouder breed.
He fled without another word or nod,
    And then I saw a Centaur, in raging storm,
    Cry: 'Where is he? Where's that surly clod?'   18
Maremma, I believe, could never swarm
    As many snakes as seethed upon his sides
    To that point where the human shape took form;
Over his shoulder, behind his head, there rides
    A dragon, wings outspread, who sets alight
    All that they meet where next the Centaur strides.   24
My master said: 'That's Cacus. Beneath the height
    Of that rock, Mount Aventine, he shed
    A lake of blood too often in his spite.
A road far from his kin he here must tread
    For all his fraud in thieving the great herd
    Lying nearby where Hercules had led.   30
His wicked actions Hercules deterred
    Beneath his club which rained a hundred blows,
    Though Cacus never felt ten that occurred.'

Just as he spoke the Centaur passed in throes,
　　And, also, right beneath us then, there came
36　　Three spirits; neither of us noticed those
Until they cried: 'Who are you? What's your name?'
　　So that account was stopped; we paid sole heed
　　To these – although our answer never came.
I didn't know them; it happened, as indeed
　　It often does, that one of them by chance
42　　Had used a name, and thus gave us a lead,
In saying: 'Where's Cianfa stopped?' A glance
　　I gave my guide, a finger to my lip,
　　To make him listen with a quiet stance.
– No wonder, Reader, if my credit slip
　　With you for what I now must truly say,
48　　Since I who saw it scarcely hold my grip.
For, as I watched them, lo, across their way,
　　A serpent with six legs dashed up and ramped
　　On one and fixed its claws into its prey.
Around the belly its mid claws were clamped;
　　Around the arms the second pair were clasped;
54　　It fixed its teeth into the cheeks and champed.
Its hindlegs round the thighs it grasped;
　　Insinuated tail between the two,
　　And up between the loins it reached and rasped.
Ivy was never rooted to a tree so true
　　As on the victim's limbs the monster wound
60　　And intertwined his own, and to him grew.
As if of heated wax they then compound,
　　And mix their colours, so that neither one
　　Nor other seemed what first it had been found;
Thus paper, over flame, turns brown and dun
　　But not yet charred and black, and all the white
66　　Retreats and dwindles out upon the run.
The other two stood gazing on the sight
　　And cried: 'Ah me, Agnello, how you change!
　　You're neither one nor two nor yet unite.'
The two heads had become a single, strange,
　　Where two appearances were in one mould
72　　But yet appeared but one features' range.
Two arms were blended out of fourfold.
　　Thighs with the legs the hidden parts became;
　　The torso and the chest – unique to behold.

The former shapes were now extinct yet same;
    Neither, yet both, the perverse image merged;
    With languid step it wandered off in shame.   78
As the lizard, in the dog-days' torpor scourged,
    From hedge to hedge, just like a lightning flash,
    Will dart across the path if need has urged,
So now a little reptile made its dash
    Towards the bowels of the other pair,
    Black as a peppercorn, in fury rash.   84
It pierced into that part of one just where
    We draw our nourishment at first, then fell
    Outstretched before him on the footway there.
The pierced thief gazed on it a little spell
    But nothing said; yet, with his legs stock-still,
    Yawned, as with sleep or fever made unwell.   . 90
He eyed the reptile; reptile, him – until
    One from the wound, the other, mouth, then rolled
    A violent smoke that met, as if by will.
– Let Lucan hold his peace – whose words have told
    Of poor Sabellus and Nasidius, and wait
    To hear what next my verses shall unfold.   96
Nor Ovid on Cadmus and Arethuse dilate,
    For if in poetic fit he turn one snake,
    The other fount, I do not grudge that trait;
For never did he yet transmute and make
    Two creatures, face to face, their opposite
    So both each other's substance were to take.   102
They mutually respond. The reptile split
    His tail into a fork; the wounded soul
    Congealed his steps in place till they were knit.
The legs and thighs together make one whole,
    And, blended so, no longer could the joins
    Be scrutinized where once they were not sole.   108
The cloven tail assumed the figure, loins
    The other lost; and supple grew the skin,
    Just as the other hardened up the groin's.
The arms towards the armpits shrank back in;
    The forefeet of the brute – which had been short –
    Extended as those shrank, to long and thin.   114
Then the hindlegs twisted together to distort
    Into those parts a man conceals; the wretch's
    Had two extra limbs from them support,

While, with new colour, the smoke veils and stretches
    Over them both, and generates the hair
120   On one, and hair from off the other fetches.
One rose erect; prostrate the other there,
    But never breaking off the impious light
    By which they each exchange the face they wear.
The erect, his drew towards the temples tight,
    And used the excess to fashion into ears
126   That from the smooth cheeks appeared to sight,
And, from the rest that did not shrink, appears
    A nose, and, fleshed out round the space
    That once was jaws, a mouth forms and coheres.
The one now prone extends his pointed face
    And draws his ears back inside his head,
132   As snails will draw their horns back into place.
His tongue, once joined and apt for words, instead
    Divides and, in his opposite, the split
    Within the fork unites – and the smoke is fled.
The soul, that now was brutish, hissed its spit
    And fled along the vale; the other bawling
138   And spitting at its back, then turned from it
His novel shoulders: 'I'll have Buoso crawling
    On all fours down this road,' he said, 'the same
    As me!' towards the other shade then calling.
I saw the seventh ballast where I came
    Changing and interchanging; if my pen
144   Errs, the unprecedented is to blame.
And, though my eyes were quite bewildered then,
    And mind dismayed, they could not flee away
    Before I knew Puccio Sciancato again.
For he, of those who first came, side by side,
    Did not transmute his form, but on he went.
150   The other person there that we had eyed
    Was he because of whom, Gaville, you lament.

CANTO 26

Dante opens with a sorrowing condemnation of Florence. Vergil then reveals the evil counsellors of the eighth chasm of the eighth circle. This leads the poet to rein in his genius. Ulysses gives him an account of his last voyage and his fearful end.

Florence, exult since you have grown so great
    That over sea and earth your wings are spread,
    And throughout Hell your name extends its state.
Among these thieves I found the five you bred,
    For which great shame is mine, nor have you drawn
    A heap of noble honours on your head.   6
But, if the dreams are truthful near to dawn,
    You'll feel, quite soon, what Prato, not to speak
    Of others, wished for you and all you spawn.
And, if already happened, as they seek,
    It had not been too early. Since it must come,
    I wish it now, than weigh my old physique.   12
We left; and on the curbstones, crashed unplumb,
    That made the stairs by which we could descend
    My guide climbed, showing me the way to come.
So, pressing on our lonely way, jag-end,
    And spur and outcrop of the cliff, the feet
    Could not succeed without hands to contend.   18
I sorrowed then, and now that grief repeat,
    When I recall what I had seen. My swift
    Genius I curb, though usually so fleet,
In case it mount where Virtue does not lift,
    So that, if kindly star, or better influence,
    Gave me this good, I may not grudge the gift.   24
As many fireflies as a peasant can sense
    While resting on a hill – those days the light
    That shines upon our world least hides from hence
And when flies cede to gnats of dithering flight –
    Can sense all down the valley, maybe, where
    He tills and gathers grapes – just so, this sight.   30
As many flames as that, the eighth gulf's air
    Revealed, all gleaming to my scrutiny,
    When I'd arrived where all lay to my stare.

As he, who was avenged by bears, could see
    Elijah's chariot rise, when the horses flew
36   Direct to Heaven, and knew where it would be
But could not track it with his eyes but knew
    It only as its flame, a little cloud
    Ascending and diminishing in the blue –
So moved these flames along the fosse they crowd.
    For none reveals the theft that their flames fan,
42   And steals away a sinner in its shroud.
Where I had climbed the bridge to see and scan
    Much more, I stood, and would have fallen down
    Unpushed, if I'd not grabbed the rocky span.
My guide, who saw me so intently frown,
    Remarked: 'Within those flames the sinners are.
48   Each swathes himself within this burning gown.'
'Master,' I said, 'what I had thought so far
    Your words confirm, as I had just now guessed,
    Already wished to ask: what sinners char
Within that fire that forks toward the crest,
    As if it wandered from the funeral pyre
54   Where Eteocles and his brother went to rest?'
He said, 'Within that torturing, double fire,
    Ulysses and Diomedes are the source;
    They run in punishment as once in ire;
Within that flame, lament the ambush-horse
    That made the way by which the noble seeds
60   Of Rome came issuing forth by fraud and force.
Within it they lament the trick that leads
    Deidamia in death to mourn Achilles still;
    For the Palladium, further pain succeeds.'
'If they may speak within those sparks, and will,'
    I said, 'I beg you, master, and I pray
66   My words may be a thousandfold in skill,
Do not forbid my chance to pause and stay
    Until the two-horned flame has wandered near.
    You see with what desire I lean that way.'
He answered: 'Praiseworthy the wish I hear,
    And therefore I agree to it; one thing:
72   You must restrain your tongue and just give ear.
I'll do the talking; what you're considering
    I know: and they, because they're still all Greek,
    Might well disdain your words and questioning.'

After the flame had reached where he would seek
   In moment and in place, he thus began,
   And, in this manner, then, I heard him speak: 78
'You, both within one flame, if, when a man
   I merited of you, if I merited
   Of you, in great or small, during my span
When I had made those noble verses, tread
   No further; stay and tell me, one of you,
   Where, having lost himself, he finished dead.'   84
The greater horn of ancient flame then blew
   And shook with murmurs from its denizen,
   As flame is troubled where the draught goes through.
Swaying its summit to and fro, came then
   A voice, as if it were a speaking tongue,
   And what it started saying opened: 'When   90
I quitted Circe who, a year, had strung
   My men and me along, near Gaeta – the name
   Aeneas gave it later, and it clung –
Neither affection for my son, nor claim
   Of my old father, nor the love I had
   To comfort Penelope, nothing could tame   96
The ardour that I felt within to gad
   The world and gain experience of all,
   And learn of humanity the good and bad.
I set out on the high seas with the small
   Company that never had deserted me,
   And with a single ship to rise and fall.   102
One shore and the other we came to see
   As far as Spain, Morocco, Sardinia; saw
   The other isles the seas bathe cleansingly.
Old, slow, we were, when happening to draw
   Toward that narrow strait where Hercules
   Assigned his landmark, fixed to overawe   108
And hinder men from risking unknown seas.
   Starboard, I left Seville; the left-hand shore,
   Ceuta, already left on a good breeze.
"O brothers," then I cried, "who through five-score
   Thousand dangers have approached the west,
   Don't deny this brief watch, of senses hoar   114
Already, the experience to quest
   For that unpeopled world behind the sun
   That lies beyond these pillars where we rest.

Consider your origins: not formed, not one,
    To live like brutish beasts, but made to find
120   And follow virtue, and knowledge to be won."
With these brief words I fired my comrades' mind
    With eagerness to see the voyage made.
    I never could have checked them or confined.
Turning our poop towards the dawn, each blade
    Then winged us swiftly on our foolish flight,
126   And, always gaining to the left, we strayed.
The other Pole already was in night
    With all the stars, and ours was down so low
    It did not rise from ocean into sight.
Five times we saw the moon's light glow,
    Rekindle and then quench since we began
132   Upon the arduous course we'd planned to go,
When there appeared a mountain in our scan,
    Dim with the distance, but it seemed to me,
    The highest mountain ever seen by man.
We rejoiced, but joy soon turned to jeopardy.
    A tempest from that new-found land arose.
138   Across our bows it launched a heavy sea.
Three times it spun the ship with such wild blows;
    The fourth sea lifted out the stern in air
And dipped the bow down – as Another chose –
    Until the waters closed above us there.'

CANTO 27

Still in the eighth chasm of the eighth circle, Dante meets Count Guido da Montefeltro, a Ghibelline leader, who asks after the condition of Romagna. With some affection and regret Dante tells him. The travellers now reach the ninth chasm.

Ceasing, the flame was straight and quieted;
    It was already moving to advance,
    The gentle poet's agreement being said,
When, from behind, another drew our glance
    Towards its tip from which, in garbled style,
    Confusing sounds escaped its troubled stance.   6
As the Sicilian bull (that first had roared awhile
    With that lament of his – and rightly so –
    Who had originally tuned it with his file)
Would bellow with the victim's voice, and, though
    It had been fashioned out of brass and cast,
    It seemed to be transfixed with pain and woe;   12
So, having at its start no channel past,
    Or issue from the fire, the dismal speech
    Was changed to noises of the fiery blast.
But quickly did they find their way to reach
    The tip, and lent it those vibrations stirred
    In passing from the tongue that would beseech: 18
'Oh you at whom I aim these words,' we heard,
    'And you who just now spoke with Lombard trait:
    "Now go; no more I ask you!" was your word,
Though I have come perhaps a little late,
    Don't let that irk you; stay and let's begin
    To talk. See: I'm not irked in flame to wait.   24
If, to this blind world, you've just come in
    From that sweet Latian land from which I bore,
    Into this dark, the burden of my sin,
Say if the Romagnoles have peace or war,
    For I am from the mountains there, between
    Urbino and where Tiber starts to pour.'   30
I still was leaning down, intent and keen,
    When my guide gave a nudge at me and said:
    'Answer; a Latian's in that flaming screen.'

And I, who had the answer pat in my head,
   Began without delay to speak my piece:
36   'O soul, concealed in flame, in darkness led,
That Romagna of yours has never, nor will cease
   To stir a conflict in its tyrants' minds,
   But outwardly when I left it was at peace.
Ravenna stands as long it has; it finds
   Polenta's eagle brooding over it,
42   And, covering Cervia with its wings, it binds.
The city that earlier was made to sit
   A long siege out, and made a massacre
   Of Frenchmen, bears again the Green Claws' writ.
Verrucchio's old mastiff, and the young cur
   Who wickedly despatched Montagna, gore
48   And fang where they habitually stir.
The cities on Lamone and Santerno's shore
   The Young Lion of the White Lair rules,
   Changing, from summer to winter, side and roar.
The other city that the Savio cools,
   Lying between the mountains and the plain,
54   Falls between freedom and tyranny's two stools.
Now, please, no charier than us, don't disdain
   To tell us who you are so that your name
   Its memory upon the earth retain.'
After the usual roaring of the flame,
   It moved its pointed summit to and fro,
60   Then breathed, and this the answer that then came:
'If I once thought my answer here might go
   To someone who'd return into the world,
   Not one tremor would this flame let show.
But, since not one, in this profound depth hurled,
   Has ever left alive – if what I hear
66   Be true – fearing no shame, this is unfurled:
I was a man of war, then cordelier,
   Hoping, so girdled, to amend. At least
   To some fulfilment of that hope came near,
But for – disaster take him – that great Priest
   Who drew me back again to my first sin.
72   I'll tell you why, and how it all was pieced.
While in the form of flesh and blood and skin
   My mother gave me, all my deeds were those,
   Not of the lion, but those the fox would win.

All wiles and subtle ploys I knew and chose,
　　And had the knack of them so well in hand
　　That, to the world's ends, rumour of me arose.　78
When I observed I'd reached shore on the strand
　　Of years where all should lower sail and mast
　　And gather up and coil the ropes on land,
I grieved on what had pleased me in the past;
　　Repented and confessed, a monk's vows swore.
　　Ah, woe, it would have saved me at the last!　84
The Prince of the new Pharisees, waging war
　　Near to the Lateran – not with Saracen,
　　Or Infidel or Jew, not any more,
For all his enemies were Christian then,
　　And none had been to conquer Acre yet,
　　Nor trafficked with the Sultan and his men –　90
Recked nothing of the highest office, set
　　His Holy Orders and my cord aside –
　　Which used to make the wearer leaner yet,
But just as Constantine, from Soracte's hide,
　　Fetched Sylvester to cure his leprous skin,
　　So this man summoned me to be his guide,　96
To cure the fever of his pride, and win.
　　He asked my counsel, but I held my peace
　　Because his words seemed drunk in origin.
And then he said to me: "Let all doubts cease,
　　For I absolve you now; so speak and show
　　Me how to raze Palestrina, piece from piece.　102
Heaven I shut and open, as you know,
　　For twofold are the keys I hold, though held
　　Light by my predecessor and so low."
Then weighty arguments quite soon impelled
　　My mind to think the silence worse. I said,
　　"Father, because you have so well dispelled　108
That guilt that now must fall upon my head:
　　Let large promise, scant observance be
　　The way to triumph for your throne instead."
When I was dead, St Francis came for me,
　　But I heard one of the Black Cherubim declare:
　　"Don't take him; don't discount my custody.　114
He must come down among my menials there
　　Because of the fraudulent counsel he evolved.
　　Since when, I've hovered ready by his hair.

For those who don't repent can't be absolved:
    It can't be done, both to repent and will
120   An act: a contradiction is involved."
Ah, wretched fool: how shocked I was and chill
    When he had seized me, saying, "You little thought,
    Perhaps, I was possessed of logic's skill."
He hauled me off to Minos, who wound and brought
    His tail around eight times behind his back,
126   And, biting it, in mighty anger fraught,
Said: "Sinner for the thievish fire's rack."
    And so I'm lost, as you can see me here,
    And, clothed in this, my grieving heart would crack.'
And, as he finished there, the flame, in sheer
    Sorrow, writhing and tossing its pointed crest,
132   Departed, and began to disappear.
Along the cliff, my guide and I now pressed
    Toward the other arch above that fosse
Where those who sowed discord and reaped unrest
    Gather their guilt and pay the price with loss.

CANTO 28

Here in the ninth chasm of the eighth circle they encounter those who spread schism and division. Mahomet is first encountered – for Dante a sectarian who had distorted the truth of Christianity. His son-in-law, Ali, is with him. Mahomet gives a warning for Dante to deliver to the contemporary schismatic Fra Dolcino. Others give further warnings. The poet ends with the meeting with the violent poet Bertran de Born.

Who, even with boundless words, could ever tell,
  By long reiteration, the wounds and gore
  That next I found in this new ring of Hell?
Every tongue assuredly would more
  Than fail because our memory and speech
  Have little room to master such a store.   6
If all the men were gathered, each by each,
  Who once upon Apulia's fateful land,
  For all their blood the Trojans shed, raised screech
And wail, with those of the long war's stand
  That ended with so vast a spoil of rings
  (As Livy writes, who errs not with his hand)   12
With those who bore such pain and buffetings
  Resisting Robert Guiscard, and those, no less,
  Whose bones are heaped at Ceperano where things
Were lost through the Apulians' treacherousness,
  And there, at Tagliacozzo's battle, where
  The old Alardo conquered, weaponless;   18
And, if one showed his limbs transfixed and there
  Another's hacked away, it would provide
  No match for the ninth chasm's gory share.
A cask with mid-base gone, or stave from side,
  Would never gape so wide as one I saw
  Ripped from the chin to sounding rump and stride. 24
Between his legs his entrails hung down raw;
  The pluck was bared, with sack that should expel
  What has been swallowed earlier at the jaw;
And, while I stood and gaped at him a spell,
  He looked at me and, with his hands, he rips
  Apart his breast: 'See, I split myself as well.   30

Look how Mahomet's mangled. Cleft from lips
   To forelock through the face, my Ali goes
   In front of me, and tears on tears he slips.
And all the others you can see are those
   Who peddled scandal or their schism abroad.
36   Here, therefore, they are split with routine blows.
A devil comes behind us in this horde
   And cruelly splits us with another hack,
   Subjecting all, in turn, beneath his sword,
When we have wandered round this grievous track;
   For all the wounds will heal before the shade
42   Has dragged himself around, and staggered back.
But who are you upon the cliff delayed,
   Postponing, maybe, punishment ahead,
   Pronounced upon your self-indictment made?'
'Death hasn't touched him yet. No guilt has led
   Him here,' replied my master, 'nor to bleed
48   In torture; but to fetch news of the dead.
It lies on me who am, though dead, to lead
   Him throughout Hell, and go from ring to ring.
   This is as true as I speak here, you heed.'
More than a hundred stopped, in listening,
   When they got wind of this, along the fosse,
54   To look on me in awe past suffering.
'Well, you who may yet see the sunlight's gloss
   Quite soon, tell Fra Dolcino, if he's
   In no real rush to join me in this loss,
To build his food reserves against the freeze,
   In case the strain and stress of snow should bring
60   An otherwise hard conquest to the Novarese.'
This, having raised his foot to tread the ring,
   Mahomet told me; then he took a stride
   And left, around the fosse continuing.
Another, with an ear gone on this side,
   His nose sliced right away up to the brows,
66   His throat transfixed, who, marvelling, had eyed
Us from the rest, before a voice could rouse,
   Opened his gorge, which outwardly was gore
   In every part, yet speech it still allows:
'You, uncondemned by guilt, I've seen before
   On Latian soil above, unless your face,
72   And some resemblance, has deceived me more.

Remember Pier da Medicina, if you retrace
    Your steps, and see again the gentle plain
    That slopes from Vercelli to Marcabo, its base.
And make it known – if foresight be not vain –
    To Guido and Agnolello, that renowned
    And worthiest pair from Fano, make it plain   78
They shall be cast out of their vessel, bound
    Past Cattolica, by the treachery
    Of a fell tyrant who will have them drowned.
Neptune had never known upon the sea,
    Between Majorca and Cyprus, such a crime;
    Pirate nor Argive did such felony.   84
That one-eyed traitor who holds, at this time,
    That land which someone by me in this tract
    Wishes he'd never seen, will use, as lime,
An invitation to negotiate, but act
    So they'll not need to raise a vow or prayer
    For fear the winds of Focara attacked.'   90
I answered: 'If that's the news you'd have me bear,
    Show me and tell me who it is I saw
    Who seemed to rue that sight with bitter air.'
And so he laid his hand upon the jaw
    Of one of his companions, worked the mouth,
    And said, 'He cannot speak or hum or haw.   96
Exiled, he quenched all Caesar's doubts and drouth
    By claiming that, to any man prepared,
    Delay is always harmful, and sent him south.'
– Ah, Curio, how ghastly now, who dared
    So much in words alone, with his tongue cleft
    Right to the gorge, and further speech despaired.   102
And one with both hands severed raised what's left
    Through that dim air so that their pulsing gore
    Ran down into his face – no longer deft.
'You will remember Mosca that much more,'
    He cried: 'I said alas, "What's done, is done!"
    And evil seed it was the Tuscans bore.'   108
'Death to your kin,' I added to that one,
    And so he went his way, gathering pain
    On pain, like someone into madness run.
But I remained to view that horde again,
    And saw a thing I should have feared revealing
    Without more evidence to make it plain.   114

But conscience reassures me, in this feeling,
    That good companion that fortifies a man
    In armour of its sense of honest dealing.
Assuredly I saw, as still I can,
    A trunk without a head come walking there,
120   Just as the others of that dismal clan.
It held the severed head up by the hair,
    Swinging it like a lantern in his hand,
    And, pointing at us, moaned in its despair.
It made itself a lamp itself and scanned
    And they were two in one and one in two.
126   How this can be He knows who had it planned.
When just beneath the bridge, in going through,
    It raised its arm up high with the whole head
    And, to our ears, its words the closer drew.
'Look, you that breathing come to see the dead.
    Take a good look at my grievous penalty.
132   Is any else as harsh as this?' he said.
'And so that you can carry news of me,
    Know I am Bertran de Born, the one who gave
    Such ill advice to the young king's majesty.
What Ahithophel launched was not more grave.
    Absalom against David he incited.
138   I made father and son as foes behave.
Because I parted persons once united,
    I lug my brain divided from its source
Upon this trunk. In this I am requited.
    The law of retribution takes its course.'

CANTO 29

Dante, near blind with tears at these horrific sights, still hopes to catch sight of his father's cousin, Geri del Bello. Vergil rebukes Dante and reports that he saw Geri making angry gestures in Dante's direction. The travellers then pass on to the next group of sinners who are the falsifiers in things, in deeds and in words. In the first class come the alchemists and forgers. This is the tenth chasm and last in the eighth circle.

So many people, diverse wounds, and deep,
    Had made my eyes so drunken that I longed
    To linger there a little while and weep.
But Vergil said: 'Why gazing so prolonged?
    Why let your eyes still weep on sights down there
    Where all the mutilated shades are thronged?   6
At other chasms you never showed this care.
    Consider, if you dream of taking count,
    The two and twenty miles of thoroughfare.
The moon's beneath our feet, and the amount
    Of time allowed is small, and other things
    Than these you are to see, which you discount.'   12
At that, I answered, 'If you knew what wrings
    This searching from me, maybe you'd persuade
    Yourself to give me time to settle things.'
Meanwhile my guide was moving on. I made
    My way behind him, furthering my case,
    And added, 'In that hollow which I stayed   18
To search so keenly, I believe, must pace
    A spirit of my kin, mourning the guilt
    Which costs so dearly in this dismal place.'
'Let no more thought shatter, nor tears be spilt
    On him,' he said; 'observe some other thing.
    Just let him stay there, for I saw him tilt   24
His fingers at you, vehemently threatening.
    I heard them call him Geri del Bello, there,
    Under the little bridge's buttressing.
Then, you were so involved in steady stare
    At him who once held Alta Forte's height,
    You never saw him. He left with angry air.'   30

'Ah, guide, his violent death and shame unite,
   Because his kin have not avenged the deed,
   To make his indignation hold me light.
And, therefore, I suppose, he paid no heed
   But stalked off so, without a thing to say.
36   It makes me pity him in all his need.'
And so, in walking on, we talked away
   Along the first part of the cliff that showed
   The other depth – if light had lent a ray.
When we'd arrived upon that jagged road
   Above the last cloister of Malebolge, where
42   We saw its lay brothers in their abode,
The lamentations pierced me through that air
   With arrows barbed with pity, so I pressed
   My hands against my ears to stop the noises there.
As if all illnesses that could infest
   The hospitals of Val di Chiana, those
48   Of Maremma and Sardinia, from earliest
July to late September, were in throes
   In that one rift – such was the suffering here;
   And stenches, as from putrid limbs, arose.
On the last bank of the cliff, long and sheer,
   Towards the left, again we made descent;
54   And then the sight became so very clear
Right to the depths where, with infallible intent,
   Justice, ministrant of the mighty Lord,
   Punishes the falsifiers she is sent.
A greater sorrow it would not afford
   To see Aegina's people so infirm
60   When such malignance in the air was stored
It killed all beasts, even the smallest worm;
   And after that, as poets hold for true,
   The ancient people there, out of the germ
Of ants were then restored – than now to view,
   Throughout that darksome gulf, the weary shades
66   Languishing in many shocks, or one or two.
One on his belly; on the shoulderblades
   Another lay; and some on all fours crawled
   Along the path of wretchedness that jades.
Step for step we moved, silent, appalled,
   Watching and listening to the groaning sick
72   Who couldn't raise themselves where they were stalled.

One pair I saw whose skin was covered thick
    With scabs, who leant against each other's weight,
    As pan is leant to pan in the warming trick.
No currycomb was plied at such a rate
    By stable boy whose master he delays,
    Or one reluctantly awake when late,   78
As each one with his nails so claws and flays
    Himself intently, in that agony
    Of itching, sole relief to ease the craze.
Their nails drew down the scurf as you might see
    A kitchen-knife remove the scales of bream
    Or other fish of large variety.   84
'Ah, you,' my guide addressed one of that team,
    'You who unmail yourself with fingernails,
    And sometimes tweezer with them, it would seem,
Tell us if any Latian spirit ails
    Within this gulf; so may your nails succeed
    Eternally to rid you of these scales.'   90
'We, so disfigured here, of Latian breed,
    Both of us,' answered one, starting to weep.
    'But who are you that ask and pay us heed?'
My guide replied: 'I'm one who leads, from deep
    To deep, this living man, and my intent
    Is this: to show him Hell, and all its sweep.'   96
Their mutual leaning broke, and both then bent
    Towards us, trembling; more shades turned my way,
    Who, near, had caught the echo he had sent.
My good master closely turned to me to say:
    'Tell them anything you'd like to speak.'
    I started as he wished without delay: 102
'So that your memory shall not grow weak
    In human minds in the first world but last
    Beneath as many suns as you would seek,
Tell us who you are, what clan and cast?
    Don't let this ugly and disgusting disease
    Frighten you from revealing all your past.'   108
'I was from Arezzo,' said one of these.
    'Albert of Siena burnt me at the stake
    But that's not why I have these scabs like fleas.
True, I did say, joking, I could make
    Myself fly through the air. Of little wit
    And foolish hope, he wished me, for his sake,   114

To demonstrate to him the art of it;
 And since I couldn't make him Daedalus,
 By one, whose son he was, my fire was lit.
But Minos, infallible and rigorous,
 For alchemy I'd practised on the earth,
120 Condemned me to the tenth of circles thus.'
I asked my guide: 'Are there, of any birth,
 A people lighter than the Sienese?
 By no means the French, for what that's worth.'
The other leper, who had eavesdropped these
 Remarks, responded, 'Save for Stricca, who
126 Contrived to spend so niggardly his fees,
And Niccolo who first devised and grew
 The costly clove fad in that garden plot
 Where such seed always roots; and then that crew
Where Caccia of Asciano spent his lot,
 Squandering his forests and his vines,
132 And Abbagliato showed his wit a jot!
But so you know who seconds you, and lines
 Himself against the Sienese, persuade
 Your eye to look: my face will give you signs,
And you shall recognize Capocchio's shade,
 Who falsified the metals with alchemy;
138 And recollect, if I know you, how I made
 As good an ape of Nature as there'll be.'

CANTO 30

Still observing the tenth chasm of the eighth circle, Dante encounters Gianni Schicchi of Florence, and Myrrha who both impersonated others for gain. He meets Potiphar's wife and Sinon who represent the falsifiers in words. Dante becomes engrossed in eavesdropping an altercation between Sinon and Master Adam. His curiosity earns a rebuke from Vergil.

When Juno was incensed against the race
    Of Thebes because of Semele, as she'd shown
    Before, and more than once to be the case,
Athamas turned insane; seeing his own
    Wife with each son held on either side,
    He ordered, 'Now let all the nets be thrown   6
That I may catch within the pass,' he cried,
    'The lioness and cubs.' And then he flung
    His pitiless talons out to clutch his pride;
Grasping the child called Learchus, swung
    Him round and dashed his head against a stone.
    She drowned herself with her remaining young.   12
When the dare-all pride of Trojans was laid prone
    By Fortune, and the king and realm had been
    Obliterated, Hecuba, alone,
Wretched, and sad, and captive, having seen
    Polyxena slain, and, utterly forlorn,
    Had recognized Polydorus on the clean   18
Sea sand, her sanity was overborne,
    And she, reduced to barking like a hound;
    By such sorrow had her soul been torn.
– Furies of Thebes or Troy were never found
    So cruel to anything – not brutes that spring,
    Nor anything in human vesture bound –   24
As then I saw two shades come ravening,
    Naked and pale, running, like the swine
    Freed from its sty, and biting, savaging.
One hurtled at Capocchio; in his spine,
    Just at the neck-joint, drove his tusks in him
    And dragged his belly, scraping the harsh decline.   30
The Aretine remaining shook in every limb.
    'That's Gianni Schicchi, the fiend,' he said.
    'He's rabid, savages anyone at whim.'

'Ah, then,' I said, 'so the second doesn't bed
   Its fangs in you, please tell us who it is,
36   Before it darts wherever it will head.'
He said: 'That heinous, ancient spirit is
   Myrrha. She loved her father with a more
   Than rightful love in her iniquities.
And when she came to sin with him, she wore
   An alien form, just as that other one,
42   Who's clearing off, assumed, so he'd ensure
He'd gain the lady of the herd – and won;
   Disguised as Buoso Donati who was dead,
   He forged his will and in the due form done.'
And, when the furious pair I'd watched had fled,
   My gaze reverted so I could observe
48   The other ill-born spirits in their stead.
And one I saw with lute-style double curve;
   If only he had had the groin cut short
   Where man is forked, this image would well serve.
The dropsy's heavy fluids, which contort
   Proportions so that features do not match
54   The bloated paunch with which they should comport,
Compelled his lips to gape and to detach,
   As does a fever patient's who, in thirst,
   Curls one lip up, one down for chin to catch.
'You, don't ask me why, from all accurst
   Punishment exempt in this grim world below,'
60   He called to us, 'look and attend me first:
I'm Master Adam, in this miserable woe.
   When I was living I had every wish;
   Now, for a drop of water craving so.
The streams of Consentino's hills that splish
   And splash into the Arno, making the course
66   So cool and moistured where they sway and swish,
Flow constantly before me, no vain force;
   Their image dries me up more than disease
   Can waste flesh from my face without remorse.
Rigorous Justice, that tries and tests me, keys
   My punishment to that place where I'd sinned
72   To make my sighs rise fast and deeper seize.
Romena lies there, where I forged and twinned
   The alloy sealed with John the Baptist's face,
   For which my body burned into the wind.

Yet, more than Branda's fountain in this place,
 I'd see the wretched Guido's soul, the shade
 Of Alessandro, or his brother's, fill their space. 78
One is already here, if that parade
 Of maddened shadows, on their rounds, speaks true.
 But what's the good when these limbs give no aid?
Were I still light enough to move a few
 Inches a century, I would have set
 Already on the road to get a view 84
Of him among the maimed. I could forget
 The circuit is eleven miles; no less
 Than half a mile the width to parapet.
They brought me to this house of wretchedness.
 They made me stamp the florin out of blanks
 With three carats of alloy in the press.' 90
I said: 'Who are that abject pair, their shanks
 Sprawled out beside you, just towards your right,
 And steaming like hands washed by wintry banks?'
'They were already here, in this same plight,
 When first I strayed to this pen; haven't stirred,
 And may not stir for this eternal night. 96
That lying wife blamed Joseph by her word;
 The other's Sinon, that lying Greek from Troy.
 Burning fever makes them reek like a turd.'
And one of them, on hearing him deploy
 Their names so darkly, struck his taut paunch
 With beating fist, as if he would destroy. 102
A drum it sounded. Adam, fixed so staunch,
 Flailed him across the face with his flung arm,
 And seemed no lighter pummelling to launch.
'Though I am stuck from moving out of harm
 By bloated limbs, I still have this arm loose
 When such contingencies may bring alarm.' 108
His answer came: 'It wasn't so much use
 When you were headed for the fire; though more,
 Much more, when coining moved it to produce.'
The dropsied one replied: 'That truth you score;
 But you were not the honest witness, plied
 In Troy with questions on the facts you bore.' 114
'If I spoke falsely once, you falsified
 The coinage,' said Sinon. 'For one fault I'm
 Punished; you, more than any demon tried.'

'Perjurer, think about the horse some time,'
 The victim with the swollen paunch then cried.
  'Your torture is: the whole world knows your crime.'
'Your torture be the thirst,' the Greek replied,
 'That splits your tongue, foul waters that produce
  That hedge-like paunch your eyes are hid inside.'
The forger then: 'You let your mouth gape loose
 To prove you wrong as usual; if I thirst
  And humours bloat me with the foulest juice,
You had head pains and burning fever first.
 You wouldn't need an invite now to lap
  Narcissus' glass, in which you are immersed.'
I stood intent on hearing every scrap;
 My master said: 'A bit more just you stay
  And gawp, and we will quarrel in some gap!'
Hearing his anger as he spoke that way,
 I turned towards him, filled with self-reproach –
  Which comes again, in memory, to this day.
As one who dreams of dangers that encroach,
 And, dreaming, wishes it were just a dream;
  Longs for what is, as if it weren't, to approach,
So I became; and speechless to redeem
 Myself, yet wishing myself to be excused,
  I was excused, although it did not seem.
'Less shame repairs a greater fault,' enthused
 My master, 'than yours has been. Therefore unload
  All of that shame with which you are suffused.
Consider: I'm always beside you on the road,
 If Fortune lead again where people verge
Upon a shouting match, with goad for goad,
 The urge to listen is a vulgar urge.'

CANTO 31

The travellers mount and cross a bank separating the tenth chasm from the ninth circle, the pit or shaft where Satan is confined. Dante is confused and fearful in the thickening fog of gloom. He encounters the ancient giants who warred against Heaven. Vergil arranges their descent into the deepest pit at the base of Hell – Cocytus where all the rivers freeze.

> One and the same tongue wounded me at first
>> So that the shameful blushes tinged my cheek,
>> But then held forth the medicine and nursed.
> I've heard Achilles, with his lance, would wreak –
>> As would his father – first a sorry gift
>> And then a goodly one, as their technique.   6
> We turned our backs on that gulf, made shift
>> To climb the bank that rings it with its height,
>> And crossed, in silence, out of that dark rift.
> Here it was neither day nor yet the night,
>> So that I saw not far before my face;
>> But then I heard a horn blown with such might   12
> It would have made the thunder dim to trace.
>> It drew my eyes back down along its course
>> Till they were pointed at the very place.
> After the sad defeat, when all the horse
>> Of Charlemagne had lost the holy war,
>> Roland never blew with such a force.   18
> I had not stared that way for long before
>> I seemed to see a crowd of lofty towers.
>> I asked my master, 'What city lies in store?'
> Yet he replied, 'Your eyesight strains its powers
>> From peering too far off, in darkness blind;
>> Imagination's hoodwinked by this sight of ours.   24
> When you are nearer to the place you'll find
>> Distance deceives the sense of shape and space.
>> So spur your step a bit. Don't lag behind.'
> He took me by the hand with loving grace
>> And said, 'Before we go much further here,
>> So that it will not seem so strange to face,   30
> Know it's not towers but giants that rear
>> Out of that pit and, planted navel-deep
>> Around the bank, like towers may appear.'

As when a mist diminishes, eyes keep
    Re-shaping, bit by bit, each form or mark
36   Which those air-crowding vapours soak and steep,
So, while peering through the noisome dark,
    Drawing nearer and nearer to that pit,
    The error fled, and terror rose up stark,
For, as along the wall that circles it,
    Montereggione crowns itself with towers,
42   So fearsome giants (Jove threatens to split
From Heaven still with thunderbolts he showers)
    Turret the parapet whose sturdy base
    Surrounds the pit that in the darkness lours.
Already I had recognized one face,
    The shoulders, chest and massive belly's swell,
48   The two arms down the sides and in their place.
– When Nature dropped that art, she acted well
    In ceasing to create beings like them,
    Keeping such agents out of Mars's spell.
Though, in deciding that she would not stem
    Her elephants and whales, all minds that plumb
54   Profoundly find a prudent stratagem:
For, where the instruments of mind succumb
    To mighty strength and evil will, men see
    That their defence is swiftly overcome. –
The face appeared as long and broad to me
    As stands the fir-cone before St Peter's shrine;
60   And, matching this, his other bones agree.
The bank, an apron from the girdle's line,
    Allowed so much to tower up in space
    Three Frieslanders would boast to reach and twine
The hair in vain. For, from shoulder-place
    Where men would latch a cloak, I clearly gauged
66   Thirty large spans to meet the torso's base.
'Raphel mai amecche zabi almi!' raged
    The savage mouth, for which there could have been
    No sweeter psalmody than this he waged.
My guide directed at him: 'Vent your spleen,
    You stupid soul, upon that horn you blast
72   When rage or passion makes you feel so keen.
Check now, and you will find the strap is passed
    Around your neck, bewildered soul, and reach
    The horn that round your mighty chest is cast.'

He told me: 'He condemns himself in speech.
   This is the Nimrod, through whose evil spurred,
   We cannot speak one language, each to each.   78
Let's leave him standing there, nor waste a word
   For every language is the same to him,
   As is his own to us, senseless, absurd.'
We moved on, bearing left around the rim,
   And, there, a bow-shot off, we found the next,
   And he was far more fierce and grim.   84
Who or what master had so caught and vexed
   Him there I couldn't tell: one arm, the right,
   Was chained behind, the left in front annexed
By links of chain that held him from neck height
   Downwards, and, all around the naked part,
   Was wound a fifth time round, and very tight.   90
My guide explained, 'This one, of haughty heart,
   Decided he would match his strength with Jove,
   And this is his reward, for all his art.
His name is Ephialtes; he, it was, drove
   So hard when giants made the gods afraid.
   He never more will move those arms that strove.'   96
And then I spoke, and this request I made:
   'If possible, I'd like to cast my eye
   Upon immense Briareus's shade.'
To which he said: 'You'll see Antaeus nearby,
   Who still can speak, and is not chained and bound;
   He'll put us where the guiltiest must lie.   102
The one you'd like to see is too far round,
   But tied the same, and built like this one here,
   Except he looks the fiercer, you'd have found.'
No earthquake shook a tower with violent rear
   As Ephialtes, all at once, began to quake
   And tremble in himself, as we came near.   108
Then more than ever I feared death would take,
   And nothing more was needed but that fear,
   If I'd not seen the chains he could not break.
We moved on then, and saw Antaeus rear
   Who rose five ells, not reckoning the head,
   Out of his shaft, into that atmosphere.   114
'You, who, in the fateful valley Hannibal fled
   With all his army, making Scipio
   The heir to glory, you who seized instead

A thousand lions for your prey; who know
    That if you had been at that haughty war
120   With all your brothers – it's still considered so –
The sons of earth had made their victory sure –
    Set us both down, and don't be shy about it,
    Where ice locks Cocytus with its freezing floor.
Don't pass us to Tityus or Typhon. Don't doubt it:
    This man can give what you would dream most worth.
127   So stoop. Don't bare your teeth in scorn, and flout it.
For he can yet renew your fame on earth;
    He is alive, and long his years should last,
    If grace permit that he fulfil his birth.'
So spoke my master. Hastily and fast,
    He took him, stretching out those mighty hands
132   That tested Hercules in days long past.
When Vergil felt the closing of those bands,
    He told me, 'Come where I can grasp you here,'
    And made one rope of our two loose strands.
It seemed to me the same as when you peer
    From under Garisenda's leaning side
138   As clouds in contrary direction steer.
So Antaeus seemed to move there as I eyed –
    It was so terrible to undergo
    I wished for other roads we could have tried.
Gently he set us in the deep below,
    Where Lucifer and Judas are held fast.
144   He did not linger long bent double, though,
    But raised himself erect, as ship the mast.

CANTO 32

This is the ninth and last circle of Hell, the ice furthest away from light. The outer ring, Caina – named after the first murderer – contains those who were violent against kindred; the inner, called Antenora, after Antenor (who was thought to have been a traitor to the Trojans, despite Homer) contains those who betray state or country. Both Guelfs and Ghibellines are here. Dante finds one, Bocca degli Abbati, the most obnoxious. Then he finds two frozen together, head to head, and hears their account in the next canto.

If I'd rhymes rough enough and full of shock
    To match the dismal hole that must support
    The mass and weight of all the upper rock,
I should extract the essence of my thought
    More fully but because I have found none,
    Not without fear I start on my report.   6
To word the whole world's sump's no task for one
    Who plays about nor for a tongue that cries
    For mum and dad like any mother's son.
But may those muses aid my verse to rise
    That aided Amphion to wall Thebes round,
    So that the facts are in the words, not lies.   12
– You, miscreated rabble who are bound
    In that place hard to speak of, better, here,
    That you as sheep and goats had walked the ground! –
When we were down in that pit dark and sheer,
    Much deeper than the giants' feet were stood,
    Still eyeing the high wall, I heard, quite near,   18
A voice complaining: 'Ah, I think you should
    Watch where you're walking so you do not tread
    Against these weary heads in wretched brotherhood.'
I turned to look and underfoot was spread
    Before my eyes a lake that in the frost
    Appeared more glass than water in its bed.   24
The Austrian Danube never yet has glossed
    So thick a veil across his winter course,
    Nor Don beneath snow skies its motion lost,
As here there lay; if Tambernic's full force
    Had fallen, or Pietrapana's hulk,
    Not even the edge would creak from such a source.   30

And, as the croaking frog will often skulk,
 Head out of water, when the peasant lass
 Dreams she is gleaning, so lay the bulk
Of these, all livid in the icy mass,
 Submerged to where the blush of shame would spread,
36 Chattering out, like storks, the vapid gas.
Each face was downward; by their eyes was shed
 Evidence of the misery in their hearts;
 And by their mouths the cold exhibited.
When I had gazed awhile at various parts,
 I looked towards my feet, and saw two pressed
42 So close their hair was mixed in tangles, darts.
'Tell me who you are, jammed chest to chest,'
 I said. And so they bent necks back and strained
 Their faces up so they might see me best.
Though only moist within, when first they craned,
 Their eyes gushed tears out at their lids, and ice
48 Bound them together again more tightly chained.
No plank pressed plank the harder in a vice;
 At which, like goats, they butted head to head,
 Fury so overcame them from the splice.
And one who'd lost both ears from cold then said,
 His face still downcast in the ice, 'Why stand
54 And gaze at us so long in this cold bed?
If you must know who those two are, their land
 Was in the valley where Bizensio descends;
 Their father Albert's, till it reached their hand.
From one flesh they sprang. Search to the ends
 Of Caina now, but you will never know
60 A shade this gel more rightfully suspends.
Not him whose breast and shadow with one blow
 Were pierced and holed by Arthur's furious hand;
 Not Focaccia; nor this wretch that so
Obstructs me with his head I've never scanned
 Beyond it: Sassol Mascheroni; you,
66 If Tuscan, what he was should understand.
And just to stop you asking what of me and who,
 Camiscion de' Pazzi I was called; I wait
 For Carlino to exculpate me when he's due.'
And then I saw a thousand in that strait
 Turned purple by the cold – since when I shake
72 Whenever I see a ford with its ice plate.

Then, moving to the centre of the lake
    Where gravity all collects, I felt the chill
    That was eternal make me shiver, quake.
Whether by chance or destiny or will
    I do not know but, passing by one head,
    My foot caught the face hard, and, shrill,   78
It railed and wailed: 'Why must you go and tread
    On me? If you've not come just to increase
    The vengeance of Montaperti, why kick?' it said.
'So I may rid myself – and have some peace –
    Concerning doubts of him, master, please wait.
    Then, as you wish, your spurring need not cease.'   84
He paused; and, to that shade in bitter spate,
    I turned to ask: 'Who d'you think you are
    In such reproach of others? Look what you rate!'
'And who are you,' he answered,' come to jar
    The jaws of us in Antenora here?
    If you'd been living you'd have gone too far.'   90
'I am alive,' I said. 'If fame is dear
    To you, you'll find it worthwhile that I write
    Your name with these that in my notes appear.'
He said: 'The opposite. Get out of my sight,
    And take yourself away for you've no skill
    In how to flatter in this lowest night.'   96
I seized him by the scalp and said: 'You will
    Reveal your name to me or not a shred
    Of hair remains with you in all this chill.'
'I won't say who I am, or show,' he said,
    'Though you should leave me bald; and even though
    You fall a thousand times upon my head.'   102
I'd wound his hair already round to go,
    And yanked a tuft out as he raised a howl,
    And kept his eyes down in the icy floe,
As someone called out, 'Bocca, why this yowl?
    Isn't this chattering enough? Why do you bark?
    Of what new devil are you falling foul?'   108
'Now,' I said, 'accursèd traitor, hark!
    I do not need your answer. To your shame
    I'll bear the truth of you when I embark.'
'Push off!' he cried, 'and make whatever game
    You please of me, but do not hold your peace
    About that wretch with tongue quick to exclaim.   114

Here, he laments the Frenchman's silver piece,
        And you can say "I saw the Duera man
        Where sinners stand and freeze without release."
And, if they ask who else is here, you can
        Reveal that there's the Beccheria whose throat
120   Was slit by Florence for his treacherous plan.
Gianni de' Soldanier, I think you ought to note,
        A bit further; Ganelon; Tebaldello, unbarred
        Faenza, sleeping, for its enemies to gloat.'
We'd left him when I noticed, frozen hard,
        Two in the same hole, so cramped, one head
126   Seemed, for the other one, a cap or guard.
But, as when hungry one would chew at bread,
        So in that neck he sank his teeth to gnash
        Just where the brain into the nape is led.
No differently Tydeus fanged, in anger rash,
        The brows of Menalippus, than he bit
132   The skull and fleshly parts that he could gash.
'You, who in brutishness reveal and pit
        Your hate against the one you fang and bite,
        Say why,' I said, 'you rage in such a fit,
So that, if you have reason for this spite,
        I, knowing who you are, and his offence,
138   May yet requite you in the world of light,
        If still my tongue be supple with its sense.'

CANTO 33

Count Ugolino and Archbishop Ruggieri of Pisa are frozen together because of the depth of their treachery to each other, and to their countrymen. Ugolino explains how he was betrayed into death with his sons. Dante and Vergil then reach Ptolomea, named after Ptolemy (see 1 Maccabees 16.11) who banqueted his father-in-law and sons and killed them when they had drunk well.

The sinner raised his mouth from the wild repast,
    Wiped it on hair of the head he'd bitten through
    And wasted round the nape, then spoke at last:
'A desperate grief you want me to renew.
    It wrings my heart to dwell on it again
    Before I find the words to speak to you.   6
But, if my words may now become the grain
    That's reaped as infamy upon this traitor
    I gnaw, you'll see me speak and weep in pain.
I don't know who you are, nor by what crater,
    Way, you've come down here, but when I heard
    You talk, your speech seemed Florentine in nature.   12
Count Ugolino, it must have since occurred
    To you, and this, Archbishop Ruggieri here;
    And that is why we're in one hole interred.
Needless to say how once he'd lent an ear
    To confidence of mine, and, by his evil goad,
    I was then put to death. That much is clear.   18
But what you cannot know, the cruel mode
    Of death I suffered, you will now be told;
    And judge if it's an injury he's bestowed.
A small gap in the mew which will always hold
    The name of Famine after me – a place
    Where others yet must be confined to mould –   24
Had, through its opening, shown the lunar face
    Several times, when I slept an evil sleep
    That tore the veil from future time and space.
This man seemed lord and master who would leap
    After the wolf and cubs on the mountainside
    That stops the Pisans seeing Lucca's keep.   30
With hounds all keen and lean and fleet in stride,
    He'd sent the Gualandi, Sismondi ahead,
    And the Lanfranchi, running at their side.

After a short run, father and sons that fled
　　Looked wearied out to me, and then it seemed
36　　　Their flanks were savaged by the fangs and bled.
And, when I woke before the dawn had beamed,
　　I heard my sons were weeping in their sleep,
　　Begging for bread in anguish as they dreamed.
– You're cruelty itself if you do not weep
　　Already at the dread my heart forethought;
42　　　And if you don't, then when would your tears seep? –
They woke; the hour at which the food was brought
　　To us, when normal, had approached quite near,
　　And they were anxious, in their dream overwrought.
And then, below, I heard it all quite clear:
　　The tower entrance nailed up well and true.
48　　　Wordless, I looked upon my sons in fear.
I did not weep, turned into stone all through.
　　They wept, and little Anselm came to say,
　　"You look so ill, father; what's troubling you?"
I shed no tears, nor answered all that day,
　　Nor all the next night till the sun's first light
54　　　Had risen on the world with narrow ray.
When that thin beam had touched our wretched plight
　　In prison, I discerned within each look
　　The image of my own return my sight.
I bit my hands in grief, and they mistook
　　The act and thought I meant I needed food.
60　　　At once they rose and, coming where I shook,
Said, "Father, less pain it would be if you'd
　　Consume us. You have given us this flesh;
　　You have the right to take it off your brood."
I calmed myself to shelter them from fresh
　　Despair. That day, the next, we all stayed dumb.
66　　　– Ah, callous earth, why did you let us thresh? –
Upon the fourth day Gaddo, then, had come
　　And thrown himself before my feet and said:
　　'Father, why don't you help me to a crumb?'
And died. As you see me, and see this head,
　　I saw them, one by one, all three, grow weak,
72　　　Till, by the fifth or sixth day, all were dead.
Already blind, I felt each face and cheek;
　　For two days further, called on them by name.
　　Then hunger had more power than grief could wreak.'

So saying, with distraught eyes aflame,
    Into that wretched skull he sank his fangs,
    Which, like a dog's, the bone would fiercely maim.   78
– Ah, Pisa, scandal which gives such shameful pangs
    To people of that lovely land of '*si*',
    Since neighbouring vengeance merely overhangs,
Let Capraia and Gorgona shift, and be
    A dam across the Arno's mouth to drown
    All souls within your streets beneath that sea.   84
Though Ugolino had that ill-renown
    As yielder of your castles, it was wrong
    To bring the children's torture on the town.
Ah, Thebes reborn, their youth, those years not long,
    Made Uguiccione and Brigata innocent,
    And both the others named within my song. –   90
We went on where the frost ruggedly pent
    Another gathering, this time in reverse,
    So that their heads were always backwards bent.
Their very weeping makes their weeping worse,
    For grief, that meets that ice-dam on their eyes,
    Drives anguish inward since it can't disperse.   96
Their first tears latch together as they rise
    And, like a crystal vizor, fill the dips
    Beneath the eyebrows' ridge, and agonize.
And, though, as in a callus, feeling in lips
    And face, because of all the bitter cold,
    Had gone, it seemed as if I felt these whips   102
Of wind; at which I questioned who controlled:
    'Master, who stirs this wind? Surely all heat
    Is quite extinguished in this frozen hold?'
He answered, 'Soon you'll reach where eye will greet
    The cause and source that sends these blasts, and find
    The answer for yourself when it is meet.'   108
One of the wretched shades in ice confined
    Then cried at us: 'O souls so cruel your place
    Down in the last station is assigned,
Remove the hardened veils that lid my face
    So I may vent the grief that stuffs my heart,
    If but a moment – till fresh tears encase.'   114
I said: 'If help you want, then, for a start,
    Say who you are; and, if I give no hand,
    May I be sent to deepest ice apart.'

He said: 'Fra Alberigo, understand.
    I ordered fruit from the evil garden; now,
120   I'm paid back date for fig, for what I'd planned.'
'Huh,' I said, 'you dead already?' – 'How
    My body copes on earth I do not know,'
    He made reply. 'Of all the frozen slough,
Ptolomea has this privilege: that, though
    Atropos has not given the soul despatch,
126   It frequently falls directly here below.
And, just to make you keener to unlatch
    The frozen tears upon my eyes, please know
    That when a soul betrays in ways that match
With mine, its body's seized by a demon foe
    That rules it afterwards until the time
132   Comes round for it to drop and fall below.
The soul falls to this sump for that one crime;
    Maybe the body of this other shade,
    Behind me, walks the earth, as in his prime.
If you've just come, you'll know this renegade.
    It's Ser Branca d'Oria; many years
138   Have passed since he was frozen in this grade.'
'I think,' I said, 'you trick me with these smears,
    For Branca d'Oria has never died,
    But eats, drinks, sleeps, wears clothes, as well appears.'
'In the Malebranches' fosse,' he then replied,
    'Where all that clinging pitch boils in its bed,
144   Michel Zanche'd not yet come to bide,
When this man left a devil in his stead
    To work his body – as did one of his clan,
    Accomplice in that treachery inbred.
But reach and open my eyes,' he next began.
    But I refused to open them for him.
150   Rudeness was courtesy to such a man.
– You Genoese, estranged from good, and brim-
    Full of corruption, why not dispersed,
    Out of the earth, like chaff on the wind's whim?
For I found one of you beside the worst
    Spirit of Romagna who, for his deeds,
156   Steeps his shade in Cocytus immersed
    While life upon the earth his body leads.

CANTO 34

Judecca, the last area of Cocytus, is named after Judas Iscariot. Here are punished with and by Satan himself the arch-traitors in Dante's eyes, Brutus and Cassius, the assassins of Julius Caesar who represents Dante's ideal of the strong secular ruler of the Roman Empire who would parallel and countervail the power of the Papacy. Dante is then led out of Hell by Vergil, who uses a baffling and frightening escape route. The opening Latin adapts a 6th-century hymn by Venantius Fortunatus. Here it means 'the regal banners of Satan advance'.

'*Vexilla regis prodeunt inferni*
    Towards us: therefore look ahead of you,'
    My master said, 'to see him as you journey.'
As when thick mist breathes, or night is due
    Within our hemisphere, a mill if swept
    By winds might seem upon a distant view,   6
That sort of thing, it seemed, as on I stepped,
    But, blown by gales, I shrank behind my guide,
    The only shelter where I could have crept.
Already (and with fear I cannot hide
    I put it into verse) I'd come where souls,
    Immersed, shone through – like glass with straw inside.   12
Some were erect; some lying in their shoals;
    One, bent just like a bow, had face to feet,
    Head uppermost were some, and others, soles.
When we had gone so far on the icy sheet
    It pleased my guide to show me that Being
    Who once had been so lovely and so fleet,   18
He moved from where his figure blocked my seeing,
    And said: 'Look, Dis; and here's the place you'll need
    Your fortitude prepared to stop you fleeing.'
How frozen I was and faint, oh, you who read
    Need never ask; my pen I cannot drive;
    What words I have to use would just mislead.   24
I did not die, and yet was not alive.
    Think for yourself, if you've a grain of wit,
    What I became if death nor life survive.
King of that grievous realm, he rose from it
    From mid breast in the ice, and I, in size,
    Nearer a giant than the giants fit   30

Into his arms. Think how the whole would rise
    To match this mass above the frozen brim;
    How mighty must he stand upon his thighs.
If he were lovely as his ugliness is grim,
    And raised his head against his Maker's will,
36   Well may the whole affliction stem from him.
With what great marvel did my vision fill!
    I found there were three faces to his head;
    The foremost one was fiery despite the chill;
The other two looked sideways out instead,
    Above the middle of each collar-bone
42   And with one crown the three were helmeted.
The right was white to yellow in its tone;
    The left, to look at, seemed to be the hue
    Of those that live along the Nile's long zone.
Beneath each head a pair of pinions grew
    Of size to match the bird; I never came
48   On sails of ships as broad as these to view.
They were not feathered; texture and form the same
    As bats' wings; he was flailing them so fast
    That three gales set off from his mighty frame.
These froze all Cocytus with their furious blast,
    And with six eyes he wept, and down three chins
54   The tears and foam of blood went gushing past.
He champed a sinner in his mouths like gins
    Or heckles, keeping three in utmost pain,
    And so he tortured them for all their sins.
The biting teeth were nothing much again
    Beside the clawing done the middle one
60   Whose back at times was flayed in skein on skein.
'That soul to whom worst punishment is done,'
    My master said, 'is Judas with his head
    Engulfed and legs outside that make to run.
And, of the pair with heads dangling,' he said,
    'Hung from the black face, Brutus. See how well
66   He writhes away, and all his words are fled.
Cassius – so sturdy – the third mouth must quell.
    But night ascends once more. We must depart
    For we have seen into the whole of Hell.'
As he desired I clasped his neck to start.
    With skill he chose his moment and his spot,
72   And, when the wings were open wide apart,

Climbed on the shaggy sides from knot to knot
    And so descended; between the tangled hair
    And crusted ice he clawed, and down he got.
When we had reached the swelling haunches there
    Where the thighs rotate, in danger on the rime,
    My guide turned down his head, his feet to air,   78
And then he grappled on, as if to climb;
    And I, a moment, thought we had turned round
    To enter into Hell a second time.
'Hold tight, for by such stairs as these we're bound,'
    He panted, like a man with forces spent,
    'And must escape the evil of this ground.'   84
And through the fissure of a rock he went,
    And issued forth, and slumped me on its rim.
    Then took a cautious step, and near me leant.
I raised my eyes to Lucifer, as grim
    As I had left him, but I saw his feet
    Turned up into the air, and fixed each limb.   90
Dull folk who miss the point in our retreat
    That I had passed, now let them be the judge
    If I were not perplexed by this strange feat!
'Get up!' my master said. 'It's time we budge.
    The way is long, and difficult the road.
    The sun's near middle tierce, and we must trudge.'   96
No palace-hall where we were stood, a mode
    Of natural dungeon with an evil base;
    An absence of all light in that abode.
When I had risen from my resting-place,
    I said, 'Before I leave the Abyss, say,
    Master, and take from me all error's trace,   102
Where is the ice? How is he fixed this way,
    Head first? How come that, in so short a space,
    The sun has made its transit to the day?'
He said, 'You think you're still in that same place
    Against the centre where I grabbed the hair
    Of that foul Serpent, piercing the world's base.   108
You were, as long as I descended, there.
    But, when I turned, you passed the point that draws
    All gravities from every part towards that lair.
The hemisphere in which you've come to pause
    Is opposite the one that arches wide
    Above the great dry land it overawes   114

In which the Sinless One has lived and died.
      You have your feet upon a little sphere,
      The other face of Judecca, its underside.
When it is evening there, it's morning here.
      The Fiend, who made our ladder with his hair,
120   Is still as fixed whatever may appear.
This is the side he plummeted through air
      From Heaven; and the land which was outspread
      Covered itself in sea, in fear's despair,
And came to be our hemisphere instead.
      What stayed this side, perhaps conceding space
126   In order to escape, rushed upward, fled.'
Furthest from Satan in his tomb's a place
      That's not to be located by the sight
      But noises of a rill the ear can trace
Trickling through the hollow that the slight
      Gradient of its meandering course has cleft
132   Into the rock since it had taken flight.
We entered on that hidden path and left,
      Returning to the bright world of the day.
      Content to press on, of all rest bereft,
We mounted up; he first; I next, that way,
      Until I made out what an opening unbars:
138   The lovely things that in the Heavens sway.
      And so we issued forth to see the stars.

PURGATORY

INTRODUCTION

Purgatory is conceived as a mountain on the underside of Hell. The extension of its vertical axis runs through Jerusalem and the centre of Hell. It is surrounded by sea. It was hollowed upward by the earth's attempt to flee from Satan as he plunged into this sea, so that his legs are sticking up beneath it, creating an exit from Hell for Dante and Vergil.

Those who are purging themselves of sin are on terraces cut in tiers into the side of the mountain. They are arranged in the following order:

THE LOWER SLOPES
Before the Gate of Purgatory:

> Cato, and the excommunicated
> The Negligent
> The Princes of this World

THE TERRACES
Above the Gate of Purgatory:

> Pride
> Envy
> Anger
> Sloth
> Avarice/Prodigality
> Gluttony
> Lust

THE GARDEN OF EDEN

CANTO 1

Leaving Hell, Dante, with some false modesty referring to his 'little boat' of genius, invokes the holy muses to aid his passage through Purgatory. He invokes as the greatest of them Calliope, who defeated in song her sisters who had praised the rebellious Titans. The writing in this canto is full of exhilarated gladness to greet the sun and the light after the depths of Hell. Dante and Vergil's way is hindered by Cato, the guardian of the purlieus of the island-mountain of Purgatory. A reader of Dante may well be surprised to find him here, since, as he was an opponent of Caesar and a suicide, one might have expected to meet him in Hell. But for medieval thinkers he was a hero-martyr in the cause of liberty. There is much symbolism of a complex, almost irrecoverable nature in this canto but what strikes is the lyric quality of the welcome to day and life and hope. The time is now before sunrise on Easter Sunday, 10 April 1300.

My cockleshell of genius sets sail to take
    Its course on better waters and now leaves
    That cruel ocean far behind its wake.
I'll sing the second kingdom which receives
    The human soul to purge it till it lies
    Worthy to ascend and Heaven achieves.   6
Holy Muses, let poetry arise
    From death again since I am yours; again
    Let Calliope a while now rise
And accompany my song with that same strain
    Whose sound the Magpies heard and so despaired
    Of pardon for their challenge made in vain.   12
Sweet tint of orient sapphire, which was aired
    On the clear forehead of the sky, bright
    And clean even to the first circle flared,
Into my eyes again restored delight
    The moment that I came from the dead air
    Which had afflicted both my heart and sight.   18
The lovely planet that moves to love was there,
    Making the whole east laugh now, while behind
    She veiled the Fishes in her thoroughfare.
I turned towards the right and fixed my mind
    Upon the other pole and saw four stars
    By none but the first people yet defined.   24

Heaven seemed to rejoice in those flaming cars;
   Poor northern climate, widowed of delight
   In them whose lovely sight your fate debars.
When I had wrenched my eyes from this great sight,
   Turning to the other pole and zone
30   From which the Wain had already taken flight,
I saw quite near a veteran, old and lone.
   His bearing drew such reverent respect
   No son toward his father more had shown.
His beard was long and touched with white that flecked
   His locks as well that plunged in double flights,
36   And with the pair of these his chest was decked.
The shining of those four most holy lights
   So lit his features with their purest beam
   I saw him as if the sun were in the heights.
'Who are you that have, against the dark stream,
   Escaped the eternal prison?' so he said,
42   Shaking those locks of venerable esteem.
'Who guided you? Who was the light that led
   You from the thick night that ever palls
   The infernal valley of the sinful dead?
Are the laws of Hell broken by thralls?
   Has Heaven's wisdom taken second thought
48   That you, the damned, can reach my rocky halls?'
My leader laid his hand on me and taught
   By word, by hand, and by his signalling,
   My knees and brow the reverence they ought;
Then answered: 'Not my idea, this journeying.
   A Lady came from Heaven through whose prayers
54   I bore him company in this wandering.
But since you wish to know of our affairs
   And how indeed this came about, to hold back
   A single thing from you my mind forbears.
His last hour hasn't come. But his wild track
   Took him so near the verge there had remained
60   But little time to try to change his tack.
I was to rescue him, as I explained
   Before; nor was there any other way
   Unless I chose this route that we have gained.
I've shown him where the guilty people stay,
   And now propose to show him those as well
66   That purge themselves beneath your charge and sway.

How I have led him this far would be to spell
    A long story out. Virtue comes from on high
    To help me guide him to hear what you will tell.
Please look on his coming with a kindly eye.
    He seeks for freedom, that most precious jewel –
    As knows the man who for her sake would die.   72
And well you know, since death was not so cruel
    To you in Utica, for her sake, where you shed
    The garb the great day brightens with renewal.
Eternal laws we neither broke nor fled,
    For he's alive and Minos binds not me.
    Your Marcia's circle I inhabited –   78
Whose chaste eyes visibly make their plea
    And prayer, O holy heart, to be your own.
    For love of her meet our exigency.
Let us across your seven realms and zone.
    Your words I will convey to her, if you deign
    Even to be mentioned there below, or known.'
                                           84
'Marcia so pleased my eyes,' he spoke again,
    'While I was yonder still, that not a grace
    She wished of me did I ever disdain.
Now that she stays and has her dwelling-place
    Beyond the evil stream, she moves no more –
    Through law decreed when I came from that race.   90
But, if a Heavenly Lady moves you, as before
    You mentioned, there's no need of flattery.
    Rest certain in the name that you implore.
Go, and ensure that your companion be
    Girdled with a smooth reed, and have his face
    Bathed so that from all filth it is set free.   96
It never would be right that any trace
    Of mist obscure his eye when he stands before
    The first minister of those in Heaven's grace.
This little isle has all around the shore,
    Where the waves beat them, rushes that grow
    Out of the softness of the muddy floor.   102
No other plant of leaf or stem lives so
    For none of them is pliant, none bends
    Against the beat and buffet of that flow.
But don't return this way; the sun ascends
    And that will show you how to climb the peak
    By an easier ascent than this way tends.'   108

And so he vanished; and I rose but speak
   I did not, drawing all attention back
   To my guide for whom alone my eyes would seek.
He started: 'Son, now follow in my track.
   We'll turn back since the plain here slopes away
114   To reach its lower limit in the wrack.'
The dawn was vanquishing the breath of day
   That fled before her so that far again
   I saw the tremor of the ocean sway.
We trudged along and trod the lovely plain
   As one returns to a missed road, and till
120   He find it seems to plod along in vain.
When we came where dew fights the sun's will,
   Being shaded where, in the cooler air,
   It's slowly scattered till the sun distil,
My master spread both hands out gently there
   Over the sweet grass; and so I raised
126   My tear-stained face, of his purpose quite aware.
And there and then he cleansed my features, hazed
   And hidden in the filth of Hell, and showed
   My true complexion to whoever gazed.
We came to a desert shore where never rowed
   Nor sailed a mariner on that vast of sea
132   Who came to landfall where those waters flowed.
To suit another's wish he girdled me.
   What marvel! That where he plucked the lovely reed
   It sprang up instantly the same as he
   First found and plucked it out to meet our need.

CANTO 2

In wonder Dante observes a strange object crossing the water towards them – an angel-propelled boat. It disembarks a group of penitents who assume that Vergil and Dante know their way about. Dante, recognizing and recognized by some, asks to hear one of the love poems made by Casella who is in these new arrivals. He takes pleasure in hearing it sung but is rebuked by Cato for lingering in the great work of purgation. The obscure remarks in line 98 refer to the fact that in the Jubilee Year, from Christmas 1299, plenary indulgences were granted to pilgrims. The Latin, line 46, means 'When Israel went out of Egypt' (Psalm 114; Vulgate 113).

The sun already had approached the line
    Of the horizon – whose meridian ring
    Covers Jerusalem at its highest incline,
And night, which turns opposed, was issuing
    From Ganges with the Scales that slip her hand
    When she exceeds the day by lengthening   6
So that Aurora's cheeks, from where I scanned,
    Lovely and rose and white, through time's advance
    Were turning orange over sea and land.
We were beside the ocean still, our stance
    Like men who wonder which direction's right:
    In heart they move; but body takes no chance.   12
And there and then – as came the morning light –
    Through the dense mists that Mars consumes to red,
    Low in the west, above the ocean's might,
Appeared a sight to me – may I be led
    To see it again – a light that crossed the sea
    So fast no flight had with such motion sped.   18
When I had turned aside inquiringly
    Towards my guide, I saw next how it beamed
    Bigger and brighter in intensity.
Then, at each side of it, I saw there gleamed
    A sort of white; and from beneath it, bit
    By bit, another white appeared, it seemed.   24
My master did not speak a word of it
    Until the first white showed as wing and wing;
    Then, when he knew the boat as definite,

He cried: 'Bend, bend the knee in reverencing.
　　Behold the Angel of God; fold hands together.
30　　Henceforth you'll see such angels ministering.
Look how he scorns man's implements whatever.
　　Oars he won't use nor any kind of sail
　　Between far shores but his own wing and feather.
Look how he turns them Heavenward to flail
　　The air with those eternal plumes that do
36　　Not change like human hair to grey and pale.'
Then, as nearer and nearer to us flew
　　The holy bird, it shone much brighter so
　　That eyesight could no longer bear to view
And I looked down, and he, approaching slow,
　　Brought to the shore so light and swift a craft
42　　The waters drew no part beneath their flow.
And that celestial pilot was standing aft,
　　On whom it seemed was written a blessedness.
　　More than a hundred spirits filled the draught.
'In exitu Israel de Aegypto' with one stress
　　And voice they sang together and would sing
48　　The rest, and duly all the psalm express.
He crossed them as a sign they were to fling
　　Themselves upon the sands and with all speed
　　With which he came he turned upon the wing.
The throng remaining seemed to look and heed
　　All their surroundings as if quite unknown,
54　　At gaze like men in places new indeed.
On every side the sun, whose bright barbs thrown
　　Had chased the Goat out of the Heaven's height,
　　Was shooting forth the day throughout the zone,
When those newcomers lifted up their sight
　　Towards us, saying: 'If you chance to know,
60　　Direct us: which way to the peak is right?'
But Vergil answered: 'You think, or it seems so,
　　That we must know this place, but we, like you,
　　Are strangers here and don't know where to go.
We only came here just before you, through
　　Another way which was so rough and hard
66　　That climbing here will seem a sport to do.'
Those souls, who of my breathing took regard
　　And realized that I was still alive,
　　Grew pale with their amazement, stunned and jarred.

As crowds towards the olive-bearer drive
 And mill about the messenger to hear the news,
 And none too shy to trample, jostle, strive,   72
So did those people fix their eyes to peruse
 My face – successful ones almost remiss
 To seek the cleansing, as they stood to muse.
And one I saw moved forward in such bliss
 Of great affection to greet me and embrace
 He moved me so to mirror him in this.   78
O shadows, void of all but outward trace!
 Three times I clasped my hands, around him laid,
 And three times drew them to my breast through space.
With wonderment I coloured up. The shade
 Smiling, withdrew, and I, eager to pursue,
 Flung myself forward as he backward made.   84
Gently it bade me pause, and then I knew
 Who stood before me and I begged him stay
 A little while and speak to me anew.
He answered me: 'Even as in my day
 Of mortal flesh I loved you, I love you freed,
 And so I'll stay: why do you go this way?'   90
'Ah, my Casella, I make the journey indeed
 Only to come this way again. But how
 Has so much time been snatched from what you'd need?'
And he replied: 'No wrong is done me now
 If he who bears off when and whom he please
 My crossing previously would not allow,   96
For of a just will he decides. And these
 Some three months past he's taken anyone
 Who wishes to embark here, with all peace.
So I, who'd reached the shore where Tiber's run
 Of waters tends to salt, was from that sand
 Gathered by him and gently was it done.   102
And even now he sets his wings to land
 Back at the river-mouth for always there
 Draw those who do not sink to Acheron's strand.'
And I: 'If there's no new law to impair
 Your memory of the love-song, or your skill
 In it, that eased my yearning with its air,   108
Please would you solace my spirit still,
 That on its arduous journey, all that way
 With its own body, is utterly drawn and ill?'

'Love that speaks in mind to me', the lay
   He then began; so sweetly that its sound
114   Is sweetness in me to this very day.
My master, and myself, and those around
   Him, seemed so glad no mind felt other care
   Or heed of anything, by music bound.
We were transfixed, attending to that air,
   When suddenly the venerable man cried loud:
120   'What is all this, you sluggard spirits there?
What negligence, why linger in this crowd?
   Hurry toward the peak and strip this grime
   That covers God from you within its cloud.'
As doves when gathering grains at feeding-time
   Assemble all together, quiet, and appear
126   To show none of their usual pride and prime,
If anything disturbs them which they fear,
   Immediately forsake their feeding, stirred
   By greater care to lift away and clear,
I saw that throng desert the song they heard
   And go towards the hillside, as one goes
132   Who feels his destination vague and blurred.
   Nor did we leave with lesser haste than those.

CANTO 3

Vergil has to calm another of Dante's sudden fears, and, in turn, the amazement and bewilderment of a group of penitents whose purgation is delayed. Manfred, one of their leaders, opens a conversation with them. Born c. 1231, he was grandson of the Emperor Henry VI and Constance (see Heaven 3*) but the natural son of Frederick II (see* Hell 10*). King of Sicily, he became leader of the Ghibellines. He was excommunicated and then defeated and killed by French and papal armies at Benevento in 1266. By order of Pope Clement IV, his body was disinterred and thrown off church lands. In line 27, Vergil refers to the fact that he was originally buried in Brindisi but the Emperor Augustus removed the body to Naples. This contrasts to the fate of Manfred's remains. The odd Latin* quia, *for 'that', line 37, stands for the 'fact', without the why and wherefore. Strictly speaking, it derives from scholastic logic where a demonstration a posteriori from effect to cause was known as* quia.

Although their sudden flight across the plain
    Was scattering them toward the mountain height
    Where Justice probes us, I drew myself again
Close to my faithful comrade. – And how slight
    Would my success have been without his aid?
    Who would have led me to the mountain right? –   6
To me he seemed by self-reproach dismayed.
    – O pure and noble conscience, how sharp a sting
    Becomes a little fault that you have made! –
And when his pace reduced its haste – a thing
    That mars the dignity of every act –
    My mind, constrained till then, widened its ring   12
Of interest eagerly until, in fact,
    My face was set toward the mountain-tor
    That rises nearest Heaven from ocean's tract.
The sun, a flaming red behind, before
    Was broken in the pattern that was thrown
    By resting rays on me and not the shore.   18
I spun to look, afraid I was alone
    When I observed the single darkness spread
    Along the earth before my flesh and bone.
My strength and comfort turned round full and said:
    'Why in distrust again? Why so afraid?
    D'you think I've gone? Deserted you and fled?   24

Now, where my body lies in which I made
    A shadow, it is already even-tide.
    Naples has it, from Brindisi conveyed.
So if no shadow falls before my stride
    Be no more startled than at Heaven's spheres,
30   How rays from one the next one cannot hide.
That Power that lets our body suffer fears
    And torments, heat and frost, does not intend
    To show its deeper workings when our mind peers.
Foolish is he who thinks to comprehend
    And compass in the mind that infinity
36   Where, in one Substance, Three Persons blend.
Rest content, then, human race, to see
    The *quia*. For if you ever saw the whole
    What need of Mary's Jesus would there be?
And you have seen men questing for that goal
    (Whose quest elsewhere fulfilment might have seen)
42   Fruitless, and in eternal grief of soul.
Plato and Aristotle, many more, I mean.'
    And thereupon he bent away his face,
    Feeling the sorrow of it sharp and keen.
Meanwhile we reached towards the mountain's base
    And met a cliff so sheer that nimble feet
48   Themselves would try in vain to scale the place.
Between Lerici and Turbia you will meet –
    Most desolate and solitary the rise –
    A climb that, matched to this, were smooth and fleet.
'Now who knows where an easier gradient lies,'
    My master wondered, halting in his pace,
54   'Where wingless ones may risk this enterprise?'
And while in thought he lowered eyes and face,
    Searching to find a way, and I had craned
    My neck to scan the rocks for footing space,
On the left appeared a crowd that trained
    Their feet towards us yet appeared, to sight,
60   Not to advance, so slow the pace maintained.
'Master,' I said, 'look up; some, there, who might
    Be able to advise us of a way,
    If you may not devise one by your light.'
He looked at them and happy he was to say:
    'Let's go to them for their approach is slow,
66   And greater hope, my son, raise and display.'

When they had still a long way yet to go
    (I mean after a thousand paces of ours.)
    As far as a good slinger hurls a throw,
They all pressed close against the rocky towers
    Of that steep cliff; transfixed and packed they stood,
    As someone halts, who goes in fear, and cowers.   72
'You whose end is happy, spirits the Good
    Has chosen,' Vergil started, 'by the repose
    That I believe you all await, please would
You tell us where this cliff-face leans and goes
    More gently down where we may scale the peak?
    For loss of time irks more the more one knows.'   78
As sheep come from the pen, the first unique,
    Then twos and threes while all the rest fight shy,
    Timid, pointing to earth their eye and cheek,
And what the first one does the others try,
    Huddling to her, if she is motionless,
    Silly and quiet, not knowing what or why,   84
So then I saw the head of that flock press
    Himself to come, so modest in regard
    And dignified in movement and address.
When those who had observed how light was marred
    And broken on the ground to right of me,
    And that my shadow pointed where rock barred,   90
They slowed and back-tracked in hesitancy,
    And those behind, not knowing what or why,
    Followed those actions for security.
'Before you ask, I will explain; your eye
    Falls on a human body which makes a blot
    Upon the ground where sunlight cannot lie.   96
Don't gape, amazed, but do believe that not
    Without the virtue come from Heaven on high
    He seeks to overcome this wall and motte.'
So said my master and they made reply:
    'Turn round and enter in before us then.'
    And with the back of their hands gestured us by.   102
'Whoever you are,' began one of those men,
    'In passing, turn your face, take heed to know
    If ever you have seen me yonder then.'
I turned to him and studied, keen and slow.
    Golden-haired he was, and fair; his mien
    Noble: but cut through the eyebrow by some blow.   108

When humbly I disclaimed I'd ever seen
    His face he said: 'Look here!' and then displayed
    A wound above his breast, deadly and keen.
Then, smiling, 'I'm Manfred,' he conveyed,
    'Grandson of Empress Constance; therefore I pray
114   That when you return yonder, give me aid.
And to my lovely daughter find your way –
    Mother of Sicily and Aragon's great glory;
    Tell her the truth if other tale hold sway.
When I was pierced and gashed by those two gory
    Lethal blows, I gave myself in weeping
120   To him who pardons willingly and surely.
My sins were horrible; but wide and sweeping
    Are the arms of infinite Good and Grace
    And welcome all that turn toward their keeping.
But if Cozena's Pastor, who in chase
    Of me was sent by Clement, had well read
126   That page in God then truly my burial-place
And bones would have remained at the bridgehead,
    Close to Benevento, under the weight
    And guard of that great cairn over their bed.
Now rain washes them outside the realm and state,
    And wind disturbs them near the Verde where,
132   With doused tapers, he had them moved so late.
No one's so lost by curses they can swear
    That the eternal Love may not return
    While hope keeps any of it green and fair.
Yet true it is that any who may spurn
    The Holy Church in contumacy, though he repent
138   At last, must stay outside this bank and yearn
Thirty-fold for all the time he spent
    In his presumption, if that stern decree
    Is not curtailed by holy prayer's intent.
See, then, if you can help and gladden me
    By telling my good Constance how I stand;
144   Speak of this ban; for great advance may be
    Achieved here through those yonder in that land.'

CANTO 4

Absorbed in the conversation, Dante loses track of sun and time. The second tercet, put simply, means that if we had a hierarchy of souls in us, as Platonists supposed, they would not all be absorbed in the one activity but we could do at least two or three things at once with total concentration. The group shows them a fissure in the rock by which they may climb. Dante follows Vergil but the way is extremely steep and discouraging. He is puzzled by the solar system – forgetting he sees things in the southern hemisphere. Vergil explains.

When through impression of pleasure or of pain
    Which one or other faculty may record
    The soul is centred on that sense as main,
It seems the other faculties are ignored;
    This contradicts the error that avers
    Soul upon soul in us, lord upon lord.   6
So when the soul hears something that deeply stirs
    Or keenly takes the eye, the time will run
    Unheeded, just as though no lapse occurs.
One faculty it is that notes the sun,
    One holds the undivided soul; the first
    Is freed from work but bound the other one.   12
I had experience of this, immersed
    In hearing and marvelling at that soul.
    The sun had fully fifty degrees traversed
But I did not perceive it move or roll,
    When we had neared to where the spirits cried
    As with one voice to us: 'Here is your goal.'   18
A peasant often blocks a gap more wide
    Than this was with the one forkful of thorn
    When the grapes are darkening with their tide;
Such was the cleft by which my guide was borne
    Upward and I behind, we two, alone,
    When once the crowd of spirits had withdrawn.   24
You reach San Leo, and descend the stone
    To Noli, climb Mount Bismantova with feet
    Unaided; this was only to be flown.
I mean with wings made swift and feathers fleet
    From great desire behind that guide who raised
    My hope and was a ray of light so sweet.   30

We climbed within the fissure and were grazed
   On either side against the rocky wall
   And planted feet upon that ground so crazed.
Once we had reached the topmost of that tall
   Cliff to the open hillside, 'Master,' I cried:
36   'Do you know which way we go at all?'
'Take no step downward,' he replied,
   'Move always upward at my back and fight
   Your way till some wise guide approach our side.'
So high the top was it surpassed my sight.
   The slope itself was steeper than the line
42   Drawn from the centre to mid quadrant height.
Weary I was when: 'Sweet father of mine,'
   I said, 'turn and see how lonely I'll tread
   Unless you slow your pace on this incline.'
'My son, just drag yourself to there,' he said,
   Pointing above toward a spot quite near,
48   A terrace circling the mountainside ahead.
His words so spurred me that I trudged that sheer
   And kept behind, forcing myself until
   Both feet were rested on that ledge, and clear.
And then we both sat down and turned to fill
   Our vision with the east from which we rose:
54   For looking back has often steeled men's will.
I looked first at the shores below, then chose
   To see the sun, and marvelled, next, to find
   That, on the left, it struck us with its glows.
The poet well perceived how my whole mind
   Was baffled how that chariot of light
60   Between ourselves and north appeared to wind.
At which he said to me: 'Now, if the flight
   Of Castor and Pollux accompanied that glass,
   Which moves its light to north and south, your sight
Would watch the glowing zodiac wheel and pass
   Its circuit closer to the Bears, unless
66   It left its ancient path among the stars.
If you would understand, in mind impress
   The image of Zion and this mountain here
   As placed upon the earth so they possess
The same horizon, different hemisphere.
   And so the course that, to his own dismay,
72   Phaëthon never knew the skill to steer,

You will observe, must needs deliver day
   On the mountain this side, and Zion's, too,
   On that – if you consider what I say.'
'Certainly, Master,' I replied, 'that's true.
   Where once my wits were lacking any notion
   I never saw as clearly, as just now I do,   78
That the mid circuit of Celestial Motion
   (Called the equator in one science) which lies
   Always between the bright sun and winter frozen,
As you have reasoned, to the northward plies
   From here as far as Jewish purlieus
   Locate it near the torrid desert skies.   84
But if it pleases you I'd welcome news
   Of how much further we will have to go,
   For the hill climbs higher than my vision views.'
And he to me: 'The mount is such that, low,
   The labour's always hardest to ascend;
   The higher you climb less tired will you grow.   90
So when you feel such pleasure rise, my friend,
   That the ascent comes easily to you
   As sailing downstream, you'll be at the end
Of this pass: hope that rest there will renew
   Your weary limbs. And now, no further word.
   For what I say I know full well is true.'   96
When he had finished speaking, next I heard
   Nearby a voice exclaim: 'Before you crest
   That rise, perhaps you'll find a seat preferred.'
We both swung round, finding ourselves addressed
   And saw, to the left, a great boulder of stone
   Which he, nor I, had seen as we progressed.   102
Closer we drew and found these people prone
   And lounging in the shade behind the rock,
   Just as one rests the lazy flesh and bone.
And one – fatigued, it seemed, as I took stock –
   Was sitting there, clasping his knees, with face
   Sunk down between and held within their lock.   108
'Oh my sweet lord, just look at him,' I said.
   'That one there, whose indolence seems to be
   Worse than if Sloth were his sister born and bred.'
He turned to us and made a scrutiny.
   Shifting his face slightly over his thigh,
   He said, 'Go on up, you with the bravery.'   114

I knew then who he was: the toil that I
   Had done still took my breath, but no delay
   That made in reaching him; and when close by
I came, he scarcely raised his head to say:
   'So you've really and truly managed to see
120   The sun, here, drives his chariot left all day!'
His laziness and terseness moving me
   To smile a little, I began and said:
   'Belacqua, I'll think no longer grievingly
Of you from now; but say why you make your bed
   Right here. Awaiting for a guide to lead?
126   Or just resuming usual ways instead?'
And he: 'What good is it to climb, indeed?
   God's wingèd angel, guardian of the gate,
   Would never let us reach the torments decreed.
The Heavens must first revolve around my state
   Out here as long as, living, they had done
132   Because I left repentant sighs so late,
Unless, before that date, a prayer from one
   Who lives in grace may rise and give me aid.
   What helps another Heaven will never shun.'
But already the poet climbed ahead and bade:
   'Come on now. See, the meridian stands
138   Touched by the sun; the tread of night's black shade
   Covers the Ganges to Moroccan lands.'

CANTO 5

Again Dante is delayed by those remarking on his shadow. These spirits are those who came to violent ends but who made a last minute repentance. He is told the story of Jacopo del Cassero, born in Fano, governor of Bologna in 1296, who was in dispute with Azzo VIII of Este. In 1298, on the journey to Milan where he was to be the governor, he was assassinated by henchmen of Azzo. In line 75, the territory mentioned was the Paduans' whose city was, according to ancient legend, founded by Antenor (see Aeneid 1.247–9). Dante regarded him as one of the arch-traitors and names part of deepest Hell after him. Buonconte was the son of Count Guido da Montefeltro (see Hell 27.) He led the forces of the Ghibellines when they were defeated by the Guelfs of Florence at Campaldino in 1289. Giovanna was his wife. Pia de' Tolomei of Siena was married to Nello della Pietra de' Pannochieschi. Wanting to marry another woman, he had her murdered in his castle.

Those shades I had already deserted,
    Following my leader's steps, when, from behind
    Me, pointing with his finger, one asserted,
Crying: 'Look, the sunlight is confined
    From shining on his left below; he bears
    Himself like one still living in mankind.'   6
Hearing, I turned to look and saw the stares
    Of deep astonishment on me alone,
    Me only, and what the broken light declares.
'Why is your mind so tangled,' the master's tone
    Inquired, 'that you should slacken in your walk?
    Why should it matter what they buzz and drone?   12
Now, follow me and let the people talk.
    Stand firm like a tower that never shakes
    Its head in winds that blow to blast and baulk;
For always the man in whom thought overtakes
    Thought moves his target further and further away
    Since one thought's weakened by the thought it wakes.'   18
What answer could I make, unless to say:
    'I'll come!' suffused a little with the hue
    That often brings men pardon day by day.
Meanwhile across the slope a gathering drew
    Toward us as we went; they chanted, verse
    By alternate verse, the *Miserere* through.   24

When they observed the light could not traverse
   My body with its rays, they changed their song
   And let an 'Oh!', so long and hoarse, disperse.
And two, in style of messengers from the throng,
   Ran up to meet us, bidding us explain:
30   'Inform us of your status, where d'you belong?'
My master answered: 'You may return again
   And tell who sent you: the body of this man
   Is truly flesh and blood and leaves this stain.
If they have stopped merely because they scan
   His shadow, as I think, this is enough.
36   Honour him; he'll be helpful if he can.'
I never noticed flaming vaporous stuff
   Cleave the bright sky at evening more swift,
   Nor August clouds at setting so scud and scuff
But they returned uphill in shorter shrift
   And there with all the others wheeled around
42   To us as may a troop on loose rein shift.
'That crowd that gathers now is large, and bound
   To importune,' the poet said. 'Don't stay,
   But, as you go, hear all they will expound.'
'O soul that go to gladness, back some day
   With friends that you were born with,' they came,
48   Shouting, 'relax your pace along this way.
Check whether you have seen a face to name
   Among us so that you may carry news
   Back yonder. Why the hurry? Pause, for shame!
We were all done to death, but people whose
   Sinning persisted right to the last hour
54   When light from Heaven made us see and choose,
So that, repenting and forgiving, our
   Lives were then reconciled to God who fills
   Us with desire to see him through his power.'
And I, 'For all my staring, it instils
   No recognition: yet if I may do
60   Something to please you, spirits Heaven wills
To peace, just say, and I'll endeavour to;
   By that peace, I swear, which, on the tread
   Of this good guide, from world to world I sue.'
'Each of us trusts your good offices,' one said,
   'Without an oath, unless your lack of power
66   Obstructs your will to stand us in good stead.

So I, who merely speak up first in our
    Assembly, pray that, if you ever see
    The land between Romagna and Charles's dower,
You may be gracious in your prayers for me
    In Fano that intercession may be made
    To purge away my deep iniquity.   72
I came from there but deep wounds betrayed
    My very life-blood till it flowed away,
    Among those sons of Antenor outlaid.
And there I thought I was as safe as they.
    The one from Este fixed the deed – whose hate
    Against me beyond all bounds of justice lay.   78
If I had headed for La Mira, straight,
    When those at Oriaco reached my back,
    Yonder where men still breathe would be my state.
I'd fled into the marsh where reeds and wrack
    Entangled me so much that there I died
    And watched the blood-pool from my veins grow black.'   84
Another said, 'That your desire be satisfied
    That draws you to this mountain's rugged climb,
    For pity ease this yearning in my side.
I came from Montefeltro, in my time:
    Buonconte. Giovanna had no care
    For me – nor had the others – here by their crime.'   90
And I: 'What chance or violence made you fare
    So far from Campaldino your resting-place
    Was never to be located anywhere?'
'Oh,' he said, 'at Casentino's base,
    A stream, the Archiano, crosses past,
    From Ermo in the Apennines its waters race.   96
There, where its name is lost, I came at last,
    Fleeing on foot, pierced right through the throat,
    Bloodying all the plain with gore broadcast.
There, eyesight went but then my dying note
    Was on the name of Mary: there I fell,
    And there my corpse was left to lie remote.   102
I'll speak the truth, and likewise you must tell
    The living: God's angel there took hold of me,
    And one from Hell cried: "Why d'you filch from Hell?
You snatch this fellow's immortality
    To safety for the sake of one small tear.
    I'll work another way – and bodily."   108

You know how dank vapours will appear
   In air and turn to moisture once again
   As soon as they climb to colder atmosphere.
He used his evil wits and will, whose main
   Intent is only evil, stirred up a mist
114   And wind by natural powers he had for bane.
When day was past he made the fog persist
   From Pratomagno to the mountain-chain
   And charged the sky with gravid clouds to list
So that the saturated air turned rain,
   And down the rills came all earth could not bear,
120   Pouring and flowing from its back and mane.
Then, when once gathered into torrents there,
   It rushed so swiftly to the royal stream
   Nothing could impede its thoroughfare.
My frozen body, at its mouth, in extreme
   Anger, the Archiano found and swept
126   It to the Arno, loosening in its teem
The cross of arms I'd made on my breast and kept
   When suffering overcame me. It rolled me fast
   Along its banks till in its spoil I slept.' –
'When you are in the world again, at last,
   Rested after your long journey, hear my plea,'
132   A third said after the second one had passed:
'Remember I am La Pia. Remember me.
   Siena made me. Maremma unmade.
And one who swore his love well knows it, he
   Who gave me marriage with a gem displayed.'

CANTO 6

Making his way through the curious spirits with promises to bear requests for prayers of intercession from the living, Dante at last gets the chance to ask Vergil to explain the apparent contradiction between this idea of mediation and Vergil's own assertion that no prayer can change fate. Vergil explains and adds that Beatrice, not himself, will deal with the deeper mysteries. The name of Beatrice spurs Dante on but he learns the length of the arduous journey. Vergil encounters Sordello who embraces a fellow Mantuan, Vergil, with great gladness. This forces Dante to digress with feeling on the internecine dissensions of contemporary Italy, particularly Florence. Here his bitterness drives him to irony and scorn.

In line 13, the Aretine was Benincasa da Laterina who visited Florence in 1282. Having sentenced to death a relative of the famous highway robber Ghin di Tacco, he was murdered by the robber while sitting as a magistrate in Rome. The second Aretine is thought to be Guccio Tarlati whose family led the Ghibellines of Arezzo. He was drowned in the Arno, either pursuing, or being pursued by, the Bostoli, refugee Aretine Guelfs. Federigo Novello, of the Conti Guidi family, was killed while aiding Tarlati. Marzucco of the Scornigiani of Pisa is said to have shown much fortitude in pardoning the murderer of his son. Other accounts suggest he did the opposite. The murder in line 19 is said to be that of Orso of Mangona by his cousin Albert in a feud between two brothers of the degli Alberti, Alessandro and Napoleone (see Hell 32). Pierre de la Brosse was chamberlain of Louis IX and of Philip III of France. De la Brosse had accused Philip's second wife, Mary of Brabant, of murdering the heir to the throne. In response, she engineered his downfall; he was hanged in 1278. German Albert was of Hapsburg; elected king of the Romans in 1298, he never bothered to go to Italy to be crowned. His eldest son died of disease in 1307; in 1308, he was murdered by his nephew John the Parricide. The great Ghibelline family of Santafiora had lost all its lands to Siena by the end of the 13th century.

Whenever the game of dice concludes, the one
    Who loses lingers, sadly repeating throws,
    And sadly realizes what he's done.
People surround the winner as he goes;
    One runs in front; some give his back a pat,
    And one, beside, reminds him who he knows.   6
He does not pause, listening to this and that;
    Those whom he reaches for no longer press,
    And so he dodges through the crowd of chat.

Such I was in that dense crowd no less,
　　To someone here, now there, turning my face,
12　　And, by some promise, freed myself from stress.
There was the Aretino who by that brace
　　Of savage arms, Ghin di Tacco's, died.
　　And also that one drowned, running in chase.
And there was Federigo Novello, beside,
　　Praying with arms outstretched; and then the Pisan
18　　Who showed Marzucco's fortitude well tried.
Count Orso I saw; that soul who claimed with reason
　　They cut him from his flesh in envy and hate,
　　Not for committing any sin or treason.
Pierre de la Brosse, I mean, and here I state
　　That while alive the Lady of Brabant take heed,
24　　Lest to a worser flock she gravitate.
When I was free from all those shades whose need
　　And plea was, every time, that others pray
　　So that their way to blessedness might speed,
I said, 'It seems that you deny, my Ray
　　Of Light, expressly in a certain text,
30　　That prayer may bend the Heaven's Will and Sway.
These pray for this alone. Is their hope vexed
　　And vain? Or have I somehow misunderstood
　　Your words, and thus my mind has been perplexed?'
And he replied: 'My writing's plain and good.
　　Their hope is not deceived, if you but think
36　　As carefully and deeply as you should.
The height of Justice is not brought to sink
　　Because Love's fire fulfils the penalty,
　　Owed by these inmates, in a moment's blink.
Where I affirm that point, the remedy
　　For that default could never be through prayer
42　　Because that prayer could never reach the Deity.
But, in so deep a question as you have there,
　　Unless she tell you, take no view as right;
　　Her ray from truth to intellect will flare.
I don't know if you understand me quite.
　　I speak of Beatrice; you will see her wait,
48　　Smiling and blest, upon this mountain's height.'
And I: 'My lord, let's speed up in our gait.
　　Already I feel less weary than before,
　　And, look, the hill casts shadow dark and great.'

'Today,' he answered, 'we will climb some more,
    And far as possible, but the outcome's one
    That differs from your judgement on this score.   54
Before you reach that point, you'll see the sun
    Return from being hidden by the peak
    Which stops you blocking light as you have done.
But, look, a soul secluded there, unique
    And lonely, stares at us. It may refer
    Us to the quickest route that we may seek.'   60
We came to it. – O Lombard soul, you were
    Disdainful and haughty, and in your eyes
    How slow and stately the movement that would stir. –
Nothing it said to us, but let us rise
    Onward, watching only, as we pressed,
    In likeness of a lion as it lies.   66
Vergil drew towards it and addressed
    His plea that it might show the quickest way.
    The spirit did not answer that request,
But asked us of our life and land to say.
    And then my gentle guide made this reply:
    'Mantua!' and the shade, rapt where it lay,   72
Leapt up towards him with this eager cry:
    'O Mantuan, I'm Sordello. That's my birthplace!'
    And one embraced the other, eye to eye.
– Italy, inn of woe, slavish and base!
    Pilotless ship against a mighty storm!
    No queen of provinces, a brothel's space!   78
That gentle spirit was so quick and warm,
    Just hearing of his city's own sweet name,
    To greet a fellow citizen's dear form.
But now the living cannot, without shame
    Of war, reside in you, and man wounds man
    Though guarded by one wall, one moat, the same.   84
Search, wretched land; around your sea-coasts scan;
    And gaze into your heartland, gaze and tell
    Which part is pleased with peace there, if you can.
What use Justinian should refit so well
    The bridle if the saddle's riderless? –
    And, but for that, your shame would be less fell.   90
Ah, race, that in obedience should acquiesce,
    And in the saddle let the Caesar ride –
    If well you knew what God's own words express.

Look how vicious the horse grows, its hide
   Never corrected by the spurs since you
96   Have raised your hands and snatched the reins and tried.
O German Albert, you desert, eschew
   The wanton that turns savage when you ought
   To mount the saddle now and ride her true.
The Judgement that is just, from the stars' court,
   Fall on your line in plain uncanny cast
102   So that your heirs may fear what has been wrought.
For you, your father before you, steadfast
   In covetousness yonder, have allowed
   The garden of the empire to waste and blast.
Montagues, Capulets, look, you man unbowed
   By pity; Monaldi, Filipeschi, observe!
108   The first saddened; the second, terror-cowed.
Come, ruthless king, and see the broken nerve,
   Your nobles in subjection; tend their blows.
   You'll see how safe Santafiori's preserve.
Come and see Rome; widowed, weeping, she goes,
   Deserted; day and night she makes her cry:
114   'Caesar, why not with me, against my foes?'
Come and see how loving your people, and why;
   And if no pity move you, think of your fame,
   Then come for fear of shame and cast your eye.
– And if it be allowed to speak your Name,
   O highest Jove, on earth the Crucified,
120   Has your all-seeing justice some prior claim?
Is this delay some plan that you decide
   In depths of all your wisdom to good effect
   That, in our vision, cannot be descried?
Italian cities burst with tyrants unchecked,
   And every rogue that raises faction's head
126   Would play Marcellus to his petty sect.
– O my Florence, you may rejoice instead
   At this digression which does not refer
   To you, thanks to your people, reason-led.
Many have justice in their hearts, yet stir
   Slowly to aim because it comes to bow
132   Not without policy – though mouthing needs no spur.
Burdens of office many refuse to know,
   But your people answer with an eagerness
   Before they're asked: 'That task I'll undergo.'!

Rejoice! You have good reason: largesse
    And riches, yours; peace, yours; wisdom, yours!
    That I speak truth the facts cannot suppress.   138
Athens and Lacedaemon, that framed the laws
    Of ancient time, and ordered well, combine
    To give a hint of true living that flaws
Beside you whose provision is so fine
    That by October you have always spun
    What mid-November hasn't got to twine.   144
How often, in your time remembered and done,
    Have you changed laws, coins, offices, customs dear,
    And so renewed your members, one for one.
If you consider well and see things clear,
    You'll find yourself just like the woman lain
Sleepless and sick on down, that by her mere   150
    Tossing and turning tries to avoid the pain.

CANTO 7

Learning who Vergil is, Sordello offers great respect and receives Vergil's moving remarks on the state of souls in Limbo. (Mantua issued coins stamped with Vergil's portrait.) Sordello explains that none may climb the mountain in the hours of darkness. He shows them where to rest. They encounter the souls of kings who have neglected their public duties in favour of personal satisfactions. Old enemies are paired off to show the making of amends.

After that dignified and joyous embrace
    Had been repeated three or four times more,
    Sordello asked: 'Who have I face to face?'
'Before these spirits – worthy to rise and soar
    To God – were sent into this mountain-height,
6   My bones were buried by Octavian of yore.
Vergil I am, and lost all Heaven's light
    For no sin else than not to know the faith.'
    So from my guide the answer came forthright.
As someone sees in front some thing or wraith
    At which he marvels in belief and disbelief,
12   Muttering: 'Is! Isn't!' till confusion swathe,
So then he seemed, and bent his brow a brief
    Spasm, and turned back humbly to my guide
    And clasped him as a youth might clasp his chief.
'O Glory of the Latins!' he replied,
    'Who made the power of our language clear!
18   Eternal tribute to Mantua, my home and pride.
What worth or favour brings you to me here?
    But, if I'm worthy now to hear you speak,
    Say if you come from Hell, which cloister, sphere?'
'Through all the circles of that woeful reek,'
    He answered, 'I come this far. From on High
24   A virtue moved me. By that I reach this peak.
Not for the doing, but not doing, have I
    Forgone the vision of the Sun that you
    Desire, but known too late to light my sky.
There is a place below, not saddened through
    Torment, but darkness, which exhales laments,
30   Not wailings, but of sighs and breaths that rue.

There I abide with childish innocents,
    Savaged and fanged by death before they were
    Exempt from human sin and its intents.
There I abide with many a sorrower
    Who, never clad in the triple virtues, knew
    And did all others without falter or demur.   36
But tell, if known, and you're permitted to,
    The route to reach as quickly as we may
    Where Purgatory proper lies in view.'
He said: 'There's no spot fixed where we must stay.
    I am allowed to move up or around.
    As far, then, as I may, I'll lead the way.   42
But see how much the day declines; such ground
    We can't at night ascend. Better, therefore,
    To think where resting places may be found.
Some souls are secluded to right a little more.
    If you agree, I'll bring you where they rest,
    Nor without joy you'll know them and their lore.   48
'How's that?' came voice. 'Would anybody pressed
    To climb by night be hindered by your view,
    Or pause because unable to make the crest?'
The good Sordello with his finger drew
    Across the ground, and said: 'D'you see this line?
    After sunset you wouldn't cross it, you.   54
Not that anything but the day's decline
    Hinders his climbing onwards; dark delays
    The will with lack of chance, not lack of spine.
By night one might, indeed, descend these ways
    And wander on about this mountainside
    While the horizon blocks the sun's blaze.'   60
At which my lord, in wonder, said: 'Then guide
    Us, therefore, where, as you have said, we may
    Have pleasure in delay, and dark abide.'
A short distance we journeyed on the way
    When I observed the mountain hollowed out,
    As may be found in valleys we survey.   66
'Now,' said the shade, 'we'll go and scout
    There where the mountain's made itself a nook,
    And so await till fresh day comes about.'
Between steep and level was the path we took
    That led us up beside the hollow vale
    Where its edge half dies away and one may look.   72

Gold and fine silver, crimson, white so pale,
   And indigo, so brilliant and clear,
   Fresh emerald just flaked to chip and scale,
Would all be far surpassed beside the sheer
   Colours of grass and flowers in that fold,
78   As lesser is surpassed by greater here.
Nature not only painted there but rolled
   In one sweetness a thousand fragrances,
   A scent unknown, indefinable, untold.
'Salve Regina' sang the companies
   Of souls I saw then as they sat mid flower
84   And grass once hidden in declivities.
'Before the sun, now setting, sinks to its bower,'
   Began the Mantuan who'd led the way,
   'Don't ask me to introduce you till that hour.
From this terrace the better will you survey
   And know their deeds and features and compare
90   Than if received within the hollowed bay.
That one, sitting highest, with that air
   Of having left undone things better done,
   Who does not move his mouth to sing his share,
He was the Emperor Rudolph, the very one
   That might have healed the death wounds of Italy.
96   Too late for any to restore her sun.
The other, seeming to comfort him, is he
   Who ruled the land from which those waters spring
   The Moldau takes to Elbe, and Elbe to the sea;
Named Ottocar, in cot-clothes a better king
   Than is his son Wenceslas of the Beard
102   Who is consumed with lust and malingering.
The snub-nosed one, in close counsel neared
   To that one with the gracious looks, you'll find,
   Raped the lily and in his flight was speared.
See how he beats his breast. That other, mind,
   Who, sighing, makes a pillow for his face,
108   There, with his cheek upon his palm reclined,
Father and father-in-law they are to that base
   Plague of France; and well they know his wrong
   And vicious life – hence their grief and disgrace.
The burly-looking one who blends his song
   In harmony with the one of virile nose,
114   Of every virtue wore the girdle-thong.

And if the youth who sits behind in repose
    Had reigned succeeding him, then would his worth
    Have passed on as a jug to goblet flows.
Which can't be said of these of other birth.
    James and Frederick possess the lands;
    Of such heredity they hold the dearth.   120
– For human excellence but rarely expands
    Through all the branches: God who bestows
    Decides it should be prayed for at his hands.
And to the big-nosed one my meaning goes,
    No less than to the other, Peter, who sings
    With him; for Provence and Apulia's woes.   126
As the shoot is poorer than the stock it springs
    From, so may Constance, more than Margaret
    Or Beatrice, boast her husband in such kings.
Look there: the king of the simple life is set
    Apart, Henry of England: much better trees
    Did the branches of that king beget   132
But, sitting on the ground, lowest of these,
    Gaze upward, William the Marquis, because of whom,
Since Alessandria's war, the Canavese
    And Monferrato grieve and weep their doom.'

CANTO 8

The hour of evening worship arrives in the valley of kings. Dante meets Judge Nino there, where Sordello leads them. Nino refers to Giovanna, his only child. She was married to a Rizzardo di Camino in 1308. After Nino's death his wife, Beatrice, daughter of Obizzo II of Este, married Galeazzo di Matteo Visconti in June 1300. Line 74 refers to the fact that married women wore veils or bende: *a widow's would be white. The Visconti were driven from Milan in 1302 and they took refuge with Beatrice's family in Ferrara. Conrad Malaspina is summoned by Nino to see the wonder of Dante's arrival. Malaspina inquires after his country of Val di Magra. Dante cannot say but points to the high reputation of the name of Malaspina. It is forecast that Dante will test this reputation in the next six years. It is known that Dante was with the family in October 1306. The closing remarks are thus his thanks. The Latin, line 13, means 'Before the closing of the day', from a hymn for compline attributed to St Ambrose.*

It was the time for those long out to sea
    That draws the yearning home and melts the heart
    At bidding friends farewell upon the quay;
That makes the novice pilgrim feel that start
    Of love if, in the distance, he should hear
6   The bell that seems to mourn that day depart,
When I had let his words slip by to peer,
    Intrigued, upon a spirit who had risen
    And craved a hearing with his hand raised clear.
It joined its palms and lifted them, its vision
    Fixed towards the east as though to say
12   To God: All else but You has my derision.
Then from his lips there came: '*Te lucis ante*'
    And so devout, so sweet, the melody
    It took my very sense of self away.
The others sweetly and devout in harmony
    Accompanied it throughout the lovely hymn,
18   Gaze fixed upon the wheels of eternity.
– Here, Reader, sharpen up your eyes that dim,
    To see the truth, for now the veil's so fine a gauze
    Surely it's easy to notice limb from limb. –
I saw that noble troop in silence pause
    And fix their gaze on high as if in hope
24   And expectation, pale and lowly in their cause.

I saw two angels, high in Heaven's cope,
    Descending with two swords of streaming flame,
    Blades broken, and lacking points to slope.
Green as are tender, new-grown leaves, their raiment
    That flowed behind their flight was fluttering, fanned
    By beating of their green wings as they came.   30
One, just a little above us, dropped to land.
    The other rested on the further bank.
    The people in the middle took their stand.
I clearly saw their fairest hair, but blank
    Their faces since my eyes dazed in my head,
    Their sense confused by the excess they drank.   36
'Both come from Mary's bosom,' Sordello said,
    'As sentries of the vale against the Snake
    That instantly will come now light has sped.'
At which, not knowing of the way he'd take,
    I swung around, chilled to the bone with fear,
    Sank in those shoulders that would not forsake.   42
Sordello spoke: 'Into the vale we'll steer;
    And with those mighty spirits talk and pace.
    Great joy they'll have at your arrival here.'
It seemed I took but three steps to that place
    Then was below and saw one gaze at me
    As though he thought to recognize my face.   48
The time was when the air hangs darkeningly
    But not so dark that what we both beheld,
    Though distance had obscured, we could not see.
He came towards me; I to him. Joy welled,
    Noble Judge Nino; how I rejoiced to see
    You there, that not amid the damned you dwelled.   54
No friendly greeting left unsaid, then he
    Enquired: 'How long then is it since you came
    To the mountain foot across the width of sea?'
And I replied: 'From in the place of shame
    And suffering, I came this morning here,
    Alive, though to the next my travels aim.'   60
And when my answer fully struck their ear,
    He and Sordello shrank from me, a pace
    Back, as folk suddenly bewildered rear.
One turned to Vergil; the other swung to face
    Someone seated, and burst out into speech:
    'Look, Conrad, what God wills in his grace!'   66

Then, turning back to me: 'Oh, I beseech
    By that special grace you owe to Him who hides
    His prime intent where path may never reach,
When you are back beyond the vast sea's tides,
    Tell my Giovanna to make her prayer for me,
72   There where innocence is heard when it confides.
No more, I think, her mother loves me; she
    Has doffed the white veil – in wretched plight
    She must be yearning for it, to be free.
Right clearly has she shown and brought to light
    How long the fire of love in womanhood,
78   If eye or touch don't kindle and ignite.
He'll make her tomb nothing so fine and good,
    The viper that leads the Milanese in the field,
    As once, she knows, the cock of Gallura would.'
Thus did he speak, his visage marked and sealed
    By signs of righteous zeal which, in due measure,
84   The burning fervour of the heart will yield.
My yearning heart turned to the Heaven's treasure,
    To that point where the stars move ever slow,
    As near the hub a wheel turns at most leisure.
My guide enquired, 'Son, what d'you gaze at so?'
    And I replied: 'At those three lights with which
90   The entire pole in these parts feeds its glow.'
He said: 'The four stars seen this morning pitch
    Down low the other side, and these ascend
    Where those once were, and thus they switch and switch.'
But as he spoke Sordello called him to attend:
    'Look, there's the Adversary!' pointing where
96   Vergil should turn his head to apprehend.
One side, the valley lacks a rampart; there
    A snake was seen, perhaps like that which gave
    To Eve the apple that was such bitter fare.
Through grass and flowers came on its evil wave,
    And, coming, turned its head now and again
102   To lick its back as grazing beasts behave.
I never saw, and therefore can't explain
    How those celestial falcons rose, but two
    I saw and glimpsed the speed that they attain.
Hearing the green wings swiftly cutting through
    The air, the serpent fled, and wheeling round,
108   Back to their watch, abreast, the angels flew.

That shade who'd drawn toward the judge, close-bound
    When Nino called him, during the whole fight
    Not once had turned from me his gaze profound.
'Now as the lamp that leads you up this height
    May find within your will the pliancy
    To bring you the enamelled summit's sight,'   114
It said, 'if you have any news for me
    Of Val di Magra, or its neighbourhood,
    Tell it. Mighty there I used to be:
Conrad Malaspina – not the elder, I should
    Hasten to add – but a descendant. Here,
    The love I bore them is purged and rendered good.'   120
'I've never travelled through your lands or near,'
    I said, 'but where in Europe do men dwell
    To whom your house is not renowned and clear?
That fame that marks your house whose lords excel
    Proclaims them and alike proclaims their land
    So those who never reach them know them well.   126
I swear to you, even as I hope to stand
    On high, your honoured kindred never smutch
    The honour of purse or sword within their hand.
Custom and nature privilege it so much
    That, though the guilty head all earth misguide,
    That land holds straight, scorning the evil touch.'   132
Then he: 'Leave now. The sun will never slide
    To slumber seven times upon the bed
    The Ram covers with all four feet astride,
Before the courteous opinion you have spread
    Shall be affixed with better studs to display
It more than other men's within your head,   138
    If the course of judgement meet with no delay.'

CANTO 9

A couple of hours or so after sunset, Dante falls into a deep sleep: he dreams he is clasped up in the talons of an eagle and raised into an orb of fire. The sensation of heat awakes him whereupon he is surprised to discover himself alone with Vergil and that they are further up the mountain. They now reach the portals of Purgatory itself. Dante mounts the steps of sincerity, contrition and love and prostrates himself at the feet of the guardian angel to beg admission. The angel carves seven P's (for Peccavi – *'I have sinned') on his brow, representing the seven deadly sins which will be purged on his journey upward. He is warned never to look back. Line 44 indicates that it is the morning of Easter Monday.*

> Old Tithonus' mistress was growing white
>   Upon the eastern terrace, slipping away
>   From her belovèd's arms, her forehead bright
> With glittering gems, appearing to display
>   The shape of that cold animal which bites
>   At people with a tail that's barbed to slay.
> And, where we were, two paces of the Night's
>   Footsteps by which she climbs were done, the third
>   Already on the downward from the heights,
> When I, who still had some of Adam, blurred
>   And overcome by sleep, sank on the grass
>   Where sat the five of us as we conferred.
> At that time when the morning comes to pass,
>   Just as the swallow starts her plaintive lay –
>   Of former woes, perhaps, the memory and glass –
> And when our mind, more wanderer and stray
>   From flesh, less prisoner of its inmost thought,
>   In vision comes so near prophetic ray,
> In dream I thought I saw an eagle athwart
>   The sky with plumes of gold and wings outspread
>   In the intent to swoop to some onslaught.
> It seemed I was where Ganymede had fled,
>   His people all deserted, when he was caught
>   Away to the high consistory overhead.
> By habit here it stoops, I said in thought,
>   In this terrain, perhaps, and prey elsewhere
>   Its talons scorn to seize – of any sort.

6

12

18

24

It seemed that, having wheeled about the air,
    Terrible as the lightning it stooped and grasped
    Me, far into the fiery sphere to fare.   30
It seemed that, there, we both were burning, clasped
    In fire, and that the visionary flames so seared
    That sleep was broken into as I gasped.
Not otherwise, Achilles woke and peered
    About him, in bewilderment, to chart
    His whereabouts, the time his mother reared   36
Him up into her arms and made a start
    From Chiron while he slept, fleeing away
    To Scyros – which Greeks, later, made him depart –
Than I did, once my sleep was fled, and grey
    And pale, exactly as would be with one
    Frozen and petrified in terror's sway.   42
Alone, beside me, was my stalwart; the sun
    Was already more than two hours spent,
    And my eyes turned to watch the seas run.
'Don't be afraid,' my lord said. 'Be confident,
    For we are in a good position: hold
    Nothing back; exert your strength intent.   48
You've now arrived at Purgatory: behold
    The rampart that surrounds it, and, just there,
    Where it seems split, the entrance to that fold.
Just now, in the dawn that heralds the sun's flare,
    While your soul slept within you on the flowers
    With which, below, the mountain blooms so fair, 54
A Lady came and said: "Give into my powers
    This man who sleeps. I'm Lucy; I will aid
    Him on his way to climb this mount that towers."
Sordello remained; so, too, the others stayed.
    She took you and, as day grew bright, ascended.
    I followed also in the track she made.   60
She placed you here: with lovely look commended
    That open entrance to us. Then, away
    Fled sleep and she together.' Thus he ended.
Just as a man in terror feels the ray
    Of reassurance and changes fear to calm
    As soon as truth reveals he's not at bay,   66
I changed; my guide perceived that fear of harm
    No longer held me, moving on till right
    Beside the rampart. I followed without qualm.

– Reader, you see the higher theme I write
    And therefore do not be surprised at all
72   If I with greater art sustain the height. –
We moved in close to where, as I recall,
    We first had seen the fissure, like the breach
    You sometimes see dividing up a wall.
I saw a gate, and three steps, and each
    Of different colour which were to enter at,
78   And, there, a warder not yet given to speech.
And as my eyes grew wide I saw he sat
    Upon the highest step, radiant of face,
    But I could not endure to look at that.
In hand he held a sword drawn from its case
    That flashed on us such bright reflections I
84   Frequently glanced in vain to fix its trace.
'Stay where you are, and what you seek reply,'
    He started; 'Where's your escort gone? Beware!
    Further advance you may most dearly buy.'
'A Heavenly Lady who well knows this affair,'
    My master answered, 'just now said to us:
90   "Go over that way; the gate is over there."'
'And may she speed your steps,' the courteous
    Guardian answered, 'to the good. Draw near
    And safely come towards the stairway thus.'
The first step reached was white marble, so sheer
    Its polish and so smooth that I could see
96   Myself reflected just as I appear.
The second step, darker than perse would be,
    Was rugged stone, calcined, crazed and cracked
    Along its length and breadth's entirety.
And, on the top, the massive third, intact,
    Seemed to be fashioned out of porphyry,
102   As flaming red as blood from veins, in fact.
God's angel had his feet on this as he
    Was sitting at the threshold which was made
    Of adamantine stone, it seemed to me.
Up those three steps with all his willing aid
    My guide escorted me, saying, 'Request
108   Humbly the bolt be slid.' And I obeyed.
Before the holy feet I bowed and pressed
    Devout, and begged that he in mercy open
    The gate, but, first, three times I beat my breast.

Seven P's upon my forehead as a token
    He cut, then, with his sword-point. 'Each of these
    Wounds you must cleanse in here.' – All that was spoken.   114
Ashes, or earth dug dry, were similes
    Of colour for the raiment that he wore
    From underneath the which he drew two keys.
One was of silver; the other golden ore.
    First with the white and then the yellow plied,
    He satisfied my wish and freed the door.   120
'Whenever either of these keys fails to slide
    Or turns uneasily against the lock,'
    He told us, 'the entry will not open wide.
One is more precious; the other takes a stock
    Of great skill and subtlety to turn free
    Because it is the one that moves the block.   126
I hold them under Peter; he ordered me,
    If people bow and bend the knee before
    The gate, to err with opening, not locking, key.'
And then he pushed aside the sacred door,
    Saying: 'Enter, but first heed my tongue:
    Who looks behind returns outside once more.'   132
And when the pivots of that portal swung
    Round in their sockets (which were forged and rode
    On metal ringing true, and strongly hung)
Tarpeia roared less loud, less harshly showed
    When good Metellus was captured and displaced
    From her, since when she was a poor abode.   138
I moved intent to hear the first sound traced.
    'Te Deum laudamus' I seemed to hear,
    In voice and music sweetly interlaced.
Such the impression it made upon my ear
    As we are used to find when voices linked
With organ music sing, and words sound clear   144
    And then unclear and blending indistinct.

CANTO 10

The door clangs shut behind them but Dante does not look round. The fissure by which they must climb is very narrow and difficult. It takes them three hours before they come to the first terrace, eighteen feet wide, a precipice on one side; on the other a frieze of marble reliefs of astonishing lifelikeness. As he is rapt in wonder at these Vergil asks him to observe the penitents of this level who are bent double under the weight of boulders which they have to bear. These are the proud brought low. The Latin, line 44, means 'Behold, the handmaid of the Lord' (Luke 1.38).

When we had crossed the threshold of the gate
    Which souls of evil love disuse and disdain
    Because they see the crooked way as straight,
I knew by its clang the gate had closed again;
    If then I'd turned my eyes to see that door,
6   For such a fault what reason might I maintain?
We climbed up through a cleft rock in that tor
    Which bent this way, then that, just as the tide
    That ebbs and rises up and down the shore.
'Here we must use degrees of skill,' my guide
    Explained, 'and keep close in, first here, now there,
12   Wherever it twists back from side to side.'
This made our steps so very slow and spare
    That the moon's orb, wandering in the sky,
    Regained its bed and sank out of the air
Before we'd clambered from the needle's eye.
    But when we'd scrambled to a level place
18   From which the mount recedes then towers on high,
I, weary, both unsure which way to face,
    Stock-still we stood, on a level terrace more
    Remote than roads that through the desert trace.
And from the precipice's edge, the floor
    Stretched three times the body's length to reach
24   The high cliff of that sheer-ascending core.
As far as eye could wing its way in each
    Direction to the right and left of me
    This terrace looked the same, without a breach.
Our feet had not yet moved when I could see
    The encircling core of cliff (which, rising sheer,
30   Blocked any chance of scaling it) to be ·

Of marble, pure and white, adorned just here
    With sculptures; not just Polycletus alone
    But Nature, too, would be ashamed as peer.
The angel that arrived on earth to make known
    The decree of peace (since mourned for many a year)
    Which opened Heaven from its ban was shown   36
To us, so life-like in its carving, so clear
    In gentle bearing that it seemed to be
    No image that was dumb but one to hear.
'*Ave!*' one could have sworn it said, for she
    Was sculptured next to him, Mary who held
    To the supreme of Love the Heaven's key.   42
Impressed in her bearing these words indwelled:
    '*Ecce, ancilla Dei!*' – as complete
    And express as figures into wax impelled.
'Don't concentrate on one place now,' my sweet
    Guide suggested then, who had me stood
    On that same side where people's hearts must beat.   48
And so I ranged my eyes wherever I could
    And saw, behind Mary, on the side
    Nearest the guide who urged me on to good,
Another story carved, and with a stride
    I crossed by Vergil, drawing close to it
    So that its form might better be descried.   54
There, carved in very marble, opposite,
    The cart and oxen drawing the sacred ark
    (Whereby one dreads the office for which unfit).
People appeared in front; one sense could hark
    And hear the whole divided in seven choirs
    And swear: 'They sing!'; 'not!' the next remark.   60
In the same way, as smoke from incense aspires,
    Pictured there, eyes and ears dispute the trace
    And countered 'Yes' with 'No' as if to liars.
Before the holy vessel seemed to pace
    The lowly Psalmist, dancing with girded loins.
    And more and less than king was, in that case.   66
Michal, figured opposite, adjoins,
    Watching like a woman scornful, sad in mood,
    Beside a mighty palace's window quoins.
I took a step or two from where I viewed
    To see more clearly another feat conceived,
    Which, behind Michal, shining white, ensued.   72

There was the great glory storied and leaved
    Of the Roman prince whose worth moved Gregory
    To that great victory that he achieved.
I speak of Trajan, the great emperor, he.
    A poor widow at his reins appeared
78   In an attitude of grief and misery.
A trampling and a throng of horsemen reared
    Around him, and, above his head, in gold,
    The eagles in the wind visibly veered.
Amid all this, the poor thing, jostled and rolled,
    Seemed to be saying: 'Lord, avenge my son
84   Who has been killed, piercing my heart so old.'
And he, to answer her: 'It shall be done
    When I return.' And she replied: 'My lord,'
    Like somebody in grief a desperate one.
'And if you don't return?' And he: 'Rest assured
    That my successor will act for you.' She, still:
90   'What's others' good-doing, your own ignored?'
At which: 'Be calm; this duty I must fulfil
    Before I move; pity constrains delay
    And justice demands that I should do her will.'
– He who saw nothing new made this display
    Of visible speech, new to us because it is
96   None of the earth's, and novel to our clay.
While I rejoiced to see these images
    Of souls so great in their humility –
    Dear, too, for their Craftsman's sake, these verities –
'Look here,' the poet called across to me:
    'Numbers of folk but few the steps they make.
102   They'll show us where the upward stairs must be.'
My eyes that were so keenly tuned to take
    In every novel sight were not too slow
    To swing to him and all their thirst to slake.
– I'd never wish you, Reader, ever to grow
    Fearful of a good purpose, because you learn
108   How God decides what debt we undergo.
Ignore the pain; think what such pain will earn.
    Think that at worst it cannot stretch or spread
    Beyond the great Day of Judgement's sure return. –
'Master, what draws towards us,' then I said,
    'Does not appear to me of human gait.
114   I can't tell what; sight wanders in my head.'

And he replied: 'Torment's grievous state
    Doubles them down to earth, so that my eyes
    At first were doubtful what to indicate.
But look with care and you'll observe what lies
    Beneath those boulders; already you detect
    How each one beats his breast; repentant, sighs.'   120
– O haughty Christians, wretched and weary sect,
    That, sick in mental vision, put your trust
    In all the backward steps that you have trekked,
Don't you perceive that we are worms of dust,
    Born to form the angelic butterfly
    And wing without defence to judgement just?   126
Why does your mind aspire to soar so high
    Because you are but insects, immature,
    And, so to speak, grubs lacking shape and dye. –
As sometimes for a corbel to secure
    Ceiling or roof, you see a figure kneel
    With legs to chest, for epochs to endure,   132
Which, though unreal, creates a sense of real
    Discomfort in the watcher – this I felt
    Observing those beneath the boulder's heel.
They bowed according to the burden dealt,
    Greater or lesser on each back they bore.
And one who had most patience as he knelt   138
    By weeping seemed to say, 'I can no more!'

CANTO 11

The souls, bent double, speak a version of the Lord's Prayer in intercession for the living and those outside Purgatory. Dante hopes the living will intercede also on the behalf of the penitents. Dante is then recognized by the miniaturist painter Oderisi who, in his new state, is prepared to allow that Franco was his master. Cimabue's school is superseded by Giotto's and thus all human glory is transitory, a shadow. Guido Cavalcanti, Dante's great friend, still living in April 1300, surpassed Guido Guinicelli of Bologna – father of the 'sweet new style' for which Dante became so famous (see canto 26). Equally, generals of famous victories are forgotten on their very fields of battle.

'Our Father in Heaven, uncircumscribed of aim
    But by the greater love you ever hold
    For your prime creatures, hallowed be your name
And worth, by every living creature extolled,
    As it is proper thanks should never cease
6   Towards your sweet effluence manifold;
And may your kingdom come to us in peace
    For we ourselves cannot attain to it
    If it come not, for all our wits' increase.
And, as the angels sacrifice and fit
    Their wills to yours alone, singing Hosanna,
12   So, too, may men surrender and submit.
Give us this day our daily bread and manna,
    For, lacking that, he treads backward this stern
    Desert who most labours to advance his banner.
As we forgive the evil of those who turn
    Against us, so may you, in loving grace,
18   Forgive our sins – not as our merits earn.
Lead not our virtue, easy to abase,
    Into the ordeal with the Enemy
    But deliver us from him who goads our race.
Lord, this concluding prayer is not a plea
    For us; there is no need; but made for all
24   Who still remain down in humanity.'
    – Thus did those shades that under burdens crawl
    (Like weights we sometimes bear on earth in dream)
    Plead their advance and ours; unequal, small

Or great their anguish, circling in extreme
 Weariness the first terrace, purging away
 The fog and mist of all the world's esteem.   30
– If a good word there be said for us, what may
 Be said and done for them by those down here
 Who have their will rooted in good, and pray?
Truly we ought to help them cleanse and clear
 The stains which they have carried over there,
 That, pure and light, they reach the Heavenly sphere. 36
'Please, as justice and pity soon may spare
 Your burdens so that you may wing your flight
 Accordingly as you desire to fare,
Show us the shortest way, to left or right,
 Towards the stairway which – if more than one –
 Offers the easier gradient to the height,   42
For he who comes along with me, still done
 Up in the weight of Adam's flesh, is slow
 To climb which thwarts his will that yearns to run.'
Who spoke the words in answer to the flow
 Of his whom I was following so near
 Was not apparent enough for me to know.   48
But this was said: 'Come with us and steer
 Rightwards along the bank and you will find
 The pass a living man may climb, though sheer.
And, if this rock that bows my haughty mind
 Did not encumber, forcing my features low,
 I'd look to tell if memory inclined   54
To recognize this man, alive, though slow
 To introduce himself, and I would make
 Him pity me the weight I undergo.
Italian, a great Tuscan's son, I take
 From Gugliemo Aldobrandesco my name.
 I don't know if it's current where you forsake. 60
The ancient line, the gallantry and fame
 Of all my forebears gave me such disdain,
 Oblivious of the common mother whence we came,
I held all men in scorn so deep and vain
 It was my death – as in Siena's well known,
 And children in Campagnatico see plain.   66
Humbert I am; but not for me alone
 Such pride brings downfall; my colleagues all
 It also drags to mishap like my own.

And therefore must I bear this load and crawl
    Among the dead till God is satisfied,
72   Because in life I always strutted tall.'
Listening, I stooped my head, and someone eyed
    Me – not the one who spoke – his body twisted
    Beneath the weight that bowed him for his pride,
And, seeing me, he knew me and persisted
    Calling me, fixing his gaze with difficulty
78   On me, as, bent, I went with them enlisted.
'Oh,' I said to him, 'are you not he,
    Oderisi, honour of Gubbio, of the art
    Illuminating – as Paris calls such artistry?'
'Brother,' he said, 'more pleasure you can chart
    In leaves that Franco Bolognese paints.
84   The honour now is his, and mine but part.
– Indeed, I'd not have shown such courteous constraints
    While living, since I had such great desire
    Of excellence my heart bent to its taints.
For such a pride the price is paid entire.
    I'd not be here but, having the power to sin,
90   I turned, at last, to God and struggled higher.
O empty glory of all human powers! How thin
    And brief a time its green endures at peak,
    Unless it brings an age of dullness in.
Cimabue once thought to hold unique
    The field of painting; Giotto is the name,
96   So that first fame is darkening and bleak.
Likewise one Guido takes the other's claim
    To glory in our tongue; and, maybe, one
    Is born already for their niche of fame.
Earthly fame is but the wind's breath spun,
    Now this way turned and now the other way;
102   It changes name with quarter under the sun.
What greater fame will come if you should lay
    Aside your flesh when old than if at the age
    Of saying 'buppy' or 'pennies' you'd had your day,
By the time a thousand years have gone – a stage
    Shorter to eternity than a twinkling eye
108   To that sphere of slowest turn it cannot gauge?
Tuscany rang with his name in days gone by,
    Him, making little progress just ahead;
    Now in Siena he's scarcely whisper or sigh,

Where he was Lord when raging Florence sped
    To its destruction; as haughty in that day
    It was as now it has turned whore instead.   114
Your fame is grass, now green, now withered away,
    As he discolours it who makes it grow
    So green and fresh out of the earth and clay.'
And I replied: 'That truth you speak and know
    Brims up my heart with holy lowliness
    And sinks my pride; who are you meaning, though?'   102
He said: 'It's Provenzan Salvani, yes,
    And he is here because he once presumed
    To snatch Siena to his grasp by his prowess.
So he has gone, and so he goes; since tombed,
    Allowed no rest; such coin he repays
    In satisfaction, who dares too high, too plumed.'   126
And I: 'If such a spirit then delays
    Repentance till the edge of life down there
    And does not climb up here, but lower stays,
Unless by benefit of holy prayer,
    Waiting the length of time his life had passed,
    How is it vouchsafed he reach this thoroughfare?'   132
'When living in his glory he once cast
    Aside all shame and in the market square
    Of Siena took his station there, steadfast,
To liberate his friend from the pain to bear
    In Charles's prison, and made his body feel
    The shivering of every vein and hair.   138
I know I speak obscurely: I'll reveal
    No more; yet but a little time will flow
Before you'll know from deeds how neighbours deal.
    – This action saved him from those confines below.'

CANTO 12

Vergil bids Dante to straighten up and proceed at a normal pace; he does so, though still bowed down in thoughts of his own presumption. He steps out, only to be asked by Vergil to observe the ground on which he walks. Here, he sees depictions of the very proud, from Lucifer to Troy, now trodden underfoot. They circle on for some time until they reach the angel guarding the climb to the next terrace. He erases the symbol for pride from Dante's brow and the next climb already seems easier. They are heading to the terrace of the poor in spirit. Dante works the acrostic for Man into the opening of consecutive verses to show him as the epitome of pride. The Latin, line 110, means 'Blessed are the poor in spirit' (Matthew 5.3).

Like oxen in one yoke, in step with him,
    I matched that burdened spirit for the space
    My sweet mentor let me have my whim.
But when he said: 'Now leave him to his case.
    Press on, for here it's best with sail and oar
6   We voyage on with all our strength and pace,'
I raised my body straight to walk once more,
    Although within my thoughts I still remained
    Bowed down and doubled almost to the floor.
I'd moved on, and with a will I gained
    Upon my master's steps; then both revealed
12   Already how fleet our feet were, unrestrained,
When he exclaimed: 'Look down: and it will yield
    You comfort on the way, be good for you
    To see what lies beneath your feet concealed.'
And as, so that their memory stay new,
    The flagstoned tombs that mark the buried bear
18   In carven figures what they were, and who –
Because of which men often weep and stare
    On them, feeling the jab of memory
    That only stirs the pitiful to care –
So, there, I saw, engraven under me,
    The whole road, levelled from the mount, displayed
24   A craft more lifelike than on earth you see.
My eyes saw there the noblest creature made,
    On one side, in the midst of his descent
    Just like a lightning flash the Heavens rayed.

My eyes saw Briareus, opposite, pent;
    Transfixed by the celestial bolt, he lay
    On earth, with death's chill weighed and spent.   30
My eyes saw Thymbraeus; Mars, in armoured array,
    With Pallas, standing by their father's side,
    Seeing where scattered limbs of giants splay.
My eyes saw Nimrod, baffled, as he eyed
    The mighty wreck of what he toiled to build,
    Staring at those from Shinar who shared his pride.   36
Ah, Niobe, with what sorrow my eyes filled
    To see you on the roadway carved and scored
    Between your seven and seven children killed.
Ah, Saul, how pierced upon your own sword,
    Dead upon Gilboa, did you appear –
    Where never more fell dew nor the rain poured.   42
Ah, mad Arachne, I saw you there so clear,
    Already half spider, wretched, on parts
    And shreds of web that wove your harm and fear.
Ah, Rehoboam, now your image darts
    No threats, it seems, but full of fear must flee
    In your own chariot when no pursuer starts.   48
Next the hard pavement showed again to me
    How Alcmaeon made the luckless ornament
    Seem to his mother such a costly fee.
Near that, his sons that flung themselves, intent,
    On Sennacherib inside the temple, killed
    Him there and, having done so, turned and went.   54
Next showed the ruin, blood savagely spilled,
    That Tomyris effected when she said
    To Cyrus: 'Blood you thirsted; with blood be filled.'
Now shown how, routed, the Assyrians fled
    After Holofernes was slain; and also there,
    Relics of the assassinated dead.   60
My eyes saw Troy in ash and ruin. How bare
    And vile, Ilium, you were recorded then,
    Noted by us upon that thoroughfare.
What master of the chisel, brush or pen
    Could so have drawn the lineaments and tone
    That awe would fill the minds of discerning men?   66
Dead were the dead; living the live were shown.
    He saw no better than I who saw the real
    In all I trod while poring on that stone.

– Now plume your pride, with haughty visage deal,
   Children of Eve, but do not stoop, in case
72   You see your evil path beneath your heel. –
Already we had swung a greater space
   Around the mountain – and the sun much more –
   Than mind, absorbed, had reckoned of our pace
When he, alert, who always went before,
   Began: 'Now raise your head; it's not the stage
78   To go in such absorption with the floor.
Look, there's an angel ready to engage
   Us. See there the sixth handmaid withdraw
   From service of the day, now come of age.
Present your face and bearing in reverent awe
   So that it may delight him now to haste
84   Our climb. No dawn renews this day you saw.'
I knew full well his counsels not to waste
   The time, so, on that topic, what he said
   To me came seldom darkly or misplaced.
Towards us now the lovely being sped
   In robes of white, his face the shimmering
90   A star at morning glances overhead.
His arms he opened and he spread his wings
   And said: 'Come; the stair is just by here
   And easy the ascent that now it brings.'
– But few this welcome greets upon the ear,
   O human beings, born to soar and fly;
96   Why at a puff of wind waver and veer? –
He led us where the rock was hewn near by,
   And there he brushed my forehead with his wings
   And promised me safe journey up on high.
As climbing up the hill where the church clings
   Above the Rubaconte bridge and lords
102   It over that city, well governed in all things,
The steep incline is eased with steps towards
   The height (steps that were hewn in bygone time
   When records and measures were still safe from frauds)
So here, the scarp's made easier to climb
   Though sheer it drops from the next stage, except
108   That on both sides encroaches the rock sublime.
And, as we turned our feet and on it stepped,
   Beati pauperes spiritu' rose in tones
   So sweet no word conveys the song that leapt.

How different these openings from the zones
    Of Hell, for here we enter through songs and airs
    But there through fiercest wails, laments and groans.   114
Now as we mounted by the sacred stairs
    It seemed to me I was in a lighter state
    Than when I walked upon the thoroughfares,
So I: 'Master, say what heavy weight
    Has been removed from me, such little strain
    I feel in climbing now at this good rate.'   120
He answered: 'When those P's that still remain,
    Though they are nearly faded from your face,
    Shall, like the first, be quite removed again,
Your feet, so conquered by good will and grace,
    Not only will not feel the toil, but delight
    They'll have, urged forward in the upward race.'   126
I acted then like those that have a mite
    Or something on their head which they can't see
    Till someone points it out to them. And right
Away the hand gives aid for certainty
    And feels and finds and does the deed that sight
    Cannot perform with any accuracy.   132
The fingers of my right-hand spread to alight
    And found on my brow but six letters styled
By him who had the keys of gold and white –
    At which my leader, looking on, just smiled.

CANTO 13

They reach an apparently deserted terrace; Vergil decides, in the absence of any one to advise him, to follow the sun. They hear voices praising generosity of spirit for they have reached the place where the envious purge themselves of the sin that made them begrudge the beauties, goodness and achievements of other people's lives. Their eyes are sealed until their envious looks are cured. Dante is uneasy to observe while unobserved and asks if there are any from Latium there. Sapia of Siena answers, telling of her exultation in seeing her nephew Provenzan Salvani defeated and killed in the battle of Colle. Dante explains that he will spend but short time in his turn on this terrace, being of no envious disposition. She asks him to clear her name among her Tuscan kin. The Sienese, trying to rival Genoa and Venice, spent time and money fruitlessly attempting to make Talamone village a port, and also in trying to find an underground stream, the Diana, to ensure a water supply. The Latin, line 29, means 'They have no wine' (John 2.3).

We'd reached the stairway's top where a second time
    A terrace cuts the peak that makes men sound
    By healing them as up its height they climb.
A cornice like the first one winds around
    The mountain – though, this time its curvature
6   Is, as height dictates, a narrower bound.
No shade is there, no figure seen to stir;
    The bank appears so bare, level the way,
    Coloured with the stone's livid character.
'If we wait here,' the poet began to say,
    'To ask the way of someone, that, I fear,
12   Perhaps may cause us much too great delay.'
And then upon the sun he turned to peer;
    Pivoting round upon his right-hand side,
    His left was wheeled toward the glowing sphere.
'O sweet light in whose trust I turn my stride
    To this new way,' he said, 'show us the way
18   As we ourselves would choose if we'd decide.
You give the world your warmth and shed your ray
    On it; if other reasons don't refute,
    Your beams must always be our guide and sway.'
A mile, as would be here, along the route
    Already in good time we'd stretched our pace
24   Because our wills were eager and acute.

Flying towards us we heard, but could not trace,
    Spirits who offered us the courteous request
    To sit at Love's table and take our place.
The first voice winging past clearly expressed:
    '*Vinum non habent!*' and flew from here,
    Repeating it behind us without rest.   30
Before the distance drew it from our ear
    Another passed us, crying: 'Orestes, I.'
    Nor did that voice delay a moment near.
'Father, what are the voices I hear cry?'
    I asked and, looking, heard a third declare:
    'Love those who do you evil!' and fly by.   36
The good master said: 'This ring is where
    The sin of envy's scourged away; it's clear
    Then that the thongs are drawn from loving care.
The curb must be of contrary sound. You'll hear
    It, I should think if I judge right, before
    Your footsteps to the pass of pardon near.   42
Gaze straight through the air, steadily pore,
    And you will see people sitting in front
    Of us against the cliff, their seat the floor.'
I opened up my eyes wider to hunt
    And looked ahead and saw some shades, each cloak
    Was coloured like the paving, dull and blunt.   48
A little further I heard the cries of folk:
    'Mary, pray for us!'; another resound:
    'Michael, Peter, and all saints we invoke!'
I don't believe this day there treads the ground
    A man so hardened that he would not be
    Pierced by compassion seeing what I found,   54
For when I'd ventured close enough to see
    Their features clearly there, a heavy grief
    Was wrung in tears and sobbing out of me.
A coarse haircloth they wore and, for relief,
    Supported with their shoulders their neighbour's weight,
    And all leant on the bank, as sheaf on sheaf.   60
The blind, lacking means, are in like state,
    Sitting at Pardons, begging for their needs,
    And one sinks down his head upon his mate,
So pity quickly in the watcher breeds,
    Not only through the sound of words begun
    But also seeing their appearance pleads.   66

And, as the blind have no use for the sun,
  So, for these spirits where I was, in speech,
  Heaven's light dispenses its largesse to none,
For all their eyelids iron wires breach,
  Knit them together, just as people do
72 To wild hawks to keep them tame to teach.
I seemed to do them wrong to go on through
  Seeing them, myself unseen; therefore
  I turned to my adviser, wise and true.
But well he'd know what even the dumb implore,
  And therefore did not wait for my request
78 But said: 'Speak, and be brief; no more.'
Vergil walked beside me on the pavements dressed
  Against the precipice where one might fall
  Since parapet was none to give arrest.
The other side of me, against the wall,
  Were the devout shades that through the seam
84 Were seeping tears out, down the cheeks to crawl.
I turned to them and started: 'You who deem
  It certain you shall see the light to come,
  Which is your yearning's one and single theme,
Now, so that grace may quickly clear the scum
  Upon your conscience till the memory
90 May cascade through it crystal clear and plumb,
Tell me (since I will hold it preciously)
  If any soul among you is Italian here;
  Perhaps good will may come to him through me.'
'My brother, each is citizen and peer
  Of a true city; but, as you'd put it, stayed
96 A pilgrim in the Italy you hold dear.'
It seemed to me this answer had been made
  From somewhere further than I'd reached, and so
  My answer to that area I conveyed.
Among the rest I saw a spirit throw
  A look of expectation – and, if you query –
102 By lifting its face as do the blind below.
'Spirit,' I said, 'who submit yourself so dearly
  To rise, if you're the one that answered thus
  Say who you are by name and city clearly.'
'A Sienese,' came answer, 'and with the envious
  I cleanse and purge the sinful life of shame,
108 Weeping to God to lend himself to us.

Not sapient, though Sapia was my name,
    I once rejoiced in other's harm and fear,
    More than in my good fortune and good fame.
To stop your thinking that I dupe you, hear
    And judge if I were mad, as I have said;
    On my downward arc already of year on year,   114
My townsmen close to Colle their army led
    Against their foes. – I prayed to God for what
    He had already willed to come to a head.
There were they chased and routed from the spot
    In bitter haste of flight, and, seeing the chase,
    My joy exceeded all else in my lot.   120
So much so, in impudence I raised my face
    And cried to God: "I'll fear you never more!"
    As does the blackbird for good weather's grace.
And on the edge of life I did implore
    My peace with God; yet my great debt would be
    Scarcely reduced by penitence but for   126
Peter the Combseller who remembered me
    In all his holy prayers, and for me grieved
    In loving-kindness and in charity.
But who are you that come and, here received,
    Enquire of our case with eyes as yet unknit
    And breathing still, as I may be believed?'   132
'My eyes,' I said, 'to darkness will submit
    But briefly here because their own offence
    In envious looks is trivial to acquit.
The fear that grips my soul in such suspense
    Is that first torment lower down, for still
    The burden waiting there weighs on my sense.'   138
And she to me: 'Who brought you up the hill
    To us, if there you think you should have stayed?'
    'The silent one beside me led me to this sill.
And I am still alive, elected shade,
    So bid me what to do, if back down there
    You wish my mortal limbs to offer aid.'   144
'This is so new a thing to hear or declare,'
    She answered, 'it must be a wondrous sign
    Of God's great love to you: help me by prayer.
By all that you desire grant this of mine:
    That if you ever visit Tuscany again
    You will restore my fame with my kin and line.   150

You'll meet them in that foolish people whose main
    Hope lies in Talamone up the coast,
Who'll lose there more than in that search so vain
    For the Diana – but the admirals most!

CANTO 14

Dante and Sapia are more or less interrupted by two speakers who discuss Dante as though he were as deaf as they are blind. Soon they address him directly; they are Guido del Duca and Rinieri da Calboli. The former utters a lamentation over the internecine state of the cities of Italy. The details of Fulcieri da Calboli's atrocities in Florence are post-1300 but fresh and bitter enough for Dante to castigate here. Governor of Florence in 1303, he tortured many Ghibelline and Guelf citizens and had them executed for treason. He returned to power in 1312. More feelingly than ever, Guido laments over his native Romagna, recalling its nobles and condemning their lacklustre successors. The canto concludes with Cain's envy of Abel and Aglauros's envy of her sister which turned her to stone. These accounts burst on the ear like thunderclaps.

'Who is this that circles our mountain sill
 Before his death has winged his flight, and who
 Opens and shuts his eyes just when he will?'
'I don't know who he is, but there are two.
 You question that one nearest you, and greet
 Him courteously so he may answer you.'   6
Like this of me two shades began to treat,
 Leaning against each other on the right,
 Then turned their faces up as though to meet
With mine and speak; one said: 'Soul, fixed tight
 In body still, but Heavenward this far,
 For charity console us and recite   12
Where you have come from here and who you are,
 For you amaze us greatly with that grace,
 As must a feat so new and singular.'
I answered: 'Through the midst of Tuscan space
 There spreads a stream, from Falterona sprung,
 A hundred miles do not exhaust its race.   18
I bring this body from those banks: unsung
 As yet, it would be vain to give my name
 Because it counts for little in any tongue.'
'Well, if my wit has caught the sense you frame,'
 The one who spoke at first then answered me:
 'The Arno seems the place from which you came.'   24
The second questioned him: 'Why then did he
 Conceal the river's name, as one would do
 With things too terrible to hear or see?'

The shade so questioned answered him anew:
    'I don't know why, but know that it is right
30   The name of such a valley fade from view,
For, from its source in the rugged range's height
    (Whence Pelorus was ripped), with stream and rill
    It teems so that few vales exceed their flight
Until it comes to yield itself and spill
    Back in the sea what's soaked up by the sun
36   So that the rivers may restore their fill,
Virtue is fled, as if a snake, by one
    And all there, goaded by the wicked lie
    Of that land, or routine ill, long done.
The dwellers in that evil valley fly
    From their old nature till they're so debased
42   It seems that Circe had them in her sty.
Among filthy hogs, more fit for acorns' waste
    Than other food prepared for men, it first
    Directs its course, so thin and feebly traced.
Then, coming down, it finds the curs whose worst
    Is snarling more than they can bite; it tracks
48   Its snout aside in scorn of that outburst.
Lower, the fuller that its waters wax,
    That most accursèd and ill-fated rine,
    The more the dogs are turned to wolfish packs.
And, coming down through many gorge and chine,
    Foxes it finds, so full of fraud they dread
54   No cunning that could snare them or entwine.
Nor will I cease for fear that what I've said
    Be overheard: it will be well for him
    To keep my true prophecy clear in his head:
I see your grandson who becomes a grim
    Hunter of wolves beside that savage water,
60   And strikes a terror into every limb.
He sells their flesh alive; all will he slaughter
    Like worn-out cattle; so many he deprives;
    Their lives and his own honour given no quarter.
He came from the sad wood gory with their lives,
    And leaves it so that a thousand years from now
66   It can't restore its trees, never revives.'
As, hearing forecast of grievous ills, the brow
    Of someone listening is perturbed and stirred,
    No matter from which side the perils cow,

So could I see the other soul who heard,
    On turning round, grow troubled and look sad
    When it had taken in each pointed word.   72
The speech of one, the other's features, had
    Me longing then to know them by their name;
    Questions I asked of them, with prayers to add.
And so the one who first had made his claim
    Began: 'You wish that I should do for you
    What you refuse to do for me, who wish the same.   78
But since God makes his grace in you shine through,
    I won't be slow to answer your desire;
    And therefore know: Guido del Duca you view.
My blood was so inflamed with envy's fire
    That if I saw a man enjoy a thing
    I was suffused with lividness entire.   84
Of all I sowed, this straw the harvesting.
    O human beings, why set the heart full square
    Where any partnership needs banishing?
This is Rinier; this the glory, the fair
    Honour of the house of Calboli, where none
    Since of his worth have been the rightful heir.   90
From peaks to Po, along the Reno's run
    To sea, not only his are stripped of the good
    Required by truth and knighthood to be done.
Within these bounds the land is choked up, stood
    In poisonous undergrowth; good husbandry
    Would labour long to clear up field and wood.   96
Where's good Lizio? Arrigo Mainardi?
    Pier Traversaro, Guido di Carpigna? You
    Romagnoles, debased to bastardy.
When in Bologna shall again a new
    Fabbro take root; when in Faenza spring
    A Bernardin di Fosco, low-born but true?   102
No wonder, Tuscan, if I weep remembering
    Guido da Prato, Ugolin d'Azzo, that pair
    Who lived near us; Federico Tignosco's following;
The Traversaro house, the Anastagi, no heir
    For either one or other of these breeds:
    The ladies and the knights that once were there;   108
The labours and the sports, the noble deeds
    We did inspired by love and courtesy,
    Where now all hearts are grown like wicked weeds.

O Bertinoro, why not break away and free
    Yourself when all your family runs away,
114   And many more, from such iniquity?
Bagnacaval does well not breeding today,
    And Castrocaro ill; worse, Conio
      Taking the trouble to breed such counts as they.
And the Pagani, if their 'Devil' go
    Away, will yet do well but never claim
120   Ever again a spotless record to show.
O Ugolin de' Fantolin, your name
    Is safe since expectation is there none
      For more to foul it with degenerate shame.
But go your way, my Tuscan, I have done.
    It comforts me the more to weep than speak,
126   So wrought my soul with how our talk has run.'
We knew that those dear spirits heard us seek
    Our way; so took their silence to convey
      Confidence in our route toward the peak.
After we left them, going on our way,
    A voice like lightning when it splits the sky
132   Struck us, crying: 'Everyone shall slay
Me when they find me!' and then fled by,
    Just like a thunderclap that peals away
      When suddenly the cloud bursts up on high.
When it gave ears a truce, a second ray,
    Behold, with such loud crash and violent shock,
138   It seemed like swift thunder on lightning's play.
'I'm Aglauros, turned to a stone block!'
    To shelter by the poet I took a stride
      To right, not going forward on the rock.
Now quiet was the air on every side,
    He said to me: 'There, that was the stern bit
144   Which should have held men in bounds that guide.
But still you take the bait, and take with it
    The ancient Adversary's hook to draw you in,
      And so the lure and curb are scant benefit.
The Heavens call you, circle round and spin
    All their eternal splendours to your view
150   Yet still your eye absorbs this earth of sin,
    So he who sees all things chastises you.'

CANTO 15

Three o'clock in the afternoon, the travellers have rounded a quarter of the mountain and now face the setting sun from the north. Dazzled by the light of the guardian angel, Dante realizes they are near the next ascent. They hear songs of the merciful behind them but Dante's mind is troubled by what Guido del Duca had said about partnership. Vergil explains. Dante has a vision in a trance of examples of meekness. They walk toward the sunset but into a pall of fearful smoke. The Latin in line 38 means 'Blessed are the merciful' (Matthew 5.7).

As much as from the end of the third hour
    And breaking of the daylight of that sphere
    That plays as does a child about the bower,
So much was still to come of the sun's career
    Towards the evening; it was vespers there
    But time was at the midnight back down here.   6
The rays were striking our faces with their glare,
    For we had so far circled round the tor
    That now directly west we came to fare.
Then I felt my brow weighed down, much more
    Than previously, by the splendour; and they were
    Amazement to me, the things not known before.   12
Therefore I raised my hands in the curvature
    To form the shield we use above our lashes
    To bar the glare of light that makes things blur.
As when a ray of light from water dashes
    Or from a mirror in reverse direction,
    Rebounding from the surface as it flashes,   18
Matches the angle struck before reflection
    (Which varies from the line of a dropped stone
    Evenly, as shown by scientific inspection);
So I seemed struck by reflected radiance thrown
    From in front of me; swiftly I turned aside
    My eyesight from the brilliance of that zone.   24
'Gentle Father, what's that I cannot hide
    My eyes from now, that makes them function ill?
    It seems to be approaching us!' I cried.
'Don't marvel if the Heaven's household still
    Dazzles you,' he answered. 'Its messenger
    Has come to bid us now ascend the hill.   30

It won't be painful soon to see the stir
    Of sights like these, but more a joy to you
    As great to feel as nature may confer.'
Then we had reached the blessèd angel who
    With gladsome voice announced: 'Enter here
36   A stairway less inclined than the last two.'
Already parted, we were climbing, tier by tier.
    'Beati misericordes!' was sung behind
    And: 'Rejoice you who overcome!' approached our ear.
My master and I, we two, alone combined,
    Were mounting and I thought I'd use the ascent
42   To profit by his words and learn his mind.
So I addressed him, asking: 'What is meant
    By that Romagnole's choosing of the word
    "Banishing" and "partnership"? What's the intent?'
At which he said: 'He knows the evil stirred
    By his greatest sin, so feel no bafflement
48   If he condemns it so less harm's incurred.
So far as your desires are centred or bent
    Where goods more thinly spread through partnership
    Envy will pump the bellows of discontent.
But if love of the highest sphere should tip
    Your yearning upward such a narrow fear
54   Would not contract your heart with such a grip;
For by as many as say "ours" here,
    So much the more of good each may attain
    And in their cloister love may burn more clear.'
'I'm fasting more from being fed again,'
    I answered, 'than if I'd held my peace at first,
60   And more confusion gathers in my brain.
How comes it that some good when shared, dispersed,
    Can make a greater number rich in it
    Than if it were possessed by few, and pursed?'
And he to me: 'Because your thoughts commit
    Your mind to earthly things again, you face
66   Darkness in the true light I have lit.
That infinite, ineffable Good will race
    To love, as swiftly as a ray will pour
    And flash upon a bright thing, not a base.
The more ardour encountered, then the more
    It gives itself; however far love reach
72   Eternal Good will stretch to it. Therefore

The more there are on high with love for each
    The more there are for Love itself to greet.
    And so more love, as mirrors in mirrors teach.
If you're not satisfied with how I treat
    Of this, you'll come to Beatrice later; she
    Will make it clear and every yearning meet.   78
Strive only that the five wounds left may be
    Erased quite soon, as were the other pair –
    For which our anguish cures the injury.'
I was about to say: 'I'm filled with your fare,'
    When I observed we'd scaled to the next round,
    And eagerness to look silenced me there.   84
I seemed at once to be enrapt and bound
    In an ecstatic dream where people press
    Crowding into the temple, as I found.
A woman, with a mother's tenderness,
    About to enter, said as she came through:
    'My son, my son, why give us this distress?   90
Look how your father and I have searched for you
    In deep concern.' Her silence fell, and cleared
    What had appeared which faded from my view.
But then another woman soon appeared,
    Her cheeks were coursing tears risen from grief
    At some resentment that another reared,   96
Saying: 'If you are truly lord and chief
    Of that city the gods quarrelled to name,
    Where all of knowledge shines from every leaf,
O Pisistratus, avenge that deed of shame
    Against those arms so much presumptuous
    As to embrace our daughter!' With placid frame,   102
Kindly and gently the lord answered thus:
    'What shall we do to those who work us ill,
    If one who loves us be condemned by us?'
Then I saw crowds, incensed with anger, mill,
    Slaying a youth, and crying to one and all,
    Loudly in encouragement: 'Kill, kill, kill!'   108
Down to the earth I saw him slip and fall
    Under the weight of death, but of his eyes
    He made the gates of Heaven, praying, in thrall
To such a torture, to his God with sighs
    And looks which unlock pity, that He should
    Forgive his persecutors and so dies.   114

And, when my soul returned to true and good
    Objects outside of it, I came to see
    My not false errors, and I understood.
My guide who saw me moving dazedly
    Like someone coming out of sleep, then said:
120   'What troubles you to lose control and be
Wandering half a league, eyes shut, and tread
    Staggering-leggèd, just like someone wine
    Or sleepiness has overcome and led?'
'If you will listen, sweet father of mine,
    I'll tell you,' I replied, 'what came to me
126   While my legs were loosened from my spine.'
'If you should wear a hundred masks,' said he,
    'Your thoughts, no matter how trivial the thing,
    Would not be hidden from my scrutiny.
What you have seen was shown you just to bring
    You no excuse at all to keep your heart
132   Closed to the peace from the eternal spring.
I did not ask what troubled you with art
    And reason with which a person asks whose eyes
    Cannot detect when sense and body part.
I asked to spur your feet; so must the wise
    Stir the slothful who are lax to use
138   To full their waking hours when they arise.'
Then we were treading through the dusky views,
    Straining our eyes forward as far as we might
    Against the shining rays and evening hues,
And then, little by little, smoke dark as night
    Was rolling towards us, nor was there the room
144   For us to try escaping it. Our sight
    And the pure air were snatched into its gloom.

CANTO 16

Dante is obliged to follow Vergil, hand on his shoulder, to find his way through the smoke. Addressed by Marco Lombardo, he requests him to explain why Italy is so degenerate. He is told the fault lies with mankind, not with the planets, particularly in that the church has confused spiritual and secular power in the hands of political popes so that there no longer exists a ruler to guide men to the just city. They emerge from the smoke near the ascent to the next terrace. The names in lines 124–5 are of leading Guelfs in Dante's time. They were Lombards; the second is praised in Convivio 4.14.12 and the third in 4.16.6. 'Guileless' may mean: one of the few Lombards not a usurer. Lines 131–2 refer to the Bible's 'among the children of Israel they have no inheritance' (Numbers 18.23).

Gloom of Hell, night of every planet void,
    Under a barren sky, darkened by cloud
    That over every part had been deployed,
Made to my sight never so thick a shroud,
    Nor pile so harsh to sense, as did that smoke
    Which covered us and with its blackness bowed.   6
It forced my eyes to close beneath its yoke.
    Therefore my wise and trusty guide drew near
    And offered me his shoulder's shield and cloak.
And as a blind man clings to his guide in fear
    Of straying, and to avoid all obstacle
    That might cause injury or death down here,   12
So did I travel through that horrible
    And bitter air, listening to my guide
    Who kept repeating: 'Stay close as practical.'
I heard these voices: each one prayed and cried
    For peace and mercy to the Lamb of God
    Who takes away all sin, for which he died.   18
Agnus Dei began each prayer and period;
    One word was on their lips, and one their stress,
    So full the concord sounded where we trod.
'Are these more shades I hear?' I asked him. 'Yes,'
    He said, 'you have indeed the answer you seek.
    They're slackening the knot of wrath, no less.'   24
'Here, who are you that wade our smoke and speak
    Of us as though you still would mark the date
    According to the calendar, though on this peak?'

So came a voice. My master said: 'Relate
    Your answer and enquire if this is the way
30   By which we may approach the upward gate.'
And I: 'O shade, that purge so that you may
    Return as pure to him who made you, a wonder
    Will you hear if heeding all I say.'
'I'll follow as far as I'm allowed to under-
    Stand you,' it said, 'and if the smoke blinds,
36   Hearing will prevent our parting asunder.'
I started: 'Wrapped in coils that death unwinds,
    I travel upward and have journeyed here
    Through all Hell's anguish and its pain that binds.
If God allows me so far here in sheer
    Grace since he wills that I should see his court
42   In ways that past all current use appear,
Do not conceal from me but now report
    Who, prior to death, you were; and tell me, too,
    If this leads to the pass; talk as you escort.'
'A Lombard, Mark, I was. The world I knew,
    And loved to aim for worth – though every one
48   Has now unstrung that bow which once he drew.
You're climbing up the right way.' He had done.
    But added, 'I beg that you will pray for me
    When you have risen closer to the Sun.'
And I to him: 'Upon my faith, your plea
    I bind myself to honour, though I'm split
54   Within by doubt, unless you set me free.
Simple it seemed at first, but double-knit
    Since your reply that makes a certitude
    Of something from elsewhere I link with it.
The world is barren, indeed, and has eschewed
    Every virtue, even as you put to me,
60   And heavy is its load of sin accrued.
I beg you, though, to show and let me see
    The cause of this, to tell to other men.
    One blames the stars; one, earth's iniquity.'
A deep sigh, grief-shortened to 'Alas!' he then
    Breathed out, and so began: 'The world is blind,
66   And, clearly, brother, you came from its den.
The living trace all causes in mankind
    Back to the Heavens alone as if they swept
    All things along by necessity designed.

If so, free-will would be destroyed, overleapt;
   No justice would there be in joy for the good,
   And sorrow for the evil-doer kept.   72
The Heavens set your urges off. (I would
   Not swear to all.) But if I did, a light
   Is given on good or evil's likelihood.
And if free-will survive its opening fight
   Against the Heavens, it will win the day
   And conquer everything, if nurtured right.   78
To a better nature, a greater power, I say,
   You, free, are subject. And this will create
   The mind in you the Heavens do not sway.
So, if today the world strays from the straight,
   The cause is you, and in you must be sought.
   I'll be the vanguard scout to show your state.   84
Out of his Hands, who loves her with fond thought
   Before she springs to life, there comes (a small
   Child who will laugh and then will weep in sport)
The simple, tender soul, ignorant of all,
   Except that, sprung from joyous Maker, she
   Willingly turns to what delights befall.   90
First, she will taste some triviality
   That's good, and is beguiled to chase that thing
   If there's no guide to curb her ardency.
Thus law was needed as this curb; a king
   Was needed who at least might see, aloof,
   The battlements of the true city towering.   96
Laws there are but who wields their reproof?
   No one at all, because the shepherd who leads
   May chew the cud but not divide the hoof.
Therefore the flock, who see the shepherd feeds
   Only on what his appetite has craved,
   Do likewise, nor seek new pasture for their needs.   102
It's clear that how ill guidance has behaved
   Is cause of the world's sinfulness and shame,
   And not the nature in you that's depraved.
Rome, that made the good world, had claim
   To two suns once which lit for every sight
   Both of the ways: the world's and God's aim.   108
One now extinguishes the other light.
   Crosier is joined with sword, paired on one route;
   Together they consort ill in wretched plight.

Neither fears the other, in combined pursuit.
   Consider the ear of corn, if still in doubt,
114   For every plant is labelled by its fruit.
Where Po and the Adige broaden out,
   Worth and courtesy were by custom found –
   Before Frederick suffered opposition's rout.
Safe-conduct is permitted through that ground
   To anyone who, silent for shame with men
120   Of virtue, would avoid where they abound.
Indeed, there are three veterans in that pen
   In whom the olden days rebuke the new;
   Tardy, they feel, God's summons from that den:
Currado da Palazzo, the good Gerard, too,
   And Guido da Castel who's better named
126   "The Guileless Lombard" as the Frenchmen do.
Henceforth, explain that Rome's church be blamed,
   Confusing these two powers as if one,
   And, in that mire, both church and charge are shamed.'
'O Mark!' I said, 'how well your reasoning's done.
   And now I understand why Levi's line
132   Was barred inheritance from son to son.
But who's this Gerard whom you cite as fine
   Example of the extinct race and shown
   To rebuke the barbarous age in its decline?'
'Either your accent deceives me in its tone
   Or tests me,' then he said. 'In Tuscan speech
138   You seem to claim good Gerard is unknown.
I know no surname for him unless I reach
   It from his daughter Joy. I'll go with you
   No further now. May God be with you each.
You see amid the smoke that light shine through,
   Growing much brighter: the angel that you seek.
144   Now I must go before I come in view.'
    He turned, and would not hear me further speak.

CANTO 17

Dante, clear of the smoke, sees a vision of the wrathful but is drawn out of this by the light of the angel at the ascent of the next terrace. When they reach the level it is dark and they must rest. Vergil takes the chance to explain the design of Purgatory, demonstrating that all humans, even the wicked who misapprehend it, are drawn by aspects of the divine love. The Latin, line 69, means 'Blessed are the peacemakers' (Matthew 5.9).

Reader, if ever, in the mountains, mist
    Has caught you, through the which you only see
    As moles do through the skin the earthy grist,
Recall how, when dense dank vapours start to flee
    And melt away, the sun reveals its sphere
    Feebly behind them, and your fantasy   6
Will lightly come to know how first I here
    Observed the sun again before my face,
    And how I saw its setting was quite near.
So matching mine to the master's trusty pace
    I issued from the clouds of smoke to rays
    Already spent on the low shore's base.   12
Imagination! that can sometimes raise
    Us from ourselves till we're aware of nought
    Although a thousand trumpets round us blaze,
What moves you when the senses cease report?
    A light moves you which takes its origin
    In the Heavens or by a will is downward brought.   18
The impress of her wicked act of sin,
    Hers, changed to a bird that loves to sing,
    On my imagination was imprinted in,
And mind was so indrawn that not a thing
    Came from external prompting that could be
    Received or enter my considering.   24
Then poured into my lofty fantasy
    One crucified, scornful and fierce of mien,
    And thus was dying on the gallows-tree.
Near him the great Ahasuerus could be seen,
    Esther his wife, and Mordecai, the just,
    Whose word and deed sincere and true had been.   30

And, as this image broke, as in a gust
    A bubble bursts because its watery wall
    Fails instantly to hold against the thrust,
There rose, in vision, a maid whose tears fall
    Scornfully to say: 'O Queen, why, why,
36   In rage decide to be nothing at all?
Not to lose Lavinia, you chose to die;
    You've lost me now. Mother, mother, I mourn
    Your death; no other's do I weep and sigh.'
As sleep breaks suddenly when light is born
    Upon the lidded eyes, and, when once broken,
42   Hovers before it fades into the morn,
So then, imagination sank as I was woken
    By light upon my face, more luminous
    Than any light of ours may give a token.
I turned to find my bearings when, imperious,
    A voice drew from me all other thought and trace,
48   Saying: 'Here is the ascent,' to us.
It gave my urge to know who showed the place
    Such eagerness that never rests at ease
    Until it has encountered face to face.
As sunlight hurts the eyes if they would seize
    Its form concealed in its excess from sight,
54   So, there, my power failed such intensities.
'This is the divine spirit that shows the right
    Way to ascend without our asking, and hides
    His form in this intensity of light.
He acts for us as someone for himself provides,
    For he that sees the need but waits the prayer
60   With those who would refuse already sides.
Let's match our step to the invitation there
    And strive to climb before the night's descent;
    Or else until next light we cannot fare.'
So spoke my guide and with him then I bent
    My steps towards the stair to climb up higher,
66   And just as over the foremost step I leant,
Near me, it seemed, the wing-stroke of some flier
    Fanning my face; and I heard someone say:
    'Beati pacifici who lack all evil ire.'
So far above us rose the sun's last ray
    Before the dark, that round us we could see
72   The stars on many sides about our way.

'Ah, strength, why have you deserted me
    At just this stage?' I asked within my thought,
    Feeling the force in my legs lose energy.
Then, to the landing of the stairway brought,
    We stood stock-still as would be with a boat
    Which had been beached on shingle and stopped short.   78
I harked a moment then to catch what smote
    The ear from this new circle, and next, urged,
    I turned toward my master on this note:
'Sweet father, tell me what offence is purged
    Here in this circle we have reached. Don't still
    Your tongue though stilled our feet where we've emerged.' 84
And he to me: 'The love of good that ill
    Performed its duty here restores its soul;
    Here it rows once lax oars with a will.
But so you understand more plainly the whole,
    Bend your mind to mine and you will hold
    Good fruit from this delaying of our goal.   90
Neither Creator nor creature,' so he told,
    'Was ever lacking in love, neither natural
    Or rational – and this you knew of old.
The natural cannot err; the rational
    May err through evil purpose, or it might
    Through excess vigour, or too minimal.   96
While to the primal good it directs its sight
    And in the secondary moderates its force,
    It cannot be the cause of sinful delight.
Twisted to evil, moved in the good course
    With lesser drive, or more than should be due,
    The creature works against its Creator-Source.   102
Thus you may understand that love in you
    Must be the seed of every virtuous deed
    And every punishable action, too.
Yet, since love cannot turn back from the need
    And welfare of its subject, everything
    Is safe from self-hatred and from it freed;   108
And since one can't conceive beings that bring
    About their own existence, from God apart,
    Affection cannot hate its Creator-King.
It follows then, if well I judge and chart
    The division, that the evil which we love
    Is other's harm, with three forms in the heart.   114

First, he who hopes to gain and rise above
    His neighbour's downfall and, just for this aim,
    Wishes him cast downward often enough.
Next, he that dreads to lose his power or fame,
    Favour or honour, since some other succeeds,
120   And, grieved, the opposite he loves to frame.
Last those who feel so shamed by insult it breeds
    The yearning for revenge and they must go
    To work the offender harm for his misdeeds.
This threefold love is mourned and purged below.
    I wish you now to grasp this further one:
126   Disoriented to the good – too keen or slow.
Each vaguely knows some good that may be won
    In which the mind may rest, wants that repose
    So each type strives to reach and find it done.
If lukewarm is the love with which he goes
    Toward the vision, or achieving it, he would
132   Bear, after penance due, this stage of throes.
The other good remains that never could
    Make people happy; not happiness, nor yet
    The Good Essence, root and crop of good.
This love, too abandoned in that, must regret
    And mourn in the three circles on high,
138   But how allotted in its threefold set
    I leave for you to fathom, by and by.'

CANTO 18

Dante enquires further as to the nature of love – a burning question among poets of his school in his younger days. Vergil explains but leaves to Beatrice the full explication of the question of the will and the nature of the love of God. Curiously, this canto has no prayer or office of the church blended into it. Presumably this is deliberate because these slothful penitents – or accidists – are not yet fervent enough for such devotions to be efficacious before God.

Concerning lines 118–126, the speaker is probably Gherardo II who died in 1187. The Emperor Barbarossa razed Milan in 1162. The illegitimate son of Alberto, Giuseppe della Scala, was abbot of San Zeno from 1292 to 1313.

My lofty teacher clinched his argument
    And then, to check that I was satisfied,
    Was gazing on my face with deep intent.
And I, urged on by greater thirst, replied
    With silence outwardly while inside thinking:
    'Perhaps these constant queries irk my guide.'   6
But that true father – who perceived my shrinking
    Wish that concealed itself – by speaking then,
    Gave me the courage to voice a further inkling:
'Master, my sight is given acumen
    And so enlivened by your light that clear
    And plain is all your words put to my ken.   12
Therefore, I beg you, father kind and dear,
    To give your definition of love to which
    You trace good action and the obverse here.'
He said: 'Your eye of understanding switch
    To me; I'll show the error of the blind
    Who set themselves as guides but to a ditch.   18
Since it's created keen to love, the mind
    Responds to each delight as soon as pleasure
    Wakens its activity of any kind.
Perception takes a sense-object's measure,
    Forms an impression which it will display
    In you and turn the mind toward that treasure;   24
If mind, once drawn to it, inclines that way
    That inclination's love; nature it is
    Which through the pleasure newly binds your clay.

Then, just as fire by its form and propensities
    Moves upward, since its nature's to ascend
30   (In materials that long endure its energies)
So to desire the loving mind must tend,
    A spiritual movement never to rest or sleep
    Till it enjoys its object in the end.
And now it may be clear to you how deep
    The truth lies hidden from all those who deem
36   All acts of love are laudable to reap,
Because, indeed, its material may seem
    Always of good: but not all impression's good,
    Although the wax may be of good esteem.'
'My grasp, attending yours, has understood
    Love's nature,' I responded, 'even though
42   It raises queries of this likelihood:
If love impinge from outside, and soul go
    Upon no other footing, what good in her
    Whether she go straight or straying to and fro?'
Then he: 'As far as reason may infer
    I'll tell you; past that point you must await
48   Beatrice; a question of faith you stir.
Every substantial form, distinct in state
    From matter, yet in union with it, contains
    A specific virtue, in itself innate;
Perceived in function only, it remains
    Unseen, except in its effects, as shows
54   The life in plants by green in leaves and veins.
Thus no one knows from whence the knowledge flows
    Of primary ideas; nor whence the drive
    Towards the primary appetites arose.
These are in you as instinct in bees to hive
    The honey, and this primary will and bent
60   No blame nor praise for merit may derive.
That every will relate to this will is pent,
    Innate within you, a wisdom to advise –
    Which ought to guard the entrance of assent.
This is the principle which supplies
    The cause of your desert, then, in so far
66   As it may winnow good from wicked guise.
Those who, in reasoning, have delved from spar
    To footings found this freedom was innate,
    And so they left ethics to the world's bar.

Suppose each love that fires you come straight
    Out of necessity, you still have power
    In you to stop that love and obviate.   72
Beatrice means by the "noble virtue" our
    Free will, and therefore bear in mind this mode
    Of hers when meeting on these heights that tower.'
The moon, late almost to midnight, showed
    The stars more thinly to us in the guise
    Of a brazier where every coal but glowed.   78
Her course against the Heavens and the skies
    Was in those parts the sun enflames when Rome
    Sees, mid Sardinia and Corsica, his demise.
That noble shade whose Pietolan home
    Is more renowned than any Mantuan town
    Let drop my burdening, leaving me to roam –   84
Having now gathered his words and noted down
    His lucid answers to my questioning –
    Like someone rambling with a drowsy frown.
But this drowsiness suddenly took wing
    As people, who had been behind our backs,
    Drew round in front of us along the ring.   90
Just as Ismenus and Asopus by their tracks
    Might see of old a furious gathering rove
    If Thebans needed Bacchus, in night's blacks,
Likewise, along the circle, came and strove
    To raise their pace, as far as I could see,
    Those whom goodwill and just love moved and drove.   96
They reached us fast, since that society
    So vast was coming at a run, and two
    Who were ahead shouted in tears to me:
'Mary hastened to the hills. To subdue
    Lerida, Caesar struck Marseilles, and raced
    Away to Spain with all his retinue.'   102
'Hurry, hurry, let no moment waste
    Through lack of love!' others cried, behind,
    'That, striving to excel, we're newly graced.'
'People – in whom this fervour of the mind
    Repairs, perhaps, the negligence and delay
    You showed, lukewarm in deeds of goodly kind –   108
This living one – and rest assured I say
    No lie – desires to climb once the sun shine.
    So say how near the entry to the way.'

This was the wording of that guide of mine.
   One of the spirits answered: 'Follow us,
114   And you shall find the cleft and the incline.
We're all so anxious to progress that thus
   We cannot linger here; forgive our haste
   Then, if this penance seems discourteous.
Myself, San Zeno's abbot, Verona, placed
   Under the good Barbarossa's rule
120   Of whom Milan still speaks with sorrow's taste.
There's one – whose foot is in the grave – one who'll
   Grieve, soon, over that monastery, and show
   How sad he'll be for ruling in that school,
Because his son – deformed in flesh, worse so
   In mind, and born in shame – that son he placed
126   In charge, and brought the true shepherd's overthrow.'
So far ahead of me by then he'd raced
   Whether he said much more I could not guess,
   But this I heard and savoured in mind its taste.
Then he, my help in every need and stress,
   Said: 'Look around and get this pair in sight
132   Who come putting a bit on slothfulness.'
Last of them all, they said: 'Each Israelite
   For whom the Red Sea parted was long dead
   When Jordan's Land first knew its heirs by sight.'
And: 'That clan which in its evasion fled,
   Deserting Anchises' son before the toil
138   Was done, sank in inglorious days instead!'
Then, when those shadows were a distant coil
   That scarcely could be seen, a novel thought
   Was forced upon me like a fertile soil
From which sprang many another sort.
   And so I wandered from this to that's extreme,
144   Shutting my eyes, in actual rambling caught,
   Until I changed my musings into dream.

CANTO 19

Dante, toward morning, has a nightmarish vision. Vergil, prompted by a Heavenly lady, reveals the unwholesomeness of the vision and encourages him to break out of his preoccupation. Vergil reveals that those who have succumbed to such things expiate themselves in the remaining three terraces. Pope Adrian, representing the avaricious, explains how hard it was to wear the papal mantle and explains how he eschewed the sins of avarice only in reaching that high office. Having informed Dante in Latin of his office on earth as one of St Peter's lineal successors as Pope, he rebukes him for showing respect for it by kneeling. There are no 'offices' in the after-life, he claims, strangely applying the biblical phrase neque nubent – 'they neither marry'. The soul is naked of such things before its maker.

The Lavagna flows into the Gulf of Genoa between Sestri and Chiaveri. The family of this pope, the Fieschi, were counts of Lavagna. Alagia de' Fieschi was the daughter of Adrian's brother Niccolo and wife to Marquis Moroello Malaspina. She was thus probably Dante's hostess in 1306. Dante places another Fieschi, Boniface, in the circle of the gluttons. In line 50, the Latin means 'those who mourn'. The Latin, lines 73–4, means 'My soul cleaveth unto the dust' (Psalm 119.25; 118 Vulgate).

In that hour when the day's heat, now subdued
    By Earth, or sometimes Saturn, can no more
    Temper the moon's coldness until renewed;
When geomancers watch Fortuna Major soar,
    Pre-dawn, towards the east, in that direction
    Which briefly through the dark its path will score,   6
A stuttering woman came, in dream's reflection
    To me, bent over her feet, squint of eye,
    Maimed in her hands, and sallow of complexion.
I gazed on her, and, as the sun on high
    Confronts the chill limbs which the night subdues,
    So did my look loosen her tongue to ply,   12
And quickly straightened up her back and thews;
    And colour came into her pallid face,
    And Love itself would have suffused such hues.
Once tongue was free, she sang with such a grace
    I would have found it difficult to steer
    Attention from her to some other place.   18
'I am,' she sang, 'that siren sweet and clear
    Who leads the mid-sea mariners astray,
    So full I am of pleasantness to hear.

And with my song I drew Ulysses away
    Out of his wandering course; whoever veered
24   But seldom left the pleasure I purvey.'
Her lips had not yet closed when there appeared
    A Lady by me, holy, alert, to rout
    Her in complete confusion as she neared.
'Vergil, Vergil, who is this?' wrath made her shout.
    At which he went for her, but never did
30   He look from this Lady honest and devout.
He seized the first and ripped her clothes that hid
    Her belly, to reveal the stench that rose
    And woke me; of that phantom I was rid.
I turned to good Vergil, who spoke to disclose:
    'Three times, at least, I've called for you to rise
36   And come and find the way that upward goes.'
I raised myself and found that day-lit skies
    Filled all the holy mountain's terracings;
    We travelled with the sun behind our eyes.
Trailing, I bent my brow, like one that brings
    It burdened with his thought, and, weighed in mind,
42   Was half-arch of a bridge with ponderings,
When I could hear: 'Come, here's the path!' in kind
    And gentle tones announced in such sweet tune
    As never heard on mortal earth confined.
With outspread wings, in swanlike stirring, soon
    The speaker indicated where the stair
48   Between the two cliffs of stern stone was hewn.
He stretched his wings and fanned us, affirming there
    Qui lugent to be blest because their souls
    Shall be so rich in consolation after care.
'What troubles you as if you search for moles?'
    My guide said to me when we both had scaled
54   A little above the angel who controls.
And I: 'In such a dread and fear I've trailed
    Through a strange vision which draws me down to it.
    My thoughts of it persist, it so prevailed.'
'Have you seen the witch for whom they sit
    And weep above us?' he asked, 'and have you seen
60   How man may break away from her and quit?
Let that suffice; and spurn the earth, and mean
    To turn your eyes above toward the lure
    The King revolves with mighty spheres serene!'

Then, like a hawk that studies its claws, then sure,
　　Turns at the call and spreads wing with desire
　　For sustenance, the prey he must procure,   66
So I became and, as the stairs aspire,
　　Cleft in the rock as passage for all those
　　Who mount, so then I reached the circle higher.
Once in the open, where the fifth ring goes
　　I saw that people, weeping, round it lay,
　　Turned face toward the ground in sorrow's throes.   72
'*Adhaesit pavimento,*' I heard them say,
　　'*Anima mea!*' so that the words, for sighs,
　　Could hardly be distinct, or sense convey.
'O God's elect, whose deep and suffering cries
　　Justice and hope alleviate, direct
　　Us on our high ascent towards the skies.'   78
'If you're excused prostration, and expect
　　To find the quickest way, keep to your right
　　The outer drop, and travel circumspect.'
So had the poet asked; ahead, a slight
　　Way off, that answer came – from which I guessed
　　What else the answer hid from casual sight.   84
I turned my look towards my lord who expressed
　　Agreement with a willing wave for me to do
　　What I in glance was yearning to request.
Once I could do just as I wished, I drew
　　Forward till standing almost over the soul
　　Whose previous answer made me note and sue.   90
I said 'Spirit, whose tears mature and make whole
　　That without which one cannot turn to God,
　　Delay for me awhile your greater goal.
Who were you? Why back up, lying where feet plod?
　　Tell me. – And if there's anything for me
　　To do for you on earth from which I trod.'   96
'Why Heaven turns our backs to it,' said he,
　　'I'll tell you so you'll know, but first propose:
　　Scias quod ego fui successor Petri.
Between Sestri and Chiaveri there flows
　　A lovely river; from its name my race
　　Takes origin of the name it knows.   102
I learnt for one month and a brief space
　　How heavy to keep from mire that mantle weighed.
　　All burdens else as feathers one could brace.

And my conversion, ah, was late; but, made
  Pastor of Rome, I soon discerned by test
108   The falseness of the life upon me laid.
I saw that there the heart was not at rest
  Nor could one rise the higher in that life.
  And so the love of this one lit my breast.
Until that time I was a soul in strife
  Parted from God, a wretch of avarice.
114   Now, as you see, I'm punished for such life.
What avarice creates is shown in this
  Purgation of these prostrate souls and no
  Bitterer penalty rings this precipice.
Just as it gazed on things of earthly show
  And never looked above, so justice would
120   Prostrate it down again to earth so low.
As avarice quenched the love of every good
  So that our labours were in vain, so here
  Justice holds us chained in lowlihood.
Bound, fettered hand and foot, as long, or near,
  As it may please the just Lord will we lie
126   Manacled and motionless along this tier.'
I'd knelt, and was about to answer; I
  Had just begun when he perceived my reverence
  Merely by listening to the voice nearby.
'Why kneel?' he asked, 'why bend and show such deference?'
  I answered: 'For the dignity of your state
132   My conscience pained me, standing as by preference.'
'Straighten your legs, brother. Stand up straight,'
  He answered. 'Make no mistake: a lowly
  Fellow servant of yours to one Potentate.
If you have ever understood that holy
  Gospel that reads: *"Neque nubent"* you well
138   Know why I say so. Leave me to purging solely.
Go on your journey. Do not stay a spell.
  Your lingering makes my tears of sorrow cease.
  They'll mature that of which I heard you tell.
Yonder I have Alagia, who's my niece,
  Good in herself if only my line does not
144   Corrupt her with wicked example and caprice.
  She's the last of mine left in that spot.'

CANTO 20

The avaricious lie weeping their sins. Dante, as author, here attacks the sin of avarice – the she-wolf of the opening canto of the Comedy. He encounters Hugh Capet, founder of the present French dynasty. Capet bewails the evil behaviour of his descendants – whom Dante blames for many evils in the Italy of his day. The current king, Philip IV, is so obnoxious to Dante that his own arch-loathing, Boniface, seems noble in defending the Papacy from him. This king was a new Pilate who attacked Christ in the form of this Pope, his Vicar on earth. The mountain then shakes with what appears to Dante to be an earthquake. He is calmed by Vergil.

The will contests badly a better will;
    Therefore, displeased to please him then, I drew
    Out of the water the sponge I might not fill.
I moved as did my leader in the few
    Gaps free; as with a battlemented top
    One hugs the wall, we hugged the rock-face too,   6
For those distilling through their eyes, drop
    By drop, the evil that fills the wide world's fold
    Crowd close towards the edge before they stop.
– Accursèd may you be, she-wolf of old,
    That have more prey than all the beasts there are,
    To feed your hunger, insatiable and bold.   12
O Heaven, by whose circling, star by star,
    Conditions here are thought to change and slew,
    When shall he come who'll rout and drive her far? –
We travelled on, our footsteps slow and few,
    Myself intent upon the shades I heard
    Piteously weeping in remorse and rue.   18
It chanced I heard, ahead, one call the word
    With tears: 'Sweet Mary!' just as a mother
    Who feels the pangs of birth would have averred.
It went on: 'So poor you were, as we discover
    From that inn where you were forced to lay
    Your holy burden in the stable's cover.   24
Good Fabricius,' next I heard it say,
    'You chose to possess virtue in poverty
    Rather than wickedness in rich display.'

These cries so pleased me that I hurriedly
    Drew forward to detect which spirit made
30   This utterance that seemed almost a plea.
It went on, telling how St Nicholas laid
    Out such largesse towards the maids to lead
    Their youth to honour. I said, 'O shade
That speak so much of good, tell me, I plead,
    Who once you were?' I asked, 'and tell me why
36   You, only, speak the praises that I heed.
Your words will not go unrewarded, if I
    Return to finish off the road, so brief,
    Of life that to its ending races by.'
And he replied: 'Not for any relief
    That I expect from there, I'll state my case,
42   But rather for the grace shown you, in chief:
I was the root of that wicked tree, the base,
    Which overshadows every Christian land
    So that good fruit there's very hard to trace.
If Douai, Lille, Ghent or Bruges were manned
    With force, revenge would soon descend on them,
48   And this I beg for from the Judge's hand.
Hugh Capet, yonder, was my name; they stem
    From me: Philips, Louises descended,
    Who late in France have worn the diadem.
Son of a Paris butcher I was. Expended
    Was the line of all their ancient kings –
54   All – but one in grey garments – ended.
I found my hands firm on the harnessings
    Of government within the realm, and power
    From new possessions, wealth of friends and things,
That on my son's own head it set the dower
    Of widowed crown, from whom there were derived
60   The consecrated bones on whom God lour.
And while the great Provençal dowry survived
    Without taint from my line, though little worth,
    At least there was no harm that it contrived.
By force and fraud, rapine seized that earth,
    And, for amends, Ponthieu and Normandy
66   It grasped; next, Gascony fed its dearth.
Then, for amends, Charles came to Italy,
    Made Conradin a victim; had Thomas thrown
    Back, for amends, into eternity.

A time I see, not far when this day's flown,
    That brings another Charles forth out of France
    To make himself and people better known.   72
Not with an army, but with Judas' lance
    He'll sally forth and, couching it, will burst
    The paunch of Florence wide in that advance.
From that he'll win, not land, but sin, immersed
    In shame, and on him the heavier will it be
    For thinking lightly of it, at his worst.   78
A third, once captive on a ship, I see,
    Selling his daughter, haggling over the price,
    As pirates with women sold to slavery.
O avarice, what worse can you do to us, vice
    That brings so many of my race to err
    So that they cast their kin to sacrifice?   84
I see – that evil past and to occur
    Seem less – Anagni entered by fleur-de-lys,
    Christ in his vicar again a prisoner.
A second time I see him mocked: I see
    The gall and vinegar renewed; see him
    Killed between living thieves in agony.   90
I see the new Pilate, cruel and grim,
    And how he is not satisfied with this
    But, lawless, to the temple sets his trim.
O my Lord, when shall I have the bliss
    To see the vengeance which, though counsel hide
    In secret, sweetens your wrath at avarice.   96
– What I had said of the Holy Spirit's Bride,
    Unique, and what had made you turn to me
    Expecting comment that I would provide,
Is the response in all our prayers while we
    Observe the day; and when it turns to night
    We start instead a note that's contrary.   102
Then of Pygmalion we all recite,
    Whom insatiate lust for gold turned thief,
    Traitor and parricide; the wretched plight
Of avaricious Midas which brought to grief
    His greedy quest – because of that, it's just
    That we should always mock this foolish chief.   108
Mad Achan next, each one recalls his lust,
    And how he stole the spoils so that the ire
    Of Joshua seems here to fang him in disgust.

Then we accuse Sapphira, her husband, dire;
   The hoofs Heliodorus felt are next extolled;
114   Then Polymnestor's name this mountain-spire
Encircles with his infamy who doled
   Out Polydorus' deathblow. Last: "You know,
   Crassus, so tell us what's the taste of gold?"
Sometimes one speaks loud, another low,
   Matching the ardour spurring us to speak
120   With stronger or with weaker force and flow.
So I was not alone before, nor unique
   In speaking of the good, but no one near
   Was raising up his voice from low and weak.'
We had already gone from him to steer
   And strive to overcome the way so far
126   As was permitted to our efforts here
When suddenly I felt the mountain jar
   Like something falling; whereupon a chill
   Gripped me like one the grasp of death will mar.
Assuredly, Delos never felt a thrill
   So vast before Latona made her nest
132   To bear the two eyes in the Heavens still.
Then from all parts a mighty shout oppressed
   My ears so that my master came beside
   To say: 'While I'm your guide don't be distressed.'
'*Gloria in excelsis Deo!*' they all cried,
   As far as I could tell from those around
138   Whose voices could be heard, and sense supplied.
Stock-still we stood, in such suspense fast-bound
   Just like the shepherds first to hear that song,
   Until the tremors ceased upon that ground.
Then on our holy pathway moving along
   We went, observing there the shades that lay,
144   And to their usual prayer returned that throng.
No ignorance – if memory do not stray –
   Had ever such impulsion given me
   To yearn for knowledge as then seemed to weigh
On me in pondering; nor was I free
   To ask because we were in haste to climb,
150   Nor could I there perceive what it might be,
   So journeyed timid and pensive for a time.

CANTO 21

A newcomer catches up with them; as they continue together he explains why the mountain appeared to quake. He reveals who he is and his great admiration for Vergil. Statius died toward the end of the first century. He has thus spent over 1,200 years in Purgatory. More than 400 were spent in the terrace of the slothful; 500 in that of the niggardly or prodigal. Statius never completed his second major work, the Achilleid. His first is the Thebaid.

That natural thirst not to be satisfied
    Except it taste the water which the poor
    Samaritan woman begged that grace provide,
Burned me – and haste was goading me the more
    Behind my leader, searching out foot-room –
    And pity, too, for the penance on that floor;   6
When, lo, as Luke has told that Christ the Groom
    Appeared to those two who were on the road –
    Already having risen from the tomb –
A shade appeared, and just behind us strode,
    Gazing at his feet and on the prostrate crowd,
    Nor did we notice till it spoke in this mode,   12
Saying: 'My brothers, with God's peace be endowed.'
    Quickly we turned and Vergil made the sign
    Befitting such a greeting; then, aloud:
'May the true court that chooses to confine
    Me in eternal exile bring you in peace
    To the councils of the blest with the divine.'   18
'How,' he asked, while our pace did not decrease,
    'If you are shades unworthy in God's eye,
    Who brings you on his stairway of release?'
My guide: 'If you observe the marks that lie
    On him, those that the angel's sword has done,
    Clearly he'll join the righteous by and by.   24
Since she who works, day, night, has not yet spun
    For him the flax that Clotho turns and loads
    Upon the distaff, for each and every one,
And since his spirit sees not in our modes,
    Though sister to yours and mine, in coming here
    Alone, he'd not have overcome these roads.   30

So I was fetched from Hell's wide jaws to steer
   His course, and I will lead him on as far
   As my school may escort him in this sphere.
But tell us why the mountain felt that jar
   And quaked – if you know why – and why all seemed
36   With one voice to ring its soft base like a bar?'
Thus did he thread the needle's eye that gleamed
   With my desire, in asking this; less dry
   My thirst became through hope itself that beamed.
'This mountain's holy rule,' he made reply,
   'Permits of nothing chance or hazardous,
42   Nothing uncustomary, nothing awry.
In this place nothing is fortuitous.
   What Heaven accepts here as its own of its own
   Occasions change; nothing extraneous.
Since neither rain nor hail nor snow is known,
   Nor dew nor hoarfrost, any higher than
48   The stair of those three steps which you were shown,
Clouds, dense or thin, do not appear, none scan
   The lightning flash, nor Thaumas' daughter's bow
   That often, yonder, wanders with its span.
Dry vapour does not rise past the top row
   Of those three steps I mentioned just before,
54   Where Peter's vicar places heel and toe.
It quakes, below, to less extent or more;
   But, at this height, the wind concealed in earth,
   I don't know how, has never jarred the tor.
It quakes here when some soul may feel her worth
   So cleansed that she may rise, start to ascend;
60   Such general shouts acclaim her newer birth.
The will alone gives proof of purging's end.
   It fills the soul, now free to change its dwelling,
   And gives the power to climb as she intend.
It wills before but, justice divine impelling,
   Desire, against the will, yields to the fine
66   And penalty as once to sin, rebelling.
And I who lay five hundred years to pine
   Under the torment – and more – only just now
   Felt the will free for higher sills than mine.
Therefore you felt the mountain quake and cow,
   And heard the pious shades upon the brink
72   Praise God – their rising may he soon allow.'

So he informed us; since we relish drink
    In measure to the dryness of our thirst,
    How much he gave I cannot say or think.
My guide said: 'Now I see the net that first
    Takes you, and how one snaps its snarling strand –
    Which makes the mountain shake with joy's outburst.   78
Who are you, please? And let me understand
    Why you have lain so many ages here.
    On these topics let your words expand.'
'When good Titus, aided in full career
    By Heaven's high King, avenged the wounds that shed
    The blood that Judas Iscariot sold so dear,   84
I bore the name most lasting,' the shade said,
    'And, yonder, honours most, and great in fame
    I was, but not in faith for which he bled.
So sweet the music of my words became
    That I, Toulousan, was drawn to her by Rome,
    And on my brow deserved the myrtle's acclaim.   90
Statius I'm known as still, on yonder loam.
    I sang of Thebes and great Achilles' name,
    But fell with the burden of a further tome.
The sparks which fired me leapt from the divine flame
    By which more than a thousand have been lit
    And were the seeds from which my verses came.   96
I speak of the *Aeneid*; that mother-writ,
    It was, nurtured my poetry; without that guide
    I'd not have weighed above a drachma-bit.
Just to have lived when Vergil breathed there, I'd
    Consent to one sun more than I have paid
    To end my exile on this mountainside.'   102
These words made Vergil turn to me; he conveyed
    A look that silently 'Be silent!' said,
    But willpower's not in everything obeyed.
For tears and laughter from their fountainhead
    In passion so directly flow they sway
    Least to the will when truth's elicited.   108
I only smiled – as one might well convey
    A hint. The shade was silent, looked me in
    The eyes where soul's most clearly on display,
And said: 'As in this feat you hope to win,
    Now tell me why your face this moment let
    A flash of laughter on me half begin.'   114

Here I was trapped between the two; one set
   Me to be silent; the second bade me tell.
   I gave a sigh which then my master met
With understanding as he said: 'Dispel
   Your fear of speaking; tell him straight and true
120   What he requests, and his great yearning quell.'
I said, 'The flash of laughter which you drew
   Excited your amazement, but I desire
   A greater marvel yet to seize on you.
The one who guides my eyes from high to higher
   Is Vergil himself from whom you drew your force
126   To sing of men and gods and sweep the lyre.
If you assume some other cause the source
   Of laughter, set it by as quite untrue.
   It was your words on him in your discourse.'
Already was he bending over to
   Embrace my master's feet. 'Brother,' said he,
132   'Don't; for you're a shade, and shade you view.'
Standing, he said: 'You know now the degree
   Of love that warms me to you when it brings
   Me to forget our insubstantiality:
   I treat our shadows still as solid things.'

CANTO 22

Vergil inquires how Statius could have become a Christian. Statius explains and, in return, inquires after their various characters and peers in classical literature. They encounter a tree that inculcates the lessons of temperance. The Latin, line 6, is a reference to Matthew 5.6, concerning those who thirst after righteousness – in the Vulgate version, after justice.

We had already left the angel behind,
    The angel who'd shown us to the sixth ring,
    Having erased the scar on my brow outlined.
And he had told us that all those who bring
    Their desire to righteousness were blest,
    And closed with '*Sitiunt*' and no other thing.   6
Lighter than at previous stairs, I pressed
    Along behind those other spirits so fleet,
    Without any labouring or need to rest,
When Vergil said, 'Love, lit by virtue's heat,
    Has always kindled love elsewhere if its flame
    Is nakedly revealed to shine and greet.   12
And therefore from the time that Juvenal came
    To us, within the Limbo down in Hell,
    And made quite clear the affection you proclaim
Goodwill for you in me began to well,
    As great as ever held for one unknown,
    So that these stairs won't seem so steep. But tell   18
Me – as a friend forgive me if my tone
    Seem over-confident and slack my rein,
    And as old friends let's talk – what made you prone
To avarice, how could you entertain
    It in that breast where so much wisdom lay,
    Garnered with all your diligence? Explain.'   24
These words made Statius smile at first, then say:
    'Each word you speak's a precious gift to me
    And token of your love; but things convey
Indeed a false impression frequently
    And lead to needless doubts because their true
    Cause lies in such a deep obscurity.   30
Your question shows me the belief in you
    That I was avaricious in yonder land –
    The circle I was in suggests your view?

Know now that avarice was too far from my hand.
   Thousands of moons in punishment I've spent
36   Because of this excess, you understand.
And, if I'd not corrected that intent
   When I considered those lines where you say,
   In wrath, as though at human temperament:
"To what extremes do you not drive astray
   The lust of mortals, accursèd greed for gold?",
42   To roll those grievous jousts had been my way.
Thus I perceived our hands could also unfold
   Their wings too wide in squandering – and I
   Repented it, with more I have not told.
How many will rise again, with shorn locks awry,
   In ignorance which blocks chance to repent
48   This sin in life and in the hour to die.
Know that a fault's reverse extreme and bent
   In this place withers of its green and dries
   Beside that sin itself, as complement.
Therefore, if I have been where avarice lies
   And weeps, this has befallen me by reason
54   Of the counter fault, sentenced likewise.'
'Now, when you sang the savage strife and treason
   Sprung from Jocasta's double sorrow,' said
   The singer of bucolic lay and season,
'By that which Clio touches on that head
   With you, it seems there that the faith had yet
60   To make you faithful; good works, without, are dead.
If this is so, what sun or candles set
   The dark alight for you to hoist your sail
   To follow after the Fisher with his net?'
He said: 'You first showed me the way to scale
   Parnassus and to drink out of those caves,
66   And, next, to God you lighted up the trail.
You have behaved like somebody that braves
   The night bearing a lamp behind him, who'd
   Not help himself but those behind he saves,
When you announced: "The world is now renewed;
   Justice returns, and the primal age of man;
72   From Heaven descends a new progeny and brood."
Through you I was a poet; through you began
   As Christian; yet, so you may better tell
   What I've outlined, I'll colour in the plan.

Already had the world begun to swell
    With true belief sown by the messengers
    Of the eternal Kingdom over Hell.   78
In such a concord with the gospellers
    Sounded those words I've cited, it became
    My custom to call upon these ministers.
They grew so holy in my sight and aim
    That, when Domitian persecuted them,
    Not without my tears their grief and shame.   84
And while I walked the earth I tried to stem
    Their injuries; the upright ways they led
    Made me scorn other sects, and all contemn.
I was baptized before the Greeks had spread
    To Theban rivers in my poem, though
    I stayed a secret Christian in my dread,   90
And a long while as a pagan made a show.
    But that faint-heartedness imposed my yoke,
    The fourth ring and four-hundred years to go.
You, therefore, who have lifted off the cloak
    That hid from me the great good that I tell,
    As we've the time, give news of other folk   96
While climbing. Where does ancient Terence dwell?
    Caecilius, Plautus, Varro? If you know,
    Say if they're damned, and in what ward of Hell.'
'Persius, they, and I, and more below,'
    My master answered, 'are beside the Greek –
    More than all poets, the Muses fed his flow –   102
In the first ring of the prison blind and bleak.
    Of the mountain, where our nurturers abide
    For ever, very frequently we speak.
Euripides is with us, Antiphon, beside,
    Simonides, Agathon, many Greeks more,
    Whose brows with laurel once were dignified.   108
Of your own people, also there, are poor
    Antigone, Deiphyle, Argia, and fair
    Ismene, sad as she was in time before.
Also seen there is she who showed them where
    Langia sprang; Tiresias' daughter; Thetis, too;
    Deidamia and her sisters; all of them there.'   114
Both poets were silent then, intent to view
    The new place, gazing, freed of the ascent
    And free from the impinging walls anew.

Four handmaids of the day by now were spent;
  Behind, the fifth was at the chariot-pole;
120   Directing up the flaming horn, she went,
When my guide said: 'Here we should turn the sole
  As previously, I think, and keep our right
  Shoulders outward round the mountain bole.'
So custom here became our guiding light.
  We chose the way with less uncertainty
126   Because that noble shade assented quite.
They journeyed on the way in front of me;
  I came alone and heard all that they said,
  Which gave me understanding in poetry.
But soon the sweet exchanges stopped. Ahead,
  We found a tree grown right amid our way:
132   Wholesome its fruit, and pleasant fragrance spread.
Now, as the pine ascends with bough and spray
  That taper as they rise, so this reversed
  The process – so that none could climb, I'd say.
A clear spring from the high rock dispersed
  Itself over and on the leaves, this side
138   On which our path was blocked by the tree's upburst.
Both poets neared the tree and stood: then cried
  A voice within the leaves: 'Famine this food
  Will give you.' And then it amplified:
'Mary considered more how to conclude
  The wedding-feast with honour than of her mouth –
144   Which answers for you now, in Heaven sued.
The Roman women always slaked their drouth
  With water as their drink. Daniel, in scorn
  Of food, put greater wisdom in his mouth.
The first age was fair as gold that morn;
  Hunger made savoury the acorn's taste;
150   And thirst made nectar flow in every bourn.
Honey and locusts in the desert waste
  Were food for John the Baptist; thus he's great
And glorious as in the Gospels may be traced
  Where you may read the truth which they relate.

CANTO 23

They encounter Forese whom Dante can barely recognize among the famished ones.
Dante has rounded the year of Forese's death up; he actually died on 28 July 1296.
Since he repented at the last minute he should still be outside the gates of
Purgatory, Dante thinks. Forese explains the purpose of the strange tree and the
cascade. In line 30, Mary comes from the historian Josephus: when Titus besieged
Jerusalem, he records, she actually cooked and ate her own child. The Latin, line 11,
means 'My lips O Lord' from Psalm 51 (50 Vulgate): 'O Lord, open thou my lips'.
Line 74 refers to Matthew 27.46, Christ's cry from the Cross.

While I was staring hard in the leafy spray
    With eyes fixed steady just like those who waste
    Their time away on birds that hawk and prey,
My more than father said to me: 'Son, haste
    Yourself along because the time availed
    To us must be more profitably traced.'   6
My face I turned, nor speed of footstep trailed,
    Towards those sages who were speaking there,
    So little cost to me the going entailed.
And lo, we heard in tears a song-like air:
    'Labia mea Domine' in such a mode
    That joy and grief at once it seemed to bear.   12
'Sweet father, what do I hear along this road?'
    I started. He: 'Perhaps the shades that tread,
    Loosening the bonds of debt that they have owed.'
Just as musing travellers, as they head
    Past strangers on the way, look back to see
    But do not loiter in the course they thread,   18
So, at our backs approaching and passing us three,
    A throng of spirits, silent and devout,
    Gazed on us, and in wonder seemed to be.
And each was dark and hollow-eyed; about
    The bones skin took the shape that underlay,
    So wasted, pale, they were, with fast and drought.   24
I don't think Erysichthon withered away
    To skin and bone like these, not even when
    He had the greatest fear how it would slay.
I said in silent thought: 'These are the men
    And women that had lost Jerusalem
    When Mary ate her child in the siege's den.'   30

Eye-sockets seemed like ouches without gem.
    Whoever reads 'omo' in the face of man
    Would clearly there have recognized the em.
Who, lacking knowledge of the cause, would scan
    And think the scent of fruit and water might
36   So work upon the appetite they fan?
Already I was astounded at the sight
    Of how they starved because I could not see
    The cause of hunger and sad scurf aright,
When, lo, a spirit turned its eyes to me
    Out of their hollow sockets, and it nailed
42   Its gaze and cried: 'That such a grace should be!'
Never would I have known the face that hailed
    Me but I found within the voice a trace
    Of what in feature was obscured and veiled.
This spark relit my memory to place
    The altered looks exactly then, and I
48   Recognized at once Forese's face.
'Ah, do not stare,' he cried, 'upon this dry
    Leprosy that discolours all my skin,
    Nor any fault the flesh brings to the eye.
But tell me all your news, and say what kin
    Are those two spirits who accompany you.
54   Don't stop yet fail to speak with me. Begin.'
'Your face,' I answered, 'which I wept to view
    Once at your death gives me no less a grief
    That moves to tears, seeing its wasted hue.
So tell me, in God's name, what strips your leaf.
    Don't make me speak in this bewilderment.
60   Poorly he speaks whom other pressures brief.'
And he: 'From eternal wisdom comes descent
    Of power in the water and the tree,
    Behind us now, that wastes me till I'm spent.
All these who weep and sing at once must be
    Resanctified by hunger and by thirst
66   For earlier excess and gluttony.
The scent the fruit exhales and that dispersed
    By all the spray diffused upon the green
    Creates the craving by which we are amerced.
And not the once alone; this pain comes keen
    Again – I call it pain but should have said
72   Our solace – as round this road we grow more lean,

For that desire leads us to the tree that led
    The glad Christ to say *"Eli!"* and set
    Us free by reason of the blood he shed.'
And I to him: 'Forese, not five years yet
    Have circled since the day you changed earth's grime
    To reach the better life that you have met.   78
If power of further sin ceased ere that time
    Came for the holy sorrow which unites
    Us once again to God, how did you climb
So rapidly up here into these heights?
    I thought to see you further down below
    Where time for time's repaid, and then requites.'   84
And he: 'Here to the torments, and to know
    The sweet wormwood my sweetest Nella sped
    Me swiftly with the tears that she let flow.
By prayer and sighs devout she thus has led
    Me from the borders where they wait and plod,
    And from the other circles saved my head.   90
So much more precious and beloved of God
    Is my dear widow whom I loved so well
    As good works isolate her from the squad.
For, in Sardinian Barbagia, women excel
    By far in modesty all those who flaunt
    In the Barbagia where I left her to dwell.   96
O my sweet brother, what would you have me vaunt?
    Already in my vision a time's prepared,
    One when this hour shall not be old and gaunt,
In which the pulpit's ban will be declared
    On those women of Florence so brazen-faced
    They flounce about with breasts and nipples bared. 102
What Barbary, what Saracen woman so unchaste
    That spiritual or other curb were needed
    To make her cover them or be disgraced?
But, if the shameless creatures ever heeded
    What swiftest Heaven prepares for them on high,
    They'd gaped their mouths in howling unimpeded. 108
For, if foresight does not mislead my eye,
    They will be sorrowing before the son
    Is downy-cheeked that now hears lullaby.
Brother, don't hide my thought from everyone.
    You see that not myself alone but all
    Of us observe how you obscure the sun.'   114

And I to him: 'If you will but recall
    What you with me, and I with you, have been
    The present memory should still appal.
From such a life the one who can be seen
    Going before turned me the other day
120   When that one's sister showed her roundest sheen.'
(And here I pointed to the sun.) 'My way
    Through the deep night of all the truly dead
    In my true flesh he's led, and I obey.
From there, his help has raised me up ahead,
    Climbing and circling the mount that straitens you
126   Who once were bent by the world you used to tread.
He promises to keep me as his true
    Companion till I reach where Beatrice must be.
    There shall I be deprived of him anew.
Vergil is he who speaks these things to me.'
    (I indicated him.) 'The other soul
132   Is he for whom this realm, shaking him free,
    Trembled and discharged from her control.'

CANTO 24

Forese refers to his sister Piccarda who appears again in Heaven 3. *Also among the famished ones Dante encounters Bonagiunta of Lucca who discusses the nature of literary style with him. He also mentions a woman, her name 'Gentucca', who will be more relevant to Dante in his coming exile. Forese prophesies the downfall of Corso Donati, his own brother, leader of the Florentine Blacks, who is here implicated in the degeneracy of Florence.*

Neither did our speech delay our tread,
    Nor movement hinder speech; talking we went,
    Strongly as ships a fair wind drives ahead.
The shades that seemed twice dead in wonderment
    Directed their vision from its hollow pits
    At me, aware my life was not yet spent.   6
And I continued talking: 'I think that it's
    The case, maybe, since he accompanies
    Someone, he slows his climbing as befits.
But tell me if you know where Piccarda is.
    Tell me if I can see people renowned
    In these that fix on me their scrutinies.'   12
'My sister whom I can't say whether I found
    The more devout, or beautiful, this day
    Enjoys her triumph on high Olympus crowned.'
He said this first and then: 'Here, we may
    Reveal the names of all because our faces
    Are fallen in with fasting, withered away.   18
That's Bonagiunta of Lucca.' (He pointed out places.)
    'Those features, just behind him there, with line
    And seam more furrowed than the other cases,
Held in his hands the Holy Church; a divine
    From Tours he was, and, fasting now, is purged
    Of eels from Bolsena and Vernaccian wine.'   24
And, one by one, so many more emerged
    As he announced them; and never a black look
    I saw, since all so named with gladness surged.
I saw Ubaldin dalla Pila took
    Thin air in hungry bites – and the Boniface
    Who pastured many flocks with staff and rook;   30

Messer Marchese, saw: he'd time and place
　　To drink at Forli, with none so great a thirst
　　As here, but eased his craving not a trace.
But as one looks and may prefer the first
　　More than another, so did I return
36　　To him from Lucca – of me, it seemed, well versed.
Muttering, he was; I seemed then to discern
　　Something like 'Gentucca' as he felt
　　The pangs of justice there with which they burn.
'O soul,' I said, 'that such yearnings melt
　　To talk with me, speak so that I may know
42　　And may be satisfied with words you've dealt.'
'A woman's born who wears no wimple,' so
　　He started,' and she'll make my city please
　　You soon, though men revile and speak it woe.
Now take this prophecy and go; if these
　　Mutters of mine misled you, then the true
48　　Facts will be clear to you when time decrees.
– But tell me, are you he that made the new
　　Rhymes which begin: "Ladies that hold
　　Intelligence of love"? Now was that you?'
'I'm one that notes,' in answer then I told,
　　'The inspiration of love, and all the while
54　　Write in the style it orders me to mould.'
'Dear brother,' he said, 'I see, beyond denial,
　　The knot that kept Guittone, the Notary, then
　　Myself, tied up short of the sweet new style.
I well see now how faithfully your pen
　　Takes down from the dictator – which I know
60　　Was never true of us, the earlier men.
Whoever searching further seeks to go
　　Has lost all sense of difference from one style
　　To the other.' He stopped, as if contented so.
As birds, accustomed to winter on the Nile,
　　Sometimes depart in aerial squadrons east,
66　　Then fly at speed, later, in single file,
So all the crowd there, facing round, increased
　　Their pace, and leanness with desire lends
　　Them speed, as if they moved towards a feast.
And, as one tired of running lets his friends
　　Go past him and then walks himself until
72　　The panting in his chest is eased and ends,

Forese let the holy flock fly past and mill,
    Then followed on behind with me to say:
    'When shall I see you back upon the hill?'
'I do not know,' I answered, 'how long I may
    Still live; yet my return won't be so soon
    But longing sooner will seek to leave that bay,   78
Because where I was put to live and commune
    Is daily stripped the more of good – appears
    Foredoomed in wretched ruin to be strewn.'
'Now go,' he said, 'for he in whom inheres
    Most blame I see dragged at tail of beast
    Towards that vale where no sin's cleansed nor clears.   84
Faster the beast goes, every pace increased
    In speed until it dashes him to lie
    Hideously disfigured and unpieced.
Those wheels' (he raised his eyes towards the sky)
    'Will turn not long before it shall be clear
    To you what here my words may not imply.   90
Now stay behind, for time is precious here
    In this domain, and I have lingered long,
    Matching my pace to yours along this tier.'
And, as a horseman gallops from the throng
    Of charging cavalry, and rides to snatch
    The honour of the first onslaught with strong   96
Strides, so he parted from us with despatch
    And I was left behind beside those two
    Who, of the world, were marshals without match.
And, when he was so far away from view
    My eyes pursued him with great difficulty –
    As did my mind those words of his pursue –   102
The green and laden boughs of another tree
    Appeared to me, and not so far away,
    For I had just reached its vicinity.
I saw a crowd beneath its boughs, and they
    Lifted their hands and shouted something out
    Towards the leaves, in a spoilt child's display.   108
They beg; and he they beg answers no shout,
    But to increase their longing holds up high
    What they desire and shows it all about.
They left as though not thwarted then; close by
    The great tree we came – that seemed to mock
    So many tears, so many pleas that sigh.   114

'Pass on without approaching; on the rock
    Above, there is another tree Eve ate;
    And this plant's been nurtured from that stock.'
So spoke a voice amid the branches set.
    Therefore Vergil, Statius and I then closed
120   Ranks, passed as near the mount as we could get.
'Recall,' it said, 'the cursèd ones, composed
    Within the clouds, who, when once gorged, had fought
    With Theseus with their double breasts exposed;
And all those Hebrews, shown as the soft sort
    In drinking, so Gideon spurned them from his force
126   When from the hills of Midian he made onslaught.'
And so beside the rock we steered our course
    While hearing of the sins of gluttony,
    Once of such woeful gain and pay the source.
Then in a single file, each solitary,
    Fully a thousand strides or more we went,
132   In contemplation, wordlessly, all three.
'What are you pondering, alone, intent?'
    Suddenly said a voice, at which I reared
    As timid beast, frightened at some event.
I raised my head to see who had appeared:
    And, in a furnace, ore or glass one sees
138   Had never glowed as red as this we neared.
He said to us: 'Pass upward now, by these.
    Here you must turn your steps, and here must go
    Any who hope to meet with peace and ease.'
His face had blinded me beneath its glow,
    So I turned back to face my guide like one
144   Who goes by hearing what the sound might show.
As the May breeze, herald of dawning sun,
    Stirs and breathes a sweetness forth that brings
    The scent of grass and flowers freshly begun,
Such wind I felt across my brow, and wings
    Indeed I felt, wafting their drifting airs,
150   Ambrosial fragrances on my sense of things.
I heard one say: 'Blessedness is theirs
    Who are illumined by such grace that lust
Of palate never stirs or overbears
    Their breast, whose hunger's for but what is just.'

CANTO 25

Dante wonders how purely spiritual beings can feel the purgation of hunger and thirst. Vergil defers to Statius for the explanation. These issues are shelved when they reach the next terrace where flames jet out from the mountain, almost blocking the way. This canto, which is mainly filled with medieval embryology, is somewhat obscure and tedious to the non-specialist reader but its extreme detail does convince that Dante really believed he was presenting objective fact. It is interesting how 'evolutionary' the explanation is of foetal development. Line 121 quotes a hymn attributed to St Ambrose: 'God of supreme mercy', sung at matins on Saturday. The Latin, line 128, means 'I know not a man' (Luke 1.34), Mary's reply to the angel at the Annunciation.

It was a time when the ascent allowed
    Of no impediment, for sun to the Bull,
    Night to the Scorpion, had left meridian and bowed.
Thus, as a man will neither halt nor pull
    Up on his way, whatever may appear,
    If spurred on by the need to reach the full,   6
So did we enter through the fissure here,
    The one behind the other, mounting the stair
    Whose narrows parted us from tier to tier.
And, as the fledgling stork that seeks the air
    Raises its wings, desiring now to fly,
    But loath to leave the nest, lowers them there,   12
Just so with me: the urge to question why
    Flared and went out, just when about to frame
    The word and mouth to speak, but running dry.
My sweet father did not pause to exclaim,
    Although the pace was swift, but called: 'Shoot
    The bow of speech, barb drawn, to point of aim.'   18
I spoke my query, confident, resolute,
    Asking: 'How can one waste away, grow lean
    Where need for food can't urge one like a brute?'
'If you recall how Meleager had been
    Consumed at consuming of the burning brand,'
    He said, 'it would not be too dark a scene.   24
And, if you note whenever you may stand
    Before the glass, your image with you goes,
    That which is hard to see were easier scanned.

But so this yearning may receive repose
    Within you, here is Statius. With him I plead
30   That he should heal the wound that you expose.'
'If,' answered Statius, 'I unfold and feed
    Him, in your presence, with eternal things
    He sees, let my excuse be: you, I heed.'
Then he: 'If you, in all your ponderings
    Mind and receive my words, they'll be a light
36   To you to show the how of your questionings.
Perfect blood – that's never drunk to requite
    The thirsty veins but left behind, like food
    That is removed from table and the sight –
Acquires, within the heart, a plenitude
    And power to form all human members, as flows
42   The blood in veins becoming what it endued;
Refined again, it sinks where silence shows
    The better form of speech to name its base.
    Thence in the natural vessel next it goes
To another's blood where both will interlace,
    Passive the one; the other active designed,
48   Because it issues from a perfect place.
And, joined, this then begins to work and bind,
    Coagulating, giving life to what
    It has solidified for its material kind.
The active principle, now soul (but not
    Unlike a plant, but for this difference:
54   It is in process; the latter its goal has got)
Develops even more to move and sense
    Like a sea-fungus; organs it next prepares
    Through which the powers it holds in germ dispense.
And now expands and spreads the virtue that fares,
    Son, from its source in the begetter's heart
60   Where nature plans all members and their shares.
But how from animal it grows apart
    To be a human being you can't see clear –
    A wiser here than you erred in his art,
For, in his lore, the reason would appear
    As quite distinct from soul because he scanned
66   No part or organ where soul might inhere.
Receive the truth that comes, and understand
    That, once within the embryo the brain
    Is perfectly organized as it was planned,

The First Mover turns to it again,
    Joyous at nature's feat, breathes and effects
    A new spirit, brimmed with virtue's main,   72
Which draws into its substance what it detects
    That's active there, and a single soul is made
    That loves and feels and on itself reflects.
So that you'll marvel less at what's conveyed,
    Look at the sun's heat that turns to wine
    When in the grape-juice it is held and stayed.   78
And when Lachesis has no more to twine,
    It frees itself from flesh and bears away
    In potency the human and divine.
The other powers – mute they all stay:
    Memory, intelligence and will more fleet
    In action than ever before that day.   84
Without delay it falls by wonderful feat
    To one of the shores. Arriving there, it first
    Discovers whichever path it is to beat.
As soon as circumscribed, in place immersed,
    The formative virtue radiates around
    In form and number as the living parts rehearsed.   90
As saturated air may well rebound
    With various colours, through another's rays,
    Which are reflected from it, and surround,
So ambient air in corresponding ways
    Accretes into the form that it must bear
    From imprint of the soul where now it stays.   96
And then, like flame which follows everywhere
    The fire may move, this new form coincides
    With every movement of the spirit there;
And henceforth since its semblance it provides
    Is called a shade and fashions out of shade
    Organs for every sense and sight besides.   102
By this, our speech; by this, our laughter's made;
    By this, our tears must flow, our sighs expire
    That on the mount you may have heard relayed.
The shade takes form according as desire
    And other affections spur us; this is why
    The leanness comes that made you first enquire.'   108
But now we'd reached the final turn and by
    The right we'd wheeled, and instantly were cast
    In depths of other problems we'd to try.

For there the rock-side flares out flames; the blast
    Up from the cliff repels them with its sweep
114   And clears them from the edge that may be passed.
So we'd to change our route, edge round the steep
    In single file; on one side was the fear
    Of fire; the other, of falling in the deep.
My guide said: 'Here the eye must be quite clear
    And bridled very well; a false step placed
120   Could easily take you off into that sheer.'
'*Summa Deus clementiae!*' then I traced,
    Sung in the heart of heat in that great blaze
    Which made me eager to turn aside in haste,
And spirits in the flames captured my gaze,
    And thus it was attention sometimes sprang
126   From step to them, divided phase by phase.
After the hymn had ended, their cry rang:
    '*Virum non cognosco!*' and so the hymn
    Softly a second time they raised and sang.
And, ended once again, the interim
    Was 'Diana kept in the wood and chased away
132   Helice who felt the poison of Venus brim.'
Then back into the hymn, and, after, they
    Acclaim the husbands and the wives all chaste
    As virtue and as marriage would have us stay.
And this mode – all the time they are embraced
    By fire – suffices them, and of such food
138   And such a treatment must they always taste
    Before the last wound be cured and renewed.

CANTO 26

They proceed precariously avoiding the flames by going along the precipitous edge.
A conversation is begun with one penitent but interrupted by Dante's observation
of a crowd moving counter to the first. After hearing the explanation, the conver-
sation resumes with Guinicelli, whom Dante regards as a father-influence on his
poetry. Guido Guinicelli of Bologna was the most important Italian poet before
Dante. He was governor of Castelfranco in 1270 and died in 1276. Dante was highly
influenced by his poem 'Al cor gentil repaira con amore' ('Within the gentle heart
love shelters'). He is mentioned in Dante's other works five times. Guinicelli defers
to Arnaut Daniel whom Dante permits to speak in his own tongue of Provençal.

While we advanced like this in single file
    Along the brink, the good master would say:
    'Take care, and follow me!' once in a while.
On my right shoulder leant the sun's ray
    That with its light already began to spread
    The western face from azure to white display,   6
And with my shadow the flames appeared more red,
    And even at so slight a sign, I saw
    Some shades paid heed, moving to pass ahead.
This was the thing that gave the chance to draw
    Into a conversation; one said to the next:
    'He's no shadow-body for flames to gnaw.'   12
Then some of them approached, their guard flexed
    Ready to stop them edging from the heat,
    But near as possible while flame still vexed.
'Oh you, behind the others, not with feet
    Of sluggard, but perhaps in deference,
    Tell me who burn in thirst and fire complete,   18
Nor me alone, for these have more intense
    A thirst than Indian's or Negro's for chill
    Water. So say how come you make a fence
Or wall that blocks the sunlight from the sill
    As if your body had not yet been caught
    Within the net of death, but living still.'   24
Thus one addressed me, and I would have taught
    Already who I was, if not intent
    Upon a second thing of strange import,

For through the middle of the flames there went
   A crowd in counter motion to this group
30   That made me hesitate in wonderment.
Then next I saw each shade of either troop
   Cursorily kiss the other without delay,
     To briefest greetings only content to stoop.
Likewise, amid their dark battalion's array
   One ant rubs muzzle with another, perhaps
36   To find where fortune lies and which the way.
As soon as all the friendly greetings lapse,
   Before the first step forward, each one tries
     To shout the louder and the other caps:
The second group: 'Sodom and Gomorrah!' cries;
   The other: 'Pasiphaë turns cow for bull
42   To hurry to the lusting of her thighs!'
Then, like the cranes that should take wing and pull
   Towards the Rhiphean mountains, or else to sands
     As shy of frost, as those of sun too full,
One group passes the other of these bands
   And, weeping, they return to previous chants,
48   And so the cry most suiting them expands.
Those who'd entreated me made their advance
   As closely as before, intent to hear,
     As one could tell from looking at their stance.
And I who'd twice seen their desire appear
   Started: 'O souls assured to reach the state
54   Of peace when it is offered, far or near,
My limbs, whether they're green or grown in gait,
   Have not remained on earth; are here with me,
     With coursing blood and joints that bear my weight.
I'm climbing upward so that I may see,
   No longer blind. A Lady, higher, earns us grace
60   And so my flesh comes through your territory.
Yet, that fulfilment take high yearning's place,
   And so that Heaven may sooner shelter you,
     Filled with all love and broadnesses of space,
Tell me, so I'll record it straight and true
   On paper, who you are and who those there
66   That move behind your back away from view.'
Not unlike those, the highlander will stare
   In dumb awe, lingering bemused and vexed,
     Raw and uncouth, encountering a city square.

So did each shade appear: but unperplexed
  Of their bewilderment which noble hearts
  Soon render calm, that shade began this text: 72
'Blessèd are you who've come into these parts
  To bear away the knowledge of these bounds
  And make for holier life in the world's marts.
These people who don't follow in our rounds
  Offended similarly to Caesar's offence,
  Against whose triumph the cry of "Queen!" resounds.   78
Therefore they are split from us, and hence
  They cry out "Sodom!" in their self-reproach,
  Helping the flames with shame that burns intense.
Our sin was hermaphrodite, and since that broach
  Of human law in following our lust
  Like brutish animals, when we approach,   84
Since we are infamous, so we have thrust
  On us the name of her turned beast, concealed
  Within the brutal framework, cased and trussed.
You know our deeds, our guilt is now revealed,
  But much too long a time we would expend
  If you expect me now each name to yield.   90
But I will satisfy the wish you extend
  Towards me: Guido Guinicelli you address,
  Purging from full repentance at my end.'
I was as in Lycurgus' bitterness
  The two sons were, seeing their mother's plight –
  But not so much emotion did I express,   96
When I heard him name himself – by right
  My father, and of my betters, whoever wrought
  Rhymes of love so sweetly and so light.
And deaf and dumbfound then I moved, in thought,
  Gazing a long time on him, but for the blaze
  I drew no nearer to him though I sought.   102
When I had satisfied my mind and gaze
  I offered, with the oath that will compel
  Belief, the ready service of my days.
And he replied: 'You leave, as I hear tell,
  Traces so deep and clear no Lethe draws
  Oblivion over them nor dims with its swell.   108
But if your word swore truth, tell me the cause
  Why you should hold me dear as indicated
  Both in your eyes and in each word and pause.'

I said: 'Because the sweet songs you created,
    As long as native speech is used and sung,
114   Ensure their very ink is venerated.'
'Ah, brother,' he said, 'I point to one among
    Us with this finger,' at a shade who'd passed,
    'A better workman in the mother tongue.
His verse of love, his prose romance, outclassed
    Us all – and let fools babble on who say
120   He was by that man in Limoges surpassed.
To rumour, not to truth, they turn away
    Their faces; they have fixed their view before
    They hear what art or reason would convey.
Thus many of our fathers used to roar
    And clamour out Guittone's praise alone;
126   But truth prevails with most now on that score.
Yet, if you've had so great a privilege shown
    You that you journey to the cloister where
    Christ's abbot of the college not of stone,
Say a Paternoster for me there
    So far as it befits us here with mind
132   And power to sin no longer ours to snare.'
Then, maybe giving place to one behind,
    He vanished through the flames now he had done,
    As fish dive to the mud and leave us blind.
I drew a little forward to the one
    He'd pointed out; my yearning I expressed
138   To bring his name the gratitude he'd won.
Eagerly he started: 'Your courteous request
    Pleases me so I can't and won't and ought
    Not hide myself from you and your behest.
I'm Arnaut that weep and sing at once: in thought
    I see my previous madness; I see sublime
144   Before me too that day of joy I sought.
I pray you by the Good that helps you climb
    And to the summit of the stair aspire,
Be mindful of my pain in due time.'
    And then he hid in the refining fire.

CANTO 27

Dante is fearful of entering the fire at the angel's command until Vergil finds a way to give him courage. Crossing the flames they reach the steps upward but night waylays them. Dante dreams prophetically of his future experiences. When they reach the top step Vergil informs him that his task as guide is finished, both because his knowledge ends here and because Dante's will, now perfect, is his own guide. The Latin, line 8, means 'Blessed are the pure in heart' (Matthew 5.8). Line 58 means 'Come, ye blessed of my Father' (Matthew 25.34).

As when he shoots his earliest beam and flare
    Where his Creator's precious blood was shed,
    While Ebro falls beneath the Scales, that lofty pair,
And Ganges burns with noon-tide overhead,
    So stood the sun; thus day was fading here
    When God's glad angel appeared before our tread.   6
He stood outside the flames along the tier,
    And sang '*Beati mundo corde,*' in ringing
    Voice much more clear than ours are on the ear.
Then, 'There's no further way unless the stinging
    Of fire bite you first: enter the flame
    And don't be deaf toward the distant singing,'   12
He said as we approached him. I became
    More like a body buried when I learned
    What he had paused in singing to proclaim.
I raised my clasped hands up, my gaze I turned
    Into the fire, and I imagined there,
    Vividly, bodies that I'd once seen burned.   18
My kindly escorts turned to me in care,
    And Vergil then explained: 'My son, it may
    Be torment, but not death, within that flare.
Remember, remember, in the evil bay
    I guided you on Geryon safe and sound.
    What shall I do, nearer to God today?   24
Be sure: if you a thousand years were bound
    Within the heart of all this flame, no harm
    Would touch a single hair with which you're crowned.
And if you think I'm lying, reach your arm
    Closer to them and make this test to see,
    Touching your garment's surface with your palm.   30

Put fear aside, put it aside,' said he.
    'Turn and come onwards safely through the heat.'
    But I was rooted, conscience accusing me.
Seeing me stubborn still with rooted feet,
    Troubled a little, he said: 'Son, look: there lies
36   Between yourself and Beatrice this wall – or street.'
As, at the name of Thisbe, Pyramus' eyes
    Opened at point of death to gaze on her
    When the mulberry reddened in its dyes,
So softened was my stubbornness to stir.
    I turned to my wise guide, hearing her name
42   That always rises in my mind as spur.
At this he shook his head: 'What, do we aim
    To stay this side?' he asked, and showed the smile
    A child, won by an apple, draws as on I came.
Before me through the fire he led the file,
    Asking that Statius follow where I'd stepped –
48   Who'd split us on the road for such a while.
Once there, in molten glass I would have leapt
    To cool myself, so immeasurable the heat
    That burned me as across the flames we swept.
My sweet father, encouraging, would repeat
    Again and again the thought of Beatrice; say:
54   'Her eyes already now I seem to meet.'
A voice was guiding us along the way
    From opposite and we, intent, were led
    To come out where the steps bid us essay.
'*Venite benedicti patris mei*,' said
    A light that shone so brightly that my sight
60   Was blinded by the dazzle that it shed.
'The sun is setting,' it added, 'and the night
    Approaches: don't delay; increase your pace
    While in the west remains a little light.'
The way rose straight into the rocky face
    So that ahead of me I blocked the sun
66   Which was already sinking to its base.
We tried a few steps but hardly were they done
    When I and both the sages saw the light
    Had set behind, since shadow was there none.
Before the horizon's immensity and might
    Had turned one colour and the dark had spread
72   Over all her dominion of the night,

Each of us made a single step our bed
    Because the nature of the mount denied
    The power, not the urge, to forge ahead.
As goats are agile on the mountainside
    And gambol prior to feeding but grow tame
    While ruminating, and peaceably abide   78
Within the shade when sun is all aflame,
    Guarded by the herdsman who has leant
    On his crook but, leaning, minds them just the same;
And, as the shepherd beneath the firmament
    Lodges and keeps a silent watch by night
    For fear his flock is spread by beasts and rent –   84
So then we were, all three: myself, as might
    Be goat, and they the herdsmen, in that ravine
    Bound by high rock on both sides of the flight.
Little of the outside could be seen
    But through the gap I saw the stars more bright
    And larger than their normal size and sheen.   90
As I was pondering this, and on their light,
    Sleep fell on me, sleep that often knows
    The news before the deed appear to sight.
At that time when Cytherea, who glows
    Forever with love's fire, first shone her beam
    Upon the peak from eastward as she rose,   96
It seemed I saw a lady in my dream,
    Lovely and young, going along a plain
    Gathering flowers, and singing on this theme:
'Know, whoever seeks my name to gain,
    That I am Leah; using my hands I fare,
    Making a garland and a flower-chain;   102
To please me in my glass I deck my hair.
    Rachel, my sister, never once she stirs
    Before her glass, and all day gazes there.
She's keen to watch those lovely eyes of hers
    As I to deck myself, to cull and roam.
    I'm active; contemplation she prefers.'   108
Now, at the splendour of pre-solar gloam,
    That spreads, for those returning, a grateful sight
    Because they lodge each night more near to home,
In all directions fled the shades of night,
    And sleep went with them; so I rose to find
    My masters risen already to the light.   114

'That sweet fruit, for which all mortal kind
    Seeks on so many boughs, will give today
    Your hunger satisfaction in soul and mind.'
These were the words I then heard Vergil say;
    And never have there been gifts to invite
120   A pleasure like the one those words convey.
So much did yearning on yearning then incite
    Me on to be above, each stride ahead
    I felt my wings grow strong to make the flight.
When once the stairs had rushed beneath our tread
    And we were on the topmost, Vergil turned
126   And fixed his eyes on me, and this he said:
'The temporal, the eternal fires that burned,
    You now have seen, my son, and reached the part
    Where I myself no further have discerned.
I've led you here by wit and by my art;
    Take your own pleasure as your guidance now.
132   Out of the steep way, out of the narrow, start.
Behold the sun that shines upon your brow;
    Behold the tender grass, the shrubs and flowers
    The ground brings forth without the hand or plough.
While the glad and lovely eyes (whose tears were powers
    That made me rush to you) are coming here,
138   You may sit down or walk amid these bowers.
No further word or sign expect to appear
    From me. Your will is free, whole, upright now.
Wrong would it be to give its voice no ear.
    Therefore I place your crown and mitre on your brow.'

CANTO 28

Dante, exploring, encounters a lovely maiden, Matilda, who explains the details of the Garden to him. It is the morning of Wednesday 13 April, the sixth day of the journey, when Dante enters the Garden of our lost earthly happiness. The Latin, line 80, means 'thou hast made me glad' from Psalm 92 (Vulgate 91).

Keen to explore both outside and within
    The divine forest, lush and green, whose sight
    Tempered the new day ready to begin,
Without delay I left the mountain height,
    Crossing the plain with lingering steps on ground
    That breathed all round a fragrance of delight.   6
A sweet, unchanging air was stroking round
    My brow with just the merest touch as made
    By a soft breeze, so in the wood I found
The boughs responsive to it were all swayed
    Freely to where the holy mountain-crest
    Casts down its earliest and longest shade,   12
Yet never swayed so much from upright rest
    To stop the little birds that still could sing
    In them and practise all their arts with zest.
They sang in all their gladness welcoming
    The earliest hours in the leaves that lent
    Their rhymes accompaniment in whispering,   18
Just as from bough to bough the sound is sent
    Through pine-woods on Chiassi's shore, set free
    By Aeolus giving the Sirocco vent.
And soon my leisured pace had taken me
    So deep a way into the ancient wood
    My entry point I could no longer see,   24
And further progress there a brook withstood.
    Towards the left its little waves were bending
    The grass that tilted from the bank so good.
The purest waters, here, contain some blending,
    Admixtures, in comparison with this stream
    That hides no single thing in all its wending,   30
Although it courses under the extreme
    Darkness of the everlasting shade
    Where neither sun nor moon may cast its beam.

My step I stopped and with my eyes I made
   Across beyond the stream so I could see
36   The great May-fresh variety displayed;
And there appeared to me, as suddenly
   A thing appears that in our wonderment
   Turns every other thought to vacancy,
A lady quite alone, following her bent,
   Singing and selecting flower from flower
42   That painted all the way on which she went.
'Fair lady who warm yourself in the ray-shower
   Of love – if I may trust looks that give clear
   Witness of the heart – I pray: empower
Me – if it may please you to draw near
   And closer to the stream,' I sent my prayer,
48   'So that what you are singing I may hear.
You make me bring to mind just what and where
   Proserpine was, the time her mother lost
   Her and she spring,' I said; and – as a fair
Lady in dancing turns, foot hardly crossed
   By foot, both close together on the ground
54   They hardly leave – so she, on floret-mossed
Yellows and reds of flowerets, turned around
   Towards me as a virgin would do here,
   Veiling her modest eyes to sight and sound,
And granted my request, drawing quite near
   So that I heard the sweetness of the air
60   And all its meaning sounded in my ear.
As soon as she had come to where the fair
   River just lapped the grass with waves, she deemed
   Her eyes might lift to look upon me there.
I don't believe so bright a light had beamed
   Beneath the lids of Venus, by her son's bow
66   Pierced, against his practice, as it seemed.
She smiled out from the right bank of that flow,
   Arranging many colours in her hands,
   That the high land bears though no man sow.
Three steps the stream estranged us – in different lands;
   But Hellespont (where Xerxes chose to cross –
72   That as a curb to pride to this day stands)
Drew from Leander no more hate for the toss
   And turmoil of its waves, than this from me –
   Despite its turbulence, Sestos to Abydos.

And she began: 'Newcomers you must be,
    And, seeing me here, smiling in the place
    Chosen for the human race's nursery,   78
Perhaps some doubt bewilders, in which case
    The psalm, '*Delectasti*', gives light to clear
    The mist in understanding that you face.
And you in front who spoke, if you would hear
    Anything further, say. To satisfy
    And answer all your questions I've drawn near.'   84
'The music of the forest, then,' said I,
    'And the water work against my fresh belief
    In something which appears to give the lie.'
She said: 'I'll tell you from what cause, in chief,
    That comes to make you wonder; and persuade
    Away the mist that draws you to the reef.   90
High Good, that alone pleases itself, had made
    Man good, and for the good, and gave this place
    As promise of eternal peace never to fade.
Through his own fault he stayed just a brief space
    Sojourning here; through his own fault he chose
    Sweat, tears, not sweet play and laughing face.   96
In order that the storms (which come from throes
    And exhalations of the earth, the water
    Beneath, that rise to join the heat that grows)
Should bring no man to any harm or slaughter,
    This mountain rose towards the Heaven's bound;
    From where it's locked, stands safe above their quarter. 102
Now then, since all the air must circle round
    Within the primal motion – unless it be
    Impeded in some areas such as high ground –
Its movement beats upon this height, all free
    In the living air, and makes the wood resound
    Because it is so dense with shrub and tree.   108
The plants so stirred with such a power abound
    They seed the air-flow with their potent worth,
    And it in circling scatters this around
So that the other land conceives, as earth
    And climate suit the seed, and brings from these
    Varied virtues varied plants to birth.   114
If this were understood, it wouldn't tease
    The mind with wonder, there, when plant or flower,
    Without apparent seed, takes root with ease.

The holy plain, where you are, is a bower,
  As you must know, for every seed, and brings
120   Forth fruit not yonder plucked by earthly power.
The stream you see wells from no earthly springs,
  Fed by the moisture which the cold condenses,
  As rivers gain or lose their showerings,
But from a constant fountain that dispenses;
  And, by God's will, regains as much as it
126   Freely expends on either side it drenches.
This side, it flows with power and benefit
  To take from men the memory of sin done;
  It gives remembrance of good deeds opposite.
Lethe, this side, and, on the other one,
  Eunoë, it is called. Nor can it heal
132   Except both sides be tasted where they run.
And this excels all savours. – If I reveal
  No other thing, the queries that you place
  Have all been clarified, and yet, I feel,
In adding this corollary as a grace
  My words to you will hardly be less dear
138   In reaching past my promise in this case.
Those, in the old poetic days, who sang so clear
  The age of gold, and all its happy state,
  Dreamed on Parnassus, perhaps, of this land here.
Innocent here was mankind's root; the date
  Of spring's eternal, as is every fruit;
144   This is the nectar each of them relate.'
I spun round on the poets standing mute,
  And saw the smiles with which they took this grace,
This last interpretation; and, resolute,
  Back to the lovely lady turned my face.

CANTO 29

This is probably the least successful in poetic terms of all Dante's cantos, based as it is on allegory rather than his lyrical and dramatic imagination. It consists of an observed historical pageant of the Christian Church which is almost lost on a modern reader.

The seven candlesticks are the seven churches of Revelations 1.12, 20. They may also represent the seven gifts of the Spirit: Wisdom, Understanding, Counsel, Might, Knowledge, Compassion, and Fear of the Lord (Isaiah 11.2–3). The seven pennons represent the seven sacraments and their rainbow colours may allude to Revelations 4.3. The 'ten-pace break' that spans them may allude to the Ten Commandments. The twenty-four elders represent the books of the Old Testament – with some amalgamations. The four Beasts are described in Ezekiel 1.4–14 and Revelations 4.6–9; they represent Matthew, Mark, Luke and John, the Gospels. The green leaves represent hope. The six wings represent the six laws: natural, Mosaic, prophetic, evangelical, Apostolic and canonical. The two wheels that bear the chariot of the Church are the contemplative and the active ways of faith. The Griffon represents the dual nature of Christ, with one of its wings standing for mercy, the other for truth/justice. The three dancers are faith, hope and charity with representative colours. The four dancers by the other wheel are the cardinal virtues; their purple represents the imperial traditions of Rome. The reverend pair are Luke, the physician, and St Paul, martyred by the sword, or bearing 'the sword of the spirit which is the word of God'. The penultimate four are James, Peter, John and Jude, authors of the general epistles. They are followed by John, author of the book of Revelations. The rose and red flowers may represent the charity expounded in the New Testament. The Latin, line 2, means 'Blessed is he whose sins are covered', Psalm 32 (Vulgate 31). The Authorized Version is 'Blessed is he whose sins are forgiven.'

Her words were over; then, as if in love,
   'Beati quorum tecta sunt peccata,'
   She sang and raised this lovely sound above.
As nymphs who used to wander off apart
   Through woodland shades, and one decide on light
   And sun, another to avoid its dart,   6
So she advanced upstream along the right,
   Walking the bank, and I, abreast of her,
   Matching her slight step with step as slight.
No hundred steps of ours were to occur
   When both banks wound in such a way I found
   I faced the east, and was her follower.   12

Nor had we gone much more when, turning round,
    My lady faced me fully as she said:
    'My brother, look! Listen to every sound!'
Lo, everywhere a sudden brilliance spread
    Throughout the great forest, so that I thought
18   It might be lightning flashing overhead.
But as the lightning ends with its onslaught
    But this endured and brighter, brighter shone,
    I thought, 'What is this light, and how's it wrought?'
Through luminous air sweet melody ran on;
    At which a righteous zeal made me reprove
24   The daring of the way that Eve had gone:
When, there, where Heaven and earth obedient move,
    That she, a woman, alone, and newly made,
    No veil could tolerate, nor yet approve;
Whereas if she'd remained devout, and stayed
    Beneath it, I'd have tasted of these joys
30   Ineffable, sooner, longer, undelayed.
While I was going where the first fruits poise
    In the eternal pleasure, enrapt,
    And yearning for still further sights and joys,
The air before us, under green boughs capped,
    Became just like a flaming fire; each chord,
36   So sweet, into a chant seemed to adapt.
– O holy, holy Virgins, if I've ignored
    Hunger, fatigue and cold to serve your art,
    The time spurs me to claim my just reward.
Now is it meet that Helicon should dart
    Forth and Urania with her choir give aid
42   To set in verse things hard for mind to chart. –
And farther off, a false appearance, made
    By the long vista from object to the eyes,
    An image of seven golden trees conveyed.
But when they neared me so the general guise,
    Which can mislead the sense, no longer blurred
48   The detail through distance and apparent size,
The faculty by which they are referred
    To reason, saw that candlesticks were there
    And, in the chant, 'Hosanna' was the word.
The lovely pageant flamed upon the air
    Much brighter than the moon, mid-month, in skies
54   Of midnight that are serene and bare.

And, full of wonderment, I turned my eyes
    To the good Vergil who answered with a face
    No less astounded in his deep surmise.
I turned my countenance back round to trace
    Those sublime things so slowly reaching us
    That brides just married would outstrip their pace.   60
The lady called to me: 'Why curious
    Only about the vision of shining light
    And to what follows quite oblivious?'
Then I beheld the people clad in white;
    They followed as behind their leaders; sheer
    Whiteness like theirs, on earth an unknown sight.   66
The water on my left was bright and clear,
    Reflecting back to me my left-hand side
    When, there, as in a mirror, I would peer.
When on the bank's edge so that the divide
    Narrowed to water only, I stopped to see
    The better, and just there restrained my stride.   72
I saw the flames advance and, trailing free
    Behind, the air was painted till it streamed
    And waving pennons now appeared to be.
And thus the air behind was streaked and teemed
    With seven bands in hues and tints that make
    The sun's bow, and in Delia's girdle gleamed.   78
These banners flowed to rearward in the wake
    Beyond the eyesight; and I judged to be,
    Between the outer pair, a ten-pace break.
Beneath the sky, as fair as shown by me,
    Came four and twenty elders, two by two,
    And each of them was crowned with fleur-de-lys.   84
And all of them were singing, 'Blest be you
    Among all Adam's daughters, and to eternity,
    Blest be your loveliness so fair and true.'
And, when the flowers and tender herbs were free
    Of those elected ones upon the bank
    That lay directly opposite from me,   90
Even as star follows star within the rank
    Of Heaven, four creatures came along behind,
    Each crowned with leaves of green, and flank by flank.
And each was fledged with sixfold wings inclined,
    The feathers full of eyes – Argus' eyes,
    Were they alive, would be of selfsame kind.   96

– I'll sprinkle no more rhymes on form and size,
   Reader, for other issues now require
   Me, so I cannot lavishly devise.
But read Ezekiel who depicts entire
   Their coming from the regions of the cold
102   With whirlwind and with cloud and with the fire.
For here, they were as you will find it told
   Within his pages, except that John is more
   With me, than him, about the wings – sixfold.
Within the space that lay amid these four,
   Upon two wheels went a triumphal car,
108   Drawn from a Griffon's neck across the floor.
He raised up both his wings upon a par
   Between the midmost and the three and three
   Pennons so that they would not cut or mar.
They rose so high their tips no one could see;
   His limbs were golden where he was a bird;
114   The coat was white and vermilion mixedly.
Neither Augustus nor Africanus stirred
   Rome to rejoicing with a chariot so fair
   That even the sun's itself were poor and blurred,
The sun's itself that, straying in the air,
   Was once consumed at earth's devout appeal
120   When Jove brought justice secretly to bear.
Three maids divine beside the right-hand wheel
   Came dancing in a round, and one so red
   That in the fire her form she might conceal.
The next had emerald, it seemed, instead
   Of flesh and bone; the third as though
126   Of newly fallen snow she had been bred.
Led by the white, they seemed, and then they go
   By her in red, and from that song the group
   Took up their tempo either fast or slow.
Beside the left wheel four came in a troop,
   Dressed in purple, festive in their dance,
132   Following a three-eyed one beside the hoop.
Behind the whole depicted I saw advance
   Two agèd men, unlike in garb, the same
   In bearing, venerable, grave of glance.
One showed himself a member of the name
   And house of great Hippocrates – made
138   By nature for her dearest creature's claim.

The other showed the opposite, with blade
    That was so sharp and bright a sword held high,
    That even on this the bank I felt afraid.
Then four of lowly bearing caught my eye,
    And, after them, an old and lonely man,
    His keen face in a trance, was coming by.   144
These seven dressed like the first, except there ran
    About their venerable brows no round
    Or wreath of lilies, but each one with a span
Of roses and other crimson blooms was crowned.
    You would have sworn, if looking from afar,
    That it was flames in which their heads were wound.   150
And then I heard, just as the holy car
    Came opposite, a thunderclap: the noble folk
Appeared to find their movement met some bar;
    Their ensigns halted and their step they broke.

CANTO 30

While the wain of Heaven is stationary Dante encounters Beatrice in a moment full of awe, and feels the shame of the years ignoring her. (The word given as 'wain' here, in Italian 'settentrion', contains the idea of seven lights, which may allude to the seven gifts of the Spirit.) Beatrice had died in 1290 so that, by the time of the notional date of the poem, Dante had not seen her for ten years.

In line 21, Dante has adapted the Latin from the Aeneid 6.883 as his parting compliment to his guide, Vergil. It means: 'Oh, give lilies with full hands'. To rhyme this, Dante uses more Latin; the first means 'at the voice of so great an elder', the second 'Blessed is he that cometh' (Matthew 21.9). Line 11 means 'Come with me from Lebanon, my spouse' (Song of Solomon 4.8), the spouse symbolizing the Church. The phrase 'ancient flame' (line 48) is another citation from the Aeneid 4.23. In line 82, the Latin means: 'In thee, Lord, we hope'; in line 84, Pedes meos refers to Psalm 31 (Vulgate 30): 'my feet'. The full sentence is: 'Thou hast set my feet in a large room.'

When this wain of the first Heaven (that never knew
    Setting nor rise nor any mists that hide,
    Except of sin, and guided all to do
Their duty there as here our Wain's the guide
    For him who steers the ship into the sound)
6   Had stopped, the people of the truth that stride
Between it and the Griffon, as I found
    At first, then turned towards the holy wain
    As to their peace; and like a herald bound
From Heaven, one of them sang this refrain
    Three times: 'Veni, sponsa, de Libano',
12   And all the others sang it out again.
As all the saints, when the last trump shall blow,
    Will rise out of the tomb with voice reclad,
    And sing their 'Hallelujah' as they go,
So from the wain there rose a hundred, glad
    To answer 'ad vocem tanti senis',
18   Messengers of eternal life, to add
These words: 'Benedictus qui venis';
    And, throwing flowers everywhere around,
    'Manibus o date lilia plenis'.
Once, at the dawning of the day, I found
    The eastern regions rosy red, elsewhere
24   The Heaven with a lovely clearness crowned,

And then the sun rise shadowed in its glare
    So that, because mist tempers it, the eye
    Could tolerate the light a long time there.
So, in a cloud of flowers that flew on high
    From those angelic hands and fluttered down
    Again inside the wain and round and by,   30
With a white veil beneath an olive crown,
    A Lady appeared to me, her mantle green
    On hue of living flame that was her gown.
My spirit that so long a time had seen
    Since I had trembled in her presence last,
    And broken with the weight of awe had been,   36
Without more reinforcement of glance cast,
    Through hidden virtue that went out from her
    Felt the great power of ancient love bind fast.
The instant that my sight received the spur
    Of that high virtue which, when I was just
    A boy, had pierced me first, my actions were   42
To turn towards my left with all the trust
    Of child in mother here, if it became
    Frightened or hurt from tumbling in the dust,
'Each drop of blood,' I wanted to exclaim
    To Vergil, 'is trembling now in every limb;
    I know the traces of the ancient flame.'   48
But Vergil had left us now deprived of him,
    Vergil, the sweetest father, Vergil to whom,
    For my salvation, I bent my will and whim.
Not all our ancient mother lost to doom
    Could help me then to keep my dew-washed face
    From turning in its tears so dark with gloom.   54
'Dante, because Vergil leaves and gives place
    Do not weep yet, do not weep yet:
    You must weep for other sword in due space.'
Just as an admiral from stern to bow will get
    To see the crews of other ships and urge
    Them on to valiant deeds in battle's threat,   60
So did I see, when sight turned to converge,
    Hearing my name (which therefore must be written
    Here), to leftward of the car, emerge
The Lady who seemed veiled at first and hidden
    Amid the festival of angels, but had bound
    Her vision to the bank where I was bidden.   66

Although the veil that hung from her head, crowned
   With Minerva's leaves, did not allow
   Her features to be clearly seen, I found
She was a queen in bearing; stern of brow,
   She still maintained herself, like one who'd dam
72   Back last the hottest words in speaking now:
'Look at me straight. Truly I am; I am
   Truly Beatrice. How dared you climb the mount?
   Didn't you know that here man's happy in the Lamb?'
I cast my eyes down to the crystal fount,
   But saw my face in it, and turned to the grass,
78   My brow weighed down with shame's prolonged account.
So, to the child, the mother seems to pass
   Harsh judgements, as then she seemed to me;
   For pity that is firm tastes sharp as glass.
She stood silent. '*In te, Domine, speravi,*'
   The angels sang, but did not go beyond
84   '*Pedes meos*' in their choristry.
As, on live rafters of Italy's back, the bond
   Of snow freezes underneath the blast
   And stress of Slavonian winds as they abscond,
Then, melting, trickles through itself at last
   If, coming out of shade, the land but breathe,
90   So that it seems flame melts the candle's cast,
So without tears I was, or sighs to seethe,
   Until that song of those who harmonize
   Their notes in music that the spheres enwreathe.
But when I heard in those sweet chords the rise
   Of their compassion, more than if they'd said:
96   'Lady, why do you shame him and chastise?',
The ice which had enclosed my heart was fled
   To breath and water, and with anguish ran
   Out of my heart; from mouth and eyes was shed.
She, standing firm beside the car, began
   And turned her words towards those angels who
102   Had pitied me: 'You angels in the span
Of everlasting day keep watch and view
   So neither night nor sleep may steal a pace
   The world takes in its course away from you;
Therefore, my answer with more care I'll trace
   So that this weeping man may comprehend
108   And sorrow's measure balance sin's disgrace.

Not only by the mighty spheres that send
    Each seed towards some aim in their design,
    According as companion stars attend,
But by largesse of graces so divine
    They pour down from such high and lofty cloud
    They can't be reached with eyes like yours or mine,   114
In early life this man was one endowed
    In essence with such talents for the good
    They'd come to wondrous proof, had he allowed.
But then the soil that's strong and fertile would
    Become more rank and wild with evil seed
    If no one cultivated as they should.   120
My countenance sustained him from misdeed
    Awhile. I showed my youthful eyes to him,
    And led him in the true life he should lead.
But as I trod the threshold, on the rim
    Into my second age of life, he drew
    Apart and to another in his whim.   126
And when I rose from flesh to spirit, grew
    In loveliness and virtue, I was less
    Pleasing to him, less precious in his view.
And so he turned his step aside to press
    Along a way not true, for lying visions
    Of good that pay no promise they profess.   132
Nor was there any use in all my missions
    To gain him inspirations, signs and dream,
    To call him back – deaf to my admonitions.
He sank so low that all ways to redeem
    His soul were useless unless it were to spread
    Before him people lost in Hell's extreme.   138
I visited the portals of the dead
    For this, and to the one who guided him
    As high as this my weeping prayers were said.
And it would break God's high decrees if the brim
    Of Lethe should be crossed, or any taste
    Be given without some penitence in him,   144
    The debt of tears for all the years of waste.'

CANTO 31

Beatrice continues, now speaking directly to Dante who is ashamed and shows his repentance. The angels appeal for her to let him see her face unveiled. He sees in her eyes the dual nature of Christ reflected. The Latin, line 98, means 'Cleanse me' (Psalm 51; Vulgate 50).

'O you upon the sacred stream's far side,'
　　She aimed her speech with point direct at me –
　　Its previous edge was sharp enough applied.
She went on without any hesitancy:
　　'Say, say if this be true: for so accused
6　　You must confess to such iniquity.'
My powers were so confounded and confused
　　That speech began and then its force had fled
　　Before it struggled from the organs used.
She waited for a little, then she said:
　　'What are you thinking? Answer me. Your sad
12　　Memories are not yet cleansed by tears you've shed.'
Confusion mixed with fear drove lips to add
　　A 'Yes!' that only could be comprehended
　　If eyes could see the look which then I had.
As breaks a crossbow if too much extended,
　　Both string and bow, and with a lesser force
18　　Towards its target flies the bolt intended,
So with this charge I burst in my remorse
　　And such a torrent of tears and sighs expired,
　　My voice in process dried up at its source.
Therefore she said: 'In all your yearning fired
　　For me which led you to the love of good –
24　　Beyond the which is nothing to be aspired –
What chains then did you find where you were stood?
　　What cross-trenches made you give up hope
　　Of passing onward, upward, as you should?
And what allurements, advantages or scope
　　Were shown you in the way others appeared
30　　That you must serve them and descend the slope?'
After heaving a bitter sigh that seared
　　I scarce had voice to answer and my lips
　　Laboured to shape the words that slowly cleared.

Weeping I said: 'Immediate things with grips
   Of falsest pleasure turned my steps aside
   As soon as your face was covered in eclipse.'   36
And she: 'If you were silent, or denied
   What now you have confessed, the fault were none
   The less observed: such is the Judge who tried.
But when self-accusation bursts to run
   From cheeks before our court, the grindstone turns
   Backward to blunt the blade – as now is done.   42
Yet, so that you can bear the shame that burns
   For your transgression, so that, another time,
   Hearing the sirens, your heart more staunchly spurns,
Set by the seed of weeping for your crime
   And listen how my dead and buried flesh
   Should have moved you to a counter-aim sublime.   48
Nature or Art never offered you so fresh,
   So great a pleasure as the lovely-limbed
   Body I wore – now dust in the wind's thresh.
And, if that highest pleasure failed or dimmed
   For you when I was dead, what mortal thing
   Beside should draw your longing? You should have
      skimmed,   54
Truly, and mounted soaring on the wing,
   After the first shot of deceptive things,
   To me, no more in such entrammelling.
Young girls, or other vanity that brings
   Such brief enjoyment, never should have weighed
   Your wings to risk more danger from the slings.   60
The fledgling's struck by two or three, but laid
   In vain the net, the arrow shot in vain,
   Before the eyes of full-fledged birds displayed.'
As children, dumb with shame, will stand and train
   Their eyes on earth and listen, self-confessing,
   And in repentance silent they remain,   66
So stood I. She said: 'Since you're expressing
   Grief for what you hear, lift up your beard
   And more grief will you feel to see your blessing.'
Strong oak's uprooted – with less resistance, upreared,
   Whether by one of our winds or one that blows
   From the kingdom of Iarbas veered –   72

Than, at her order, I raised up chin and nose,
    And when she named my face by saying 'beard'
    I well knew the venom of the point she chose.
And when I'd raised my face and straight appeared,
    My eyes observed the primal creatures resting
78   After strewing round the flowers as she neared.
And then my eyes, not steady in their questing,
    Saw Beatrice turned towards the Beast that is
    One single Person, two natures investing.
Beneath her veil at the river's distances,
    To me she seemed to surpass her old self there
84   As, here, she passed all other presences.
Repentance stabbed me so, I could not bear
    Of all things else the single thing that drew
    My longing and my love beyond compare.
Remorse so gnawed my heart it overthrew
    Me and I fell down. What I then became
90   She knows who was the cause I yielded to.
Then when my heart restored to me the claim
    Of outward things, the lady I'd seen alone
    Was gazing on me. I heard her to exclaim:
'Hold on, hold on to me!' To the neck-bone
    She'd drawn me in the stream and, pulling me
96   Behind her, crossed, light as a shuttle flown.
When near the blessèd bank I seemed to be,
    I heard '*Asperges me!*' so sweetly sung
    I can't recall, recount its melody.
The lovely woman, her arms wide open flung,
    Grasped my head and pushed it in the flow
102   So that I swallowed water as I clung.
She pulled me out, bathed, and made me go
    To join the fairest ones within the dance,
    And with their arms each sheltered me below.
'Here we are nymphs; in Heaven as stars advance.
    We were ordained her handmaids long before
108   Beatrice descended to the world of chance.
We'll bring you sight of her; those three more,
    Across the other side, who deeper gaze,
    Upon the joyous light will help you pore.'
So, singing, they began, and led my ways
    Towards the Griffon's breast where Beatrice stood
114   Turning on us those eyes of dazzling rays.

They said: 'Make certain not to hide or hood
   Your eyes; we've set you before the emerald
   From which Love drew on you his shafts of good.'
A thousand desires hotter than flames scald
   Held my eyes bound to those shining eyes
   That stayed upon the Griffon, fixed, enthralled.   120
As sun within a mirror, not otherwise,
   The twofold beast within her pupils shone:
   One nature then the other seemed to rise.
Think, reader, if I marvelled, gazing on
   The thing that in itself was motionless
   Yet in its image change had undergone.   126
And while my soul in wonder and joyfulness
   Was tasting of that food which, satisfying
   Itself, still leaves a thirst for it to bless,
The other three, whose bearing was implying
   They were of higher order, forward swept,
   In their angelic dancing unifying: 132
'Turn, Beatrice, turn your holy eyes; accept
   Your faithful one who just to see your face
   Through such long journeyings has stepped.
Unveil; do us the favour of your grace,
   Show him your mouth so he may have in sight
   The second loveliness you hide from trace.'   138
O splendour of the living eternal light!
   Who that has grown so pale in Parnassus' shade,
   Or drunk so deeply at its well, but might
Not seem to be too cumbersome and staid
   Of mind in trying to record, express
How you appeared, Heaven's harmonies arrayed   144
   Above you, when you showed your loveliness?

CANTO 32

Beatrice speaks in a more kindly way after Dante has nearly lost his sight through gazing on her radiance. She suggests he should be a forester guardian of the Church with her. Dante observes weird events happening to the holy chariot. These allegorize the history of the church in terms of the heresies and misdirections it has suffered. One of the chief of these, in Dante's view, is its entanglement with secular government through the Donation of Constantine – not to mention the she-wolf of avarice.

My eyes were so intently fixed to fill
    Their ten-year thirst that every other sense
    Was quenched in me and rendered dull and still;
To either side they had a wall and fence
    Of heedlessness, so well the holy smile
6   Drew them to itself in toils of long hence;
But then, perforce, my face was turned awhile
    To left as those divine ones caught my ear,
    Saying: 'Too long you gaze; too fixed a style.'
And that condition of the eyes that peer
    Too long into the sun made me remain
12   A little while with sight obscured and blear.
When it restored itself enough again
    To see the lesser (lesser, I mean, in respect
    To greater which it could no more sustain),
I saw the glorious host had wheeled and checked
    On the right flank, returning with the sun;
18   The seven flames before its face erect.
As, under shields, a troop turns on the run
    And wheels around behind its colours before
    It can completely change its van as one,
So did the ranks of Heaven's soldier-corps
    That made the van wheel past within our view,
24   Before the pole brought round the car once more.
The maids returned to the wheel; the Griffon drew
    The hallowed burden so that not a plume
    Was ruffled on it as it processed through.
The lovely lady who'd brought me through the spume
    Was following – and so were Statius and I –
30   The wheel that made its turn in lesser room.

Crossing the lofty forest, emptied by
    Eve's credence in the Snake, the angels' song
    Gave us the timing for our steps. But nigh
On three flights of an arrow passed along,
    Perhaps, advancing through that holy land,
    When Beatrice descended in that throng.   36
I heard them murmur 'Adam!' and take their stand
    Around a tree with leaf and flower shed
    From every single bough on either hand.
The more it rises so the branches spread
    Its crown the wider; it would be a tower
    Of wondrous height to forest Indians. All said: 42
'Blessèd are you, Griffon; you don't devour,
    Rending with your beak, this tree so sweet
    To taste – that turns the belly sick and sour,'
Around the sturdy tree. The beast, complete
    In dual nature: 'The seed of righteousness
    Is thus preserved.' And, turning round to meet   48
The shaft he'd drawn, toward the blossomless
    And widowed tree he dragged it, left it bound,
    Using a branch, that grew there, like a jess.
As plants of ours as the great light round
    Them falls when blended with the rays that beam
    Behind the Heavenly Carp spring from the ground,   54
Their colour new, before the solar team
    Is yoked beneath the next stars circling there,
    So spreading colour, less than rose would seem,
But more than violet, the tree grew fair,
    And had renewed itself where once each limb
    And branch had been so naked and so bare.   60
I did not understand, nor is the hymn
    The people raised sung here, nor could endure
    Outright the anthem of that interim.
If I could show how eyes, ruthless and sure,
    Could fall to sleep when told of Syrinx, eyes
    Whose length of vigil cost so dear a cure,   66
As painter from a model I'd realize
    And picture how I'd fallen off to sleep;
    Paint drowsiness whoever can devise!
So to the time I wakened now I'll leap
    And say a bright light ripped my sleep from me
    And then the call: 'Arise, why sleep so deep?'   72

As to see some florets of the apple tree
 (That makes the angels hunger for its fruit
 And spreads perpetual marriage-feast in Heaven's lea)
Peter, John and James, brought to that root
 And overwhelmed, came to themselves to hear
78 The Word that broke a sleep more absolute,
And saw their band begin to disappear
 As Moses and Elias vanished, while yet
 Their Lord's robe was transfigured, so, here,
I came round; my returning vision met
 The lady of pity bending, looking on,
84 Who'd earlier led me by the rivulet.
Deeply confused, I said: 'Where's Beatrice gone?'
 And she replied; 'Look, there she has her seat
 Upon that root beneath the leaves, new-shone.
Behold the company circled at her feet;
 The rest ascend, and after the Griffon go,
90 Raising a song profounder and more sweet.'
But, if she said much more, I do not know
 Because before my eyes was she whose worth
 Had shut me off from every other show.
Alone she sat upon the naked earth,
 Left there to guard the chariot made fast,
96 Bound by the twofold Beast to the tree's girth.
The seven nymphs had made a ring and passed
 A fence around her, those lights in their hands
 Which are secure from north or south wind's blast.
'You'll be a forester here in these lands
 A brief time and eternally with me
102 Citizen of Rome, where Christ, a Roman, stands.
Therefore to help the wicked world to see,
 Carefully watch the car; and mind you say
 And write, back yonder, what you see shall be.'
So Beatrice; and I who would obey
 Her every command then turned my eyes and mind
108 To look as she directed by her sway.
Never did fire in densest cloud confined,
 From the remotest region so rapidly
 Plummet in its descent upon mankind,
As I observed Jove's bird swoop on the tree,
 Tearing its bark, and, likewise, at its flowers
114 And all those leaves of freshest greenery.

He struck the car with all his mighty powers.
    It listed like a vessel, mast and spar,
    Starboard and larboard lashed by sea that towers.
And then I saw a fox, after that jar,
    Gaunt in its fasting from all proper food,
    Leap in the triumphal chariot's car.   120
Rebuking it for sin and turpitude,
    My Lady put it to as swift a flight
    From her as fleshless bones could have pursued.
Next, from where he first appeared to sight,
    I saw the eagle swoop into the car
    And with his plumes he fledged it with his might.   126
And, in the tones of a heart that sorrows jar,
    A voice came out of Heaven; these words it spoke:
    'How vilely loaded, my little boat, you are!'
It seemed that then the earth beneath it broke;
    Between the wheels a dragon, bursting through,
    Had staved its flooring in with one tail stroke.   132
And, as a wasp pulls out its sting, withdrew
    His spiteful tail and, wrenching part away,
    Ripped from the base, went wandering anew.
And what was left – as does the fertile clay
    With dog's-tail grass – with all those feathers, gift
    Of sincere and kind intent, made an array   138
And covered itself again in every rift,
    Both wheels and pole as well; so swift an act
    That from a sigh to silence mouth's less swift.
And so transformed the holy artefact
    Put forth these heads: first, three were on the shaft,
    Then one above each corner grew intact.   144
The first had horns like oxen used for draught,
    The four had one each, central on the brow.
    Nothing was ever as monstrous as this craft.
Safe as a fortress on a steep hill now,
    A whore with open robe appeared to me,
    She sat with roving looks that none could cow.   150
As if she'd never slip his company,
    I saw a giant take stance at her side.
    From time to time they kissed, now he, now she.
And when she turned her roving eye and plied
    Me with her looks, her lover, fierce and mean,
    Scourged her from head to foot and whipped her hide.   156

Then filled with jealousy, his fury keen,
    He loosed the monster, dragged it through the wood
Some distance till the trees became a screen
    To shield from me where whore and monster stood.

CANTO 33

Beatrice draws Dante level with herself to tell him to put away shame and fear. She
shows him the error of his ways and takes him to drink of Eunoë, the part of the
river that gives remembrance of good deeds. The opening Latin refers to Psalm 79
(Vulgate 78): 'O God, the heathen are come into thine inheritance; thy holy temple
have they defiled.' It refers to the destruction of the Temple in Jerusalem. In line
10, the Latin refers to John 16.16: 'A little while, and ye shall not see me; and again,
a little while, and ye shall see me.' This was a promise given by Christ. In line 17,
the nine to ten steps might refer to a period of over nine years, from 1305 when
Clement V was persuaded by Philip the Fair to move the Papacy to Avignon, until
1314 when both men died.

'*Deus, venerunt gentes,*' the ladies, now three,
  Now four, alternately began to sing
  Weepingly in their dulcet psalmody.
Beatrice, compassionate, sighed in listening,
  And was so altered that but little more
  Was Mary changed at the Cross of suffering.   6
When these gave place, then Beatrice rose before
  Them, stood erect to answer in this way –
  Her colour like that in the fire's core:
'*Modicum, et non videbitis me,*
  Et iterum, belovèd sisters, *modicum*
  Et vos videbitis me.'   12
Then she positioned them in front, and, dumb,
  By nod alone, she motioned me behind,
  The lady and the sage as well, to come.
So she advanced and, as I bring to mind,
  She had not put a tenth step to the ground
  Before she fixed me, eye to eye, to bind;   18
And in a quiet manner spoke this sound
  To me: 'Catch up, brother, so if I confide
  You'll be well placed to hear what I expound.'
As soon as I was with her where I'd abide
  In duty, she asked me: 'Why don't you pose
  Your questions, brother, now we're side by side?'   24
And, as in presence of their elders, those
  Too lowly in their speech can't clearly lift
  Their voice to lips and say what they propose,

So then with me. I launched upon my drift
    Without full voice: 'My Lady, you know my need
30   And know from that what would be a good gift.'
And she: 'I wish that you should now be freed,
    Released from shame and fear, so that you spoke
    No longer as a dreaming man might heed.
Know that the vehicle the serpent broke
    Was and is not; but he to blame should know
36   God's vengeance brooks no sop to stay its stroke.
Not for all time without an heir shall go
    The eagle that left its plumage as the car's –
    Which turned it monster first, then prey brought low.
I surely see and so foretell of stars
    Already near that make a time arrive
42   Free from all hindrance or any block that bars,
Wherein a five hundred, ten and five
    Sent down by God shall slay the thief, and slay
    The giant with her, who such sins contrive.
Perhaps obscure, this dark tale I convey,
    As those the Sphinx and Themis told, and less
48   Convincing, since it darkens the mind's day.
But soon the facts will be the Naiads to guess
    And solve this hard enigma – though the rye
    And flocks will not be lost for this success.
Take note exactly of the words that I
    Now speak; make sure to teach, and show them true
54   To those whose living is the race to die.
Keep well in mind, when writing them, you do
    Not hide how you have seen the holy tree
    That twice has been despoiled in leaves and hue.
Who robs and injures it, with blasphemy
    In act offends against our God who for his own
60   Service alone has made its sanctity.
For eating there, the first of souls was thrown
    Five thousand years and more in pain, and yearned
    For Him who avenged that taste on Himself alone.
Your wit sleeps if it has not yet discerned
    That for good reason was this tree raised high
66   And near the top transposed like this and turned.
And if your idle thoughts didn't calcify
    Your mind – like Elsa's waters – and your delight
    In them a Pyramus to the mulberry's dye,

Then by such things alone you'd see how right,
    Morally, was the Justice of our God
    In placing on the tree his interdict.   72
And yet because I see your mind's a clod
    And turned to stone of such a tint the light
    My words give dazes you till vision nod,
I also wish that if you cannot write
    It down, you'll bear it pictured in the mind
    As pilgrim staffs return in palms wound tight.'   78
And I: 'As wax beneath the seal is signed
    And the imprinted figure cannot change
    So well you've stamped my brain and underlined.
But why do your words, so long desired, range
    And soar beyond my sight, so that the more
    I peer the more it blurs and looks most strange?'   84
'So that you know the School you followed before,'
    She said, 'and see how far its teachings keep
    Pace beside these words that I outpour;
And so that you may see your path to sweep
    As far a distance from the holy way
    As earth to Heaven's swiftest sphere is steep.'   90
Therefore I answered her: 'I call no day
    To mind when I removed myself from you;
    Not for that cause does conscience gnaw my clay.'
'Well, if you can't remember that as true,'
    Smiling, she answered, 'consider how you drank
    From Lethe; only this very morning, too.   96
And if from smoke they argue fire, this blank
    Forgetfulness must clearly prove a fault
    In your desire – elsewhere intent and frank.
But now my words shall be quite clear, but halt
    Before they reach to parts they should not show
    Beyond the range that your blunt sight can vault.'   102
At once more coruscating, with steps more slow,
    The sun maintained the meridian's ring
    Which varies with position to and fro,
When halted – as would a person piloting,
    As scout before a group, if face to face
    With some strange object or unusual thing –   108
Those seven maidens just before the trace
    Of a pale shadow such as the Alps would cast
    On cool streams where green leaves and dark boughs lace.

In front of them Euphrates running past
        I seemed to see, and Tigris from one source,
114   And part like friends that linger to the last.
'O Light, Glory of Humankind, what course
        Is this of waters springing from one well,
        That self from self then wind away their force?'
And at that plea: 'Bid Matilda tell
        You what they are.' The lady made reply
120   As someone thought to blame might fault dispel.
She said: 'This, and other details, I
        Have told him earlier today; I swear
        That Lethe's water has not blurred his eye.'
Then Beatrice: 'Perhaps some greater care,
        That frequently bereaves of memory,
126   Has made his mind's eye darken with its glare.
But look, the flowing Eunoë. Let him be
        Brought to it and, as accustomed to,
        Revitalize his flagging strength for me.'
As a gentle soul makes no excuse in lieu,
        But makes her will of someone else's will
132   As soon as it discloses what to do,
So then the fair maiden moved to fulfil
        The task and took me there; with queenly mien,
        Saying to Statius, 'You come with him still.'
– Ah, reader, if I had, or there had been
        More space to write, I'd sing at least in part
138   Of that sweet drink that quenched yet made more keen.
But, seeing all the pages set to chart
        This second canticle are filled, and close,
        I may no further stretch the bounds of art. –
I came forth from the holiest of flows,
        As new plants with new leaves repair their scars;
144   Remade and pure and ready I arose,
        Prepared for my ascending to the stars.

HEAVEN

INTRODUCTION

Dante's physical Heaven is based on the ancient geocentric Ptolemaic system now unfamiliar to many readers. Stated simply, it asserts that the planets and stars revolve around the sphere of earth, not the sun. The land is conceived as floating in an engirdling ocean. The mountain of Purgatory rises into this ocean. All orbits were considered circular, and the elliptical movement of bodies was explained by having them move in epicycles on circles. These circular orbits represented a perfect geometrical and eternal form and were considered to be made of an invisible crystalline substance. The moon, sun and planets had their own crystalline spheres; there was one vast sphere containing all the stars.

All of the spheres took their motion from the *Primum Mobile* which surrounded the universe, and was itself contained in the Empyrean, the dwelling of God. The universe is also based on astrological principles that purport that the configuration of the Heavens at birth contribute to the character and destiny of the new-born infant. Dante is constantly qualifying this idea to move it away from fatalism and to introduce scope for free will and moral responsibility. In his actual Heaven, the souls of the good appear on different levels of the geocentric universe. This is not in order to express a hierarchical society in Heaven but to provide pictures of different levels of spirituality to make understanding easier for mere mortals.

Here is a schematic representation of Dante's arrangement:

BENEATH THE SUN
These represent a spirituality tinged with or limited by earthly concerns or endeavours:

> *The Moon*
> Inconstancy of various types

> *Mercury*
> Service tinged with earthly ambition

> *Venus*
> Earthly love spoilt by wantonness

> *The Sun*
> Wisdom (broadly interpreted); theologians

ABOVE THE SUN

These represent a purer spirituality:

Mars
Fortitude in the good; warriors for the good

Jupiter
Justice; rulers

Saturn
Temperance; contemplatives

The Stars
The Church Triumphant; meeting place of souls
of the saved

Primum Mobile
Where Dante meets the angels

The Empyrean
The Trinity; The Virgin, angels and saints; the still
point which is God

CANTO 1

Dante realizes the awesome task ahead of him and invokes Apollo to come to his aid as well as the other muses who previously have supported him. He finds Beatrice gazing at the sun and copies her, finding that his powers of vision are now adequate. He hears the music of the spheres and sees, in some agitation, the great light until Beatrice explains how he is no longer on earth but amid the Heavens; she explains how he transcends his bodily heaviness. The light referred to at the opening is the Empyrean.

Glory of him who moves all penetrates
    The universe, and shines in one part bright
    And less in other parts irradiates.
Within the Heaven that most receives his light
    I was: and there I saw such things that none,
    Descending, has power or knowledge to recite,   6
Because our intellect, when it has run
    So near to its desire, sinks in so deep
    No memory can trace what it has done.
And yet whatever memory could keep
    And treasure from that holy realm shall be
    The subject now with which my song shall leap.   12
Make such a vessel of your power from me,
    O good Apollo, on this last work bound,
    To merit of your cherished laurelry.
Thus far one peak of Parnassus have I found
    Enough; but, needing both of them, I must
    Now enter in upon this holy ground.   18
Make entrance in my heart; inspire me just
    As when you drew Marsyas from the case
    That sheathed and shielded all his limbs from dust.
O power divine, if you come to me by grace
    So that some shadow of that holy land,
    Imprinted on my mind, I still may trace,   24
You'll see I reach your chosen tree to stand
    And crown myself with leaves for which I may
    Seem worthy through my theme, your guiding hand.
– So rarely, father, gathered in our day
    For triumph for a Caesar or poet-seer
    (Since sin and shame of human will betray)   30

That the Peneian frond may bring forth sheer
　　Delight in the joyous Delphic Deity
　　When it sets any thirsting for it here.
A tiny spark can set a great flame free;
　　And, maybe, after me shall prayers arise,
36　　And better voice win Cyrrha to agree.
– The lantern of the world, the sun, may rise
　　To mortals here through various different straits;
　　But, when four rings make three crosses, plies
A more propitious course than other gates,
　　United with a more propitious star,
42　　And marks the mundane wax more with its traits.
This strait had almost made the morning far
　　And evening close: that hemisphere was bright,
　　The other darkling, where the shadows are,
When Beatrice I saw; she turned her sight
　　Leftward toward the sun. No eagle may
48　　Focus so fixedly upon that light.
And, as a second follows a first ray,
　　Rising again, as does a pilgrim, intent
　　On reaching home again since long away,
So, from her stance (which through my vision went
　　Straight to imagination) my own I drew,
54　　And looked into the sun, against our bent.
For much not granted here our powers to do
　　Is granted there by virtue of the place
　　Made, for the human race, so fit and true.
I looked for neither long nor short a space,
　　But well enough to see its dazzling round,
60　　Like iron issued from the furnace base.
And, suddenly, it seemed to me that day
　　Added to day as though He with the might
　　Had gloried Heaven with a second sun's ray.
Beatrice was standing with her sight
　　Fixed on the eternal wheels. To see
66　　Her more I turned my eyes from all that light.
And, watching her, I seemed myself to be
　　Like Glaucus when he ate the herb and came
　　To swim, a fellow of the gods of sea.
Beyond the human bound, words cannot frame.
　　Therefore let this example stand to show
72　　Experience to those whom grace may name.

O Love, that rules the Heaven, you must know
    If only what you made anew of me
    Was what you lifted up from here below.
When that wheel you create to eternity
    In yearning so toward yourself then drew
    My mind towards itself with harmony   78
You temper and define, so much of Heaven grew
    Kindled with the sun's blaze, no river might,
    Nor rain, create so wide a lake to view.
The newness of the sound, and the great light,
    Kindled in me a longing for their cause;
    I never yearned so strongly for that sight.   84
To give my agitated mind some pause,
    She who saw me as I saw myself,
    Opened her lips before I moved my jaws,
And said: 'You make yourself so dense with wealth
    Of false imagination, cannot see
    All that you would if you had freed yourself.   90
You are not on the earth, but think to be.
    No lightning, flying from its site, has darted
    As fast as you, returning earthbound, flee.'
If by that smile-pointed discourse parted
    From my first confusion, I was tight
    Entangled in a further one she'd started.   96
I said: 'I rest at ease now from the height
    Of a great marvelling, but still amazed
    How I transcend these bodies all so light.'
At which, sighing with pity then, she gazed
    On me, and with that look a mother shows
    Her delirious child her answer phrased: 102
'A mutual order all things must compose.
    This is the form that makes the universe
    Resemble God. In this, the higher are those
That see the impress of the Eternal Worth's,
    Which is the purpose and the very goal
    For which the system has been made. By diverse   108
Apportion in this order derives the whole,
    Approaching either distantly or near
    To that one principle their forms extol.
Therefore to different ports they each one veer
    On the vast sea of being; each moves right,
    With instinct given it to guide and steer.   114

One bears the fire to the moon in flight;
    One is the motion in hearts of things that die;
    One draws the earth together to unite.
Not merely creatures without mind must fly
    Shot from this bow, but also all of those
120   That have both intellect and love comply.
The Providence that regulates these shows
    Maintains the Heaven quiet with its light
    Where spins the next sphere that the swiftest goes.
The power of that bow-string wings our flight
    As to a place appointed; whatever's sent,
126   It aims towards a target of delight.
Though, it is true, the form with the intent
    Is sometimes not accordant in an art,
    Because the matter's slow to take its bent.
So creatures having power will sometimes part,
    Once shot, out of their proper course and bend
132   Toward some aim for which they did not start,
As fire may dart from cloud but then descend,
    If its first flight be drawn aside to earth
    By false-appearing pleasure as its end.
Now you – if yet my judgement has much worth –
    Should no more marvel that you rise and soar
138   Than that the streams flow down the mountain's girth.
The true marvel would be if, free once more
    From all impediments, you settled back below,
As would be stillness in the flames that roar.'
    At which she turned her gaze to Heaven's glow.

CANTO 2

With Beatrice Dante enters the moon – without any sense of irruption. Puzzled, he asks Beatrice the reason for the variations in the colour of the moon. She convinces him of the error of his own theory with possibly the earliest scientific experiment recorded in literature as such – though the experiment does not demonstrate what she affirms. In line 51, the reference to Cain with his bundle of thorns reflects the common medieval idea that this was what the marks on the moon's surface represented.

O you that in your little skiff far back,
　　In such longing to hear, follow the wake
　　Behind my keel that sings upon its track,
Turn tail to visit your own shores, and take
　　No risks on open sea, for losing me
　　You would be lost, not knowing where to make.　　6
For no one's ever crossed before this sea
　　I sail. Apollo guides, Minerva blows.
　　The Muses show me where the Bear must be.
– You few who crane your neck, unlike all those,
　　For bread of angels (which gives life to ease
　　The hunger which, though sated, never goes)　　12
You may commit your craft to these high seas,
　　And follow in my course, safe in my wake
　　Before the water lapses level by degrees.
Those glorious ones who crossed the sea to make
　　Colchis weren't so amazed as you will be
　　When they saw Jason to the ploughing take.　　18
The inborn and perpetual thirst to see
　　The godlike realm had carried us up there,
　　Swift as a glance sees Heaven instantly.
Beatrice gazed up; on her I fixed my stare.
　　Swiftly we rose; as quarrel nocked to string
　　And fired, perhaps, we hurtled through the air.　　24
I found myself arrived where a wondrous thing
　　Attracted all attention; therefore she,
　　For whom my deeds lack any covering,
As much in joy as beauty turned to me:
　　'In gratitude to God, direct your thought.
　　He's brought us to the first star's entity.'　　30

I seemed enclosed in cloud of a strange sort:
    Dense, it was, shining, firm, with polished play,
    Just like a diamond the sun has caught.
As water-drops encapsulate a ray
    Yet never split, that pearl's eternal glow
36   Absorbed us in itself, not giving way.
If body I was – and if we cannot know
    How one dimension another could enfold,
    As must be if body into body go,
The more should longing stir us to behold
    That Essence where we shall discern the way
42   God and our nature blended in one mould.
There, what we hold by faith we shall survey,
    Not demonstrated but self-known, in figure,
    Like the primal truth believed by human clay.
I answered: 'Lady, with devoutest vigour
    As I may, I thank him for his grace
48   That raised me from the world of mortal rigour.
Tell me, what are these darkenings I trace
    On this body which, below on earth, has made
    Folk tell the tale of Cain upon its face?'
She smiled a little while and then conveyed:
    'If mortal thoughts go wrong where key of sense
54   Cannot unlock the door of obscure shade,
Surely the shafts of wonder should not hence
    Pierce you, since, even when the senses guide,
    You see that reason's wings lack competence.
You tell me what you think.' And I replied:
    'What seems diverse to us, in this high place,
60   I think are bodies dense or rarefied.'
She answered: 'You'll discover, in this case,
    Your thought's thrown deep in falsity, if well
    You note the points I make against its base.
The eighth sphere shows you many lights that dwell
    In it; the countenance of each is seen
66   Varied in scale and brightness, as you tell.
If density or rarity had been
    The cause, a single virtue variously spread
    Would underlie each one, whatever sheen.
Different virtues must be the fruit instead
    Of formative principles, but these could be
72   One, only, where your reasoning has led.

Further, if darkening sprang from rarity,
　　As you suggest, either in part, or run
　　Right through, the matter would lack constancy
Within the planet: or, as fat and lean is done
　　Within a body, it would alternate
　　The pages of its volume, one and one.   78
If premise one were true, the thinner state
　　Would be revealed by eclipses of the sun
　　Which through its rarer stuff would penetrate.
Not so. Therefore let's test the other one,
　　And if, by chance, I make this too appear
　　False, then I've proved your reasoning undone.   84
If rare stuff doesn't go right through the sphere,
　　There must be points at which some density
　　Prevents its passage penetrating clear.
A sun ray then would be cast back and be
　　Like colour that is thrown back by a glass
　　Which has some lead to back it, as you'd see.   90
You'll argue that the darkening comes to pass
　　Because the ray's reflected well behind
　　Those rays from areas of different class.
Experiment should disentwine your mind
　　(If you will make the test) that spring and fount
　　Of all the flowing science of mankind.   96
Take three mirrors, and one pair mount
　　At equal distance from you; the third you fit
　　Between, but from the eye more distance count.
With light behind your back so placed to hit
　　All three, next look at all the rays
　　And note the light cast back and measure it.   102
The distant third seems smaller but conveys
　　A light as bright as both the others show,
　　As you may surely measure with your gaze.
Now, as at first touch of sun, the snow
　　Is stripped of both its colour and its cold
　　To its substrate by all the warming glow,   108
So you, stripped in intellect, I'd fold
　　In light so living that it's tremoring
　　As you fix your gaze upon it and behold.
In the Heaven of peace divine revolves the ring
　　Of one body and in its virtue lies
　　All it contains, the being of everything.   114

The next sphere that so many lights comprise
   Allots this being in essences diverse,
   Distinct yet held in it in various guise.
The other spheres by differences disperse
   Their own distinctive qualities decreed
120   To seed and end as they direct and nurse.
These organs of the universe proceed
   From grade to grade, as you may see, deriving
   Power from above and working down they lead.
Note how I make the passage here, arriving
   At truth for which you yearn; thus you will know
126   How you may cross the ford alone yet thriving.
Motion and virtue of these wheels must flow –
   As hammer's art from hand of smith who smites –
   From the blessèd movers' influence, fast or slow.
The Heaven, lovely with so many lights,
   Takes image from the mind that makes it roll,
132   And makes of it the seal to what it writes.
And, as within your dust the living soul
   (Through varied members formed for various ends)
   Diffuses itself and spreads throughout the whole,
So that intelligence deploys and sends,
   Multiplied through the stars, its goodness and rotates
138   In its own unity that comprehends.
Diverse virtue diverse alloy creates
   With the precious body that it vivifies,
   Bound with it as, through yours, life permeates.
Because of the glad nature from which it plies,
   The mingled virtue makes each body bright,
144   As gladness scintillates in living eyes.
So comes what seems the variance of light and light,
   And not from rarefaction and things dense.
This is the formal principle of white
   And dark, according to its excellence.'

CANTO 3

Perhaps the talk of mirrors misleads Dante but he sees figures and swings round to see them in reality. Beatrice sets him right and he meets Piccarda (see Purgatory 23). She was Simone Donati's daughter, sister of Dante's friend Forese. Her talk of her vocation and its loss gives Dante pause for question which he raises in the next canto. Line 97 refers to St Clara (1194–1253), friend and disciple of St Francis of Assisi, who founded the order of the Poor Clares, and line 106 to the fact that Piccarda's brother Corso had compelled Piccarda to marry Rossellino della Tosa, a truculent, violent man, to try to cement an alliance. The 'three blasts' were: Frederick Barbarossa, his son, Henry VI and his grandson, Frederick II. Constance was heiress of the Norman dynasty that had conquered the Saracens and taken from them Sicily and southern Italy in the eleventh century.

The sun which first had warmed my breast with love
     Thus showed me, both by proof and argument,
     The lovely countenance of truth above.
And I, to show my error and convinced assent,
     As would have been most fitting, raised my head
     To give expression to my clear intent.   6
But at that moment rose to me, instead,
     A sight that so compelled my eyes to gaze
     It drove acknowledgement out of my head.
As, from transparent glass of polished glaze,
     Or from a pool of water, still and clear,
     Yet not so deep the bottom is in haze,   12
Our faces are reflected but appear
     So faint a pearl upon the whitest brow
     Would come no easier to the vision here,
So could I see such faces float – and how
     Eager to talk! – and counter-error made
     From him who, in the fountain, came to bow.   18
No sooner seen than thought reflections played;
     I swung my eyesight round to find who they
     Might be whose figures there had been portrayed.
Nothing was there. I turned back to the ray
     Of my sweet guide's light whose holy eyes
     Were shining on me as she smiled to say: 24
'No wonder if I smile at your surmise,
     Your child-like thought that cannot trust the weight
     Of its dull feet upon the truth to rise,

But turns, according to its custom, straight
   To vacancy. True substance these you flee.
30   Because they broke their vows, this is their state.
Speak with them, listen and believe: you'll see
   The light of truth that illuminates their pace
   Permits no step from it to error's scree.'
As in yearning long confused, I turned my face
   Toward the soul who seemed most keen for speech,
36   And so this discourse started in that place:
'O spirit well created, you who reach –
   In rays of life eternal – sweetness none,
   Unless they taste, may understand or teach,
Merely to know your name and what you've done
   Would satisfy me, if you'd deign to tell.'
42   With eager smiling eyes she'd soon begun:
'Our charity would no more bar, repel
   A just desire, than His would do whose worth
   He yearns to see in all His courts excel.
I was a virgin sister on the earth.
   Search in your memory and you will find
48   My greater beauty not hide my name and birth.
You'll recognize Piccarda, in your mind,
   Who's placed with all the blessèd ones to treasure
   Their blessèd state on the slowest sphere to wind.
Here, our affections, kindled only in pleasure
   Of the Holy Spirit, joy and delight,
54   Indwelt by his true guidance and his measure.
This level, seeming low, is theirs who slight
   The vows they swore – and ours, in various ways,
   We failed to keep or follow as was right.'
And I replied: 'Something divine, in rays
   Shown in your wondrous face, seems to transmute
60   You from my memory of former days.
And that is why my memories dispute
   Among themselves. But what you now make clear
   Has rendered recollection more acute.
But tell me, though your blessedness lies here,
   Do you then never yearn for higher grace
66   To see much more and to become more dear?'
She turned and smiled among the souls a space,
   And then she spoke with such a joyous thrill
   That love's first flame appeared to light her face.

'The power of charity becalms our will,
    Brother, and makes us yearn for nothing more
    Than this that leaves no other thirst to fill.   72
If ever we desired further to soar,
    Our longing would be discord from his Will
    Who ranks us in these places and this shore.
These circles cannot harbour such an ill,
    You'll see, if of necessity we're here
    In charity – and its nature your thought distil.   78
No, it's the essence of this blessèd sphere,
    Indeed, to fold ourselves within God's Will
    So that our wills are one and co-inhere.
Therefore our ranking is, from sill to sill,
    To all the realm, a joy as to the King
    Who wills our will to what he would fulfil.   84
Our peace is in his will; and everything
    That it creates, or nature may create,
    Toward that sea is ever journeying.'
Then it was clear to me how every state
    In Heaven is Paradise, and even though
    The Supreme Good pours grace at varied rate.   90
Yet, as may happen, one dish here below
    May cloy while taste for other food remain;
    We ask for that, give thanks for this to go;
So I, by word and sign, to see quite plain
    The pattern of the weave in which she held
    The shuttle poised, not drawn right through again.   96
'Perfection of the life, worth unexcelled,
    Enskied a lady higher whose rule some take
    On earth, and wear the veil by her impelled,
So that till death they may both sleep and wake
    With that Bridegroom who finds each vow of worth
    That charity conforms to please him for her sake.   102
To follow her, I fled the ways of earth
    In girlhood; sworn to her order in his name,
    Closed in her habit, her girdle round my girth.
But men, less used to good than sin and shame,
    Tore me from that sweet cloister's ways,
    And God knows what my life since then became.   108
This second splendour who reveals her blaze
    To you, upon my right, kindling her ray
    With all the light our lovely sphere displays,

Has, like myself, the same tale to convey.
    She was a sister; from her head they tore
114   The holy wimple's shade in selfsame way.
Yet, thrown back so into the world once more,
    Against good usage and her will and right,
    She never lost the veil that her heart wore.
She is the great Constance; this is her light
    Who, from the second blast of Swabia, bred
120   And bore the third and final of their might.'
She started – concluding all that she had said –
    To sing *Ave Maria*, vanishing in her song,
    Like some great weight to a deep water's bed.
My sight, that followed after her as long
    As possible, then turned to see that goal
126   Of longing much more deep and much more strong,
And bent on Beatrice my entire soul;
    But she so dazzled in my eyes that they
Could not at first endure a light so whole.
    This made me slow of question on the way.

CANTO 4

Dante raises two queries with Beatrice: why should people forced to break their vows by external pressure be penalized; and, seeing that the inconstant are domiciled with the moon, was Plato right to suggest people's souls descend from the planet germane to their characters and return to the same planet at death. The first query is explained by the difference between the wish to fulfil a vow and the consent under pressure to its breaking. Secondly, the planetary levels on which Dante meets the elect are emblematic. Beatrice is pleased with these questions, which show the soul on its way to the truth of God.

Between two pleasing equidistant dishes
    The man who's truly free would starve and die,
    Before he could decide which filled his wishes.
A lamb would stand stock-still, confronted by
    Two ravening wolves, in dread of both; a hound,
    Between two does, not know which one to try.   6
Therefore, if I held my peace when found
    Between perplexities, in the same way,
    I take no praise or blame, since necessity bound.
My peace I held, but my desire, as day,
    Was painted on my face; my question must
    Have shown more warmly than if word should say.   12
And Beatrice took the role on Daniel thrust
    In saving Nebuchadnezzar from the ire
    That rendered him so cruel and unjust.
She said: 'I see how this and that desire
    Attract you so that your own eager brain
    Tangles itself in knots and can't enquire.   18
You query: "If the right will should remain,
    By what justice can another's violent act
    Lessen for me the merit I attain?"
And more perplexity comes to distract
    You by the semblance of the souls returning
    To stars – as Plato's doctrine frames the fact.   24
These are the questions that are twinned and burning
    Upon your will: therefore I shall assay
    The latter first, more noxious to discerning.
The Seraphim most sunk in God's own ray,
    Moses, Samuel, whichever John you chose –
    None, not Mary herself, I dare to say –   30

Dwell in any other Heaven than those
    Spirits who recently appeared to you;
    Nor have their beings more or less repose,
But all make lovely the first circle, too,
    And share sweet life, in various measures weighed,
36   As they may sense the eternal breath blown through.
These have appeared here, not because some grade
    Allots them to this sphere, but to reveal
    They are the least of the celestials arrayed.
Such images your faculties require; they deal
    In sense-data, and from these proceed, extend
42   To shape things for the mind to think and feel.
Therefore the Scriptures have to condescend
    To your capacity, give to the Divine
    Such hands and feet, but deeper truths intend.
Likewise, the Holy Church must thus assign
    Human aspects to Michael and Gabriel, too,
48   And him that cured Tobit – to your depth confined.
What Timaeus argues of souls is not quite true
    Of what is here; he seems to think things are
    Exactly as he states, and hides no deeper view.
He says the soul returns into its star,
    Believing it's separated from its sphere
54   When Nature gives it form on earth afar.
It may be that he has some meaning here
    Different from what the words seem to suggest,
    Some sense, not risible, though never clear.
If he should mean honour and blame, that rest
    Upon their influence, return to those wheels,
60   Perhaps his arrow strikes some truth at best.
Misunderstood, this theory turned the heels
    Of almost all the world aside to name
    Mercury, Mars, and Jove, as down it kneels.
The other question baffling you may claim
    A weaker venom since its spite could wind
66   Nowhere away from me to error's shame.
If Justice appear unjust to human mind,
    Then that would seem to be an argument
    For faith and not to heresy inclined.
But, since you seem to be intelligent
    Enough to pierce this truth, just as you mean,
72   I'll put at ease your mental discontent.

If force is force when victims do not lean
    Towards its will, it follows these that vowed
    Could never claim that case for what they'd been.
For, if the will determines, it can't be cowed,
    But does as nature does when in the flame,
    And, wrenched a thousand times, it is not bowed.   78
But, if it swerve a little in its aim,
    It lends itself to violence of the act.
    Not seeking shrine again, these bear that blame.
If will had held as firm as Laurence, racked
    Upon the grid, or Mucius, resolute
    Against his own right hand, with will intact,   84
It would have thrust them back upon the route
    From which they were waylaid, as soon as free.
    But will so firm is all too rare a shoot.
Now, with these words, if you have followed me,
    As certainly you should the argument,
    What's troubled you becomes vacuity.   90
Another pass impedes on your ascent,
    As you observe: before you made your way
    Alone you would be wearied and forspent.
I've shown you how no blessèd soul could say
    A lie because it dwells forever now
    Beside the Primal Truth, and cannot stray.   96
But then you heard Piccarda telling how –
    And seemingly to contradict me there –
    That Constance kept her truth to veil and vow.
Many times before, brother, be aware,
    Things better not were done under the stress
    Of fleeing peril that was brought to bear.   102
Thus Alcmaeon felt his father's pleading press
    Him on to kill his mother – not to forsake
    His filial duty he acted pitiless.
And here, I'd have you know, violence may take
    Suggestion from the will and they so act
    That, in offence, there's no excuse to make.   108
Absolute will does not condone the fact,
    Yet acquiesces in so far as it's afraid,
    In drawing back, to be more cruelly racked.
So, when Piccarda spoke like this, she made
    A point about the will called absolute;
    But I, the other; both have truth conveyed.'   114

Such rippling of the sacred stream to shoot
    Out of the Fount from which all truth must flow!
    It brought a peace, a longing more acute.
'Love of the Primal Lover,' I answered so,
    'Divine one, you whose words suffuse and thrill

120   So that I quicken more the more I know,
My love lacks depth sufficient to fulfil
    Grace for grace; but may the one who sees,
    And has the power, answer for me still.
I see now intellect can't be at ease,
    Or satisfied till truth is shone on it.

126   Beyond which range no other verities.
There it may rest as a wild beast may sit
    Inside its den as soon as it arrives,
    As well it may, or longing's a futile fit.
Thus, at the roots of truth always survives
    Such querying, a shoot that always grows

132   And, branch by branch, towards the topmost strives.
And this persuades me further to propose,
    And gives me nerve, my Lady, now to plumb
    Another truth that seems as dark as those.
Can men, then, satisfy you with goods or sum
    In lieu of slighted vows, and have dispelled

138   The weight lost when the scales of Justice come?'
Beatrice looked on me; her eyes so welled
    With sparks of love that all my vanquished mind
Turned away; like someone lost, I held
    My gaze downcast upon the ground, behind.

CANTO 5

Dante wishes to raise the question whether, once a vow has been made, it may be remitted for something else. Beatrice explains that, in respect of monastic vows, this is hardly possible because no other offering can be equivalent to its total commitment of life and will. Others may be remitted as the Church permits by additional sacrifice. But not all vows are acceptable to God. Discussion is interrupted by their rising to Mercury, emblematic of souls whose good deeds were tainted by earthly ambition. Dante is met by Justinian, the codifier of Roman Law.

'If I should dazzle you in warmth of love,
    Beyond what you have witnessed on the earth,
    And overwhelm your vision from above,
Don't marvel, for this springs from growing birth
    Of perfect vision which, as it apprehends,
    Draws closer to the apprehended worth.   6
I clearly see how, in your mind, resplends
    The eternal light that always, merely seen,
    Will kindle love wherever it descends.
If something else seduce your love, its sheen
    Is nothing but a trace of holy light,
    Ill-understood, but shining in things mean.   12
You want to know if other service set right
    The reckoning for broken vows so well
    The soul is safe from dispute in this plight.'
So Beatrice began this theme to swell –
    As those unwavering in word express –
    Continuing the sacred progress as I tell: 18
'The greatest gift God made in his largesse
    At the creation, the closest in agreeing
    To his perfection, most prized in godliness,
Is freedom of the will, with which each being –
    One and all that are intelligent –
    Have been endowed, in powers of mind and seeing.   24
That, if you draw the inference, will present
    To you the high worth of a vow intact –
    If made so God consent when you consent.
When God and man agree, in such a pact,
    The sacrifice is given of this treasure,
    As I defined it, by its own will and act.   30

What recompense may offer equal measure?
   If consecration's put to other good,
   It's charity from plunder – nothing lesser.
The main point now you should have understood,
   But since the Church finds dispensations fit –
36   Which seems to counter truth that I unhood –
You, at the table, must still calmly sit
   Because the austere food that you partake
   Needs more assistance for digesting it.
Open your mind to what I say, and take
   It in and fix it there; not to retain
42   Once understood – scant knowledge that would make!
Two things essential to the vow pertain:
   First, the details of which it is composed;
   Second, the actual compact, straight and plain.
This last cannot be cancelled or disposed,
   Except by being kept; concern for this
48   Has made precise what's now to be disclosed.
It follows, then, the Jews could not dismiss
   The sacrifice at all, though substitute
   They were allowed to make – you must know this.
The former, shown as content, they may commute
   And interchange with other things, indeed,
54   Without offence or any real dispute.
Let none, then, shift the load he shoulders, heed
   His own judgement, without the turn of white
   And yellow key, and let him be agreed
That any change is folly and a slight.
   But if the thing remitted bear the thing
60   Assumed as four to six, it may be right.
So, if the gift bear weight enough to swing
   Every balance with its virtue's worth,
   There is no substitute that you could bring.
Let mortals never vow in sport or mirth.
   Keep faith, yet doing so, not as squint-eyed
66   As Jephthah was, in his first vow on earth.
Better he should have said, and not complied:
   "I made an error!" than worse should have occurred.
   Of the same folly you may accuse, beside,
The great leader of the Greeks whose foolish word
   Made Iphigenia mourn her lovely face,
72   And wise and simple mourn the rite they heard.

Christians, in your direction firmly pace;
    Not like a feather in the wind, nor hold
    That any water cleanses you by grace.
You have the Testaments, both New and Old,
    The Shepherd of the Church to be your guide.
    Let these suffice to reach salvation's fold.   78
If wretched greed proclaim aught else beside,
    Be men, not senseless sheep, in case the Jews
    That live among you see this and deride.
Don't gambol like the lamb that leaves the ewe's
    Milk – silly, wanton, tripping its own feet,
    And struggling with his limbs across the dews.'   84
So Beatrice to me as written on this sheet;
    Then turned in utter longing to that place
    Where all the world is quickened as by heat.
Her sudden pausing and transfigured face
    Enjoined a silence on my eager wit
    Which had already more questions to trace.   90
But as an arrow finds the mark is hit
    Before the bow has ceased to hum and sing,
    So, in the second realm, we then were knit.
My Lady was, I saw, so glad to wing
    Into the light of this new Heaven the sphere
    Itself had brightened with her brightening.   96
And, if the star was changed and laughed so clear,
    What then did I who by my nature lie
    Subject to change, in various guise to veer?
As, in a fishpool, still and clear, the fry
    Approach whatever falls out of the air,
    If they assume it is some food supply,   102
I noticed over a thousand splendours bear
    Towards us, and, from each one there, I heard:
    'Look! One who will increase our loves moves there.'
And, as each approached, the soul was stirred
    And filled with joy, as showed well by the glow
    That, beaming out, as light in light occurred.   108
– Think, reader, if what I started telling go
    No further here, how anguished you would wait
    In hunger and in famine more to know,
And, in yourself, you will perceive how great
    My longing was to hear from light and light,
    As soon as seen, concerning their estate.   114

'O, happy born, whom grace concedes the right
    To look on the eternal Triumph's Thrones
    Before abandoning your time of earthly fight,
The light that ranges through all Heaven's zones
    Enkindles us, so if you wish to draw
120   Our light, fulfil your wishes in your tones.'
So spoke one of the devout souls I saw;
    And Beatrice urged: 'Speak, speak your mind outright,
    And trust them as if deities in awe.'
'Indeed, I see you nestle in your light,
    And how you draw it forth out of your eyes,
126   Since, when you flash a smile, it dazzles sight.
But, worthy soul, I do not recognize
    You yet, nor why you're in this sphere immersed
    By the sun's rays and veiled from men's surmise.'
And thus I spoke, addressed towards the first
    That spoke to me; its radiance, though bright,
132   Grew brighter than before we had conversed.
And, as the sun hides in excess of light
    When all its heat has swallowed up the dense
    Steaming of vapours that obscure his might,
So, by access of joy, that sacred light intense
    Was closed, most closed, and hidden in its beams,
138   But answered me in such a style and sense
    As the next canto descants on his themes:

CANTO 6

Justinian begins with a history of the Roman Empire as the disseminator and inculcator of the arts of peace and civilization. (This idea is central to Dante's thought, as he sees a strong empire and emperor as the countervailing power to the secular ambitions of the Papacy.) The Guelf and Ghibelline factions are condemned as misusers of imperial insignia and ambition when compared to Rome in history, the cradle of Christianity, the avenger, in Titus, of the Crucifixion. Lines 100–1, the Guelfs opposed the French arms and influence against the Empire. The Ghibellines took over the name of the Empire for divisive political purposes. Lines 127–142 refer to Raymond Berengar IV, who reigned in Provence 1209–45. Romeo of Villeneuve (1170–1250) was his devoted servant.

'After Constantine had counter-wheeled
    The Eagle from the course the Heavens rolled,
    Following Aeneas who made Lavinia yield;
A hundred years, another hundred told,
    And more, God's Eagle dwelt on Europe's border,
    Near to those mountains where first fledged of old.   6
And there he ruled and brought the world to order
    Under the shadow of his sacred wings,
    From hand to hand, till I became his warder.
Caesar I was; Justinian am; those things
    Excessive or defunct in law I shed;
    Done, I now feel, by Primal Love's determinings.   12
Before I fixed my mind on the task ahead,
    I held that Christ was of one nature made;
    And, with that faith content, my life I led.
But blest Agapetus, high pastor, swayed
    Me to the Faith without alloy or blend,
    By all his disquisitions and his aid.   18
Him I believed; but here I apprehend
    His faith as clearly as your minds conceive,
    In contradictions, true and false contend.
Once with the Church I stepped out to believe,
    God, of his grace, inspired me with the deed
    I dedicated my being to achieve.   24
My armies I chose Belisarius to lead –
    Whom Heaven's right-hand gave so much support
    It signalled me to yield them as agreed.

My answer to your first question stops short
    At this point, but its bearing makes
30   Me add some further things to this report.
So you may see with what right one side takes
    And abrogates the standard as its own,
    While others stand opposed for their own sakes,
Observe what great virtue has made it known
    And worth all reverence – starting from the day
36   When Pallas died to give it power alone.
You know how long in Alba it would stay,
    Three hundred years or more until the close,
    When three fought three for mastery and sway.
You know what it achieved, between the woes
    Of the Sabine women till Lucretia's shame,
42   Through seven monarchs conquering neighbour foes.
You know full well what it achieved of fame
    When chosen Romans conquered Brennus' tribes,
    Pyrrhus and more, princes and powers of name.
Of whom Torquatus, Quinctius – whose name describes
    His unkempt locks – the Decii and Fabii, won
48   Such fame my joyous memorial thus ascribes.
It cast the Pride of Arabs down and done,
    That followed Hannibal through Alpine snow,
    From which, ah, Po, your waters glide and run.
Beneath it, Scipio and Pompey triumphed, though
    Still young; and bitter did its soaring seem
54   To those hills where your life began to grow.
Then, near the time when Heaven's will and theme
    It was to give the world its peaceful mood,
    Caesar, at Rome's behest, seized it, supreme.
And what it did from Var to Rhine was viewed
    By Loire, Isère, and all along the Seine,
60   And every vale with which the Rhone accrued.
What it achieved when he had issued plain
    Out of Ravenna, and crossed the Rubicon,
    Was such a flight that pen or tongue is vain.
Towards Spain, it wheeled its powers next, and on
    Towards Durazzo; after that, it took
66   Pharsalia, so that the Nile in tremors shone.
Antandros and the Simoïs – it once forsook –
    Were reached again, and Hector's resting-place,
    And (sad for Ptolemy) its feathers shook.

On Juba, then, it swooped at lightning pace,
　　And wheeled towards the west, once it had heard
　　Pompey's trumpet blasting out its case.　　　　　　　72
For what it wrought by the next marshal stirred,
　　Brutus and Cassius howl aloud in Hell:
　　Modena and Perugia uttered their doleful word.
Still wretched Cleopatra weeps as well
　　Who, as she fled before it from her land,
　　Caught from the viper death so black and fell.　　　78
With him, it swept into the Red Sea's sand;
　　With him, established peace on such a scale
　　That Janus saw his temple locked and banned.
But what the standard that compels my tale
　　Had done, or what it was ordained to do
　　In the mortal realm, its subject, seems to pale　　84
And dim, if once we come to clearer view
　　Of it beneath the third-come Caesar's control,
　　With a keen eye and heart that's pure and true.
For living Justice, that inspires my soul,
　　Granted that, in his hand, it should now win
　　For vengeance of his wrath the glorious role.　　　90
Now marvel at the revelation I begin:
　　Afterwards, under Titus, it then bore
　　Vengeance on vengeance for the ancient sin.
And when the Lombard teeth savaged and tore
　　The Holy Church, victorious Charlemagne,
　　Beneath its wings, protected her once more.　　　96
Now you may judge those I accused again
　　Just now, and of their sins – which are the sources
　　Of all your suffering and all your pain.
One sets against the public standard's courses
　　Its yellow lilies; one links it with a faction.
　　Who knows which sin is worse between these forces?　102
The Ghibellines should set their arts in action
　　Beneath another standard – they follow ill
　　That sever justice from it by infraction.
Nor let the new Charles strike it down at will
　　With all his Guelfs, but let him fear the claws
　　That, earlier, flayed a mightier lion still.　　　108
Many a time have fathers been the cause
　　Of children's tears; so let him not suppose
　　That God trades crests with lilies and their flaws.

This little star adorns itself with those
    Good spirits driven and obsessed to seek
114   That fame and honour laud them with its shows.
Now when desire diverts towards this peak,
    So do the rays of true love pour with less
    Intensity, in life and vigour weak.
In the balance of reward with our success
    And merit lies our joy, in part: we find
120   It less nor more than is our worthiness.
In this, the living Justice sweetens mind
    And our affections so they cannot bend
    Or warp to malice of whatever kind.
Variety of voices on earth will blend
    To make sweet harmony; degrees, like those,
126   Make sweet harmony from these wheels ascend.
And, in the very pearl, the brilliance glows
    Of Romeo whose beautiful and noble act
    Was given such wicked payment through his foes.
The last laugh those Provençals won't protract;
    And so misplanned such course has always been
132   That twists a good deed till the doer's racked.
Four daughters, and each one turned a queen,
    Had Raymond Berengar, and this achieved
    For him by Romeo, an alien of lowly mien.
Suggestions slyly spoken then deceived
    Him to demand account from this just man,
138   Through whom, for every ten, twelve were retrieved.
Then, old and poor, his wanderings began,
    Begging his life, crust after dry crust,
And if the world knew the heart within the man,
    Though praising well, a greater praise it must.'

CANTO 7

When Justinian goes, Beatrice enlarges on his remarks with respect to the Crucifixion and Atonement. Man could not bear the punishment for sin in himself because he could not abase himself as low as he once in hubris attempted to rise. Therefore another would have to bear it. The Incarnation allowed a God and a Man to make that atonement. But the indignity of the crucifixion borne by God required the vengeance of Titus. She further points out that God made the Heavens, the angels, and Adam and Eve; the angel-powers made all the other elements of sublunar nature. Therefore, with the penalty of sin lifted, man was immortal again. Line 70 refers to the idea that whatever God creates without intermediary, such as the angels, Heavens, mankind, is eternal. Those things created through intermediary forces are mortal. See lines 133–8 for further explanation.

This canto has three more lines than usual texts, as I have translated the first tercet as an additional second tercet. For comparison with other texts 3 should be deducted from the line numbers after this opening.

'Osanna, sanctus Deus sabaoth,
    Superillustrans claritate tua
    Felices ignes horum malacoth!'
'Hosanna, Holy God of Hosts who light
    With added radiancy of your own shining
    The happy fires in these realms so bright!'   6
Thus, wheeling to his own notes, combining
    The two-fold light I saw that being sing
    And he and all the others intertwining
Their movements in the dancing of the ring
    Until like briefest sparks they all were sped
    And veiled from sight in sudden distancing.   12
In doubt, 'A word to her, one word,' I said,
    'To her,' within myself, 'a word to her,
    My Lady who slakes my thirst with sweet drops shed.'
But, though for B and ICE, as once it were,
    The reverence that mastered me had bowed
    Me as a man who sleeps and cannot stir,   18
Brief was the instant Beatrice allowed
    Me; speaking out, she cast a smile's rays
    That might have blessed a man in the flame's shroud.
'According to my insight – that never strays –
    How justly could a vengeance already just
    Be so avenged? has put your thought in a maze.   24

I'll quickly clear your mind now, yet you must
    Listen with care, for what I say will make
    The gift of highest doctrine for your trust.

Because he would not tolerate a brake
    Upon the power of will, that man not born
30   Condemned himself and heirs in dread mistake.

For which the human race lay sick and worn
    Many an age down there in error's blindness,
    Till it pleased the Word of God to come, that morn,

To share man's nature (that had wandered mindless
    Of its Creator) in one person with his own,
36   By single act of his all-loving-kindness.

Now fix your sight on what I next make known:
    This nature, united with its Maker, as when
    Created, was undebased and good alone.

But by its self-will ceased as citizen
    Of Paradise, because it swerved, distracted,
42   Out of the path of truth and life to men.

As for the penalty the Cross enacted,
    If measured by the nature taken on,
    A juster sentence never was exacted.

Yet never so great a wrong was undergone,
    If you regard to Whom it was applied,
48   The Victim in whose Person this nature shone.

So, from one act, diverse results divide.
    God, and the Jews, in one death rejoice.
    Earth shuddered; Heaven opened wide.

No longer, then, should it seem harsh to voice
    A saying that just vengeance was, at last,
54   Avenged by a just court and a just choice.

But now your mind, from thought to thought flown fast
    Into a tangled knot, I see, is yearning
    For some assuagement to be swiftly cast.

You say, "Your meaning I am learning,
    But why God willed Redemption in this way,
60   And only this, is veiled from my discerning."

This decree is buried, truth to say,
    My brother, from the eyes of all who yet
    Are not matured in love's flames that purge away.

But since this target frequently is set,
    And understood so little, I shall express
66   Why such a way was worthy of the debt.

Divine Excellence, spurning envy's stress,
    Burning within itself, emits such rays
    As to display the eternal loveliness.
Whatever it distils directly from its blaze,
    Without some agent, is a deathless thing,
    Since that seal's mark there's nothing can erase.   72
All things that, without mediation, spring
    From it are wholly free, because their flight
    Is never prone to change or faltering.
It most approves what most conforms to light,
    Because the holy radiance that shines on all
    Lives most in what's most like its dazzling might.   78
On all these advantages mankind may call,
    So, if one failed, then by necessity
    The race in all its nobleness must fall.
But sin alone exiles humanity
    To differ from the Highest Good, and spurn
    The light, till it instil less radiancy.   84
To dignity it never will return,
    Unless it fill the void that sin must be,
    And serve the sentence evil pleasures earn.
When, in its seed and its entirety,
    Your nature sinned, just as from Paradise,
    So from these dignities it turned to flee.   90
Nor might they be recovered in such vice,
    If you consider deeply, in any way,
    Unless the crossing of either ford suffice:
Either God in his beneficence should pay,
    Or else man of himself should face all this
    And for his folly the penalty obey.   96
As closely as you may, on the abyss
    Of the Eternal Wisdom, fix your gaze,
    And trace the path with my analysis:
Within the limitation of his ways
    Man lacks the means to pay this penalty,
    Because he never could so humbly abase   102
Himself by late obedience as firstly he
    Designed in disobedience to rise so high.
    Through him, no satisfaction could there be.
Thus, God must of himself redignify
    Mankind in his own ways, and reinstate
    To perfect life – and one or both ways try.   108

Moreover, since a deed you instigate
    Will be more gracious if the more it shows
    The goodness of the heart that would create,
Divine Good which imprints the world then chose
    To work in both these ways to lift your plight
114   And raise you back where earlier you rose.
Nor was there made, between the last night
    And first day, nor shall there ever be
    In either course, a deed of nobler height.
God was more generous, giving himself to free
    Humanity to life itself again,
120   Than if by choice he waived the penalty.
All other modes fell short of justice then,
    Except the Son of God, in lowliness,
    Were made and fashioned in the likeness of men.
– To grant your every wish, I now digress
    To explicate a passage till you'll read
126   As clearly there as I myself profess.
"I see the fire and water," you proceed,
    "The air and earth, in every mix and blend,
    Come to an end, and little time they speed."
– These were created, so what I contend,
    If it were true, would make them all secure
132   From such corruption and coming to an end.
The angels, brother, and this region so pure
    Where you have come, may be declared to be
    Created in entirety to endure.
Those elements you name, the variety
    Of things made out of them in any mould,
138   Derive from powers created in degree.
Created the material that they hold,
    Created the informing virtue's power
    That circles round them in the stars untold.
The life of every living thing, of flower
    And creature, is drawn from compounds taking force
144   From beams and motions of these lights that shower.
Yet yours is breathed by no mediate course,
    But by the Supreme Good is made to stir
    Toward itself in yearning for its source.
Therefore you may go further, and infer
    Your resurrection, if you will recall
150   The method of creation when our parents were
    First fashioned on the earth before the Fall.'

CANTO 8

They rise to Venus, level of those whose love of the divine was mixed with too much love of created things. They encounter Dante's old friend Carlo Martello, once heir to Provence and the kingdom of Naples, actual ruler of Hungary, though Sicily had revolted from this kingdom because of evil government. Dante, with astrological preoccupations, wishes to know how good parents may produce evil offspring. Carlo explains that the Heavens supply through their influence the variety of human attributes and faculties required for society – but not by lineage. Since the system was made by a perfect God there is a proper place for all of these qualities to function within the community. Unfortunately, human interference assigns individuals to their work not by their natural proclivities but by their rank and birth. This leads to most of the disorders within society.

    The world, to its peril, held that, from above,
        The lovely Cyprian, rolling in the third
        Epicycle, rayed down the folly of love,
So they not only honoured her, and conferred
        On her their sacrifice and votive plea –
        Those ancients who in ancient falsehood erred –   6
But Dione they honoured; her mother, she,
        And Cupid as her son; they gave the news
        He lay in Dido's lap its currency.
From her I started with they took to use
        Her name for that star which courts the sun,
        Now from the nape, now from the brow it woos.   12
I had no sense our rising had begun.
        My Lady gave me confidence of being there,
        Because I saw her grow a lovelier one.
And as we see a spark in flame now flare,
        And as a voice in voices may be heard
        If one hold, another vary on the air,   18
So, in that light, I saw how others stirred,
        Torches that move in circles swift or slow
        As vision of the eternal vision spurred.
From chill cloud no blasts that ever blow,
        Seen or unseen, have speed that wouldn't seem
        Hindered or lagging to any one below   24
Who had observed those lights towards us stream,
        Leaving the circle that begins among
        The exaltation of the Seraphim supreme.

And, in the foremost of them, I heard sung:
    'Hosanna!' with such music that, to this day,
30   I've yearned ever again to hear that tongue.
Then one drew nearer and along to say:
    'We all are ready here to do your will,
    So you may have with us your joy and way.
With those celestial princes we roll and thrill
    In one circle, one orbit and one thirst
36   – To whom you once remarked, when on earth still:
"You who by understanding," so you versed,
    "Move the third Heaven". – Such love we feel
    That, to please you, quiet will please us first.'
When I had raised my eyes in mute appeal
    And reverence to my Lady, and she had made
42   Me certain of her assurance, I made them wheel
Back to the light that previously displayed
    The generous offer of itself; I said
    'Say who you are!' with great affection conveyed.
Ah, how I saw its brilliance brighten, spread
    At this new joy, augmenting all the rest,
48   To hear the question then with which I'd led.
So, changed in light, it answered my request:
    'Briefly the world held me – had it been more,
    Much evil that must come would not infest.
My joy, it is, conceals me from you, for
    It rays round, hiding me, like a worm bound
54   And swathed within its own silken store.
You loved me much, and good cause you'd have found,
    Since, if I'd stayed below, I would have shown
    You much more of my love than leaves unwound.
The left bank, that is washed and rinsed by Rhone
    After it joins the Sorgue, awaited me
60   To be the timely lord upon its throne;
So would the Ausonian corner have me be,
    Citied by Bari, Gaeta, and Catona, down
    Where Tronto and the Verde meet the sea.
Upon my brow already shone the crown
    Of that land the Danube waters when it's slid
66   Beyond the banks and shores of German renown.
And fair Trinacria – that darkens there amid
    Pachynus and Pelorus over the straits
    That Eurus troubles as it ever did

(Not from Typhoeus but sulphur that congregates) –
    Would from my lineage still have sought its kings,
    Sprung from Charles and Rudolph to those states,   72
Had wicked lordship – which at all times wrings
    The heart of subject folk – not moved and driven
    Palermo to shriek: "Death! Death!" in its ravenings.
And had my brother foreseen this he'd have striven
    To shun Catalonia's greedy poverty
    Already, long before offence were given.   78
And, truly, he, or others, needs to be
    Prepared, or else upon his ship some weight
    More burdensome shall swamp it in the sea.
His nature – mean descendant of a great
    And generous forebear – needed soldiery
    Who aren't concerned with coffers and estate.'   84
'Sire, since I think the joy you pour in me
    Through your discourse, there, where all good receives
    Its source and end, is – clearly as I see
It – clear to you yourself, it therefore leaves
    Me greater pleasure; and I hold it dear
    That such your eye, gazing on God, perceives.   90
You fill me with rejoicing: now make clear
    For me this query your remarks suggest:
    How from good seed may bitter fruit appear?'
So I. And he: 'If I can manifest
    A certain truth, you'll see before your eyes
    What lies behind your back – and end your quest.   96
The Good, that circulates and satisfies
    The whole realm which you ascend, creates
    Its providence to be the power which lies
In those great bodies; the Mind – whose only state's
    Perfection in itself – provides for creatures
    Of varied types and on their welfare waits.   102
So what this bow lets fly is fit and reaches
    A well-provided end, as does a shaft
    That is directed at the target's features.
This Heaven you cross would lack all art or craft
    If this were not the case, and its effect
    Would cause confusion and a ruined draft.   108
This could not be unless each Intellect
    That moves these stars were lacking; lacking, too,
    The Prime One, not perfecting its elect.

D'you wish for more to clarify this view
    Of truth?' And I: 'No, now I clearly see
114   Nature can't lack in all it has to do.'
And he again: 'Then tell me, would it be
    Worse for a man to be no citizen
    On earth?' 'Yes,' I said, 'undoubtedly.'
'And can he be? – except some earthly men
    Be different with different offices? No!
120   Not if your Master writes the truth again.'
Up to this point, deduction made the flow.
    Then, in conclusion: 'The roots therefore
    Of your effects must then diversely grow.
Therefore, one is born a Solon, or
    A Xerxes, Melchisedek, or one whose flight
126   Lost him his son in daring so to soar.
The art of circling nature is done right,
    And seals the mortal wax, having no need
    To favour one house or on another light.
So Esau's line differs from Jacob's seed;
    And Quirinus derives from a sire so base
132   That he is then ascribed to Mars indeed!
The nature born would always have to trace
    A course like its begetters, if divine
    Providence had not overruled the case.
What was behind will now before you shine;
    I'll have you cloaked in this corollary
138   To show you what delight in you is mine.
Always, if nature's out of harmony
    With fortune, scant achievement will it find,
    As, out of region, seed grows stuntedly.
Yet, if the world below would set its mind
    To the foundation nature lays on earth
144   And build there, it would be good for humankind.
But still you wrench a person who, by birth,
    Should be a swordsman to religion; king
You make of one whose sermons show his worth.
    So out of the road your tracks go wandering.'

CANTO 9

Carlo turns back to the contemplation of the divine, after giving Dante further warnings about troubles to come to his lineage. Cunizza, sister to Ezzelino 'the firebrand' (Hell 12), mistress to Sordello (Purgatory 6) – and several others – speaks of Can Grande's defeat of the Paduan Guelfs in 1314. She introduces Folco to illustrate her complaint that current Venetians no longer seek such fame and achievement. Folco himself, once troubadour, then bishop, deserts the celestial ring to speak with Dante. He commends Rahab the harlot who helped Joshua to win the Holy Land; he condemns the Popes for neglecting the need for Crusades to recover it. Finally, he condemns Florence for corrupting the world with the 'flowers' of its florins in pursuit of wealth.

Clemence, line 2, was the widow of Carlo Martello; their son's throne was usurped by Carlo's younger brother Robert, who seized Naples in 1309. Richard, line 51, the evil lord of Treviso, was murdered in 1312. The Bishop of Feltro betrayed some Ferrarese Ghibellines, refugees in his protection, to their enemies in Ferrara. They were executed in 1314. ('Malta' here is the name of a Papal prison.) The extraordinary play on words in line 123 is on the victory palm and the palms of Christ's hands nailed to the Cross.

> Then when your Carlo had enlightened me,
> > Fair Clemence, he told of treacheries his heirs
> > Would come to, but he spoke in secrecy,
> Adding: 'But hold your peace on these affairs,
> > And let the years revolve.' – So all I say:
> > Your wrongs shall bring on well-earned woes of theirs.   6
> The life of that holy light had turned away
> > Already to the Sun that fills its view –
> > As to the good the all-sufficient ray. –
> Ah, souls deceived, ah, wicked creatures who
> > Crook your heart awry from such a good,
> > And turn your minds to vanity anew! –   12
> When, there, another of those splendours stood
> > Before me, signifying of its will
> > To satisfy me; brightening to show it would.
> The eyes of Beatrice were fixed so still
> > On me as previously; their loved assent
> > Assured me to allow desire its fill.   18
> 'Ah,' I said, 'quickly make my wish content,
> > O blessèd spirit; give me proof that I
> > May cast reflection on you of my thought's bent.'

The light so new to me made this reply,
    Out of the depth in which it ceased its song,
24   As someone, happy to do good, might fly:
'In that depraved, Italian land, along
    From the Rialto, before the source and site
    Where Brenta and Piave gush and throng,
Rises a hill – but not of such a height –
    From which there sprang a firebrand who, enflamed,
30   Brought on the land a dire onslaught of might.
I sprang from that same root, and I was named
    Cunizza. Here I glow because the light
    Of this star overwhelmed me and reclaimed.
I gladly pardon in myself the blight
    That caused my lot, nor do I sorrow here –
36   Which may seem strange, perhaps, in your crowd's sight.
This shining, precious gem of our Heavenly sphere
    Who is the nearest to me has much great fame
    Remaining, and, before it withers sere,
This centennial shall five recyclings claim.
    Should not a man then make himself excel
42   So that the first make further life its aim?
The current rabble never think or tell
    Of this where Tagliamento, Adige enclose.
    Never do they repent, though beaten well.
But soon shall come to pass, in the swamp's throes,
    That Padua shall stain the waters that cool
48   And bathe Vicenza, since duty they oppose.
Where Sile joins Cagnano, one holds rule,
    And holds his head up high. – The net to take
    Him is already woven off the spool.
From Feltro shall a cry in due time break
    For its godless shepherd's perfidy, so low
54   That none were jailed in 'Malta' for like sin's sake.
The vat to catch Ferrara's blood, full flow,
    Would be so cumbersome that it would wear
    The man out, weighing, ounce by ounce, the woe
That this obliging priest shall give, not spare,
    To prove himself a party man. The land condones
60   Such gifts as that – and with its ways they square.
Mirrors there are above – you call them Thrones –
    That send God's rays of judgement down on us.
    Therefore we may approve these words and tones.'

Here, she was silent, and her semblance thus
    Seemed someone's whose attention travelled on,
    Watching to join the wheel as previous.   66
The other joy, declared illustrious, shone
    Into my vision like a ruby while
    The sun is striking through its polygon.
– Brightness is won up there by joy, as a smile
    On earth; but down below the shade grows dim
    Outwardly should mind through sorrows file.   72
'Our God sees all and your seeing's in Him,'
    I then replied, 'so there is no desire,
    Blest spirit, that can hide from you its whim.
Why is it that your voice, gladdening the choir
    Of Heaven endlessly, in unison
    With these, the godly flames that cowl and attire   78
Themselves with six wings, won't fulfil my one
    Longing? If I were oned with you, as you
    In me, I'd not have waited, as I've done.'
'The greatest valley water stretches through,'
    His words restarted then, 'out of that main
    That garlands all the earth, between those two   84
Discordant shores extends so far its terrain
    Against the sun's course it makes meridian where
    Earlier the horizon had been lain.
I was a shoresman of this valley, there
    Between the Ebro and the Magra's brief run
    That parts the Genoese and Tuscan pair.   90
Almost alike for rise and set of sun
    Lie Bugia and my place of birth whose own
    Blood warmed its harbour once – by Caesar done.
Folco I'm called by those to whom I'm known,
    And this Heavenly sphere is stamped by me
    As I am stamped and marked for it alone.   96
For Belus' daughter burned less ardently,
    Wronging alike Sichaeus and Creusa, than I,
    As long as it became my locks – and she,
The Rhodopeian girl, burned less, whom sly
    Demophoön deluded; less, Hercules
    Who'd shut Iole in his heart to lie.   102
But here we do not feel repentance seize.
    We smile, not at our sins that never rise
    To mind, but at the Power that rules and frees.

So here we gaze on the Art that beautifies
    Its great effects, and, here, discern the Good
108   Wheel world above for world that underlies.
But so that you may bear away, and should
    Fulfil all wishes born within this sphere,
    I needs must speak that more be understood.
You wish to know who stands beside me here,
    Hidden in light that dazzles like a sun-
114   Beam sparkling on to water that is clear.
Now know that it is Rahab who's the one
    In peace; and, when she joined our order's ring,
    It marked itself, in her, as noblest done.
By this Heaven – touched by the shadowing
    Point which your earth casts – she was received
120   Before all else in Christ's triumphant harrowing.
Indeed, most fitting she should be retrieved
    By some Heaven here, as trophy of the victory
    By palm and palm so loftily achieved,
Because she aided Joshua when he
    First gained the victory in the Holy Land –
126   Which scarcely jogs the Papal memory!
Your city – offshoot of his who turned his hand
    And back upon his Maker first, whose sour
    Envy brings such lamentation – shall expand,
And grow and propagate that cursèd flower
    Which set the flock astray since it deflected
132   The Shepherd into wolf that will devour.
Through this, with Gospels and great doctors neglected,
    Now the Decretals hog analysis –
    As all the margins show, if they're inspected. –
The Popes and Cardinals are bent on this;
    To Nazareth they never turn the mind
138   Where Gabriel spread his wings to speak our Bliss.
The Vatican, and other parts enshrined
    Of Rome, the cemetery of soldiers led
By Peter, speedily and soon shall find
    They are set free, and all that whoredom fled.'

CANTO 10

They rise to the sun, emblematic of wisdom and understanding. Dante remarks on the wonders of the solar system to encourage people to marvel at God's wisdom and his provision for the earth. The spirits in the sun are so brilliant that they even stand out against the sun's light. He encounters Thomas Aquinas, the representative of theology, who informs him of others there whom Dante uses to represent areas of wisdom that he thinks are important. Albert of Cologne is another theologian; Gratian represents ecclesiastical and civil law; Isidore, natural science; Bede, church history; Richard, contemplation; Siger taught in the Street of Straw (Vicus Straminis, line 137) ideas for which he was accused of heresy and opposed by Thomas Aquinas. In Heaven they are now in harmony. Solomon represents royal wisdom; Boethius, the wisdom of philosophy.

The Primal and Ineffable Power and Worth,
    Gazing on his Son, in that love they brim
    Each other with, created all the earth,
And all that circles mind, or space's rim,
    With such design that all, who see it turn,
    Are not without some trace or taste of Him.   6
Then, reader, raise your eyes with me, discern
    Amid those noble wheels the region where
    One and the other motion interturn.
And from that point take pleasure as you stare
    Upon the Master's art who loves it so
    Within his heart, his eye is anchored there.   12
Note how the circle spirals with the row
    Of planets which administer the world
    That calls upon their aid from here below.
Yet, if their circuit weren't obliquely whirled,
    Much power in the Heaven would be vain,
    And dead most potency of earth be furled.   18
And, if it moved much less or more again
    Out of the straight, how great would be the wrench
    To world order, high or low, would show quite plain.
– Now stay, good reader, seated on your bench,
    And on this foretaste of it think and brood;
    You'll be well pleased before you tire and blench.   24
I've laid your table, banquet on the food,
    For the great matter I've set myself to write
    Draws to itself my total care and mood.

The greatest minister of nature whose light
   Measures our time for us, and stamps the world
30   With all the worth of Heaven in our sight,
One with that part just called to mind, now swirled
   Upon those spirals where he'd rise to view
   Always earlier and earlier as he whirled.
And I was with him; but I no more knew
   Of my ascent than is a man aware
36   Of what will be his next thought to pursue.
Beatrice, it is, that leads from Good to fare
   Towards the Better, and so instantaneous
   Her action that it fills no moment there.
How that itself must be so luminous
   Which, in the sun that I had entered now,
42   Shows not by colour but its light to us!
Never on mind could word of mine endow
   That image, though genius, art, tradition aided –
   But trust me, and let men long to witness how.
Yet, if our fantasies are low and jaded
   For such an exaltation, small wonder why!
48   No eye can penetrate the sun unshaded.
This was the fourth household of the High
   Father who satisfies as only he can,
   Showing how he breathes and begets to the eye.
'Give thanks, give thanks!' Beatrice began,
   'To the Angels' Sun who, by his grace,
54   Has raised you to this sun of sense you scan.'
No heart of mortal man, in time or space,
   So drawn into devotion, nor so keen
   To yield to God its will as, in this case,
I was to hear these words; so wholly had been
   My love committed to him, it caused eclipse
60   Of Beatrice – forgotten and unseen.
Yet she was not displeased; and on her lips
   A smile; the splendour of her laughing eyes
   Split my one mind into the many's grips.
I saw such lights, living and victor, rise
   And make a centre of us; the crown they made,
66   Sweeter in voice than shining to our eyes.
Latona's daughter we sometimes see displayed
   Like that, when vapour's so gravid to retain
   The thread that, round her zone, we see arrayed.

In Heaven's court from which I've come again
 Are many gems so lovely and so dear
 That may not be removed from their domain.   72
The song of all those lights was one; and here
 Whoever cannot fledge himself and wing
 Up there must wait for news the dumb make clear!
When, singing so, those burning suns in ring
 Had circled round us thrice, like stars around
 The neighbouring fixed poles circuiting,   78
They seemed as ladies, not from the dance unwound,
 But pausing, hushed and listening to hear
 The notes renewed of all that lovely sound.
In one I heard these words rise: 'Since the clear
 Beaming of Grace – at which true love is lit,
 And then, by loving, grows till it appear   84
Increased and spread – so lights and makes you fit
 To tread the stairway which, but to ascend
 A further time none ever descends by it,
Whoever, in your thirst, refused to lend
 His wine-flask were no more free than is the flow
 Of water that never in the sea shall blend.   90
You'd learn what plants within this garland grow
 That lovingly round the lovely maiden rings
 Who strengthens you for Heaven from below.
I was a lamb in the flock Dominic brings
 The goodly pasture's way, if none are prone
 To roam away upon their wanderings.   96
Next, on my right, is Albert of Cologne;
 He was a brother and a master to me;
 As Thomas of Aquino I was known.
If now you want to know the rest you see,
 Direct your eyes round as my words shall name,
 Circling the blessèd wreath accordingly.   102
This is the smile of Gratian, the next flame;
 He served both forums well and gave such aid
 It pleases Heaven with its noble aim.
The next to grace our choir: Peter, who laid
 His treasure – like the widow who was poor –
 Before the Holy Church, a gift well made.   108
The fifth light, fairest of all that here adore,
 Breathes from a love of which the world below
 Is thirsting to receive the news and lore.

There is the lofty mind once granted so
   Profound a wisdom that, if truth be true,
114   No second rose to the vision it could show.
Look at that taper light, the next in view,
   That, in the flesh below, fathomed the deeps
   Of the angelic nature, its ministry, too.
Now, in the next little light, there leaps
   That advocate of Christian times and ways,
120   From whose discourse Augustine sows and reaps.
Now, if from light to light you track my praise,
   In your mind's eye, your thirst already grows
   To see the eighth to come into your gaze.
In seeing good that sainted spirit glows,
   Rejoicing in that which strips away, divests
126   The world's deceit – for whoever hears and knows.
The body it was driven from still rests
   Below, in Cieldauro; to this peace he came
   Himself through martyrdom and exile's tests.
Next, the glowing breath of Isidore; the flame
   Of Bede, and that Richard, there, you see,
132   In contemplation more than man became.
That one from whom your gaze reverts to me
   Is the light of that soul whose depth of thought
   Felt that his death approached too sluggishly:
Siger's eternal light, it is, who taught
   In the *Vicus Straminis* to propound
138   By syllogism, truths invidious and fought.'
Then, as the clock that tells us with its sound
   The hour when the Bride of Christ will rise
   And sing her matins, for her Groom's love bound,
Where one part draws or drives the next, and plies
   So sweet a chiming note that, at the sound,
144   The well-tuned spirit swells with loving sighs,
So saw I, then, the glorious wheel go round
   And render voice to voice in harmony
And sweetness that may not be known or found
   Except where joy is felt eternally.

CANTO 11

This canto, mainly in the voice of Thomas Aquinas, is a record of St Francis of Assisi's love-affair with the Lady Poverty. Despite its powerful poetic simplicity it is derived fairly directly from St Bonaventura's Legend of the Blessed Francis. *It was customary for a Dominican to speak on St Francis' Day and a Franciscan to speak on St Dominic's Day. Dante follows this pattern here and in the next canto. The account ends with an attack on modern Dominicans for their shift away from the principles and rule of the original founder, whose virtues are praised in the next canto.*

Aphorisms, line 4, was the title of a famous book by Hippocrates (469–399 BC), a founder of the study of medicine. In line 27, 'distinction' reflects a technical term in logic which meant to find that the inference is not true, though the premises are, because the sense of the terms has altered to produce the conclusion. Both cities, in line 48, were controlled by the Angevins whom Dante hated. 'Ascesi' is an old spelling of Assisi, and could mean 'I have risen'.

O senseless cares of mortals: how untrue
    The arguments which make you beat your wings
    Downward to earth, no matter what you do.
One chases Law; one, Aphorisms; one clings
    To priestcraft, while another goes for power
    By violence and quibbling in all things.   6
And yet another loots; one spends his hour
    In business; one languishes in his ease;
    One tires himself in lusts of flesh and bower.
Meanwhile, I was released from all of these,
    And, gloriously with Beatrice received,
    I was amid the Heavens in their degrees.   12
When each had circled us and so achieved
    His first position, there he paused once more,
    As candle in a chandelier perceived.
Within the light that spoke to me before,
    Again I saw a smiling start to shine,
    As it increased in brightness from the core.   18
'As I reflect its rays, these eyes of mine,
    Gazing in Light Eternal, apprehend
    What causes you to think along that line.
You query, want to know what I intend –
    In clear and detailed discourse aimed to reach
    Your understanding – in speaking to this end: 24

"The goodly pasture's way," a turn of speech
    I used just now, and next, "no second rose".
    Here we need fine distinction, each from each.
The Providence that rules the world (and shows
    It such a wisdom that created eyes
30   Are foiled before the bedrock interpose)
In order that the Bride of Christ, whose cries
    Of pain espoused her with his blood so blest,
    Might move to the delight for which she sighs –
Secure herself, to him the faithfullest –
    Ordained two Princes on each side to be
36   Her guards, and help and guide her for the best.
One was seraphic in his ardency;
    The other, in his wisdom on the earth,
    A splendour of cherubic light was he!
I'll tell you of the one, because the worth
    Of both is spoken when either one is praised,
42   No matter which: to one end their deeds gave birth.
Between Topino and the stream that's raised
    Upon the hill the blest Ubaldo chose,
    From lofty height there slants a good slope grazed.
Perugia, from this mountain, either froze
    Or sweltered through the Porta Sole vent;
48   Nocera and Gualdo weep the yoke of woes.
Here, where this slope has levelled its descent,
    Was born into the world a very sun,
    Even as ours from Ganges in the Orient.
Therefore, whoever mentions it to anyone
    Should never say "Ascesi" – much too curt,
54   But "Orient" rightly names where he'd begun.
Not far from there, he started to alert
    The world to his great power, and brought to her
    A certain reinforcement where she lay inert.
In youth, for such a Lady did he spur
    To war against his father. Willingly none,
60   No more than to his death, unlocks to her.
And, in his father's presence, then, this son,
    Before his spiritual court, became united
    With her in love that grew each day begun.
She, deprived of her first husband, unrequited
    A thousand years and more, obscure, despised,
66   Until he stood beside her, uninvited.

No good it did her, though men realized
 He that the world feared had with Amyclas found
 Her fearless at his voice, unterrorized.
No good it did her to remain so sound
 In faith, so fearless, that when Mary stayed
 Below, she on the Cross with Christ was bound.   72
But, fearing I proceed too darkly: the Maid
 Was poverty; Francis her lover here,
 Clearly in simple speech is now conveyed.
Their harmony, and all their joyful cheer,
 Spread love and wonder, and their tender look,
 The cause of sacred thoughts both far and near.   78
And so the venerable Bernard shook
 His sandals off and ran to find that peace;
 And, chasing, mused how long his running took.
O wealth unrecognized! O rich increase!
 Egidius unsandals; Sylvester unsandals, they
 Follow the bride whose joy was such release!   84
So father and master true went on the way
 Beside this lady, binding the humble cord
 Already round the household in her sway.
Upon his brow no heaviness was scored
 From being son to Pietro Bernardone, nor
 From the contempt or wonder of the horde.   90
His stern intent he then revealed before
 Pope Innocent, and had from him first seal
 And imprint for his order of the poor.
When throngs in poverty trailed at his heel –
 Whose wondrous life it would be best to sing
 In Heaven's glory where the sainted wheel –   96
The will of this chief shepherd a second ring ·
 Encircled, by being crowned by Honorius,
 And by the Holy Spirit's visiting.
In thirst for martyrdom, he preached victorious
 Christ and his followers before the face
 Of the proud Sultan – too vainglorious   102
He found them, set against conversion's grace;
 And, not to waste his time, returned to reap
 The harvest of his own Italian race.
Between Tiber and Arno, on a harsh steep,
 He then received Christ's final mark and seal,
 That on his limbs for two years he would keep.   108

When God, who chose him in such good to deal,
    Was pleased to take him to the prize he'd won
    In being so lowly in the commonweal,
His dearest lady, to each brother – as son
    And heir to him – he pledged, and bade them cleave
114   To her, and keep their faith, as he had done.
And then his glorious spirit chose to leave
    From her embrace for its own realm again
    And let no other bier his corpse receive.
Think what his colleague should be, fit to maintain
    The true course that the ship of Peter plies,
120   Steady towards its mark across the main.
Such was our Patriarch; those who rise
    To follow him, as he commands them be,
    Laden themselves with goodly merchandise.
But still his flock has grown to gluttony
    For fresher foods – which cannot be, except
126   They wander various glades in vagrancy.
The more his sheep strayed from him and stepped
    Into the distant pastures they discern
    The emptier they came to fold where they are kept.
There are a few, indeed, who fear to spurn
    The fold, and stay beside the shepherd – so few
132   That little cloth for cowls will serve their turn.
Now, if my words have not been vague to you,
    And if you have attended well to me
    And can recall what I have said, it's true
Your wish must partly be fulfilled. You'll see
    The plant from which they whittle; you'll ponder
138   The rebuke intended, as was meant to be,
    In "way of goodly pasture" if none wander.'

CANTO 12

Bonaventura, General of the Franciscans from 1256–74, now returns Thomas's
compliment by speaking of St Dominic. Ubertine of Casale and Matteo of
Acquasparta were leaders of two factions of Franciscans who disagreed over strict-
ness or liberalness in interpreting the Franciscan rule. Hugh of St Victor was the
master to Richard of the same famous abbey. Pietro Mangiadore was a commenta-
tor, from St Victor also. Pietro Hispano was a logician who became Pope John XXI.
The prophet Nathan confronted David with his sin (2 Samuel 12). Anselm was the
famous Archbishop of Canterbury; Donatus composed a grammar – a subject
regarded as most important in those times. Rabanus was a German scholar and
historian. Joachim wrote a commentary on the Apocalypse. The first ring of the
two garlands, line 19, represents individuals of the Thomistic-Aristotelian tradi-
tion of the church; the second represents the Platonic-Augustinian. Franciscans
tended to the latter view while Dante preferred the former which maintained the
pre-eminence of intellect and vision.

Once the blest flame had said the final word
    The sacred quern, which had not paused for long,
    Began to turn; the round had not occurred
Before a second ring, a circling throng,
    Had caught its motion up into its own,
    And harmonized its song into the song –   6
Song that so excelled those of our Muses known,
    Our sirens in those sweet pipes, as the first Splendour
    Excels what it reflects within its zone.
As two rainbows, over thin mist, that render
    The same hues parallel, when Juno makes
    Request to her handmaiden, and the centre   12
Gives birth to the outer bow that takes
    The style of speech from that poor nymph consumed
    By love, as sun consumes the haze that quakes –
And makes the people know earth won't be doomed
    To flood again, by virtue of the pact
    That God made Noah, when the dry land loomed: 18
So those two garlands made their rings and tracked
    Their eternal roses round us so that one
    Answered the inner circle, act for act.
Soon as the dance and great high festival, spun
    Alike from song and flashing light with light,
    Blithely and benign, in all accordance done,   24

In point of time and act of will, were quite
　　Becalmed (as eyes which, dwelling on the joys
　　That move them, lift in concord, closed to sight)
Out of the blaze of one new light deploys
　　A voice that turned me compass to the pull
30　　Of that one star that drew me to the noise.
It said: 'That love which makes me beautiful
　　Bids me to praise the second leader here –
　　For whom my own was found so laudable.
And right it is that where the one appear
　　The other should, for, as in partnership
36　　They warred, their glory should, as one, shine clear.
Christ's army, so dear to re-equip,
　　Was following the standard, lagging, strayed,
　　Dispersed, thin-ranked, and in fear's grip.
Therefore the King who rules forever made
　　Counsel for his soldiers in danger's height,
42　　Not in their own worth, but his grace arrayed.
As said, he had two champions whose might
　　Was strong at his Bride's side. At their great feats
　　The straggling squadrons grouped again to fight.
In that part where sweet Zephyr stirs and greets
　　The new leaves till they open, and Europe sees
48　　Herself reclothed in foliage from its heats,
Not far from those pounding waves beyond whose seas
　　The sun is sometimes hidden from the eye
　　Because of all their long immensities,
The fortunate Calahorra happens to lie,
　　Beneath protection of a mighty shield
54　　Where lion submits, and, next, subdues near by.
This friar, ardent in Christian faith and field,
　　Was born there, sacred athlete, kind to friends
　　But cruel to his foes until they yield.
No sooner than conceived, his mind extends
　　So full of living virtue that, in the womb,
60　　He made his mother prophet of his ends.
Now, once the pledge was made between this groom
　　And this Faith, beside the holy baptistry
　　Where they swore mutual salvation in that room,
The mother who assented for him then could see
　　The wondrous fruit that would appear, in dream,
66　　Destined to spring from him and his heirs to be.

That he might be what he was in name and theme –
    A spirit from up here – they made his name
    The possessive of whose he was, supreme.
Dominic was he named: I speak to claim
    Him as the husbandman chosen by Christ
    To tend his orchard as his single aim.   72
He proved himself the messenger of Christ,
    And his familiar, indeed, for his first
    Love was the first counsel given by Christ.
And often was he found by her that nursed
    Him, silent and awake upon the floor,
    As if to say: "For this I came!" – well versed.   78
Felix was his father, truly; more,
    His mother was Giovanna, if the word
    Translated be what it is taken for.
Not for the world for whose sake men are stirred
    To labour after the Ostian and Thaddeus,
    But for love of true manna was he heard.   84
He quickly came to be a studious
    And mighty teacher, setting out to tend
    The vines that wilt when dressers fail to truss.
And from the seat which, once, was more the friend
    To the just poor – not in itself, but him
    Who sits degenerating – not to spend   90
Two or three for six, and not to brim
    With fortune of the coming vacancy, not
    For tithes from God's own poor was it his whim
To ask, but for the right to aim his shot
    Against the erring world, to save the seed
    Of these twenty-four plants that ring your plot.   96
Then, with teaching and the will, he gathered speed,
    And, with the apostolic office, rose
    Like some torrent that a deep vein has freed.
His impetus struck among the stumps that chose
    Heresy, strongest where resistance, rife,
    Was most determined, stubborn to oppose.   102
From him, next, various rills sprang to the strife,
    By which the Catholic orchard is so watered
    And refreshed its shrubs have sturdier life.
If, in the chariot by which the Church has ordered
    Its defences, this was the one wheel
    By which she won in open war, unslaughtered,   108

It should be clear for you to see and feel
    The excellence of the other one with whom,
    Before me, Thomas was good enough to deal.
The course for which his orbit made the room
    Has been neglected, so that now is found
114   Where good crust was the mould begins to bloom.
His retinue that went where he was bound
    Has turned its back, so that its toe must tread
    The imprint of its heels and so lose ground.
The crops to which such wretched tilling led
    Shall soon be seen when tares shall wail because
120   They are excluded from the bins instead.
I do concede that any who should gloss,
    Leaf after leaf, our volume still would see
    A page which reads: "I am what once I was."
Not from Casale, Acquasparta would that be,
    From which come to our rule one sort whose goal
126   Evades and one that reads too rigidly.
Bonaventura of Bagnorea's living soul
    I am, who set aside the left-hand care
    In the great offices in my control.
Illuminato and Augustine, the pair
    Here, of the first brothers, unshod and poor,
132   Who in the cord became God's friends. And there,
Hugh of St Victor's with them; many more:
    Pietro Mangiadore, Pietro Hispano, the man
    Who shines on earth in twelve books of his store.
And Chrysostom, the Metropolitan;
    Nathan, the prophet; Anselm, and then the
138   Donatus whose hand designed the first art's plan.
Rabanus is here, and, shining next to me,
    The Calabrian abbot, Joachim, endowed
    With all the spirit of true prophecy.
I'm moved to praise this paladin aloud
    In emulation of the ardent courtesy
144   Of brother Thomas' well-judged speech; this crowd
    Of saints was also moved along with me.'

CANTO 13

Dante compares the two circles of Heavenly luminaries with the fifteen stars of the first magnitude in the astronomy of his day, the seven stars of Ursa Major and the brightest two of Ursa Minor. Aquinas clarifies his remarks concerning Solomon's kingly wisdom. He warns Dante of the risks of intelligence in jumping to obvious but mistaken conclusions. In line 59, the 'subsistences' seem to be the nine orders of angels.

Let him imagine this, who'd truly know
    What next I saw (and, as I speak, to cling
    To the image, like firm rock in the flow):
Fifteen of those stars that, in the varying
    Regions, enliven the sky with such a light
    They pierce the knitted air through which they swing;   6
Let him imagine next the Wain that, night
    And day, is pleased with the bosom of our skies
    So that it always circles in our sight;
Let him imagine the mouth of the Horn that flies,
    Starting from the axle where the prime
    Sphere its own revolving multiplies;   12
Imagine these themselves had shaped, sublime,
    Two signs in Heaven, as Minos' daughter made
    When she felt the chill of death's cold time;
And one with beams inside the other rayed,
    And both as spinning so that one should lead,
    The other follow as if it had obeyed –   18
And he should have an inkling, if he heed,
    Of the constellation of the twofold dance
    Which circled round the point I was indeed.
For it transcends our customs and our glance,
    As does, surpassing all, the Empyrean
    The motion of the Chiana's slow advance.   24
There they were expressing, not the Paean,
    Not Bacchus, but Three Persons in the One,
    And all, as human, in one Person's mien.
And, when the song and circling next had spun,
    They turned to us, sacred lamps that rejoice,
    Passing from duty to duty to be done.   30

Then, from that harmony divine, a voice
    Broke in the silence from the light that told
    The wondrous life of God's poor man and choice,
Which said: 'Since one sheaf's threshed, and garners hold
    Its store already, sweet love bids me thresh
36   The one remaining into ears of gold.
You think that in his breast – out of whose flesh
    The rib was drawn to make the lovely cheek
    For whose palate the whole world pays afresh –
And into that pierced by the lance (to wreak
    Satisfaction for past and future, and heave
42   The scale against all sin in man so weak)
Such light as human nature may receive
    Was all infused by that same Worthiness
    That made both first and second, as we believe.
Therefore you muse at what I seemed to stress
    When I declared the good inherent in
48   The fifth light had no second nonetheless.
Open your eyes to what I now begin
    To say. You'll see how that and what you believe
    Strike truth as centre of the circle's spin.
What never dies, and all that death will grieve,
    Is nothing but the Idea's reflected glow
54   Our Lord, in loving, chooses to conceive,
Because that living Light (whose rays can flow
    Out of their source yet so they never part,
    Nor from the love that triples it they go)
Out of its goodness points its rays to dart,
    As though reflected, in nine subsistences
60   That, one eternally, reveal his art.
From these, it falls to lesser potencies,
    From stage to stage becoming such as breed
    Such transient and mere contingencies,
Contingencies that grow out of a seed,
    Or others which are seedless that the sphere
66   Of Heaven generates beneath its speed.
The wax for these, and that which moulds it clear,
    Are not of selfsame mode, and, under seal
    Of the Ideal, its translucence varies here,
So that it happens that one tree will deal,
    According to its kind, good or poor fruit;
72   So men have varied skills in the commonweal.

But, if the wax and mould should truly suit,
 And, if Heaven had reached its supreme power,
 The signet's light would shine through, absolute.
But nature makes it faulty in its hour,
 Behaving as the artist who has skill
 In his technique but trembling hands that cower.   78
Therefore, if warm Love and clear Vision will,
 With Primal Power dispose and seal, entire
 Perfection is acquired which they instil.
Thus was the clay made worthy to acquire
 The full perfection of the animal,
 The Virgin, pregnant with that Love's desire.   84
So I admit your doubt is rational,
 That human nature never was, nor yet
 Shall be, as with those two, perfect in all.
But if I say no more I'll be beset:
 "How then was he so peerless?" I'll be tasked
 With further query which must now be met.   90
That what is not apparent may be unmasked,
 Consider who he was, and what should bring
 Him – bidden "Choose!" – to beg what then he asked.
I speak so you may note: he was a king,
 And chose the wisdom such a sovereignty
 Might need to suit the work of governing.   96
Not: how many spirit-movers there might be;
 Nor if a necessary and contingent premise should
 Result in necessary conclusion; no, not he!
Nor: whether to grant a *primum mobile*; nor: could
 There be, from rim to semi-circle's base,
 A triangle without right-angle stood!   102
So, if this and all I've said you face,
 Royal wisdom, it was, the arrow of my mind
 Meant as the matchless vision, in this case.
And, if to "rose" you wisely look, you'll find
 It holds for kings alone; and though there be
 So many, good are rare of any kind.   108
Shown this, accept what I propose, and see
 That then it well agrees with what you hold
 Of the first Father and our Felicity.
And let this always make your feet lead-soled
 To slow you down just like a weary man
 To either "Yes" or "No" in things untold.   114

For he is well down in the fools who can
   Affirm, deny, without distinction brought,
   Between one case and next that he should scan.
Thus often happens that the swift-formed thought
   Leans the wrong way, and then conceit the more
120   Ties the intelligence until it's caught.
It is much worse than vain to leave that shore,
   Since none returns as he set out who sails
   To fish for truth but lacks the art and lore.
The world has open proof of this: the trails
   Of Parmenides, Melissus, Bryson – those who
126   Set forth not knowing where, or what avails.
As did Sabellius, Arius, that foolish crew,
   Who were a polished sword to Holy Writ,
   Making the straight countenance look askew.
Let people never rashly in judgement sit,
   Like those who count the sheaves across the field
132   Before the harvest comes to gather it.
For I have seen at first the thorn revealed
   All winter through, forbidding, harsh and keen,
   And then upon its top a rose will yield.
And once I saw a ship go straight and clean
   And swift on course across the sea, yet sink,
138   Foundering at the last as harbour's seen.
Let neither Dame Bertha nor Squire Martin think,
   If they observe one thieve, one offering,
They see with divine wisdom, link for link,
   For one may rise, the other fall and swing.'

CANTO 14

*Dante wonders how the resurrected body will be able to withstand the incandescent
light of the Heavenly spirit. He receives an explanation. A third circle encom-
passes the first two, signifying the mystery of the Holy Spirit. They then rise to the
red planet Mars, emblem of the spiritual warrior, the martyr-soldier. These are
symbolized by a shining crucifix on which they move.*

From centre to the rim, and from the rim
    To centre, water tremors in a bowl
    As it is struck inside or at the brim.
Suddenly came this thought, just as the soul
    Of glorious Thomas lapsed to silence – seized
    From the comparison the mind's eye stole   6
Between where Thomas spoke and Beatrice was pleased,
    As soon as he had finished then, to say:
    'This man has another need to be appeased,
That neither in his speech will he convey,
    Nor yet within his thought reveal: to trace
    Into another truth as well you may.   12
Tell if the light you blossom with shall grace
    And clothe your being everlastingly,
    As now it covers you; and, in that case,
Say how, when back to visibility,
    The eyesight will not wither or be quelled
    To look upon such intense radiancy.'   18
As if by surging joy filled and impelled,
    At once, all those who wheeled upon the dance
    Quickened in rhythm, and their voices swelled.
So, at that eager devout prayer, the rings advance
    Their wheeling and their wondrous melody,
    And, with a freshened joy, their step enhance.   24
Whoever grieves that here we die that we
    May live above has never been contemplative
    Of those fresh showers of eternal radiancy.
The One, the Two, the Three that ever live
    And ever reign in Three and Two and One,
    Not circumscribed but circumscribing all they give,   30
Three times were hymned, by each spirit done
    With such a melody that it was fit
    Reward for any merit ever won.

And then I heard from the holy light that lit
    The smaller ring an unassuming tone –
36   The Angel's to Mary might resemble it –
Answering: 'While the feast of Heaven is thrown
    Our love, as long, shall clothe us in its rays
    With such a garment as is in this zone.
Its brightness matches to our ardour's blaze;
    Our ardour, to our vision which may grow
42   As great as grace – beyond our merit – raise.
When in our flesh, holy and glorified, we go
    Again, our person will become more pleasing
    Because it will its full perfection show.
Then we'll be given whatever our increasing
    Of unwon radiance the Highest God permits,
48   Radiance to let us see him without ceasing.
Therefore the vision must enlarge on its
    Focus; the ardour lit by that increase,
    And so increase the ray ardour emits.
But like a coal that gives the flames release,
    And by its lively glowing excels its light
54   So that its own appearance does not cease,
So shall this splendour which enwraps us quite
    Be conquered in appearance by flesh and bone
    Which earth's clay covers over now in night.
Nor shall the light fatigue us, in that zone,
    For every organ of the flesh grows strong
60   Towards what may delight us to be known.'
So swift and keen they were, after that song,
    To cry 'Amen' – both inner and outer choir –
    They showed, indeed, how much for flesh they long.
Not just, I think, for self do they desire,
    But for their mothers, fathers, others, dear
66   Before they wore eternal light's attire.
And lo, around them rises what would appear
    A brightening horizon, over what shone there,
    Of even splendour, radiant and clear.
And as, in earliest of the evening air,
    New objects to be seen appear on high
72   So that their image shows, then not, you'd swear,
I started to notice new arrivals ply
    A circle which was out beyond the two
    Perimeters familiar to my eye.

Oh, the Holy Spirit, dazzlingly true!
 How sudden and candescent there it wheeled!
 My vanquished eyes could not withstand the view. 78
But Beatrice, so lovely, smilingly revealed
 Herself to me – it must remain with those
 Visions the memory can never yield.
From her my eyes regained their sight and rose,
 And so I saw myself transported, lone,
 But for my Lady, to a higher state that glows. 84
Surely I saw myself raised up a zone
 By enkindled smiling of that planet won,
 That showed a more than usual reddened tone.
Within the heart – and in that tongue that's one
 To all – a sacrifice and burnt offering
 I made to God for this new grace he'd done. 90
That ardent offering was no completed thing
 Within my heart before I knew the prayer
 Had been received with favour on the wing,
For, with such radiance and reddened flare,
 Inside two beams, these splendours came to me.
 I cried: 'Divine Sun, whose blazon they wear!' 96
As, marked with major and minor lights, you see,
 Between the Universe's Poles, the Milky Way's
 White gleam that leaves the wise perplexity,
So, deep in Mars, these constellated rays
 Set forth the reverenced sign that quadrant lines
 Drawn in a circle make, with all their blaze. 102
My memory outruns the mind's confines,
 For that cross there so emanated Christ
 I find no image worthy of those signs.
But he who takes his cross and follows Christ
 Shall yet forgive me all I leave unsaid
 When, in that glow, he sees the gleam of Christ. 108
From horn to horn, from base towards the head,
 Were moving lights that brightly coruscated
 In meeting and in passing as they sped.
So, here, we see straight, wry, swift, belated,
 Variable-seeming, long and short, reflect
 Those particles of atoms congregated 114
And passing through a beam of light they've specked,
 At those times when it's streaked a canopy
 Of shade that art or skill of men erect.

And as the viol and harp in harmony
　　Of many strings convey a sweet accord
120　　　To one that hears, not notes, but melody,
So did those lights I followed there afford
　　Upon that cross a melody that bound
　　Me, though I couldn't follow hymn nor chord.
It did, I knew, in lofty praise resound,
　　Because there came to me a 'Rise and conquer!'
126　　　As one not following may catch a sound.
I was so much enraptured there, no longer
　　Was there anything that ever bound
　　Me captive in more dulcet chains, or stronger.
– Too rash, perhaps, that saying may be found,
　　As slighting the delight of those fair eyes,
132　　　Gazing on which my yearning finds her ground.
But those who call to mind how, as they rise,
　　Those living signs of every loveliness
　　Increase in power; how I'd not turned my eyes
On them again, may excuse me my express
　　Accusation, made in my excuse, and see
138　I speak the truth, including it, no less:
　　Rising, that sacred joy raises its purity.

CANTO 15

Dante encounters his great-great-grandfather, Cacciaguida, whom he represents as courageous in the Second Crusade, 1147–9. Cacciaguida condemns the current depraved state of Florence. The Latin, line 28, alludes to Vergil's account of Aeneas' meeting with his father in the underworld, Aeneid 4.679: 'O blood of mine, O grace of God so lavish! To whom was Heaven's gate ever opened twice, but to you.' Conrad III led the Second Crusade. The Law referred to is that of Islam.

The benign will – in which the true scent
    Of love distils, as, in the grudging will,
    The stench of cupidity is given vent,
Bade the sweet lyre be silent, rendered still
    The sacred strings which Heaven's right hand
    Plucks and releases with its lovely skill.   6
Nor could those souls be deaf to understand
    The righteous prayers, but tacitly agreed
    To stir my will, and plea to them expand.
Right is the boundless grief of those whose heed
    And love for what is not enduring strips
    Them everlastingly of love indeed.   12
As through the pure and tranquil sky there slips,
    From time to time, a sudden flaming trace
    So that a fixed gaze glances up, then dips,
From what appears a star changing its place,
    Except that where it lit no star is gone,
    And that its light endures but little space –   18
So, from the horn extended right, and on
    To foot of that same cross, a star was seen
    To shoot in this constellation that so shone.
The gem, not leaving from its ribbon's sheen,
    Along the radiant strip towards me made,
    Like fire behind an alabaster screen.   24
With selfsame tenderness Anchises' shade
    Greeted his son (if we grant our greatest muse a
    Measure of credit) in Elysium's glade.
'O sanguis meus, o super infusa
    Gratia Dei – sicut tibi, cui
    Bis unquam coeli janua reclusa?'   30

Thus that light; I listened to his words to me,
    Then turned my glance towards my Lady awhile;
    But stunned awe, there and here, took mastery.
For in her eyes was shining such a smile,
    I thought, with mine, I touched the very bound
36   Of Paradisal Grace beyond denial.
Then – joyous, both in terms of sight and sound –
    That spirit added to his opening, things
    I could not comprehend because profound.
He did not obfuscate; necessity brings
    His thought from higher regions than a man
42   Has power to comprehend up in those rings.
But, when love's ardent bow was eased to span
    Within the range of man's capacity,
    The first words that I understood began:
'Blessèd be Thou, Thou One-in-Three
    Who art so greatly courteous to my line!'
48   And then continued clear enough to me:
'A clear, long-cherished hunger in which I pine,
    Drawn from the reading of the mighty tome
    Where neither black nor white to change incline,
You have assuaged, my son, in this my home
    Of light from which I speak to you; thanks be
54   To her who fledged your flight to this lofty dome.
Your thought, so you believe, proceeds to me
    Out of the Primal Thought as, once it's known,
    Five, six irradiate from unity,
So that you don't ask why it is I've shown
    More joy in you than others at this feast
60   Nor who I am who greet you like his own.
You judge correctly for the greatest and least
    Of spirits in this life gaze in that glass
    Where, ere you think, you spread your thought uncreased.
But so that sacred love may come to pass –
    In which I gaze unendingly – that lends
66   This thirst and sweet desire, be not sparse
Of word but voice the longing that now pends;
    Sound forth your wishes, bold and confident,
    And joyously. My answer, decreed, attends.'
I turned to Beatrice who heard of my intent
    Before I spoke, and granted me a sign
72   That made my wings expand for their ascent.

'Once the Primal Equality chose to shine
    On you, an equal weight was made between
    Wish and performance in your every design,
Because the Sun that poured on you its keen
    Warmth and its light has such equality
    All similes fall short of what they mean,'   78
I'd started. 'Yet will and means in men must be –
    For reasons clear to you – suited much less,
    And fledged upon their wings unevenly.
And therefore I, a mortal, feel the stress
    Of this imbalance, and only in my heart
    Give thanks for the fatherly welcome you express.   84
I can and do entreat you at the start,
    O living topaz, gem in this coronet,
    Tell me your name before you must depart.'
'O leaf of mine – who gave delight when yet
    Only expected here – I am your root.'
    This was the first answer that I met.   90
He added, 'He from whom your kindred bruit
    Their name – who has a hundred years or so
    Circled the Mount, the first tier of the route –
Was son to me, your grandfather's father, know.
    It is befitting now your prayers should spare
    Those years of toil he has to undergo.   96
Florence, within its ancient bounds, from where
    She still hears tierce and nones, reposed as yet
    In peace, sober and chaste, serene and fair.
There was no bracelet then, no coronet;
    No embroidered gowns; no girdle's sway
    That strikes the eye before the person met.   102
Those days the daughter's birth caused no dismay
    To fathers; on the bride's side and the groom's,
    Both age and dowry in due measure lay.
No mansions were deserted to the glooms;
    Sardanapalus had made no arrival
    To show what acts may be indulged in rooms.   108
Montemario was unpassed by your rival,
    Ucellatoio which, as it has surpassed
    In rising, shall surpass in ruin's deprival.
Bellincion Berti have I seen to cast
    Leather and bone about him, and his wife
    Turn from her mirror plain-faced, shamefast.   114

I've seen dei Nerli's and del Vecchio's life
    Content with hide tunic, untrimmed of lace,
    And at the flax and spindle each one's wife.
Ah, happy clan! secure of their burial place!
    And none was left deserted in her bed
120   Because of France and those it drew apace.
One watched the cradle, spoke and often said
    The soothing words that first put such delight
    Into a mother's and a father's head.
One, drawing threads from the distaff, would recite
    And tell her household of the Trojan tale,
126   Of Fiesole, and Rome in all her might.
A Chianghella, a Lapo Salterello'd avail
    As great a marvel then, as now might stir
    A Cincinnatus or Cornelia, on your scale.
To such a restful, so fair a life in her,
    To such a citizenship, so loyal in aim,
132   To such a kindly inn for the traveller,
Mary gave me with loud cries on her name,
    And there, within your ancient baptistry,
    Cacciaguida, and a Christian I became.
Moronto and Eliseo were brothers to me.
    My wife came from the Po Valley; from hers
138   Your surname is derived, as you may see.
I followed the Emperor Conrad who gave me spurs
    Within his knighthood, I so rose, in his sight,
    By deeds of valour among his followers.
With him I marched on the infamy and might
    Of that same Law whose people now still lord –
144   Shame to your pastors – what is yours by right.
And there I was dismissed by that vile horde
    From that deceitful world of which the love
Stains so many souls; from there I soared
    Through martyrdom up here to peace above.'

CANTO 16

Cacciaguida continues his lament over the decline of Florence. He lists the noble families whose influence is no more. Line 145 refers to events surrounding Buondelmonte's betrothal to one of the Amidei. He was foolishly persuaded to court one of the Donati women. The injured parties debated whether the insult merited death or something less vigorous. Mosca advised that once a thing was done it was over with. So Buondelmonte was assassinated at the foot of the statue of Mars. Thus began the feudings in the Florence of this period.

Ah, petty pedigree of our nobleness,
    If people glory in you here below
    Where our affections sicken, I'll express
Small wonderment because I gloried to know
    It there where appetite is never bent;
    I mean, within the Heavens' eternal glow.   6
Truly, it makes a cloak of shrinking extent,
    So, if we do not daily add some more,
    Time, shearing round, will leave it clipped and rent.
Then, with that *you* the Romans used before,
    Though now her citizens least persevere,
    My words began again that style of yore.   12
At which Beatrice, standing off, though near,
    Smiled, so she seemed the one who coughed to see
    The first recorded lapse of Guinevere.
I started: 'You're my father who raises me
    So much it gives me boldness now to speak
    Because I'm more than I myself could be.   18
So many streams of gladness fill the creek
    Of mind, it gives me joy that it can swell
    With such a spate and neither burst nor leak.
Tell me, dear root from which I sprang, ah, tell
    Your ancestry, what was recorded on
    Your boyhood memory as the years befell.   24
Speak of St John's sheepfold, how great it shone,
    And which the families worthiest to bear
    The foremost offices in times bygone.'
And, as an ember glows into a flare
    At the wind's breath, so then I saw the glow
    Increase to hear my tender words and care.   30

And, as to sight it grew the lovelier, so
    With voice more sweet and gentle, but not versed
    In this the modern dialect we know,
He said: 'From when *Ave* was said first,
    To the birth in which my mother, sainted now,
36   Unburdened herself of what her body nursed,
Five-hundred, fifty and thirty times allow
    This fire returned to his own lion's lair,
    Rekindling beneath its feet where he would bow.
My ancestors and myself were born right there
    Where, in your annual games, the ones who run
42   Reach the ward furthest in their thoroughfare.
Concerning them, let this suffice and have done:
    Of where they came from, what they must have been,
    Silence were better than discourse long-spun.
At this time all of those stirring between
    Mars and the Baptist, fit for waging war,
48   Were but a fifth of those now on the scene.
The people – debased with Campi now, and more
    From Certaldo, Figline – knew it was pure
    Down to the humblest of its stock and poor.
These folk I name were better, I am sure,
    As neighbours; and your boundaries should close
54   At Galluzzo and Trespiano, not immure
These, and so bear the stench that reeks and flows
    From that peasant from Aguglion, that swine
    From Signa who for jobbery still has the nose.
And, if the race – the most degenerate line
    On earth – not Caesar's stepmother, but instead
60   Had been a mother to her son, benign,
One now a Florentine and moneychanger had fled
    To Semifonte, where his grandfather went
    Traipsing, and begged to find his daily bread.
Still would Montemurlo be a battlement
    Of the Counts; Cerchi, in Acone parish bounds,
66   And, in the Val di Greve, the Buondelmonti content.
The mix of people from the start laid grounds
    For all the city's woes, as would be food
    Towards the body when excess confounds.
A blind bull falls more heavily, conclude,
    Than does the blindest lamb; many a time
72   One sword cuts cleaner than some five had hewed.

If you regard Luni and Urbisaglia's prime,
    How they have gone, and how they're followed now
    By Chiusi and Senigallia in their crime,
It won't seem new, nor a hard thing to allow
    How families undo themselves, though high,
    And cities have their end, and come to bow.   78
Your business has its death, as you must die,
    But that, in long enduring things, escapes
    The notice since your lives are brief and fly.
And as the rolling of the Moon's orb drapes
    Repeatedly, and bares the sandy shore,
    So Fortune acts on Florence, and reshapes.   84
So it should hardly as a wonder floor
    You, hearing tell of noble Florentines
    Whose fame lies buried under Time once more:
The Ughi, Catellini, Filippi, in decline;
    Greci, Ormanni, Alberichi – citizenry
    I've seen whose fame, once, no one could outshine.   90
I've seen, as great as long their ancestry,
    Della Sannella with dell' Arca, and, as well,
    Soldanieri, Bostichi and Ardinghi.
Over the gate – laden with fresh and fell
    Perfidy of such weight it soon will lead
    To wrecking of the barque beneath the swell –   96
Were once the Ravignani, from whose breed
    Descends Count Guido and all those, since then,
    Who take the name of noble Bellincion's seed.
Della Pressa knew how to govern men
    Already, and Galigaio, in his court,
    Had hilt and pommel already gilded then.   102
The pale of vair already great in report:
    Sachetti, Giuochi, Fifanti, Barucci;
    Galli; those blushing for bushels they sold short.
The stock from which have flourished the Calfucci
    Was great already; already drawn to hold
    The curule office, Sizii, Arrigucci.   108
What greatness have I seen, by pride untold
    Now fallen; Florence flowering in feat and deed
    Illustrious beneath the spheres of gold.
Thus behaved the sires of either breed
    Who, when the church is left with vacancy,
    Fatten themselves in counsels lacking speed.   114

The outrageous clan that, after those who flee,
   Turn dragon but, to those that show a fang –
   Or purse – look quiet as a lamb might be,
Was rising, but from humble folk they sprang,
   So Ubertino Donato felt scant delight
120   When his father-in-law kinned him with that gang.
Caponsacco had come from Fiesole's height
   Already, to the market place; the fame
   Of Giuda and Infangato was already bright.
– An incredible but true thing, all the same,
   I'll tell you: the inner circle had a gate
126   To which was given the della Pera name.
Each one who bears – though distant he relate –
   The fair arms of the great baron whose name
   And worth St Thomas' feast will celebrate
From him derived their knighthood, and privilege claim;
   Though he who adds the border now has urged
132   The cause of all the people as his aim.
Already the Gualterotti, Importuni surged;
   Though Borgo would still be quieter if those
   Newer neighbours never had converged.
The house from which your flowing tears arose
   Because of a just and killing wrath which set
138   An end to all your joyous life's repose,
Was honoured with its associates. Ah, yet
   How wickedly Buondelmonte you had quit
   That wedding, and another's prompting met!
Many had been in joy who sadly sit,
   Had God to the Ema first committed you
144   The day you reached the city and entered it.
But it was fitting a victim's blood was due
   To that wasted stone that guards the bridge from fair
   Florence in that last peace she ever knew.
With these people, and others living there,
   I looked on Florence in such a full repose
150   She had no cause for wailing as her share.
With these I watched as all her people rose
   So glorious and just; the lily on the shaft
Was not reversed, nor yet by faction's woes
   Dyed crimson red with all its bloody craft.'

CANTO 17

Phaëthon's visit to Clymene is the opening parallel to the way in which Dante is to learn more from Cacciaguida of the dark intimations concerning his future life – which Dante has already received in the two previous realms of the after-life. In explaining clearly what is to befall Dante, Cacciaguida emphasizes the independence of the will from the influence of the stars. He instructs Dante to reveal to all how justice will descend on the evil-doers who have maligned him. The Gascon, line 82, was Clement V, first of the French Popes at Avignon, puppet of Philip IV of France, who sided first with the Emperor Henry VII but was secretly plotting against him. Clement died in 1314.

As came to Clymene for assurance of what
    He heard against himself, he who still sways
    Fathers to caution with sons – such was my lot;
And such was seen to be, then, by the gaze
    Of Beatrice and that light who moved to yield
    Already his position for her rays.   6
'Express the flame,' my Lady thus appealed,
    'Of your desire so that it's issued clear,
    Marked with your internal stamp, and sealed;
Not that our knowledge will increase to hear
    Your words, but so that you may learn, when dry,
    To ask for drink, and have it offered.' – 'Dear   12
Foundation of mine, who have been raised so high
    That, as an earthly mind distinguishes
    How two obtuse angles cannot lie
In one triangle, so, of contingencies,
    You are aware beforehand, since you gaze
    Upon the point where, present, all time is.   18
While I was led by Vergil on my ways
    Along the Mount that cures the souls, and down,
    Going through the dead world, a heavy phrase
Was said about my future life and renown.
    And as I feel able to stand foursquare
    Against the blows of fortune on my crown,   24
So would my will be well content to share
    The news of what disaster comes on me;
    The shaft foreseen is much less hard to bear.'

I spoke this to that light which recently
    Had talked with me; as Beatrice had said,
30   Confessed my wish to know what was to be.
In no dark sayings, such as once misled
    The foolish peoples of the ancient days
    Before the Lamb who takes all sin had bled,
But in clear words and most precise in phrase
    That father-love replied to me, concealed
36   And yet revealed by his own smiling rays.
'Contingency that can't outreach your field
    Of matter is seen in the Eternal Eyes;
    No more necessity does that foresight wield
Than would the motion of a boat that plies
    Downstream derive from its reflection made
42   In eyes of those who watch it dip and rise.
Thence, as sweet organ harmonies pervade
    The hearing, so there comes into my sight
    The time in store for you, clearly displayed.
As Hippolytus, cast from Athens by the sleight
    Of his stepmother, cruel and faithless one,
48   So out of Florence you must take your flight.
So it is willed, now plotted, soon to be done
    By him who ponders on it in that place
    Where, day to day, they put on sale God's Son.
Upon the injured party, blame and disgrace
    Shall lie, as usual, then; but vengeance will bear
54   Witness how Truth dispenses justice in the case.
And everything you loved most dearly there
    You shall abandon. This opening shaft the bow
    Of banishment will shoot into the air.
How salt another's bread is you shall know;
    How hard the step will tread, mount or descend,
60   Upon a stranger's stairs where you must go.
And what will most of all weigh down and bend
    Your shoulders is the venomous and foul
    Mob that will walk with you to this vale's end.
For all of them will turn ungrateful, howl
    Impiously against you; but soon will betide
66   Their cheeks, not yours, shall redden round the jowl.
Of their brute folly their deeds shall soon provide
    The proof; so it will be your honour to make
    A party of yourself, quite unallied.

First refuge and first lodging you will take
    By courtesy of the great Lombard who bears
    The sacred eagle on the ladder's rake.   72
So kindly shall he look on your affairs
    That out of acting and being asked shall be
    First what others make second in such pairs.
And there with him you shall most surely see
    The man so stamped by this strong star at birth
    That all his deeds shall be as notable as he.   78
People have little heeded his great worth
    Because he's young, for only nine years' span
    These wheels have rolled around him on the earth.
But, ere the Gascon deceives great Henry's plan,
    Sparks of his virtue shall appear and shine –
    Through his largesse in silver, his toils as man.   84
His munificent deeds shall soon be thought so fine
    That even enemies shall hardly choke
    Their tongues to silence which they would consign.
Look to him, and his benefits; many folk
    By acts of his shall alter in their state
    From wealth to beggary by his stroke.   90
And you shall carry this in your mind's freight
    But not reveal it.' He told me things that, past
    Belief – even of those who'll see them – lie in wait.
And then he added: 'Son, this gloss is cast
    On what was hinted to you; now beware
    The snares a few revolving years hide fast.   96
Nor would I have you envy neighbours there
    Since you'll outlive them and the time now laid
    When vengeance falls as their perfidious share.'
When silence in the sacred flame conveyed
    He'd finished setting up the woof athwart
    The warp that I had offered to be made,   102
I said, as someone doubting seeks support
    And counsel from another who sees things straight
    And wills aright and loves one as he ought,
'I do well see how time spurs at a rate
    Towards me, aiming to fetch me such a blow,
    Heaviest to those uncautioned of its weight.   108
Therefore it would be well in foresight to grow
    And arm myself that, should my dearest place
    Be lost, my songs may save all else I know.

Down in the world endlessly bitter and base,
   Along the Mountain from whose lovely crest
114   My Lady's eyes uplifted me by grace,
And since, from light to light, as Heaven's guest,
   I've learned what, if I broadcast it below,
   Holds, for so many, sour herbs to digest.
And if I am a shrinking friend to show
   The truth, I fear to lose the life renowned
120   To those who'll call this period long ago.'
The light – in which the treasure I had found
   First smiled – blazed, as a golden looking-glass,
   Struck by the sun's rays, bursts the rebound,
Then answered: 'Darkened consciences will class –
   Dark in themselves, or other's shame – your speech
126   In truth as harsh in judgements that you pass.
Nevertheless, set every lie, and each,
   Aside; and make your whole vision manifested.
   So let them scratch whatever itch they reach.
For, if your speech be bitter when first tested,
   Yet it shall leave a vital nourishment
132   Afterwards, when its pith has been digested.
This cry of yours shall move as the wind's bent
   That strikes the highest summits with its threat –
   No small point this, in honour's argument.
For this reason, in the spheres, you've met –
   And on the Mountainside, and sorrowing Glade –
138   Only those souls that fame has heeded yet;
Because the soul who hears is never stayed,
   Nor fixed in faith by samples dark and strange
Whose roots lie hidden and obscure; nor swayed
   By inconspicuous arguments to change.'

CANTO 18

The soldier heroes zooming along the cross of light are named. Then Dante rises with Beatrice to the incandescence of Jupiter, emblematic of good rulers – who first show themselves in the pattern of the Latin words for 'Love righteousness, you judges of the earth' and then in the form of the Roman Eagle. Dante expresses his yearning for the return of such justice and the Papacy is condemned for its concentration upon John the Baptist, whose image appears on the Florentine florin, rather than the example of St Peter and St Paul.

Already, then, that blessèd mirror rejoiced
    Only in its own discourse; I, in the taste
    Of mine – blending bitter with sweet he'd voiced.
The Lady who my path to God had traced
    Said: 'Change your thoughts and think that I
    Am near to Him who lifts all error's waste.'   6
I turned towards the loving sound near by,
    My strength; but to describe the love I found
    In those most sacred eyes I will not try.
Not only since I feel my skill unsound
    But since the memory cannot remount,
    Without a guide, so far above its ground.   12
So much, concerning this, I may recount:
    That, as I gazed upon her, my affection
    Was freed – all other longings could discount,
While joy eternal, without indirection,
    Which shone on Beatrice, fully satisfied
    Me with its light in that fair-faced reflection.   18
Conquering me with light of a smile, my guide
    Said: 'Turn to listen now, for you will find
    Other than in my eyes a Heaven beside.'
As, here, we'll read affection sometimes outlined
    Upon the features when they're so concerned
    They take up all the feeling of the mind,   24
So, in that flaming brow to which I'd turned,
    I noticed how the wish, within him still,
    For further words to me had thrilled and yearned.
He said: 'In this fifth range of the tree that will
    Forever fruit and never shed a leaf,
    That lives from summit to the roots' deep drill,   30

Are blessèd spirits who were great and chief
   In fame, below, before they rose on high,
   So that they would enrich each muse as fief.
So, to this cross's horns direct your eye:
   Each one I name shall make as lightning flame
36   Within a cloud across an earthly sky.'
As soon as said, I saw, at Joshua's name,
   A blaze of light drawn out along the cross,
   Nor heard the word before the action came.
At Maccabaeus' name, the flashing gloss
   Of one more, wheeling – whose joy was like the lash
42   That keeps the spinning top from motion's loss.
Then Charlemagne, Roland, I caught the flash
   Of two more in my keenest scrutiny,
   As eye follows the winging hawk's panache.
Next, William and Renouard drew my eye to see
   Along the cross; and then, Duke Godfrey came,
48   And Robert Guiscard's flame in front of me.
And last, amid those lights, that soul of flame
   Who had discoursed with me revealed his art –
   In singers of that Heaven mingling his aim.
I turned to my right for Beatrice to impart
   My duty, either by some turn of phrase
54   Or by some gesture hinted to my heart.
I saw her eyes: so clear, so joyous their gaze,
   That her appearance surpassed her former mien
   And passed the latest of her lovely ways.
And, as by feeling a delight more keen
   In well-doing, a man perceives, from day
60   To day, his virtue gain a brighter sheen,
So I saw my circling in the Heavens' sway
   Had then increased its arc, seeing this sight,
   That miracle in such a brighter ray.
And such a change as swiftly comes to light
   Upon a lovely woman when her face
66   Is freed from weight of shame, such was the white
Shown to me, when I turned around a pace,
   Because of that temperate star's white glow,
   The sixth that had received me in its space.
In Jove's torch then, I saw the sparkling flow
   Of love which signalled there into my eyes,
72   Using the language that I speak and know.

As birds that soar from banks into the skies
　　As though rejoicing, over fields they hang,
　　In flocks now round, now long, as each one flies –
So, in their lights, the sacred beings sang,
　　And, in their patterns, made at first a D,
　　Then I, and then an L as their music rang.   78
Singing, they moved to their own melody;
　　Then shaped the letters by formation, line,
　　And paused in them and ceased their minstrelsy.
– O Goddess Pegasean – who assign
　　To genius its glory and length of days
　　As it, through you, gives cities, realms – now shine,   84
Enlighten me yourself so I may phrase
　　Their shapes as I perceived them there, and show
　　Them clearly. In brief verse you power blaze. –
They shaped themselves, and I took note to know,
　　In five times seven vowels and letterings,
　　As they appeared to speak to me below.   90
DILIGITE JUSTITIAM, in the imagings,
　　The first verb and noun, then came the last:
　　QUI JUDICATIS TERRAM, shaped by their wings.
Then, in the fifth word's M, they held fast,
　　So Jupiter seemed all a silver-white
　　Pricked out just there with gold in their broadcast.   96
And then I saw additional gleams alight
　　On the M's crest, and settle into place,
　　Hymning, I think, the Good that draws their sight.
Then, just as when you strike a brand, you trace
　　Innumerable sparks – on which the fools
　　Would forecast and their augury would base –   102
It seemed there rose more than a thousand jewels
　　Of light, some sinking down, some rising high,
　　According as the Sun that lights them rules,
And, when each came to rest where it should lie,
　　I saw an eagle's throat and head outlined
　　By all the points of light before my eye.   108
(Who paints with these has none to guide His mind,
　　But He Himself guides, as from Him is sent
　　The power by which nest-building is designed.)
Other blest spirits seemed at first content
　　To turn the M a Lily, and a small flight
　　Carried out the pattern that was meant.   114

– O sweet star, that made clear to my sight,
    With worth and wealth of gems, how justice of ours
    Is the effect of Heaven you gem with light. –
Therefore, I pray the Mind from which your powers
    And motion spring should study well that place
120   Which blocks your light with smoke that swirls and lours,
So that once more its wrath may blaze in face
    Of buying and selling in the temple's court
    Whose walls were miracles, martyrdom its base.
Soldiers of Heaven whom I see and report,
    Pray for those who're gone astray on earth
126   By following example of such evil sort.
Once wars were made with swords and valour's worth;
    Now it is made denying bread, first here
    Then there, our Father bars from none at birth.
But you who just to cancel write so clear,
    Reflect that Peter and Paul, who died to guard
132   The vineyard you lay waste, live and give ear.
Well may you argue: 'I have set so hard
    My longings for him who lived a solitary span,
Drawn dancingly to martyrdom, that my regard
    Has scanted old Paul and the Fisherman.'

CANTO 19

The just kings in the form of the eagle speak as one, suggesting the universality and uniformity of true justice. Dante enquires as to the justice of excluding virtuous heathens from Heaven – a thought that has long troubled him. He is told that created minds cannot fathom the justice of the uncreated Godhead but must trust that justice because of the goodness and perfection of God. He is told that some who call on the name of Christ will be farther off from Him than others who never knew the name. Furthermore, Dante includes some heathens in his Heaven so the answer to the question is also given poetically. The kings cited in lines 115–41 are the Emperor Albert (see Purgatory 6*), who invaded Bohemia in 1304; Philip IV of France, who was killed by a boar in 1314; Edward I and the Wallace, who fought over Scottish independence from England; Ferdinand of Castile; Wenceslaus of Bohemia (see also* Purgatory 7*); Charles II of Naples, who was the titular king of Jerusalem, father of Carlo Martello (see canto 8). The counting of his deeds is, of course, in Roman numerals. Frederick II of Sicily deserted Dante's beloved imperial cause in 1313. His uncle and brother were respectively kings of the Balearic Islands and of Aragon; Dionysius was king of Portugal; Hakon, of Norway. Stephen was king of Serbia and forged the Venetian ducat in base metal.*

The lovely image, wings spread, was before me,
    Made by the interlinking souls who rise,
    Rejoicing in fruition of their glory.
Each seemed a ruby where the sun's ray lies
    Enkindling it so that it was reflected
    Straight back to my fixed and marvelling eyes.   6
What I write now no voice has ever projected,
    No wit recorded, nor has the fantasy
    Ever comprehended or suspected.
For then I saw and heard the beak to be
    Discoursing, and to use both 'Mine' and 'I'
    When, in conception, it was 'Our' and 'We'.   12
'For being just and merciful, here I fly,
    Exalted to such glory,' it began,
    'That yearning never could aspire more high.
I left such memory on earth to man
    That even evil-doers commend it there
    But don't advance the story as they can.'   18
As we may feel from many coals one share
    Of heat, so from those many souls there broke
    The one voice of that image in the air.

'Perpetual blooms of joy eternal,' I spoke
   At once, 'oh, you, whose individual tangs
24   One fragrance of your fame to me evoke,
Breathe forth and end the lengthy fast whose pangs
   Of hunger kept me starving down below,
   Since neither food for it, nor fruit there hangs.
And though divine justice, as well I know,
   Is mirrored in another Heavenly sphere,
30   Yours sees without a veil all it will show.
You know how keen I am and set to hear;
   You know what question it has been that made
   Me fast myself so many a long year.'
And as a hawk unhooded from its shade
   Shakes his head and beats his wings to blaze
36   His spirit and his beauty all displayed,
So did I see that ensign, woven from praise
   Of grace divine, with songs which are but known
   To those who are rejoicing in those rays.
It said: 'Now he whose compass drew the zone
   Enclosing the universe within its round
42   And crammed it with variety, both shown
And veiled, could not have stamped the whole and bound
   His Power except his Word should still remain
   Infinite in its excess; proof may be found
In that the first Spirit, proud and vain,
   Who, though the summit of creation, fell
48   Unripe, not waiting for the light to reign.
It's clear that lesser natures are a cell
   Too small to hold that Good of boundless sway
   That, by itself alone, is measured well.
Therefore our sight (which needs must be one ray
   Of that Mind which suffuses through all things)
54   Can't by its nature have such power it may
Not see its own origination springs
   From far beyond all that appears to sight
   Or anything that its perception brings.
And so the vision, given your world, throws light
   Upon eternal justice as the eye
60   Is lost in depths of all the ocean's might.
Near shore, it sees the bed, yet on the high
   Seas it cannot fathom out the bed,
   For so profound the depth where it must lie.

Light there is none, unless it be that shed
  From this clear sky unclouded; all else is dark,
  The flesh's shadow, or its poisoned bread.   66
The hiding-place is open now to mark,
  That veiled the living justice from your eyes,
  And made you ceaselessly on queries to embark.
"A man is born by Indus," so you surmise,
  "Where there is none to tell of Christ and none
  To read, and none to write to make him wise,   72
Yet all his will and all his deeds are done
  In goodness, as far as human reason knows,
  Sinless in life and discourse was this one.
He dies unbaptized; without the Faith he goes.
  Where is the justice that condemns him? Where,
  In not believing, does his fault repose?"   78
Now who are you that wish to take the chair
  Of judgement, from a thousand miles away,
  With sight that carries but a span of air?
For one who goes subtly to work there may
  Indeed appear – were not the Scriptures stood
  Above – a splendid ground for queries you lay.   84
– O earthly creatures, gross minds that hood! –
  The Primal Will, in essence good, can't bend
  From its own self, which is the highest good.
And all is just that harmonizes with its end.
  No good created warps it to its being,
  But it, by shining forth, makes that ascend.'   90
As, over the nest, the stork, after feeding
  Her brood, is seen to sweep, and one, just fed,
  Looks up to her to keep her in its seeing,
So did (and so did I) uplift its head
  That blessèd image, beating wings made strong
  By all the many counsels as they spread.   96
Wheeling, it sang and told: 'As is my song
  To you who do not understand, so seems
  Eternal Judgement to mortals earthbound long.'
When those bright flames of the Holy Spirit's beams
  Were still again in the standard which had won
  The Romans reverence to the world's extremes,   102
It spoke again: 'This realm is reached by none
  Who had no faith and no belief in Christ,
  Before or since his nailing up, fordone.

But see: many there are who cry "Christ, Christ!"
    Who, at the judgement, shall be much less near
108   To him than some who never knew the Christ.
Such Christians the Ethiop will condemn, severe,
    When those two colleges make the split that brings
    Riches forever to one, and one strips clear.
What may the Persians not say to your kings,
    Seeing the volume opened to proclaim
114   The wretched infamy that round them clings?
Seen there shall be, in deeds of Albert's fame,
    One action (which moves its pen again)
    That gave the realm of Prague a desert's name.
Seen there shall be that woe upon the Seine
    Brought by the one who had the coins debased.
120   He, by the wild boar's stroke, shall yet be slain.
Seen there shall be that pride whose thirst shall haste
    And madden Scot and Englishman until
    They cannot stay in bounds where they are placed.
In it be seen the lust, the soft life's frill,
    Of Spain and also that Bohemian king
126   Who never knew of worth, nor good could will.
I for his excellence shall be the numbering
    Seen for Jerusalem's cripple; M be seen
    To mark the number of the counter-thing.
In it be seen that avarice so mean,
    The baseness of the one who rules the isle
132   Of fire where Anchises ended life's long scene.
Needed to detail how immense and vile
    His paltriness, the record shall be made
    In shortened forms to cram much in the file.
Next, plain to all, the foul deeds be displayed
    Of uncle and brother whose adultery
138   A choice family and two crowns betrayed.
Norway and Portugal's kings there will you see,
    And that of Rascia who, in evil hour,
    Brought coins of Venice to his treasury.
Ah, happy Hungary, if she should cower
    Beneath no further mauling! Happy Navarre,
144   If armoured with the skirting mountains' power!
And all should take it as a pledge so far
    Of this, that Nicosia already grieves,
And Famagusta shrieks beneath the jar
    Of their own beast who keeps place with these thieves.'

CANTO 20

The just rulers who form the shape of the Eagle are identified. Dante thus reveals that Ripheus the Trojan is there in Heaven as well as Trajan. An explanation is given as to how they came to be there without any breach of divine law. Dante is comforted by the mysterious ways of divine justice in the hope that it gives and in its exceeding of human understanding.

When he that lights the whole world descends
    Out of our hemisphere and day is done
    Away on every side to the earth's ends,
The sky which has been lit by the sole sun
    Instantly makes its presence re-appear
    In many lights reflected from the one.   6
This change of sky came into mind so clear
    When once the world's standard and its guides
    Had stilled its beak and silence met the ear,
Because those living lights on all the sides
    Shone brighter and began their melody
    From which my memory wavers, slips and slides.   12
– O sweet love, clad in smiles, you seemed to be
    So ardent in those flutes where breathed alone
    Such holy thoughts and made their harmony.
When those dear lustrous stones, that gemmed the zone
    Of the sixth Heaven I saw, had once more made
    A silence in the angel chime and tone,   18
It seemed I heard a murmurous cascade,
    Clear, as from rock to rock tumbled a beck
    Which from its source in full torrent played.
And, as the note is formed in the lute's neck,
    Or, at the opening of the pipes, the air
    That entered issues forth without a check,   24
So delay of expectation ended there:
    The murmur of the eagle reached its throat
    As if its neck were hollowed to declare.
Then it became a voice, and I took note
    Of words it issued from its beak – for which
    My heart awaited then, and there I wrote: 30
'My seeing parts that mortal eagles pitch
    Against the sun,' the voice began to say,
    'You must now fix your vision on, nor switch.

For of the lights that frame my form, each ray
   That scintillates within my head for sight
36   Is chief in all the ranks that I display.
The central, like a pupil shedding light,
   Was Singer of the Holy Spirit's songs –
   Who bore the ark from house to house in flight.
He knows now what merit to his lay belongs,
   As far as it was fashioned in his mind,
42   By the reward apportioned in these throngs.
And, of the five by which the brow's outlined,
   Closest the beak is he who once consoled
   The widow who had lost her son and pined.
He knows now how dear a cost is told
   Not following Christ, by knowing this sweet place,
48   And of the opposite, in the other fold.
The next that follows, on the curve I trace
   Upon the upper arch, made death delay
   By his true penitence and God's good grace.
He knows now that eternal judgement's sway
   Is not diverted when a worthy prayer
54   Moves to tomorrow what is for today.
The next turned Greek with laws and me – a fair
   Intention which has born an evil fruit –
   To give the Roman Pastor of his share.
He knows now the evil, sprung from the root
   Of that good act, can do no harm to him,
60   Though all the world is wrecked and destitute.
The one upon the downward-curving rim
   Was William, mourned by the land whose hands now wring
   That Charles and Frederick live out their whim.
He knows now how Heaven loves the just king,
   And, in the splendour of his shining mien,
66   He shows his knowledge in its shimmering.
Who would believe on erring earth and mean,
   The Trojan Ripheus would reach this sphere,
   Fifth of those holy lights now to be seen?
He knows now much of divine grace here
   That the low world has not the power to see,
72   Although the depths he cannot focus clear.'
And, as the lark soars in the air so free,
   First singing, then with silence is content,
   Of such sweetness more filled than melody,

Such seemed to me that image to present,
 Seal of the Eternal Joy that, longing to gain,
 All things become themselves, as they were meant. 78
Yet, though I was to my question like a pane
 Of glass upon a colour, still it would not wait
 Nor bide its time, in silence to remain.
Broke from my mouth: 'How can this be?' So great
 Its weight and force, it issued on its own.
 At which I saw the lights so coruscate 84
And, straight away, with eye more brightly shown,
 The blessèd standard answered me, to stem
 The agony of wonder I had known.
'I see you trust these things since I tell you them,
 But how you cannot see; and, though believed,
 They seem as hidden as a stratagem. 90
You're like a person who has but perceived
 A thing by name but cannot really sense
 Its quiddity till shown the thing conceived.
The Kingdom of Heaven feels a violence
 From fervent love and living hope which may
 Conquer the divine will, not in the sense 96
That man subdues a man to wound or slay,
 But conquers it because it wills defeat,
 And won like that its goodness wins the day.
The first and fifth life in the eyebrow meet
 Your wonderment because you see this zone
 Of angels decked with them in Heaven's seat. 102
But not as Gentiles they left their flesh and bone,
 As you suppose, but Christian, trusting the Feet –
 One, to be pierced; next, as pierced, to atone;
Since one from Hell (where no soul, as is meet,
 Turns to right will) to flesh and blood returned –
 For living hope, this was reward complete, 108
The living hope that gave prayer force that yearned
 To God for grace that He should pluck him out
 So that the chance to change his will was earned.
That glorious soul whose life I speak about
 Returned to flesh and, staying a short time,
 In Him who can give help believed, devout. 114
And, so believing, sprang to flame sublime
 In very love; thus, when he came to die
 Again, was worthy to this joy to climb.

The next by grace (that wells from the supply
  That springs from such a depth no sight could press
120   To see the first surge with created eye)
Set all his love below on righteousness,
  For which God opened his eyes, from grace to grace,
   To our Redemption yet to come and bless.
And he believed, allowing not a trace
  Of paganism's mire, but reproved the sin
126   Of those perverse concerning things so base.
And those three ladies whom you saw within
  The right wheel stood as baptism for him
   A thousand years before it could begin.
Predestination! Oh how dark and dim
  Lies your deep root from all such sight concealed
132   That cannot hold the First Cause in its rim!
You mortals, hold back firmly in the field
  Of judgement: even we who see God here
   Have not had all the chosen ones revealed.
And such a lack we feel as sweet and dear
  Because our good in this good is refined:
138   That what God wills we will and we revere.'
So, by this divine image, clearing my mind
  Of partial vision, was administered
   A medicine to me most sweet and kind.
As a good harpist makes the chord he stirred
  Accompany a good singer's cue
144   Which makes the song more pleasant and preferred,
So, while he spoke, as I recall, the two
  Blest lights I saw trembled their flame
Just as the blinking of the eyes might do
  In unison upon the words that came.

CANTO 21

They rise to Saturn in the constellation of Leo. Dante is directed to look at a Jacob's ladder stretching beyond his focus into Heaven. On this ladder rise and descend the spirits of contemplation. Dante speaks to a spirit that pauses nearest to him. He wishes to know why of all spirits this particular spirit has paused, and inquires why there is no music and hymnody in this sphere. Dante is not quite satisfied with the answer that any spirit is happy to perform the will of God. The spirit reminds Dante that no created mind may fathom the intentions of the uncreated Godhead. Through Dante, the spirit warns humanity away from attempting to plumb too deeply into the mind of God which even the risen spirits cannot know. Dante, rebuked, learns that the spirit who speaks is Peter Damian, also called Peter the Sinner. Peter denounces the pomp and sumptuousness of current churchmen. Dante is stunned by a sudden cry of the saints descending to surround Peter.

Already, on my Lady's lovely face,
    My eyes were locked – and mind, too, latched to know,
    So every other interest had yielded place.
She gave no smile but said: 'Were I to show
    One smile, like Semele would you end,
    When she was turned to ashes long ago.   6
Because my beauty, which, the more we ascend
    The stairs of the eternal palace, the more
    Intensifies – as you've seen and comprehend,
If not so moderated, such a light would pour
    That, at one flash, your mortal force would sear
    And be like boughs all split by thunder's roar.   12
We've risen to the seventh splendour's sphere
    That, underneath the fiery lion's chest,
    Shines down, combining power on the year.
Fix your mind behind your eyes to rest,
    And let them mirror the image now to be,
    Within this mirror, clearly manifest.'   18
Whoever knows what grazing I could see
    Within this blessèd prospect when I chose
    Another interest for my scrutiny,
Would recognize how great the joy that rose
    In my obedience to my Heavenly guide,
    If weight of one against the other pose.   24

Within the crystal sphere, circling the wide
    World, bearing name of its illustrious king,
    Under whose rule all wickedness had died,
Tinted like gold that shone back shimmering,
    I saw a ladder raised on high so far
30   That, with these eyes, there was no following.
Further I saw upon each rung and spar
    So many splendours that it seemed there shone
    From all the sky the light of every star.
And as, in nature's way, as day comes on,
    The daws set out in flocks into the air
36   To warm their chilly plumes, and some are gone
Not to return, and others still repair
    To their old roost, while others yet will stay
    And wing their wheeling spirals over there –
Such change, it seemed, was in the sparkling play
    Of lights which came in company as soon
42   As it had touched a certain step or way.
The one that lingered nearest in that festoon
    Became so bright that in my mind I said:
    'I see the love you signal as my boon,
But she whose cue I wait on to be led
    To speech or silence, pauses, and I do well
48   To counter wish, and give no question head.'
At which she, who perceived my silent spell
    Within His sight who sees the whole, remarked:
    'Let out your keen desire which yet you quell.'
'My spirit is not worth,' I then embarked,
    'Your answer but, for sake of her who let
54   Me ask this question here which you have sparked,
O blessèd life who hide in gladness, yet
    Explain to me what cause has made you stay
    So near to me upon the ladder set.
And tell me why, within this sphere the lay
    And sweet symphony of Heaven are mute,
60   That sounded so devout throughout my way.'
He answered: 'You've the eyes and ears to suit
    A mortal. That Beatrice gives no smile, that there's
    No song you may to the selfsame cause impute.
And I descend the sacred ladder's stairs
    This far merely to welcome you with speech
66   And with the light that my rejoicing wears.

No greater love made me so swift to reach
    You here; for more, and so much love, up there
    Is burning – as the flares and flashes teach.
But that deep love which binds us in its care
    As ready servants of the Wisdom that sways
    The world, appointed me – as you're aware.'   72
'Yes, so I see, O lamp of sacred rays,
    How love unstinted suffices in this court
    For full obedience to Providence's ways,
But what seems hard to follow is the thought
    Why you were singled out from all the rest,
    Predestined to an office of this sort.'   78
I hadn't reached the end of my request
    Before the light upon its point rotated
    Just like a whirling quernstone in its zest.
And then the love that was within it stated:
    'A light divine is focusing on me
    And through this where I'm wrapped has penetrated.   84
Its virtue, combining with my power to see,
    Raises me from myself so far I discern
    The Supreme Essence from which it issues free.
From this derives the joy with which I burn,
    For to my sight, in measure as it's clear,
    I match the flame's intensity in turn.   90
But Heaven's most illuminated seer –
    That Seraph with his eye on God most bound –
    Has never given answer to your question here,
Because the thing you ask lies so profound
    In the abyss of the Eternal Decree
    That no created vision sees that ground.   96
And when you turn back to mortality,
    Take this report: that it should not presume
    A step toward so great a secrecy.
The mind illumined here, on earth must fume.
    Consider therefore how it could have force
    On earth when Heaven itself will not illume.'   102
His words proscribed me so I had recourse
    To nothing further on it, curbing my urge
    To ask him who he was, in lowly remorse.
'Between the coasts of Italy emerge
    Those crags (not very distant from your land)
    So high that under them the thunders surge.   108

They make a ridge called Catria; they stand,
   And there's a hermitage, hallowed and blest,
   That formerly for prayer alone was planned,'
So he began the third discourse expressed;
   Proceeding, said: 'To God's service, there,
114   I grew so rooted then and so addressed
That with my meat in olive juice as fare,
   I lightly passed the heat and cold, content
   With contemplation as my better share.
That cloister once with goodly fruit was bent
   Towards these Heavens, but now it's grown so wild
120   That soon must be revealed the harm's extent.
There I, Peter Damian, was domiciled
   In Our Lady's house, on the Adriatic shore;
   Peter the Sinner I was also styled.
Of mortal life remained but little more
   When I was called to bear the mitre's weight,
126   That goes from bad to worse man than before.
Came Cephas, came the Holy Spirit's great
   Vessel, lean and unshod, taking what fare
   From any hostel offering him a plate.
Now modern pastors needs must have a pair
   Of buttresses each side, a third ahead
132   To lead, so fat they are, and one to bear.
Their mantles on their palfreys now they spread
   So that two beasts travel in one hide.
   O patience that must bear with heavy tread!'
And, at this cry, I noticed more flames glide
   From step to step, and every whirl they made
138   So they appeared to be more beautified.
Together round the first they gathered, stayed,
   And raised a cry so deep in sound that here
I cannot find a simile that conveyed –
   Nor understood, such thunder swamped my ear.

CANTO 22

Beatrice comforts Dante in his terrified daze and explains the cry as a great burst of prayer for God's vengeance on the degenerate church. Benedict of Monte Cassino comes to answer his query before he voices it. Dante is eager to know if he might see Benedict's real appearance in its undiminished glory and learns that he will do so when he reaches the Empyrean Heaven. Benedict points out that none in the current monastic tradition now use the ladder of contemplation to achieve vision because the tradition is degenerate. Beatrice now raises Dante behind the ascending saints to his natal sign in Gemini, whose aid he now seeks in his task of recording his ascent. Beatrice suggests he measure his progress so far by looking down towards the earth before he enters the eighth sphere.

Stunned with the shock, I turned round to my guide,
    As would a little child who always goes
    Where he has had most reason to confide.
And she, just as a mother quickly knows
    What soothes her child gasping and pale with fear,
    With voice so used to calm him and compose,   6
Said: 'Have you forgotten we are here
    In Heaven? Have you forgotten Heaven as such
    Is holy; and this was righteous zeal voiced clear?
Now how the song would have confounded with its touch,
    And I, by smiling, you may realize
    Since that outcry has moved you quite so much;   12
From which, if you had understood their cries
    Of prayer, you would already hear and know
    Of vengeance you'll see before your body dies.
Not rash, nor slow, the sword that swings below
    From Heaven above – except within the mind
    Of those who wait in fear, or hope, its blow!   18
But turn towards the others you will find,
    If you direct your gaze where I suggest:
    Many illustrious spirits move and wind.'
I moved my gaze to follow her request,
    And saw a hundred little spheres that were
    The lovelier in their mutual beams caressed.   24
I stood as one resisting against the spur
    Of his desire, not presuming to enquire
    For fear of what presumption might incur.

And then the greatest and most dazzling fire
        Of all those gems came forward to assuage,
30   Concerning him, my wish and my desire.
'If you could see the love,' I heard that sage,
        'That burns in us, as clearly as I do,
        Your thoughts would have been spoken by this stage.
But, lest delay should make you miss your true
        And lofty aim, I'll only answer that thought
36   Of which you are so circumspect of view.
The mountain where Cassino lies was sought
        And thronged, a while ago upon its peak,
        By people ill-disposed, deceived, or thwart.
And there I was the one, the first, unique,
        To take the Name that brought to earth down there
42   The truth that lifts us high – if we would seek.
Such grace was shone on me that I could tear
        Those places back from the impious wicked cult
        That had seduced the world with heathen fare.
These other, contemplatives, exult,
        Kindled by that warmth that generates the fruits
48   And holy flowers that blossom as result.
Here's Macarius, Romualdus here transmutes,
        My brothers who have kept the cloistered walk,
        And kept their hearts sound, and strait their routes.'
And I: 'The love you show in that you talk
        To me, and all the obvious favour that glows
54   In your appearance, are as is a baulk
To strengthen me in confidence, and compose,
        Just as the sun's radiance opens wide
        To fullest loveliness the folded rose.
Therefore I beg you, father, please confide
        Whether I may have the favour yet
60   To see your face behind these rays that hide.'
To which he answered: 'Brother, you will get
        Your high desire when in the final sphere
        Where all desires – and mine – will then be met.
There, all we yearn for's perfect, ripe and clear;
        And there, in it alone, is every part
66   Where it has always been; it is not here
In space, and does not turn on poles you chart.
        Our ladder reaches right into its zone
        And so it soars where your eyes cannot dart.

Straight to that height, the Patriarch Jacob alone
　　Saw it when it appeared to him sublime,
　　Crowded with angels reaching to the throne.　　　　72
But now no foot is raised from earth to climb
　　Its height, and my own rule but lingers there
　　To make a waste of parchment with its time.
The walls that used to be a house of prayer
　　Have now become but dens, and wretched grain
　　Crams up the cowls and the hoods they wear.　　　78
Harsh usury's not exacted for such gain,
　　So contrary to God's will, as the fruit
　　That makes the hearts of monks so mad and vain.
All the Church holds is for those whose suit
　　Is made to God by prayer, and not for kin
　　To take, or for more brutish ones to loot.　　　　84
So soft is mortal flesh that even in
　　A good start on the earth there lies no sure
　　Sign acorns will crown the oaklings that begin.
Peter began without silver and gold to procure
　　His gathering; I, with prayers and fast;
　　And Francis, in lowliness to endure.　　　　　　90
But, if you study each one's start, and cast
　　Your eye where it has gone astray,
　　You'll see the white turn grey before much passed.
Yet Jordan's flowing back, the giving way
　　Of seas before God's will, more wondrous sights
　　To see than would be succour here some day.'　　96
He spoke, and joined his gathering on the flights;
　　The assembly closed around, together rose,
　　Like a whirlwind swirling up into the heights.
My sweet Lady thrust me after, though she chose
　　But sign to shift me up the ladder's stair,
　　My nature vanquished by the power she shows.　　102
Nor was there ever here a motion where
　　We climb and descend, by way of nature's law,
　　That might in swiftness with my wings compare.
– O reader, as I may hope some time to draw
　　Near to that devoted triumph, in which aim
　　I frequently lament each sin and flaw –　　　　108
You've never drawn and thrust your hand in flame
　　Before I saw the sign – so swift the time –
　　That trails the Bull, and into it I came.

O glorious stars! light gravid with sublime
   Power, from which my genius is sprung,
114   Whatever it might be, to build this rhyme,
Rising with you and hiding there among
   Your beams was he, the sire of mortality,
   When first the air of Tuscany filled my lung.
When grace was given me to enter and see
   The lofty wheel that turns you in your gyres
120   It was your region that was assigned to me.
To you devoutly now my soul respires
   To gain the strength for the hard pass ahead
   That draws her on, and up, where she aspires.
'You are so near,' Beatrice then said,
   'The supreme good that you should keep your eyes
126   Clear and keen to watch where they are led.
And so, before you even further rise,
   Towards that point, look down and see how great
   A universe, beneath your feet, now lies,
So that your heart, rejoicing in its state,
   May be presented to the triumphant throng
132   That, joyous through round ether, greets your gait.
I turned my eyes back down, and all along
   The seven, all and each, upon their flight;
   Wry-smiled at earth, so sorry and so wrong.
And that advice I most approve would indict
   It as the least of all; any who yearns
138   For other things is truly called upright.
I saw Latona's daughter as she burns
   Without those marks that earlier had made
   Me think her rarefied or dense by turns.
Hyperion, your son's gaze I surveyed
   Unharmed, and saw how Maia and Dione spun
144   About and near him as the motion bade.
Next, temperate Jove between father and son;
   And there, quite clear to me, the change and shift
   They make in their positions as they run.
All seven were displayed to me; how swift
   And great they are; how distantly in space
150   Lie their positions from each other's drift.
The threshing-floor which makes us fierce and base,
   As I with the eternal Twins was rolled,
Lay shown to me, from ridge to river-race.
   Then those fair eyes, my eyes turned to behold.

CANTO 23

Beatrice is gazing towards Cancer, region of the summer solstice, to the east of Gemini. Dante follows her gaze in keen expectation and sees the Heaven lit by the host of the triumphant souls in Christ; the blinding radiance is the light of Christ. Dante is overcome but recalled to reality by Beatrice who instructs him to behold the garden of Christ, the Virgin Rose and the Lilies of the Apostles. Christ withdraws on high to spare him the searing of his radiance. Gabriel descends to crown the Virgin who reascends.

Then, as a bird in her belovèd tree,
    Who's brooded her sweet nestlings through the night
    (Which covers things so that we cannot see)
And, eager to find them food, and have the sight
    Of them which makes her heavy labours sweet
    To her, anticipates the breaking light   6
And with her ardent love she waits to meet
    The sun's first rays upon the open bough,
    Fixedly staring where the dawn will greet –
So was my Lady standing, eager now,
    Erect toward the region under which
    The sun its slowest motion may allow,   12
So that as I beheld her reach that pitch
    Of longing and suspense, I was one then
    Wishing for what he lacks, by hope made rich.
But short the time from one to other when,
    I mean, of my expecting the uttermost,
    And seeing Heaven grow brighter yet again.   18
Then Beatrice suggested: 'Look, the host
    Of Christ's triumph – all the fruit now stored
    And gathered by these spheres, their only boast.'
Her features seemed to glow, and gladness poured
    Out of her eyes so that needs must my style
    Pass over undescribed how she adored.   24
As, in clear night of full moon with Trivia's smile
    In the eternal nymphs who decorate
    The sky in every facet of its dial,
I saw above thousands of lamps that coruscate,
    One Sun which kindled each and everyone,
    As we see ours light those that circulate.   30

And, through the living light of very Sun,
    The shining Substance so outshone, intense,
    I could not bear to look, all sight fordone.
Oh, Beatrice, sweet guide and dear, spoke thence:
    'What overcomes your eyesight is the might
36   Against whose power exists not one defence.
The Power and Wisdom lie within that light
    Which opened paths between the Heaven and earth
    When long desire had yearned for such a flight.'
Just as the flash bursts from the cloud's girth,
    Because it so expands, it lacks the space
42   And, contrary to nature, dashes to the earth,
So was my mind expanded from its place
    With all the wealth of food, and issued free;
    What it became, cannot recall or trace.
'Open your eyes, and what I am now see.
    You have seen things that strengthen you in sight
48   So you may bear the smile that comes from me.'
I was as one come to himself from delight
    Of some lost vision, striving in vain to cast
    His mind back to its brightness from the night,
When first I heard this offer renewed at last,
    Worthy of gratitude never to be
54   ·Extinguished from the book of all the past.
If all those tongues should raise their harmony
    That Polyhymnia with her sisters made
    Richest with their sweetest milk, in aiding me,
It would not mount into a thousandth's grade
    Of truth in hymning of that sacred smile,
60   Nor how deep and clear the sacred face portrayed.
And therefore, picturing Paradise awhile,
    The sacred poem has to leap, and seem
    As if its path were cut by some defile.
– Those who consider well the weighty theme,
    The mortal shoulders with the load to bear,
66   Won't blame them if they quake in this extreme.
No voyage for a little barque to fare,
    The daring prow is cleaving with its speed,
    Nor for a helmsman with himself to spare. –
'Why do you love my face so much you heed
    None of the fair garden where flowers shine
72   Beneath the rays of Christ that ever feed?

There is the Rose in which the Word Divine
    Made itself flesh; there, Lilies for whose scent
    The good way was followed like a line.'
So Beatrice; and I, keen and intent
    On her advice, surrendered all my powers
    To struggle with my eyelids, feeble, spent.   78
As once my eyes observed a field of flowers
    Under the rays of sun through broken cloud
    While sheltered by the shade, as if from showers,
So I beheld the throngs of splendours crowd,
    Shone on from above by ardent rays,
    But never saw the Source of the light endowed.   84
Benign Power which imprints them, since my gaze
    Must lack the power, you made yourself ascend,
    And yielded place so that my eyes might raise.
The lovely Flower's name that, dawn, day's end,
    I ever invoke absorbed me utterly.
    Till, on the greatest fire I could attend.   90
When my two eyes could hold the quality
    And power of that living Star whose light
    Surpassed in Heaven, as here, in ardency,
A torch descended from the Heaven's height
    And circled round in likeness of a crown,
    Surrounding her within its wheeling flight.   96
Whatever melody sounds the sweetest down
    On earth, and most draws out the soul to hear,
    Would seem a burst cloud thundering to drown,
Compared with music of that lyre so clear
    Which crowned the lovely Sapphire whose pure light
    Ensapphired Heaven whose brightness is most sheer.   102
'I'm the angelic love circling the height
    Of gladness that is breathed out of the womb
    Which was the inn of our desire for light.
I'll circle, Lady of Heaven, till you assume,
    In following your Son, the supreme sphere
    And make it more divine, giving you room.'   108
The circling melody concluded here,
    And all the other lights rang out the name
    Of Mary with a resonance so clear.
The royal surcoat, most fired with the flame
    Of God, most quickened by his breath and state,
    Round the revolving spheres providing aim,   114

Had inner lining at a height so great
　　That how it looked from where I fixed my eyes
　　Did not appear for me to contemplate.
And so my eyes lacked power to trace the rise
　　Of that crowned Flame as she rose and soared,
120　　Behind her offspring, to the Empyrean skies.
And, as an infant reaches out toward
　　His mother when he's finished with her breast
　　(Since impulse kindles into flame outpoured)
So each, there, reaching up its flame, expressed
　　And showed to me that deep love which they held
126　　For Mary in that yearning manifest.
Then they remained within my sight and swelled
　　Their hymn 'O Queen of Heaven', so sweetly sung
　　That my delight has never been dispelled.
O what great wealth, crammed down in there, among
　　These richest coffers which, below on earth,
132　　Were goodly husbandmen, and true seed flung.
Here they have life and joy in just that worth
　　Of treasure, earned in banishment and weeping
　　In Babylon, and scorning gold for dearth.
Here triumphs, beneath the Son and Mary, sweeping
　　In his victory, together with the bands
138　　Of old and later counsellors, he whose keeping
　　Retains the keys of glory in his hands.

CANTO 24

Beatrice asks the saints to allow Dante to drink from their table. St Peter comes from the host as representative of Faith and catechizes Dante on the strength and truth of his own commitment to the Faith. Dante convinces St Peter of his genuineness and the saint circles him thrice in approval.

'O fellowship, elected to the great
   Supper of the Lamb who feeds you all,
   Filling your desires so they abate,
Since this man foretastes the crumbs that fall
   From your table by the grace of God before
   Death has appointed him his final call,   6
Give heed to his unmeasured yearning, pour
   Him something: you drink forever from the spring
   Whose flow his mind is fixed on, more and more.'
So Beatrice said; and those souls, gladdening,
   Formed into spheres upon fixed poles, and threw
   Out light, like mighty comets, from each ring.   12
And just as different cogs in clockwork do:
   The first one, as you watch, seems not to wind,
   The last to whirl and fly in easy view –
Those carols brought that image to my mind
   With all their differing speeds, this swift, that slow,
   According as their varied wealth inclined.   18
I saw such blissfulness of flame to flow
   Out of the loveliest that none beside
   Had greater magnitude of light to show.
It swept round Beatrice thrice, and, with its glide,
   Sang so divinely that imagination
   Could not repeat it, though it tried and tried.   24
Therefore my pen skips over the narration;
   With delicacy of fold, fancy – no less
   Than speech – is far too brash in pigmentation.
'Holy Sister of mine, who pray and press
   Us so devoutly by your love that glows,
   You draw me from this sphere of loveliness.'   30
The breath that so discoursed, as I disclose,
   Was turned toward my Lady by that flame
   Of blessedness, on coming to repose.

And she: 'O light eternal of that same
    Great soul to whom our Lord allowed the keys
36   Of this great joy he brought down when he came,
Test this man yourself here, as you please,
    Upon the points, both great and small, concerning
    That faith by which you walked upon the seas.
Whether he loves well and hopes well, in yearning
    And in believing, is not concealed from you,
42   For you can see where all must meet discerning.
But, since this realm receives men through the true
    Faith as its citizens, it's only right
    That he should speak and give the glory due.'
Then, as a bachelor arms himself to cite,
    But holds his peace, until the master air
48   The question, and reason, not result, invite,
So with every reason did I prepare,
    As she was speaking, and for such a master
    And such confession, I might then declare.
'Good Christian, speak; reveal before this pastor
    What faith is.' Whereupon I raised my head
54   Towards that light which was the Word's broadcaster;
Then looked to Beatrice who signalled me, instead
    Of speaking, keenly to let the waters rise
    Out of my inner fountain till they spread.
'May grace that lets me confess before the eyes
    Of the chief Centurion of the Faith,' I started,
60   'Ensure my thoughts find utterance clear and wise.'
And I continued: 'Father, as was charted
    For us by your dear brother's truthful pen –
    With whom, for Rome, the true way you imparted –
Faith is the substance of things hoped for; then,
    It is the evidence of things not seen.
66   I take this as its quiddity, Fisher of Men.'
I heard; 'And right, then, has your judgement been,
    If well you see why it is firstly placed
    In substance, then evidence. What does this mean?'
And I, 'The deep things (which have so richly graced
    Me by appearing here) are veiled from gaze
72   Of people still below who must then taste
Of them in their belief alone, and raise
    A lofty hope; and this would characterize
    It, therefore, as substance that supports and stays.

And from this same belief we syllogize –
    As needs we must without the higher sight –
    So it holds the character of evidence, likewise.'   78
I heard: 'If all that was acquired by light
    Of teaching, down below, were understood
    So well, the sophist's wit would lose its bite.'
So breathed that ardent light of love and good,
    Then added: 'This coin's weight and alloy now
    Has stood the test as well as ever it should,   84
But is it in your purse? Come, avow!'
    And I: 'Indeed, it is so round and bright,
    And no "perhaps" has circumscribed the brow.'
Then issued from the glow of that deep light:
    'This precious jewel on which all virtue grows,
    By what means has it reached you with such might?'   90
And I replied: 'The ample shower that flows
    Out of the Holy Spirit and is poured
    On Old and New Parchments, as it chose,
Is syllogism that has brought it to assured
    And sharp conclusion for me; compared to it,
    All demonstration's blunted, hacked and scored.'   96
I heard: 'The Old and New Premise and Writ
    That brings you this conclusion, why trust its tongue?
    Why for divine discourse hold it fit?'
And I: 'The proof that shows the truth is hung
    Upon the deeds which followed – for which acts
    Nature has forged no iron, nor anvil rung.'   102
The answer came: 'Say who assures, enacts
    The proof that these things were? Words that attest
    Themselves, and nothing else, swear you these facts.'
'If the wide world turned Christian,' I confessed,
    'Without the aid of miracles, it makes a case
    Stronger a hundred times than all the rest.   108
For you had come, hungry and poor, to face
    The battle, to sow good plant, once vine,
    But now turned thorn to those who seek for grace.'
This ended and the high court so divine
    Raised *Te Deum Laudamus* through the spheres
    In the melody and song that there combine.   114
The Baron who had led me up the tiers
    From branch to branch, assaying, till we were brought
    Close to where the leafy crest appears,

Began again: 'The grace that with your thought
Holds loving conversation, up till now
120   Has moved your mouth to speak right as it ought,
So what has come I sanction and allow,
But now you must reveal what you believe
And where it came to your belief, and how?'
'Holy Father, spirit who now perceive
What was belief so strong in former year
126   To reach the Tomb – and younger feet to leave,'
I started: 'you wish me now to make quite clear
The form of my belief; and next, inquire
What made its strength; both I will answer here;
I believe in one God, eternal, sole, entire,
Who moves the Heavens, himself unmoved,
132   Suffusing it with love and with desire.
And such belief I find not only proved
In physics and metaphysics, but given to know
By all the truth rained down, which it behooved
Moses to give, the Prophets, the Psalms to sow,
The Gospels and yourself who wrote your versions
138   After the Fiery Spirit hallowed you below.
And I believe in three eternal Persons,
Believe them one in essence, so unique
Yet triune, matching "is" and "are" 's assertions.
Of this profound and holy state I speak,
The Gospel teaching often stamps its mark
144   Upon my mind whenever I would seek.
This is the beginning; this the spark
Which leaps into a living flame and glows
In me, a star of Heaven in the dark.'
Then, as a master, hearing what pleases, goes
Up to embrace his servant the instant he
150   Has fallen silent, pleased with news he shows,
So, singing benedictions, the radiancy
Of the Apostle who requested me to tell,
Circled me thrice when I stood silently,
Because I'd pleased him with my words so well.

CANTO 25

Dante vows to receive his poetic laurels at the font of the lovely church where he was christened. St James now joins them to question Dante regarding the nature of Christian hope. St John comes to question him over the nature of Love but Dante is gazing hard to see his physical body. St John points out that it is buried on earth. Jesus and Mary, as yet, are the only persons to have risen with their physical bodies. The harmony of Heaven ceases and Dante turns in vain to find Beatrice.

If ever it should be this holy song
    (To which both Heaven and earth so set their hand
    That I have grown more lean as years wear long)
Should overcome the cruelty which has banned
    Me from the lovely fold where I slept sound,
    A lamb, but foe to wolves that waste the land,   6
Voice changed, fleece changed, I will retrace that ground,
    A poet, and at my baptismal place
    I shall assume the chaplet and be crowned;
For there it was I joined the Faith whose grace
    Makes souls beknown to God; and Peter, then,
    Because of it, circled my brow and face.   12
Thereafter came a light to us again,
    Out of that sphere from which had drawn to me
    That stem of all the Vicars Christ left men.
My Lady, full of joy, exclaimed: 'See! See!
    The Baron for whose sake they turn their feet
    To Galicia down below. Look, it is he!'   18
As, when a dove comes near his mate, they greet
    And pour out mutual love, in circling near
    And murmuring, as together they will meet,
So one great glorious prince received his peer,
    As I could see, rejoicing in the will
    That feasted them on high within that sphere.   24
But when the greeting ended each stood still;
    Fixed so dazzling in front of me, the flare
    Subdued my countenance. They gazed their fill.
'Illustrious life,' said Beatrice, smiling there,
    'By whom our great cathedral's bounteous might
    Is chronicled, as well your words declare,   30

Let hope resound within this lofty height;
    You can – who were the type of it below
    When Jesus favoured three with greater light.'
'Lift up your looks, be reassured and know;
    For what comes from the mortal world up here
36   Must ripen in the rays we dart and throw,'
The second flame said, conquering my fear.
    At which I raised my eyes towards the hills
    Which bowed them earlier with weight so sheer.
'Since, by his grace, our Lord and Sovereign wills
    That, prior to death, in his most secret court,
42   You may encounter with the saints he fills,
That, seeing all its truth, your full report
    May strengthen, in yourself and others, the hope
    That makes men love the good – as well they ought –
Say what it is, and how your mind's slope
    Flowers with it, and tell me how it came.'
48   The second flame then followed with this trope.
The gentle one who trained my fledgling aim
    To such a lofty flight, forestalled my say
    In giving him an answer, to exclaim:
'Church militant has not a child today
    Richer in hope as written in the Sun
54   That over all our host directs its ray.
Therefore was he permitted to be one
    To come from Egypt to Jerusalem
    To see her long before his fight was done.
And those two other points – neither of them
    Asked to enlighten you but so he'll bear
60   Word how this virtue pleases you, root and stem –
I leave to him. They're not a hard affair
    For him, nor cue for boasting. So let him say,
    And may God's grace concede this to his care.'
As pupil follows teacher, keen to obey
    In all where he is expert to reply
66   So that his excellence is on display:
'Hope is certain expectation,' said I,
    'Of future glory; it is product of grace
    And of precedent merit, twofold in ply.
From many stars derives the light I trace;
    But that Singer supreme, of Lord supreme,
72   In psalm bedewed my heart in the first place:

"Let them hope in Thee," is his song's theme,
        "Who know thy name"; who knows it not? – if he
        Possess my faith in God who shall redeem?
Beside those showers, you showered it on me
        In your Epistle, so I'm full and start
        Your rain to shower others unstintedly.'   78
While I was speaking this, within the heart
        Of living flame quivered a sudden light,
        Repeated like the lightning with its dart.
Then breathed: 'The love with which I still burn bright
        Towards the virtue that followed me by deed
        To palm and issuing from the field by right   84
Wills that I breathe on you who are so keyed
        To such delight in her; further, accord
        This pleasure: tell where hope's promise may lead.'
And I: 'The New and Older Scriptures afford
        The sign (and this directs my mind straight there)
        For all the souls made friends with God the Lord.   90
Isaiah says that each of these will wear
        A double garment in their native land,
        And their native land's this sweet life and fair.
And then your brother makes us understand
        This revelation much the clearer where
        He treats of the white robes of that band.'   96
Immediately I'd finished rang out there
        Above us first: 'Let them hope in Thee!'
        And all the dancers, answering, sang that air.
Then one shone from them – and there would be
        A winter month turned to unbroken day
        If the Crab had such a crystal's radiancy.   102
And, as a joyous virgin stands, and makes her way
        To join the dance in honour of the bride,
        And not in any lightness to display,
So then I saw that sheer splendour side
        With these two, wheeling on in such a way
        As burning love persuaded them to glide.   108
Their music then it joined, and joined their lay.
        My Lady fixed her gaze on them, a bride,
        Silent, unmoving, as she watched them sway.
'The one who lay upon our Pelican's side,
        Against his breast, and chosen from the Tree
        For the great service that he must provide,'   114

So said my Lady, but, whether she spoke to me
    Or kept her peace, she never moved her eyes
120   From their intended point of scrutiny.
Like one who strains his vision to the skies
    To see the sun eclipsed for a brief space,
    And, through such staring, finds his eyesight dies,
So was I with this flame till, to my face,
    Word came: 'Why are you dazzled as you stare
126   To see a thing which here has not a place?
Earth in the earth my body is, and there
    Remains with all the rest till numbers reach
    The purpose the Eternal brings to bear.
With both robes in the blest cloister are each
    Of those, the only lights that ever rose;
132   And this you will take back below and teach.'
At this voice the ring of flame came to repose,
    Together with the sweetly woven round
    Made by the triple breathing as it goes,
As, to avoid weariness or danger found,
    The oars that sweep till then the water by,
138   Together cease, hearing the whistle's sound.
Ah, how my mind was wrenched, turning to eye
    Beatrice, not seeing where she was, since this –
Though I was right beside her up on high,
    Within the world of all our hope and bliss.

CANTO 26

*St John comforts Dante over his lost sight and questions him concerning the nature
of Love. Dante satisfies St John's questioning: God as good in himself must of
necessity be loved; God as good to man must be loved as the Creator of the world,
of the individual, as author of our Redemption and the provider of the Heavenly
life. Dante's sight is restored and he notices a fourth flaming spirit, Adam, who
answers his unspoken queries concerning Adam's creation, his language in the
Garden of Eden, his time there, and the first name used for God.*

While I remained in fear for my lost sight
    I was made conscious by a breath that came
    From that resplendent flame that quenched my light,
Saying: 'Until your sight which, seeing my flame,
    You have consumed, is once again remade,
    You should compensate by talking of your aim;   6
So start and say on what your mind has rayed
    Its focus; rest assured your sight is just
    Bedazed and not destroyed in endless shade,
Because the Lady who conducts your dust
    Through this divine region has power that lay
    In Ananias' hands within her trust.'   12
'At her convenience, now or later, may
    Help come to eyes that were the gates she burst
    Through with the fire that burns me, night and day.
The good which satisfies this court is first
    Alpha and Omega of the Scripture's Writ
    That love reads loud or low to me immersed.'   18
The voice, that had removed my sudden fit
    Of terror at the dazzling, set my drift
    Again upon the discourse, saying of it:
'Yes: through a finer mesh you now must sift.
    Now you must tell me what it is that trained
    On such a target's aim the bow you lift.'   24
'By philosophic arguments,' I explained,
    'And by authority that has descended,
    The stamp of such a love on me has deigned.
For good, as good – as far as comprehended –
    Must kindle love; and as its excellence
    Increases, so the more of love's extended.   30

Therefore to that Essence whose pre-eminence
   Is that, outside it, whatever good is found
   Is just reflection of its radiance,
More than to anything else the mind is bound
   In love, for all of those who truth discern,
36   On which this reasoning is rested sound.
This truth is stated for my mind to learn
   By him alone who has established for me
   The primal love eternal beings yearn.
It's set forth by the Author of Truth where he,
   In speaking of himself to Moses, said
42   To him: "All goodness shall I make you see."
In your sublime announcement, at its head,
   You set forth, below, the mystery of this place
   Above, with more light than others shed.'
I heard: 'With human reason as the base
   And by authorities agreeing, as you saw,
48   The highest of your loves seeks God and Grace.
But tell me if you feel more links that draw
   You to him so that you may testify
   With what teeth this love holds you in its jaw.'
The holy aim of Christ's eagle did not lie
   Deeply concealed for I perceived just where
54   He wished to lead my own profession by.
'All those teeth,' I started to declare,
   'Which have the power to bow to God the soul
   Have worked to build the charity I bear.
For my existence, and the world's as a whole;
   The death he bore that I might live; that, too,
60   Which I and all believers hope, as goal,
With the living assurance I spoke of, drew
   Me from the sea of love perverse, and laid
   Me on the shore of love that's just and true.
The leaves with which the garden has been made
   By the eternal Gardener I love and treasure
66   In measure of his good in leaf and blade.'
The instant I was silent a sweet song's pleasure
   Rang through the Heavens, and my Lady spoke
   And sang; 'Holy, holy, holy!' in their measure.
And as a sleeper whom a keen light woke,
   Because the visual spirit swiftly darts
72   To meet the glare that pierces cloak on cloak,

Abruptly stirs, and shrinks away, and starts
    At all the sights, so unaware he is
    Till comprehension comes to use its arts,
So Beatrice chased away the obscurities
    In my eyes with her own, those lovely rays
    That shone a thousand miles their brilliances.   78
And better than before I saw; my gaze
    Bewildered, though, I queried much to find
    A fourth was there among us with his blaze.
'Within those rays,' my Lady then outlined,
    'The soul created first, by the first Power,
    Holds loving conversation with his maker's mind.'   84
And, as in gusts a branch's tip will cower
    Its head down and then lift it up again
    By its own pliancy within the bower,
So while she spoke I was bemazed and then
    Restored to confidence with the urge to speak
    Burning with ardour in the body's pen.   90
I said: 'O single fruit, produced at peak
    Of your maturity, Father of yore,
    Each bride your daughter, daughter-in-law unique,
Devoutly as I may I now implore
    That you may speak to me. My will you know,
    And sooner to hear you now, I say no more.'   96
Sometimes a creature shifts, though veiled below
    Some cover, so that its movement may be seen
    Since what conceals it moves with it, to and fro.
Just so, the first soul, through its shield and screen,
    Made its elation show with what great joy
    To bring me pleasure it advanced its sheen.   102
And from it breathed: 'Though you do not employ
    A word I see your wish far better here
    Than you have seen what's certain, man or boy,
Because, in the glass of truth, I see it clear
    From Him who is reflector of all things,
    Though nothing fully reflects his light so sheer.   108
You want to know how long my sojournings
    Since God had put me in the Garden where
    She prepared you for the long stair to these rings;
How long I looked on that delightful fare;
    And the true cause of the great indignity;
    The tongue I made and spoke you'd have me declare.   114

Now understand, my son, tasting the tree
    Was not itself the cause of banishment,
    But breaking the command, that made us flee.
In that sad place from which your Lady sent
    Vergil, four thousand, three hundred and two
120   Revolutions my longing for this gathering went.
I saw the sun, and watched him passing through
    All of the lights upon his annual course,
    For nine hundred and thirty times anew.
The tongue I spoke long since quenched its discourse –
    Before the work they never could effect,
126   Started by Nimrod's people in their force.
For no result that reason may project
    Can last forever, since all human choice
    Varies as motions of the Heavens direct.
It's nature's doing that man is given voice,
    But this or that tongue nature leaves to you,
132   As best it seems to men in their employs.
Before I sank to infernal pain, I knew
    "I" as the name of the supreme Good on earth –
    From whom the gladness comes that robes my view.
"El" was he called thereafter, in the dearth;
    And that is fitting, since all mortal gear
138   Is leaves that drop before the next have birth.
I was upon the Mount, that rises clear
    Out of the sea, life pure, and life disgraced,
From the first hour until the sun appear
    In its next quadrant, on the sixth hour traced.'

CANTO 27

*Dante observes the glory of Heaven but then sees St Peter glow red with indigna-
tion at the behaviour of Pope Boniface VIII. All Heaven shares the mood and
Beatrice flushes as would a woman hearing of such shame. St Peter denounces
Clement the Gascon and John of Cahors, promising that justice and vengeance
will descend on them in due time. Dante is told by Beatrice to look at the earth.
They are in Gemini, the sun is in Aries with Taurus between; as a result the half
of the earth lit by the sun does not entirely match what Dante sees. The earth
appears like the moon past the full. The light spreads west of Gibraltar to the
shores of the Levant. The darkened portion lies further east. He turns back to
regard Beatrice and they rise to the Primum Mobile. Beatrice explains the workings
of this sphere and then considers the poor depraved and deprived earth which is
degenerate not in essence but because there is no ruler to keep it in check. She
asserts that in short time this course shall be reversed.*

'Glory to the Father, Son, and Holy Ghost!'
    All Paradise began the hymnody
    So that sweet song enraptured and engrossed;
And what I was observing seemed to be
    A smiling of the universe; so flowed
    Through hearing and through sight the ecstasy.   6
O joy, ineffable happiness bestowed!
    O life compact of love and peacefulness!
    O wealth secure that longing cannot goad!
Before my eyes the four lamps incandesce
    And then the one that first approached me bloomed
    With greater verve and greater liveliness;   12
It seemed as Jupiter might be presumed,
    If he and Mars were birds and so had changed
    Their markings round with which they each were plumed.
The Providence that assigns and has arranged
    Service and office imposed silence through
    The blessèd choir on every side it ranged,   18
And then I heard: 'If I transform this hue
    Don't marvel over it, for you will face,
    Just as I speak, the others changing, too.
He who usurps my place on earth, my place,
    My place (that in the sight of the divine
    Presence of God, the Son, is a vacant space)   24

Has made my burial-place a conduit and rine
    For blood and filth by which the devious Foe
    Who fell from here is soothed in his decline.'
I saw all Heaven immediately grow
    The colour clouds are painted by the sun
30   In early morning or at evening, low.
And as a good woman, sure in all she's done,
    Yet merely hearing of another's fault,
    Will suddenly become the shamefaced one,
So Beatrice changed her look: so the vault
    Of Heaven was eclipsed, I think, upon that day
36   When the Almighty suffered in our default.
Then his discourse proceeded on its way
    With voice transmuted so much in its tone
    Not even his appearance so changed its ray.
'The Bride of Christ was never built on bone
    And blood of mine, of Linus, of Cletus, then,
42   To be misused for gain of gold alone.
But, for reward of this glad life, such men
    As Sixtus, Pius, Calixtus, Urban, poured
    Their lifeblood, after tears and tears again.
Nor did we mean the people of the Lord
    Should sit, one half on our successor's right,
48   And half upon the other at Christ's board.
Nor that the keys, entrusted me, by sleight
    Should change to ensign on a standard borne
    Against the baptized in unholy fight.
Nor that I be the profile to adorn
    The seal of sold and lying privilege bought –
54   At which I redden, shoot out flames of scorn.
In guise of pastors, ravening wolves disport
    In all the pastures, as we see from here.
    Oh God of our defence, why sleep, not thwart?
Cahorsines, Gascons prepare to drink our dear
    Blood. O fair beginning to what a low
60   Ending must your downfall persevere!
But highest Providence which, with Scipio,
    Defended the glory of the world for Rome
    Will soon bring help, I judge, and overthrow.
And you, my son, who, for your mortal loam,
    Shall go below once more, open your lips;
66   And do not hide what I've not hid; speak home.'

As our air showers down the flakes and slips
    Of frozen vapour when time comes the horn
    Of the Heavenly Goat feels sun at its tips,
So did I see the ether then adorn
    Itself, and all of those triumphant flakes
    That met us, snowing upwardly were borne.   72
My gaze was following their drifting sakes,
    And traced them till the medium, by excess,
    Prevented me from following their wakes.
At which my Lady saw me relieved the stress
    Of peering up, and said: 'Look to the ground;
    Consider how you wheel and how progress.'   78
And, from the time I'd first looked down, I found
    That I had moved right through the arc that's made
    From middle to the end of the first clime's bound,
So that I saw, beyond Cadiz portrayed,
    The mad course Ulysses took and, this side,
    Almost the shore where Europa a sweet load weighed.   84
More of this threshing-floor I had descried
    Had not the sun advanced beneath my feet
    A sign and more away upon its glide.
My love-struck mind that always holds a sweet
    Dalliance with my Lady burned much more
    Than ever to look up and her face to meet.   90
Whatever provision nature or art explore,
    Or make, to captivate the eye or take
    The mind with limb and image to adore,
If all united, nothing would they make
    Beside the divine delight that shone on me,
    Once turning to her smiling face and sake.   96
The power her look had given set me free,
    And drew me out of lovely Leda's nest,
    And thrust me in the swiftest Heaven instantly.
Its parts – the nearest and the highest – possessed
    Such uniformity I cannot tell
    In which part Beatrice brought me down to rest.   102
But she, who saw at once my yearning swell,
    Began, smiling with such gladness in her beam
    That in her face God's own joy seemed to dwell:
'The nature of the universe supreme
    (That holds the centre still and spins all round)
    Here, as from its source, begins to stream.   108

And this Heaven has no other where, or bound,
Except the Mind Divine where love is lit
That turns it and rains its power on the ground.
Light and love grasp it in one circle knit,
As it holds all the others; he who whirs
114   This cincture is the single Mind in it.
Its motion from no other circle's stirs.
It metes out all the movements of the rest
As ten to half and to the fifth refers.
And how Time has its roots planted and pressed
In this same vase, and grows its leafy head
120   Within the rest may now be manifest.
– O greed that draws men's eyes down to your bed
So that not one can lift his gaze away
Out of those breakers where it's plummeted.
Though, true, the will of men has power and sway,
But such continual downpour turns true plum
126   To mouldy cankered fruit before its day.
Faith and innocence are found to come
Only in little children; then both flee past,
Even before hair clothes the cheeks of some.
Many a lisping child observes his fast
Who, later, when his tongue is loose devours
132   All food in every month as if his last.
And many a lisping child in his brief hours
Loves and obeys his mother, who, later on,
Wishes her dead when tongue has all its powers.
And so the fair skin blackens, and is gone,
First meeting the fair daughter of him who brings
138   The dawn and leaves the evening grey and wan.
And you, in case you lapse to marvellings
At such a thing, reflect that there is none
To guide earth's household from its wanderings.
Before all January out of winter's run,
By reason of the hundredth part ignored,
144   On earth, these higher wheels shall shine their Sun.
So the event, long waited and implored,
Shall turn the bows to stern so the pursuit
Of the fleet's directest course shall be restored,
And from the blossom there shall grow true fruit.'

CANTO 28

Dante perceives in the eyes of Beatrice the reflection of something not previously observed. It is a point of the intensest light with nine concentric circles whirling round it, brighter and faster as their orbits are nearer to the point of intensity. It is the still centre from which the universe depends. Dante needs explanations as to why the physical appearance of these angelic orders seems to contradict their order of magnitude as they are shown in the nine spheres of the Ptolemaic universe. He learns that the two appearances are parallel in their virtue, not in their spatial extensions. Beatrice explains the nine orders of angels, siding with Dionysius against Gregory's deviation from that view.

When she, then, who emparadises my mind
    Had so declared the truth as contrary
    To current living of our mortal kind,
As, shining in a mirror, you may see
    A torch's light when lit behind you, though
    You never saw or thought it previously,   6
And so you veer around at once to know
    Whether the mirror's view be verified,
    And see them match as words to music go,
So, memory records, I must have tried,
    Gazing upon those eyes whose lovely light
    Love made the noose to draw me to her side.   12
I turned, and mine were struck, then, by the might
    Of what appears within that volume's theme
    Whenever eye is focused on it right;
I saw a point which shot so keen a beam
    The vision that it strikes must needs be closed
    Against intensity of such extreme.   18
Whatever star's the smallest one exposed,
    Down here, would seem a moon, presented near,
    As star with star in some conjunction posed.
Perhaps as close as a halo round the sphere
    That tinges it, when vapours bearing it
    Are thickest and support its glimmer here,   24
At such a distance round the point was lit
    A fiery ring, so swift it would have passed
    That speed in which the world is bound and knit.

A second circled this, and, round that cast,
    The third; round third, a fourth, and, outside four,
30   The fifth; the sixth, beyond the fifth, spun fast.
And then the seventh came, stretching its tour
    Already so far out the messenger
    Of Juno, rounded, were too tight a door.
And so the eighth and ninth, beyond, occur;
    And each one moved more slowly, as it drew
36   Away from unity its integer.
The clearest flame was in that ring that flew
    Nearest the pure spark because, I think,
    It sinks the deepest into all that's true.
My Lady, seeing me struggle on the brink
    Of deep wonder, declared: 'From that point
42   Hangs Heaven and all of nature, link by link.
Look on that circle which is most conjoint
    With it, and realize its speed is swift
    Because love's fires kindle and anoint.'
'If the universe,' so went my drift,
    'Were ranged in ranks, like these I notice here,
48   I'd be content with what I see and sift,
But, in the universe of sense, it's clear
    To see, the wheels, according as they wind
    Remote from centre, more divine appear.
Therefore, if it behoves my longing to find
    Its goal in this angelic wondrous shrine
54   (That has but light and love to make and bind)
I need to hear and know why the design
    And copy do not apparently comply –
    But now I vex in vain these eyes of mine.'
'Well, if your inept fingers can't untie
    A knot like this, it's small wonder there;
60   It's grown so hard because you never try.'
So said my Lady, adding: 'What I declare
    To you, accept – if you wish to see straight,
    And wind your wit round it with better care.
Material bodies spread from small to great
    Accordingly as great virtue or less
66   Is interfused throughout their whole estate.
The greater excellence, the greater blessedness;
    The greater blessedness, the greater host,
    When all parts perfection equally express.

Therefore, this sphere (that moves and has engrossed
    The total universe) must be the ring
    That comprehends the most and loves the most.   72
So that, apply your measure to the thing
    Itself – the virtue, not appearances,
    Of spirits that appear as spheres – to bring
Out what a marvellous consonance there is
    In each Heaven with its Intelligence, of less
    With smallness and of more with immensities.'   78
Just as it's left shining in tranquilness,
    The hemisphere of air, when Boreas blows
    His gentler cheek and makes mists evanesce
Or flee that once obscured, and Heaven bestows
    The smile of all its lovely realm to beam
    On us, so I was when my Lady chose   84
To offer there the clearly shining gleam
    Of her reply to me, and, like a star
    Of Heaven, the truth shone lucid and supreme.
And when she ceased, not otherwise, a bar
    Of iron melting, shoots out sparks of light,
    Than did those circles sparkling near and far.   90
And every spark followed its blaze in flight
    And all those numbers were thousands beyond
    The doubling of the chessboard, black and white.
From choir to choir I heard 'Hosanna!' respond,
    Sung to that still point that keeps and keeps
    Them ever to that where, always their bond.   96
And she who saw my questing thoughts in deeps
    Of mind said: 'The first circles have now shown
    The Seraphs and the Cherubs in their glorious leaps,
So fast they trace the loopings of their zone
    To be most like the point, and, as they seem
    Sublime in vision, so success they own.   102
Those other loves which course around their stream
    Are named the Thrones of the divine sight,
    Closing the first ternary with their gleam.
And you should understand they all delight
    In measure as their vision deeper plumbs
    The truth where every mind must still its flight.   108
So may be seen that being blessèd comes
    From act of seeing, and love is not the base,
    But follows after, when the eye succumbs;

And that extent of sight's the merit grace
    Provides, and the righteous will, and thus it goes
114   From rank to rank towards the furthest place.
The second ternary that flowers and grows
    In this eternal spring which never a night
    The Ram brings on can spoil or discompose,
Ceaselessly sings Hosanna's rite,
    With triple airs that sound within the three
120   Orders of joy upon their three-fold flight.
In this hierarchy are three ranks of divinity:
    First are Dominions, next the Virtues; round
    Them spin the Powers in this ternary.
Then, in the last but one triad are found
    Principalities, Archangels; last remain
126   All of the Angels that disport and bound.
These orders all look up; and downward train
    Such potency that all below they draw
    – As they are also drawn – to God again.
And Dionysius, with such yearning awe,
    Set himself to contemplate their state
132   And named, as I, what he distinctly saw.
Yet Gregory, later, differed in this debate
    But then, as soon as seeing in this sphere,
    Smiled at his own expense and saw it straight.
And if such arcane truth were spoken clear
    By mortal men on earth, these are not things
138   For wonderment, for he who watched it here
      Revealed it, and much more about these rings.'

CANTO 29

Beatrice, gazing in the divine Light, anticipates Dante's queries. It is pointless to ask what God did before creation. Creation was not an act in time; time is a result of Creation. She explains that angels have no memories because they see all simultaneously and instantly and therefore need no recall. She denounces flippant teachers and preachers, and points out how innumerable are the angels that inform with their virtue the diverse operations of the universe.

When, covered by the Ram and Scales, Latona's pair
    Of children make the skyline seem to be
    Their girdles and that selfsame moment share
As long as from the moment when you see
    The zenith hold them balanced in that belt
    Till both change hemispheres, and from it flee,   6
So long, smile traced upon her face, she dwelt
    In silence, gazing fixed upon that locus
    Whose overmastering power I had felt.
'I tell, not ask, what you would hear,' she spoke thus,
    'For I have seen it there where every *where*
    And every *when* is brought to that one focus.   12
Not for himself to gain any good there
    – Which cannot be – but that his splendour blaze,
    And in reflection its *I am* declare,
Beyond time, and beyond all bound or gaze,
    In his eternity, as was his pleasure,
    Eternal Love was shown in new loves' displays.   18
Nor did he lie, as in a sleepy leisure,
    For no before, nor since, could ever be
    Till God moved on the waters in his measure.
Form and matter, joint and in entity,
    Were issued into being, flawless, perfected,
    As from a three-stringed bow three arrows flee.   24
And as in crystal, amber, glass projected,
    A ray alights so that, from first touch played
    To its pervading all, no time's detected,
So the threefold creation of its Lord rayed
    At once into existence, radiated
    Without priority in being made.   30

Order was co-woven and co-created
    For spirit substance; the summit these were made
    Of the world and pure activity instigated.
Potentiality was the lowest level laid;
    And, in between, potentiality tied
36   With act a plait that never could be frayed.
Jerome told you of ages stretching wide,
    In which the Angels were created, when
    Nothing was in the universe beside.
The truth I tell's on many a page, by pen
    Of writers of the Holy Spirit; you'll learn
42   Of it, if well you study there again.
And reason sees a part which might discern
    That those movers should not too long repose
    Without their full perfection in their turn.
And now you know the where and when he chose
    To make these loving spirits; and the how.
48   So three flames quench now in your yearning's throes.
Nor would one count as far as twenty now
    Before one section of the Angel host
    Convulsed your lowest element – which you plough.
But, of the angels, loyalty held most
    Who, given to this art – which you've descried,
54   Have such delight their rings maintain their post.
The outset of the Fall was that cursed pride
    Of him whom you have seen held and restrained
    Where all the universe's weight's applied.
Those that you watch were modest, and maintained
    Themselves derived from that same Excellence
60   Which made them quick to know the good they gained.
Therefore, illuminating Grace their sense
    Of vision raised, as did their merit raise
    It, so their will is full, free from offence.
And you must never be in doubt or haze,
    So be assured: it is merit to receive
66   Such grace by open affection for its ways.
Concerning this consistory, you may achieve
    Much in your contemplation, without aid –
    If what I say is gathered up to sheave.
Yet, since in schools on earth, it is conveyed
    In lectures that angelic nature's such
72   That understands, remembers, wills, as made,

I shall now add, so you may see and clutch
    The truth in purity – which, in that place,
    Equivocating discourse blurs so much:
Since first they gathered joy from God's own face
    (From which nothing is hidden) these angels' sight
    Has never been removed from it a moment's space.   78
Thus, novel things can never come to light
    Before their eyes, so they will never need
    Abstractions to recall the past from flight.
Although they're not asleep, they dream indeed
    Down there, believing – or not believing – they speak
    The truth. From one, more shame and blame proceed.   84
On earth, it's never the single path you seek
    When you philosophize; the love of show,
    And thoughts of it, misguide you slant, oblique.
Yet, here, that meets less indignation, know,
    Than when the Holy Scriptures are ignored,
    Or misinterpretation undergo.   90
They don't consider the cost of blood once poured
    To sow it in the world, nor how he pleases
    Who humbly stays beside it safely moored.
Each strains his wits to make a show and eases
    His invention in; these, the preachers take
    And then a silence on the Gospel seizes   96
One reckons that the moon drew back to break
    The sun's light, blocking it from earth below,
    When Christ was suffering for our wretched sake.
And others, that the light refused to glow –
    In which case that eclipse would then appear
    For Indian, Spaniard, not just Jews to know.   102
Florence breeds fewer Lapos and Bindos a year
    Than tales and fables of such kind are taught
    In every part by priest and pulpiteer,
So that the sheep (who little know of thought)
    Return from pasture fed with wind; and no
    Excuse is their not seeing as they ought.   108
Christ did not tell his first assembly: "Go
    And preach of trifles to the world!" but gave
    To them the true foundation they should sow.
That, and only that, they spoke to save,
    And thus they made the Gospel shield and lance
    To kindle faith in men, in battle brave.   114

Now they go forth with jokes, pull faces, prance
    To preach and, if the laughter rises loud,
    The hood swells up and nothing else need chance.
But such a bird is in the hood-tail, the crowd,
    If they could see it nestling, would then see
120   What pardon they are trusting in that shroud.
And so, on earth, spreads such vacuity
    That, without any proof, the people leap
    At any promise without a guarantee.
By this, Anthony fattens his swine to keep,
    And others, too, more swinish still than they,
126   With money lacking imprint, pay up cheap. –
But, since we have digressed enough this way,
    Turn back your sight to the true path sought,
    So that our journey-time meet no delay.
The angels rank so great in number, thought
    And speech of man has never stretched to yield,
132   As yet, the total number in this court.
And, if you see what Daniel revealed,
    You'll know that in his thousands, determinates
    Of number vanish, from all sight concealed.
And here the primal Light that radiates
    On all is felt by them in as many ways
138   As there are splendours which it penetrates.
Therefore, since the affections follow the phase
    And act of conceiving, the tenderness of love
    Glows with different aspects in their gaze.
See now the height and breadth, in all above,
    Of the eternal Good, since it has made
144   So many mirrors where it facets its love,
    Yet stays the One as ever it has rayed.'

CANTO 30

The angels disappear as do the stars in the dawn sky. Dante turns to Beatrice and finds her transcendent beauty impossible to put into words. She tells him they are now in the Heaven of Light and Love, the still centre. His sight is strengthened by a blinding flash so that he can see the real forms of the saints. He notices a vacant place among the elect appointed for the emperor Henry who will try to set Italy right but will be defeated by the avarice and greed of the Italians and the hypocrisy of Pope Clement whose fate Beatrice forecasts. The closing lines refer to Henry of Luxembourg, elected Emperor Henry VII in 1308 but dying at Buonconvento in 1313. Line 142 refers to Clement V who died in 1314; the last, to Boniface VIII – Dante's arch enemy.

It's noon some six thousand miles away
    And this world already slopes its shade
    As if toward a level bed that lay,
When Heaven's centre, deep above arrayed,
    Changes so that now here, now there, a star
    Loses its power to shine on the earth's glade   6
And as the brightest maid of the sun so far
    Advances that the Heaven closes, light
    By light, till gone the loveliest are;
Just so, the triumph in eternal flight,
    Dancing around the point that vanquished me,
    Seemingly clasped by what it clasped so tight,   12
Little by little doused what I could see,
    So seeing nothing – and my love – impelled
    Return to Beatrice of my scrutiny.
If all said of her, up till now, were held
    In one award of praise it were too slight
    To serve the present need, for it excelled,   18
The beauty I observed, surpassed the might,
    Not merely of our measure, but, I vow,
    Her Maker only knew its full delight.
At this I yield defeat – a greater now
    Than ever tragic or comic poet's, quelled
    By some point in his theme and brought to bow.   24
For, as the sun in quavering sight is held,
    Remembrance of the sweetest smile so shears
    My memory from itself that all's dispelled.

From the first day when, in this life of years,
    I saw her face, until this sight, my rhyme
30   Has never lost or left the course it steers,
But my pursuit must here desist, this time,
    From tracing in my verse her loveliness
    Since there's a bound to every artist's climb.
I leave a greater herald to express
    Her than my trumpet is – which brings its flight
36   Towards the end of the hard theme I address.
With voice and stance of guide who'd shown the height,
    She spoke again: 'We've left and come – above
    The greatest body – to the Heaven of pure light.
Light intellectual, light filled with love;
    Love of true goodness, brimmed full of joy;
42   Joy that transcends all sweetness far above.
You'll see the first and second host deploy,
    Levies of Paradise, and see the first,
    As at the Judgement Day, in twin alloy.'
As, on the vision, lightning's sudden burst
    Can rob the eyes of power to specify
    The solidest of objects it's traversed,
48 So shone around me a living light, till I
    Was swathed in such a web of shiningness
    That nothing else was visible near by.
'The Love that calms the Heaven will ever impress
    Into itself with welcome of this sort,
    To prepare the candle for the flame's caress.'
54 No sooner were those brief words said and brought
    To me than I felt myself surmount and rise
    Beyond my normal powers of sight and thought,
And, fired with new-born sight my earthly eyes,
    There is no light so bright in anything
    I might not hold in view and scrutinize.
60 I saw light in form of a river shimmering,
    Gleaming in splendour in its pair of banks,
    And both of them painted with marvellous spring.
Out of the river, on both its flanks,
    Fountained these living sparks which, after, fell
    Into the blossoms like rubies in golden ranks.
66 Then, as if drunk upon the fragrant smell,
    They plunge again into the marvellous flow
    Whence others leap when they rejoin the swell.

'The high desire that burns in you to know
　　More of these things on which you gaze and think
　　Pleases me more the more that it can grow.　　　　　　72
But of this water here you first must drink
　　Before so great a thirst be slaked,' so she
　　To me, the sun of my sight upon that brink.
'The river, the topaz gems that leap out free
　　And find the flow again, the smiling grass,
　　Are shadowy forecasts of their reality.　　　　　　　78
Not as themselves imperfect must you class
　　Them, since the defect lies on your side still,
　　Because your sight's not reached the highest pass.'
Child never threw itself with such a will
　　Upon its milk, when happening to rise
　　Much later than its normal daily drill,　　　　　　　84
As I bent swiftly down to make my eyes
　　Still better mirrors from the waters streamed
　　To make us perfect as it clarifies.
And, once the eaves of my eyelids drank, it seemed
　　To me, the river's length appeared to change
　　Into a circularity that gleamed.　　　　　　　　　90
Then, as those who wear a mask quite strange
　　But, when they take it off their face and head,
　　They alter features in our vision's range,
So, in my eyes, these sparks and flowers spread
　　Into a greater festival: I saw
　　The dual courts of Heaven revealed instead.　　　　　96
– O Splendour of God by which I looked and saw
　　That high triumph of the truth's domain,
　　Give me the power to tell of all I saw. –
A light there is that makes the Creator plain
　　And clear before the creature who only finds,
　　In seeing Him, his perfect peace again.　　　　　　102
It spreads so wide a circle that it winds
　　Too vast to close the sun inside the sway
　　Of the immense circumference it binds.
Its whole expanse is made of a single ray,
　　Reflected on the curving of the first-
　　Moved sphere, which gains its motion in this way.　　108
And, as a hill reflects itself, immersed
　　In water at its foot, gazing as bound
　　In its beauty, rich with grass and flowers dispersed,

So, mounting over the light, around, around,
  Reflecting, I saw more than a thousand rows
114   Of those who'd journeyed homeward from the ground.
And, if the lowest row gathers and glows
  With such a brilliant light, what magnitude
  Upon the further petals of that Rose?
Sight was not lost in height and breadth I viewed,
  But fully grasped the nature and the scope
120   Of all the joy and gladness in the mood.
Neither distance nor nearness to our hope
  Adds or subtracts a jot where God is King,
  Since nature's laws no longer need to cope.
Within the Rose's eternal yellow, that, ring
  On ring, expands and breathes its fragrant praise
126   Towards the Sun, and makes it lasting spring,
Myself – as one who wants to speak but lays
  Silence upon his tongue – Beatrice drew and said:
  'Look! How large the white-robed concourse sways!
See how our city sweeps, how vast outspread!
  Look how many thrones are filled! How few
132   Have still to take their seats from years ahead.
On that great seat, where you have fixed your view
  Because it bears already a crown's acclaim,
  Before your presence at this feast is due,
Shall sit the soul (on earth, imperial its fame)
  Of lofty Henry who shall come to set
138   Italy right – before it's her own aim.
The blind greed that cursed you made you fret
  Like a spoilt brat who, hungry, still would pine,
  Yet chase its nurse away with sulky threat.
And he who holds the court of things divine
  Shall be the sort that, open or underhand,
144   Shall tread a different path from his design.
But brief the time that God will let him stand
  In sacred office; down he shall be thrown
Where Simon Magus for his worth lies banned;
  He from Anagni, to a lower zone.'

CANTO 31

The elect are seen as filling petal on petal of the mystic Rose. Dante gazes, rapt, and turns to ask Beatrice a question but panics when unable to find her. Bernard, symbol of contemplative vision and love of Mary, comes at Beatrice's request to lead Dante to the peak of his desire by directing him to take that straight look at the actual appearance of the divine for which Beatrice has prepared his soul. He looks first at Beatrice and pours out his gratitude. He looks in awe at Bernard on discovering who he is and then directs his vision on to the Virgin whose glory is like the dawn. The oriflamme, line 127, was the standard said to be given by the angel Gabriel to the ancient kings of France to make them invincible. 'Pacific' is an ironic contrast with the current rulers.

Then, in the form of a white rose, was displayed
    To me that sacred soldiery Christ brings
    To be his Bride for whom in blood he paid.
The Angel host that, flying, sees and sings
    The glory of Him who fills it with his love
    And excellence – from which its being springs –   6
Just like a swarm of bees that, now above,
    Enflowers itself and, after, will resume
    To where its toil is turned to sweetest stuff,
So constantly descended to the great bloom,
    Decked with so many leaves, and then arose
    To where its love forever makes it room.   12
Faces of living flame had all of those,
    Their wings were gold, the rest a sheen of white
    That is unmatched by any of our snows.
When they descended to the flower, from flight
    To flight, they offered peace and ardour gained,
    By that fanning of their sides with wings so bright.   18
Nor did the coming of such swarms, sustained
    Between what was on high and this fair flower,
    Impede the vision of the Splendour that remained,
For light divine so penetrates its power
    Throughout the universe, to the degree
    Of worthiness, that nothing blocks that dower.   24
This safe and joyous realm of monarchy,
    Thronging with old and new folk, near and far,
    Held look and love on one sign they could see.

– O threefold Light which, in a single star,
   Contents them all, in sparkling on their eyes,

30   Look down upon our earthly storms that jar.
If the Barbarians – from the zone that lies
   Where Helice overarches every day,
   Wheeled, with the son she loves, across the skies –
On seeing Rome, her mighty works and sway,
   When the Lateran transcended mortal things,

36   Were dumbstruck there, what, then, of me to say –
Who, to divine, from human reckonings,
   From time, to all eternity had passed,
   From Florence, to just and reasoned gatherings?
In what astoundment was my mind then cast;
   Truly, between all that and this joy amazed,

42   I wished to hear and speak nothing – dumbfast.
And, like a pilgrim renewed, who stood and gazed
   Within the temple of his vow and yearned,
   Looking around, to tell of it unhazed,
So, traversing through the living light, I turned
   My eye along the ranks – up, down – to see,

48   Then round in circles till all was discerned.
Faces persuasive of love were clear to me,
   Adorned by Another's light and their own smile,
   And gestures graced with worth and dignity.
My glance had taken in the form and style
   Of Paradise in general, as a whole,

54   Pausing on no especial part awhile.
I turned, with urge renewed, to ask a scroll
   Of questions to my Lady, concerning things
   Which held in such suspense my mind and soul.
One thing I purposed; another, answer brings.
   I thought to look on Beatrice, but beheld

60   An elder like the glorious in coverings.
His cheeks were streaming and his eyes had welled
   With benign joy; in kindly gestures he came,
   A father in his tenderness impelled.
But 'Where's she gone?' I suddenly exclaim.
   At which he said, 'Beatrice drew me here

66   To you so that your wish should meet its aim.
You'll see her if you look up to that sphere
   That's third from highest rank, upon the throne
   On which her merit assigns her to appear.'

No answer I returned but to that zone
    I raised my eyes and saw her make a crown
    As she reflected the eternal radiance shown.   72
Though plunged beneath the ocean, deepest down,
    No mortal eye is further from the sky
    That thunders highest in the clouds that frown,
Than was my sight from Beatrice, throned on high,
    But that did not perturb me, since I saw
    Her image, clear of medium, reach my eye.   78
'O Lady in whom my hope finds strength to draw,
    Who, for my salvation, did endure
    To leave your footprints right across Hell's maw,
Of all things I've observed, I see the pure
    Grace and its might through power of yours in me,
    And, through your excellence, my eyes are sure.   84
From slavery you drew and made me free
    By all the paths and all the ways that lay
    Within the power of your activity.
Keep your munificence in me so may
    My spirit now that you have made it sound
    Escape the body pleasing you.' – So did I pray.   90
And she, who was at such a distant bound
    As then she seemed, just smiled and looked my way,
    Then back to the eternal Fount turned round.
'To consummate,' the elder started to say,
    'Your journey in perfection – to which end
    Prayer and holy love bade me obey –   96
Run your eyes across this garden; bend
    Your look on it, and that equips your sight
    Easier through divine rays to ascend.
The Queen of Heaven, for whom I am alight
    With love, will grant us every grace required
    Since I'm her Bernard and her faithful knight.'   102
As one who, say, from Croatia has aspired
    To come and see our Veronica, and though
    His old hunger's not satisfied, inquired
In thought the whole time that it was on show:
    'My Lord Jesus Christ, True God, was this
    Then how you looked on earth so long ago?'   108
So I, beholding the living love, in bliss,
    Of him who, in this world by contemplation,
    Tasted that peace in this earth so amiss.

'Son of Grace! This joyous being and station,'
   He started, 'won't become well known to you
114   By pinning all your looks on the foundation.
Look at the circles to remotest view
   Until you see the Queen enthroned, to whom
      This realm is subject, devoted, through and through.'
I raised my eyes and, as at dawn, the gloom
   Of where the sun declines is overpowered
120   By all the oriental regions as they bloom,
So, as from valley up where mountain towered,
   With my own eyes, I saw part of the bound
      Surpassing all the rim with light it showered.
And, as, where we await the chariot's round
   That Phaëton misguided, the part's ablaze,
126   Whereas, on either side, less light is found,
So that pacific oriflamme quickens its rays
   Within the midst; but, out on either side,
      Tempers its radiance in even ways.
More than a thousand angels I descried
   In that part, wings outstretched, in festive mood,
132   And each distinct in light and function plied;
And saw a loveliness that, smiling, viewed
   Their sports and games – she was a joy to each
      And every saint that watched the interlude.
Though, if I had a wealth equal in speech,
   As in conceiving, I'd not dare to try
138   A part of that delight in her to teach.
Bernard, seeing my fixed and eager eye
   Upon the glowing source of his own glow,
Again turned eyes to her with love so high
   He made my own burn more to see and know.

CANTO 32

Bernard enumerates the saints and their positions in the Rose which is divided down the centre into those who precursed Christ and those who came after his birth. Across this division spreads the circle of the infants who are there as a result of the faith of others and their correct observances. Finally Dante is advised to turn in prayer to Mary for the grace to be able to look directly on the Primal Love.

With love to his delight, the contemplative
    And saint freely assumed the office to teach,
    And started, then, this sacred lore to give:
'The wound that Mary closed, anointing the breach,
    Eve, who is so lovely at her feet,
    Opened, and pierced with her hand's reach.   6
And, in the third rank's order, is the seat
    Of Rachel under her, with Beatrice, see,
    Even as your eyes reach out again to meet.
Sarah, Rebecca, Judith, and there sits she
    From whom, descending third, that singer came
    Who, grieving at his sin, cried, 'Pity me!'   12
These, rank by rank, as I announce each name,
    In moving down the Rose, you now may know,
    As petal after petal I proclaim.
From seventh rank more Hebrew women go,
    As to that point they reach, dividing all
    The tresses of the flower, as they show.   18
For these are as a boundary and wall,
    Parting the sacred stairway, in the degree
    That they had looked to Christ who heard their call.
And this side, where the bloom is full, you see,
    In all its petals, sit those who'd believed
    Upon the Christ still yet to come and free.   24
And where the semi-circles still are cleaved
    With vacant seats, upon the other side,
    Are those who saw Christ come, in flesh conceived.
And, as on one side is a great divide
    The Lady of Heaven's throne, and those below
    Create, so, opposite, you see allied   30
That great John's seat, who bore the desert's woe,
    And, ever holy, a martyr's death, and grim
    Hell for two years after that to know.

Extending the distinction under him,
    Are Francis, Benedict, Augustine; and more
36   Progress towards this point from rim to rim.
Now marvel at divine prevision, for
    Both of the aspects of the Faith, as peers,
    Shall cram this garden full of goodly store.
Notice that, down from the central rank that shears
    The two distinctions, those are given place
42   Who have no merit of their own brief years
But have another's – on set conditions' base –
    For these were spirits freed before they could
    Enact true choice within the human race.
You well may see this from their looks, and should,
    Also, by their childlike voices if you observe,
48   And if you listened carefully you would.
Perplexed now in perplexity, you preserve
    Your silence: but I will loosen the tight knot
    In which your subtle thought has lost its nerve.
Within this realm's expanse may be no spot
    For chance, no more may sadness here be found,
54   Nor thirst, nor hunger, find a place or lot,
Because whatever you may see or sound
    Is founded on eternal law all through
    To match exact, as ring to finger's round.
Therefore this gathering, hurried to the true
    Life, are here, and, not without good cause,
60   Higher or lower ranged in order due.
The King – through whom this realm may ever pause
    In such great love, and such a great delight,
    That will has never dared beyond its laws –
As he created minds in his own glad sight,
    So, at his pleasure, he endows them each
66   Diversely; here let fact persuade you right.
And this, express and clear, the Scriptures teach
    And show, concerning those twins whose ire
    Was stirred within their mother's womb and breach.
And so needs must the lofty light attire
    And chaplet them, according to their worth,
72   And to the shades of locks that grace inspire.
Therefore, with no reward for doings on earth,
    They are accorded different ranks and stages,
    According to their primal vision at birth.

And so it is that, in the recent ages,
    To be redeemed – though innocence commend –
    The parents' faith alone suffices and assuages.   78
But, when the first ages reached their end,
    Male children needed to have circumcision
    To make their wings of innocence ascend.
But, in the time of grace, the new provision
    Was only in the pure baptism of Christ,
    Or innocence remained in Limbo's prison.   84
Now look upon the face most like to Christ;
    Its brightness and no other has the power
    To make you worthy to behold the Christ.'
I saw rain down upon that face such shower
    Of joy (carried on sacred minds, created
    For flying through that lofty region's flower)   90
That I was never held by such a bated
    Suspense and wonder by any previous thing;
    Nor seen such likeness to God irradiated.
That loving spirit who came down to sing
    To her 'Hail, Mary, full of grace!' now spread
    His wings before her in his worshipping.   96
The divine canticle was answered, said
    On every side by that most blessèd court
    So that serenity filled each face and head.
'O holy father, who, for my sake, have thought
    To suffer being here, leaving your place
    So sweet that the eternal judgement wrought,   102
Who is that angel gazing in our Queen's face
    And eyes with so much love and such delight
    He seems to be alight and all ablaze?'
So I had turned again for his teaching aright
    Who drew his beauty from Mary as morning star
    Derives it from the sun so fresh and bright.   108
And he: 'Exaltation, gladness are
    In him as much as they may be in soul
    Or angel; and we would have him filled so far
For he's the one who brought the palm to extol
    Mary when God's Son was himself intent
    To bear in full the burden of our role.   114
But follow with your eyes as I present
    In words, and note the great patricians here
    In this most just and holy realm's extent.

Those two who sit up there, most blest, most near,
    Beside our Empress, are as if the two
120   Roots from which our Rose has risen clear.
The next, upon her left, is the father who
    So rashly tasted that the human race,
    Since then, has tasted bitterness and rue.
To right, observe and see the holy face
    Of that ancient Father of the Church to whom
126   Christ gave the keys of this fair flower's grace.
And he who, before his death, saw all the gloom
    Of grievous seasons come to that fair Bride,
    Won by the nails and lance by her good Groom,
Sits at his side, and, on the other side,
    Resides the mighty leader that fed with manna
132   That mutinous, fickle race, and was their guide.
Opposite Peter, see the seat of Anna;
    She sits to gaze upon her Daughter, eyes
    So fixed they turn not even for Hosanna.
Facing the greatest family father, lies
    The seat of Lucy, too, who, when you bent
138   To your destruction, made your Lady rise.
But time, that holds you sleeping, flies, is spent;
    Let's end here as a skilful tailor designing
    According to his cloth the coat he meant.
And, to the Primal Love our sight confining,
    You may so gaze and penetrate your eye
144   As far as possible into His shining.
And yet, in case, in winging up to fly,
    Imagining to soar, you waver short,
    By prayer you must seek grace before you try –
Grace from Her whose power may support;
    And with such love now follow me with care
150   So that your heart not lose my words and thought.'
    Then he began to say this holy prayer:

CANTO 33

Bernard offers a prayer to Mary on Dante's behalf. In answer, she looks into the Light of God to gain acceptance of the prayer. Dante looks into that Light – an experience the memory cannot contain or record. Nevertheless, he has a feeling that he saw the unity and harmony of the entire universe in a single flame of love. He sees eventually a representation of the triune God in a human form. But power of imagination and invention fail him in recording with exactitude his mystical experience. It has unified his will and his desire to move in accord with the Love that moves the stars.

'Virgin Mother, Daughter of your Son,
    Lowly yet exalted more than any being,
    Eternal Wisdom's purpose, fixed and won,
You so ennoble human nature that, seeing,
    Our own Maker scorned not to assume
    Its mould and form, his nature there agreeing.   6
That love was lit again within your womb,
    The love whose warmth, in the eternal peace,
    Has opened out this flower into bloom.
Our noon torch of charity you are, nor cease
    To be – for mortals still upon the earth –
    A living spring of hope and of release.   12
Lady, so great you are, and have such worth,
    That, if there be a person seeking grace
    Elsewhere than you, his hope's a wingless birth.
Your loving-kindness helps all those who place
    Their hope in you, and often before a due
    Request is made, anticipates their case.   18
In you compassion is; pity, in you;
    In you, largesse; as one, in you, is found
    All in creation that's excellent and true.
This man that, from the deepest pit and bound
    Of all the universe, right to this height,
    Has seen the spirits, one by one to sound,   24
Implores you, of your grace, for so much might
    As to be strong enough to lift his gaze
    The higher – to the final bliss of light.
And I – who never was so much ablaze
    For my own vision as his – offer my prayer
    Of prayers and pray, also, its power sways,   30

That you may scatter every clouding air
>   From his mortality through your own pleas
>   So that the supreme joy he yet may bear.
And more I pray, O Queen: after he sees
>   So great a vision, keep his affections pure,
36   Since you may do whatever you will and please.
His human impulses, your care keep sure.
>   Look how Beatrice, and saints how many, bow,
>   Clasp hands to join my prayer and so secure.'
Those eyes, beloved and known to God, their brow
>   Fixed on the praying one, showed us how prayer,
42   Devoutly made, was pleasing to her now.
To the eternal Light, they turned then, where
>   We never could suppose an eye to look
>   So steadily and clearly in the glare.
And I, who drew so near the aim that took
>   All of my yearning, quenched the ardency,
48   As was most meet, of longing that in me shook.
Bernard's smile then signified to me
>   That I should look on high, but my accord
>   Already was as he would have it be,
Because my sight, becoming purged, explored
>   Deeper and deeper into the eternal Ray,
54   The deep Light, true in itself, that poured.
From then, vision was more powerful a way
>   Than discourse which must fail at such a sight;
>   And memory, at such excess, loses sway.
As someone sees in dream, once dream takes flight,
>   Has only passion still impressed, but none
60   Of all the detail comes to mind or light,
Even such am I; an almost vanished one,
>   My vision is; and yet the sweetness that flows
>   Within my heart, from it, is never done.
Thus the snow unseals at the sun's glows;
>   Thus, on the wind was lost, on leaves so light,
66   The wisdom that the Sibyl would disclose.
O Light Supreme, uplifted to such height
>   Above all mortal thoughts, lend to my mind
>   Again a little of what was in my sight!
And give my tongue the power of such a kind
>   That, of your glory, it may leave one spark
72   That all the people yet to come might find,

For, by returning memory something to remark,
    By sounding a little in the lines I write,
    Your triumph will be better known through your clerk.
For in that magnitude of living Light
    That I endured, I had been lost, I hold,
    If I had turned aside from it my sight.   78
As I remember I was made more bold,
    And bore the brilliance of it for so long
    Till my gaze reached the Infinite Good untold.
– O Grace abounding, in which I dared prolong
    My look, and in eternal Light immerse,
    Till power of vision waned at beams so strong.   84
Within its depth I noticed intersperse,
    By love within a single volume bound,
    The scattered leaves of all the universe.
Substance, accident, and relation, found,
    As though together fused, in such a way
    A simple light is what I would expound.   90
I think I saw, of this complex array,
    The universal form, because I feel
    My joy expand in telling what I say.
A single moment makes oblivion conceal
    Deeper for me, than twenty-five centuries wrought
    On Neptune's bafflement at Argo's keel.   96
Thus, in a rapture, was my whole mind caught,
    And fixed immovably intent to gaze,
    And always kindled by the gazing thought.
And, at that Light, a man becomes so he
    Could never turn from it to other sight,
    For that is past all possibility,   102
Because the good, which is the will's right
    Object, is one and whole there; elsewhere
    Is defective what is perfect in that Light.
Now further short shall fall what I declare,
    Even of what my memory can store,
    Than babe whose tongue still bathes in milky fare.   108
Not that the living Light ever had more
    Than one aspect where I fed my sight,
    For it is ever what it was before,
But, as my sight increased in power and might
    The more I looked, the sole appearance changed
    In that I changed in gazing at the Light.   114

In that profound clear ground of light there ranged,
 Before my eyes, three rings of three hues beamed,
 And of the same extent, in light unchanged.
One by the other – as rainbow, rainbow – seemed
 Reflected, and like a fire was the third
120 That, equally from both, was breathed and gleamed.
But oh, how poor and feeble, speech and word!
 How weak to my conception! For what was shown
 Me there, to call this slight, would be absurd!
O Light eternal, self-indwelt alone,
 Only self-understood, self-understanding,
126 And understanding, love and smile on your own!
Those rings that had appeared to me as banding
 Of light reflected, as my eyes conceived,
 Those moments that my vision held their stranding,
Within itself, in self-colour, seemed relieved
 With human image; seeing which, my eye
132 Was wholly dedicated, and there it cleaved.
As the geometer who means to try
 Squaring the circle but cannot find,
 Think as he may, the principle to apply,
Such, at this new sight, was I in mind;
 I would perceive how image could inhere
138 Within the circle yet remain defined.
But my own wings were not sufficient gear
 For that – had not a flash then come to me
 By which what I had wished was made quite clear.
Here, power failed for this high phantasy;
 But, now, as a smooth wheel – without any jars –
144 My will and my desire turned evenly
 Through Love that moves the sun and other stars.

The Illustrations

The half-title illustrations in this book are black-and-white reproductions
of watercolours painted by William Blake (1757–1827) for a series of engravings
for *The Divine Comedy* (1824–7), which he did not live to complete:

Hell, *The Simoniac Pope*
(Watercolour 52.7 x 37.2 cm)
Tate Gallery, London

Purgatory, *Dante and Virgil Ascending the Mountain of Purgatory*
(Watercolour 52.7 x 37.2 cm)
Tate Gallery, London

Heaven, *Dante Adoring Christ*
(Pen, ink and watercolour over pencil and black chalk, 52.7 x 37.2 cm)
Felton Bequest, 1920. National Gallery of Victoria, Melbourne

Index of Proper Names

Abbagliato, 118
Abel, 18
Abraham, 18
Absalom, 114
Abydos, 254
Achan, 223
Acheron, 15, 58, 149
Achilles, 22, 48, 104, 123, 177, 227
Acone, 344
Accorso, Francesco d', 61
Acquacheta, 65
Acquasparta, 330
Acre, 109
Adam, 16, 120, 121, 176, 185, 259, 271
Adige, 47, 208, 316
Adriatic, 366
Aegina, 116
Aeneas, 9, 20, 105, 303
Aeolus, 253
Aesop, 91
Africanus, 260
Agapetus, 303
Agathon, 231
Aglauros, 200
Agnello, 100
Agnolello, 113
Aguglion, 344
Ahasuerus, 209
Ahithophel, 114
Alagia, 220
Alardo, 111
Alba, 304
Alberichi, 345
Alberigo, Fra, 134
Albert, 117, 128, 166, 321, 358
Alcmaeon, 189, 297
Aldobrandesco, Gugliemo, 185
Aldobrandi, Tegghiaio, 64
Alecto, 37
Alessandria, 171
Alessandro, 121
Alessio Interminei, 74
Alexander, 49, 56
Ali, 112
Alichino, 86, 89
Alps, 55, 277
Alta Forte, 115
Amphiaraus, 80
Amphion, 127
Amyclas, 325
Anagni, 223, 402
Ananias, 383
Anastagi, 199
Anastasius, Pope, 44
Anaxagoras, 20
Anchises, 7, 216, 339, 358

Andrea, Jacomo da Sant', 54
Anna, 410
Anselm, 132, 330
Antaeus, 125, 126
Antandros, 304
Antenor, 161
Antenora, 129
Anthony, 398
Antigone, 231
Antiphon, 231
Apennines, 65, 161
Apollo, 283, 287
Apulia, 111, 171
Aquarius, 95
Aquino, 321
Arachne, 67, 189
Aragon, 154
Arbia, 42
Arca, dell', 345
Archiano, 161, 162
Ardinghi, 345
Arethuse, 101
Aretine, 87, 119
Aretino, 164
Arezzo, 117
Argenti, Filippo, 33
Argia, 231
Argive, 113
Argo, 413
Argus, 259
Aristotle, 152
Arius, 334
Arles, 38
Arnaut, 248
Arno, 54, 61, 93, 120, 133, 162, 197, 325
Arrigo, 27
Arrigucci, 345
Arthur, 128
Aruns, 80
Ascesi, 324
Asciano, 118
Asdente, 82
Asopus, 215
Assyrians, 189
Athamas, 119
Athens, 47, 167, 348
Atropos, 134
Attila, 50, 54
Augustine, 322, 330, 408
Aulis, 81
Augustus, 6, 52, 260
Ausonian, 312
Aventine, Mount, 99
Averroës, 20
Avicenna, 20
Azzo, Ugolin d', 199
Azzolino, 49

Babylon, 374
Bacchiglione, 61
Bacchus, 80, 215, 331
Bagnacaval, 200
Bagnorea, 330
Barbagia, 235
Barbariccia, 86, 87, 88, 90
Barbarossa, 216
Barbary, 235
Bari, 312
Barucci, 345
Bears, 156
Beatrice, 10, 11, 164, 171, 203, 214, 215, 236, 250, 264, 268, 269, 271, 272, 275, 278, 284, 287, 294, 295, 298, 299, 301, 302, 307, 315, 320, 323, 335, 337, 340, 343, 347, 348, 351, 352, 364, 370, 371, 372, 373, 375, 376, 379, 382, 385, 388, 389, 399, 402, 404, 405, 407, 412
Beccheria, 130
Bede, 322
Belacqua, 158
Belisarius, 303
Bellincion, 345
Bello, Geri del, 115
Belus, 317
Benaco, 80
Benedetto, San, 65
Benedict, 408
Benevento, 154
Berengar, Raymond, 306
Bergamese, 80
Bernard, 325, 405, 406, 412
Bernardin di Fosco, 199
Bernardone, Pietro, 325
Bertha, Dame, 334
Berti, Bellincion, 341
Bertinoro, 200
Bindos, 397
Bismantova, Mount, 155
Bizenzio, 128
Blacks, 98
Bocca, 129
Bologna, 94, 199
Bolognese, 72, 93, 186
Bolsena, 237
Bonatti, Guido, 82
Bonagiunta, 237
Bonaventura, 330
Boniface, 76, 237
Bonturo, 84
Boreas, 393
Borgo, 346
Born, Bertran de, 114
Borsiere, Guglielmo, 64
Bostichi, 345
Brabant, Lady of, 164

Branca d'Oria, 134
Branda, 121
Brennus, 304
Brenta, 59, 316
Brescian, 80
Briareus, 125, 189
Brigata, 133
Brindisi, 152
Brosse, Pierre de la, 164
Bruges, 59, 222
Brunetto Latini, 59, 61
Brutus, 20, 136, 305
Bryson, 334
Bugia, 317
Bulicame, 57
Buonconte, 161
Buondelmonte, 346
Buondelmonti, 344
Buoso, 102

Caccia, 118
Cacciaguida, 342
Caccianemico, Venedico, 72
Cacus, 99
Cadiz, 389
Cadmus, 101
Caecilius, 231
Caesar, 20, 52, 113, 165, 166, 215,
    247, 283, 303, 304, 305, 317, 344
Cagnano, 316
Cagnazzo, 86, 89
Cahors, 45, 388
Cain, 82, 288
Caina, 23, 128
Calahorra, 328
Calboli, 199
Calcabrina, 86, 90
Calchas, 81
Calfucci, 345
Calixtus, 388
Calliope, 143
Camilla, 7, 20
Camonica, Val, 80
Campagnatico, 185
Campaldino, 161
Campi, 344
Canavese, 171
Capaneus, 56
Capet, Hugh, 222
Capocchio, 118, 119
Caponsacco, 346
Capraia, 133
Caprona, 85
Capulets, 166
Carentana, 59
Carlino, 128
Carlo, 315
Carpigna, Guido di, 199
Carrarese, 80
Casale, 330
Casalodi, 81
Casella, 149

Casentino, 161
Cassino, 368
Cassius, 136, 305
Castel, Guido da, 208
Castor, 156
Castrocaro, 200
Catalano, Friar, 93
Catalonia, 313
Catellini, 345
Cato, 55
Catona, 312
Catria, 366
Cattolica, 113
Caurus, 46
Cecina, 51
Centaur, 48, 49, 50, 99, 100
Ceperano, 111
Cephas, 366
Cerberus, 25, 38
Cerchi, 344
Certaldo, 344
Cervia, 108
Ceuta, 105
Charlemagne, 123, 305, 352
Charles, 77, 161, 187, 222, 305, 313,
    360
Charon, 15, 16
Charybdis, 28
Chiana, 116, 331
Chianghella, 342
Chiassi, 253
Chiaveri, 219
Chiron, 48, 49, 177
Chiusi, 345
Christ, 223, 225, 235, 248, 272, 303,
    318, 325, 328, 329, 337, 357, 358,
    360, 371, 372, 379, 384, 388, 397,
    403, 405, 407, 409, 410
Chrysostom, 330
Ciacco, 26
Cianfa, 100
Cieldauro, 322
Cimabue, 186
Cincinnatus, 342
Circe, 105, 198
Ciriatto, 86, 88
Clemence, 315
Clement, 154
Cleopatra, 22, 305
Cletus, 388
Clio, 230
Clotho, 225
Cluny, 92
Clymene, 347
Cocytus, 58, 126, 134, 136
Colchians, 73
Colchis, 287
Colle, 195
Cologne, 321
Conio, 200
Conrad (Malaspina), 173, 175
Conrad (III), Emperor, 342

Conradin, 222
Consentino, 120
Constance, 154, 171, 294, 297
Constantine, 77, 109, 303
Cornelia, 20, 342
Corneto, 50, 51
Corsica, 215
Corybantics, 57
Cozena, 154
Crassus, 224
Crete, 47, 57
Creusa, 317
Croatia, 405
Cunizza, 316
Cupid, 311
Curio, 113
Currado da Palazzo, 208
Cyprus, 113
Cyrrha, 284
Cyrus, 189
Cytherea, 251

Daedalus, 118
Damian, Peter, 366
Damietta, 57
Daniel, 232, 295, 398
Dante, 263
Danube, 127, 312
David, 18, 114
Decii, 304
Decurion, 88
Deianira, 48
Deidamia, 104, 231
Deiphyle, 231
Delia, 259
Delos, 224
Democritus, 20
Demophoön, 317
Devil, 94
Diana, 196, 244
Dido, 23, 311
Diogenes, 20
Diomedes, 104
Dione, 311, 370
Dionysius, 49, 394
Dioscorides, 20
Dis, 33, 45, 48, 135
Dolcino, Fra, 112
Dominic, 321, 329
Domitian, 231
Don, 127
Donati, Buoso, 120
Donato, Ubertino, 346
Donatus, 330
Douai, 222
Draghignazzo, 86, 88
Duca, Guido del, 199
Duera, 130
Durazzo, 304

Ebro, 249, 317
Egidius, 325

Egypt, 380
Elbe, 170
Electra, 20
Elias, 272
Elijah, 104
Eliseo, 342
Elsa, 276
Elysium, 339
Ema, 346
Empedocles, 20
Empyrean, 9, 331
Ephialtes, 125
Epicurus, 40
Erichtho, 36
Erinyes, 37
Ermo, 161
Erysichthon, 233
Esau, 314
Este, 49, 161
Esther, 209
Eteocles, 104
Ethiop(ia), 97, 358
Euclid, 20
Eunoë, 256, 278
Euphrates, 278
Euripides, 231
Europa, 389
Europe, 175, 303, 328
Eurus, 312
Euryalus, 7
Eurypylus, 81
Eve, 174, 190, 240, 258, 271, 407
Ezekiel, 260

Fabbro, 199
Fabii, 304
Fabricius, 221
Faenza, 130, 199
Falterona, 197
Famagusta, 358
Famine, 131
Fano, 113, 161
Fantolin, 200
Farfarello, 86, 89
Farinata, 27, 41
Felix, 329
Feltro, 7, 316
Ferrara, 316
Fiesole, 60, 342, 346
Fifanti, 345
Figline, 344
Filipeschi, 166
Filippi, 345
Flemings, 59
Florence, 42, 65, 98, 103, 130, 131,
    166, 187, 223, 235, 341, 345, 346,
    348, 397, 404
Focaccia, 128
Focara, 113
Folco, 317
Forese, 234, 235, 239
Forli, 65, 237

Fortuna Major, 217
Fortune, 29, 61, 119, 122
Fosco, Bernardin di, 199
France, 77, 170, 222, 342
Francesca, 24
Francesco d'Accorso, 61
Francis, St, 109, 325, 369, 408
Franco Bolognese, 186
Frederick, 43, 52, 92, 171, 208, 360
Frieslanders, 124
Fucci, Vanni, 98
Furies, 37, 119

Gabriel, 296, 318
Gaddo, 132
Gaeta, 105, 312
Galen, 20
Galeotto, 24
Galicia, 379
Galigaio, 345
Galli, 345
Gallura, 174
Galluzzo, 344
Ganelon, 130
Ganges, 147, 158, 249, 324
Ganymede, 176
Garda, 80
Gardingo, 93
Garisenda, 126
Gascony, 222
Gaville, 102
Gentucca, 238
Gerard, 208
Germany, 67
Geryon, 69, 70, 71, 249
Ghent, 222
Ghibellines, 305
Ghin di Tacco, 164
Ghisolabella, 72
Gideon, 240
Gianni de' Soldanier, 130
Gianni Schicchi, 119
Gilboa, 189
Giotto, 186
Giovanna, 161, 174, 329
Giovanni, San, 75
Giuda, 346
Giuochi, 345
Glaucus, 284
Godfrey, Duke, 352
Gomita, Friar, 89
Gomorrah, 246
Gorgon, 37
Gorgona, 133
Governolo, 81
Graffiacane, 86, 87
Gratian, 321
Greci, 345
Greece, 81
Gregory, 182, 394
Greve, 344
Gualandi, 131

Gualdo, 324
Gualdrada, 64
Gualterotti, 346
Gubbio, 186
Guelfs, 305
Guerra, Guido, 64
Guido, 113, 121
Guido (Cavalcanti), 41, 186
Guido, Count, 345
Guido da Castel, 208
Guido da Prato, 103, 199
Guido del Duca, 199
Guinevere, 343
Guinicelli, Guido, 247
Guiscard, Robert, 111, 352
Guittone, 238, 248

Hannibal, 125, 304
Harpies, 51, 53
Heaven, 14, 15, 19, 27, 36, 38, 44, 46,
    60, 104, 109, 124, 138
Hebrews, 240
Hector, 20, 304
Hecuba, 119
Helen, 22
Helice, 244, 404
Helicon, 258
Heliodorus, 223
Hell, 7, 14, 21, 26, 27, 33, 41, 64, 71,
    89, 99, 103, 111, 112, 117, 136, 137
Hellespont, 254
Henry, 349, 402
Henry of England, 171
Heraclitus, 20
Hercules, 99, 105, 126, 317
Heresiarchs, 39
Hippocrates, 20, 260
Hippolytus, 348
Hispano, Pietro, 330
Holofernes, 189
Homer, 19
Honorius, 325
Horace, 19
Hugh of St Victor, 330
Humbert, 185
Hun, 80
Hungary, 358
Hyperion, 370
Hypsipyle, 73

Iarbas, 267
Icarus, 69
Ida, 57
Ilium, 7, 189
Illuminato, 330
Importuni, 346
Indus, 357
Infangato, 346
Innocent, Pope, 325
Interminei, Alessio, 74
Iole, 317
Iphigenia, 300

Isaiah, 381
Isère, 304
Isidore, 322
Ismene, 231
Ismenus, 215
Israel, 18
Italy, 7, 38, 80, 165, 170, 222, 264, 365, 402

Jacomo da Sant' Andrea, 54
Jacopo Rusticucci, 27, 64
Jacob, 314, 369
James, 171, 272
Janus, 305
Jason, 73, 77, 287
Jehoshaphat, 40
Jephthah, 300
Jerome, 396
Jerusalem, 147, 233, 358, 380
Jesus, 152, 380
Jew, 94, 109, 300, 301, 308
Joachim, 330
Jocasta, 230
John (the Baptist), 54, 120, 232, 295, 343, 407
John (the Evangelist), 260, 272, 295
Jordan, 216, 369
Joseph, 121
Joshua, 223, 318, 352
Jove, 56, 124, 125, 166, 260, 272, 296, 352, 370
Joy, 208
Juba, 55, 305
Judas, 36, 126, 136, 223, 227
Judecca, 137
Judith, 407
Julia, 20
Juno, 119, 327, 392
Jupiter, 353, 387
Justinian, 165, 303
Juvenal, 229

Lacedaemon, 167
Lachesis, 243
Lamone, 108
Lancelot, Sir, 24
Lanfranchi, 131
Langia, 231
Lano, 54
Lapo Salterello, 342
Lapos, 397
Lateran, 109, 404
Latian, 20, 88, 107, 112, 117
Latini, Brunetto, 59, 61
Latona, 224, 320, 370, 395
Laurence, 297
Lavinia, 20, 210, 303
Leah, 251
Leander, 254
Learchus, 119
Leda, 389
Lemnos, 73

Leo, San, 155
Lerici, 152
Lerida, 215
Lethe, 58, 247, 256, 265, 277, 278
Levi, 208
Libicocco, 86, 88
Libya, 97
Lille, 222
Limbo, 18
Limoges, 248
Linus, 20, 388
Livy, 111
Lizio, 199
Loderingo, 93
Logodoro, 89
Loire, 304
Lombard, 6, 89, 107, 165, 349
Louise, 222
Lucan, 19, 101
Lucca, 74, 131, 237, 238
Lucia, 11
Lucifer, 126, 137
Lucretia, 20, 304
Lucy, 177, 410
Luke, 225
Luni, 80, 345
Lycurgus, 247

Macarius, 368
Maccabaeus, 352
Maccabees, 77
Magra, 98, 175, 317
Magus, Simon, 75, 402
Mahomet, 112
Maia, 370
Mainardi, Arrigo, 199
Majorca, 113
Malacoda, 85
Malaspina, Conrad, 175
Malebolge, 71, 83, 96, 116
Malebranches, 134
Malta, 316
Manfred, 154
Mangiadore, Pietro, 330
Manto, 80
Mantua, 6, 10, 81, 165, 168, 170
Marcabo, 113
Marcellus, 166
Marchese, 237
Marcia, 20, 145
Maremma, 99, 116, 162
Margaret, 171
Mark, 206, 208
Mars, 54, 98, 124, 189, 296, 314, 337, 344, 387
Marseilles, 215
Marsyas, 283
Martin, Squire, 334
Mary, 152, 161, 173, 181, 193, 215, 221, 232, 233, 275, 295, 325, 336, 342, 373, 374, 380, 407, 409
Marzucco, 164

Mascheroni, Sassol, 128
Matilda, 278
Matthias, 77
Medea, 73
Medicina, Pier da, 113
Medusa, 37
Megaera, 37
Melchisedek, 314
Meleager, 241
Melissus, 334
Menalippus, 130
Mercury, 296
Metellus, 179
Michael, 28, 296
Michael Scott, 81
Michal, 181
Michel Zanche, 89, 134
Midas, 223
Midian, 240
Milan, 216
Milanese, 174
Mincio, 81
Minerva, 264, 287
Minos, 21, 53, 80, 110, 118, 145, 331
Mira, La, 161
Modena, 305
Moldau, 170
Monaldi, 166
Monferrato, 171
Mongibello, 56
Montagna, 108
Montagues, 166
Montaperti, 129
Montefeltro, 161
Montemario, 341
Montemurlo, 344
Montereggione, 124
Mordecai, 209
Morocco, 105
Moronto, 342
Mosca, 27, 113
Moses, 18, 272, 295, 378, 384
Mucius, 297
Muses, 231, 287, 327
Myrrha, 120

Naiads, 276
Naples, 152
Narcissus, 122
Nasidius, 101
Nathan, 330
Navarre, 88, 358
Nazareth, 318
Nebuchadnezzar, 295
Nella, 235
Neptune, 113, 413
Nerli, dei, 342
Nessus, 48, 49, 51
Niccolo, 118
Nicholas, St, 222
Nicosia, 358
Nile, 136, 238, 304

Nimrod, 125, 189, 386
Nino, 173, 175
Ninus, 22
Niobe, 189
Nisus, 7
Noah, 18, 327
Nocera, 324
Noli, 155
Normandy, 222
Norway, 358
Novello, Federigo, 164

Obizzo, 49
Octavian, 168
Oderisi, 186
Olympus, 237
Orestes, 193
Oriaco, 161
Ormanni, 345
Orpheus, 20
Oria, Branca d', 134
Orso, Count, 164
Ostian, 329
Ottocar, 170
Ovid, 19, 101

Pachynus, 312
Padua, 59, 68, 316
Pagani, 200
Palazzo, Currado da, 208
Palermo, 313
Palestrina, 109
Palladium, 104
Pallas, 189, 304
Paris, 22, 186, 222
Parmenides, 334
Parnassus, 230, 256, 269, 283
Pasiphaë, 246
Paul, 9, 354
Pazzi, Camiscion de', 128
Pazzo, Rinier, 50
Pelorus, 198, 312
Penelope, 105
Pennino, 80
Penthesilea, 20
Pera, della, 346
Persians, 358
Persius, 231
Perugia, 305, 324
Peschiera, 80
Peter, 321
Peter (King), 171
Peter, St, 8, 9, 72, 77, 124, 179, 193,
    226, 272, 318, 326, 354, 369, 379,
    410
Peter the Combseller, 195
Peter Damian, 366
Phaëthon, 69, 156, 406
Pharisees, 93, 109
Pharsalia, 304
Philip, 222
Phlegethon, 58

Phlegra, 56
Phlegyas, 32
Phoenix, 97
Pholus, 48
Photinus, 44
Pia, La, 162
Piave, 316
Piccarda, 237, 292, 297
Piceno, 98
Pietrapana, 127
Pila, Ubaldin dalla, 237
Pilate, 223
Pinamonte, 81
Pisa, 131, 133, 164
Pisistratus, 203
Pistoia, 98, 99
Pius, 388
Plato, 20, 152, 295
Plautus, 231
Plutus, 27, 28
Po, 23, 81, 199, 208, 304, 342
Pola, 38
Polenta, 108
Pollux, 156
Polycletus, 181
Polydorus, 119, 224
Polyhymnia, 372
Polymnestor, 223
Polyxena, 119
Pompey, 304, 305
Ponthieu, 222
Porta Sole, 324
Portugal, 358
Prague, 358
Prato, 103, 199
Pratomagno, 162
Pressa, della, 345
Priscian, 61
Proserpine, 254
Provençal, 222, 306
Provence, 171
Provenzan Salvani, 187
Ptolemy, 20, 304
Ptolomea, 134
Puccio Sciancato, 102
Pygmalion, 223
Pyramus, 250, 276
Pyrrhus, 50, 304

Quarnero, 38
Quinctius, 304
Quirinus, 314

Rabanus, 330
Rachel, 11, 18, 251, 407
Rahab, 318
Raphel, 124
Rascia, 358
Ravenna, 108, 304
Ravignani, 345
Raymond Berengar, 306
Rebecca, 407

Red Sea, 97, 216, 305
Rehoboam, 189
Reno, 72, 199
Renouard, 352
Rhea, 57
Rhine, 304
Rhiphean mountains, 246
Rhone, 38, 304, 312
Rialto, 316
Richard, 322
Rinier, 50, 199
Ripheus, 360
Roland, 123, 352
Romagna, 108, 134, 161
Romagnole, 107, 199, 202
Romans, 61, 71, 304, 357
Rome, 6, 57, 104, 166, 207, 208, 215,
    220, 227, 260, 272, 304, 318, 342,
    376, 388, 404
Romena, 120
Romeo, 306
Romualdus, 368
Rubaconte, 190
Rubicante, 86, 88
Rubicon, 304
Rudolph (Emperor), 170, 313
Ruggieri, Archbishop, 131
Rusticucci, 27, 64

Sabellius, 334
Sabellus, 101
Sabine, 304
Sachetti, 345
Saladin, 20
Salterello, Lapo, 342
Salvani, Provenzan, 187
Samuel, 295
San Leo, 155
San Zeno, 216
Sannella, della, 345
Santafiori, 166
Sant' Andrea, Jacomo da, 54
Santa Zita, 84
Santerno, 108
Sapia, 195
Sapphira, 223
Saracen, 109, 235
Sarah, 407
Sardanapalus, 341
Sardinia, 89, 105, 116, 215
Sassol Mascheroni, 128
Satan, 28, 138
Saturn, 217
Saul, 189
Savena, 72
Savio, 108
Scarmilione, 85
Schicchi, Gianni, 119
Sciancato, Puccio, 102
Scipio, 125, 304, 388
Scott, Michael, 81
Scyros, 177

Sea, Red, 97, 216, 305
Seine, 304, 358
Semele, 119, 363
Semifonte, 344
Semiramis, 22
Seneca, 20
Senigallia, 345
Sennacherib, 189
Serchio, 84
Sestos, 254
Sestri, 219
Seville, 82, 105
Sextus, 50
Shinar, 189
Sibyl, 412
Sichaeus, 22, 317
Sicily, 49, 154
Siena, 162, 185, 186, 187
Siger, 322
Signa, 344
Sile, 316
Simoïs, 304
Simon Magus, 75, 402
Simonides, 231
Sinon, 121
Sismondi, 131
Sixtus, 388
Sizii, 345
Socrates, 20
Sodom, 45, 246, 247
Soldanier, Gianni de', 130
Soldanieri, 345
Sole, Porta, 324
Solon, 314
Soracte, 109
Sordello, 165, 168, 169, 173, 174, 177
Sorgue, 312
Spain, 105, 215, 304, 358
Sphinx, 276
Statius, 227, 229, 240, 242, 250, 270, 278
Stricca, 118
Strophades, 51
Styx, 30, 38, 58
Sultan, 22, 109
Swabia, 294
Sylvester, 109, 325
Sylvius, 9
Syrinx, 271

Tacco, Ghin di, 164
Tagliacozzo, 111
Tagliamento, 316
Talamone, 196
Tambernic, 127
Tarpeia, 179

Tarquin, 20
Tartar, 67
Tebaldello, 130
Tegghiaio, 27
Terence, 231
Thaddeus, 329
Thaïs, 74
Thales, 20
Thames, 50
Thaumas, 226
Thebes, 56, 99, 119, 127, 133, 227
Themis, 276
Theseus, 37, 240
Thetis, 231
Thibault, 88
Thisbe, 250
Thomas, 222
Thomas (Aquinas), St, 321, 330, 335, 346
Thymbraeus, 189
Tiber, 107, 149, 325
Tignosco, Federico, 199
Tigris, 278
Timaeus, 296
Tiresias, 80, 231
Tisiphone, 37
Tithonus, 176
Titus, 227, 305
Tityus, 126
Tobit, 296
Tomyris, 189
Topino, 324
Toppo, 54
Torquatus, 304
Toulousan, 227
Tours, 237
Trajan, 182
Traversaro, Pier, 199
Trent, 47, 80
Trespiano, 344
Trinacria, 312
Tristan, 22
Trivia, 371
Trojan(s), 7, 51, 111, 119
Tronto, 312
Troy, 119, 121, 189
Tully, 20
Turbia, 152
Turnus, 7
Tuscany, 98, 186, 195, 370
Tydeus, 130
Typhoeus, 313
Typhon, 126
Tyrol, 80

Ubaldin dalla Pila, 237

Ubaldo, 324
Ucellatoio, 341
Ughi, 345
Ugolin d'Azzo, 199
Ugolin de' Fantolin, 200
Ugolino, 131, 133
Uguiccione, 133
Ulysses, 104, 218, 389
Urania, 258
Urban, 388
Urbino, 107
Urbisaglia, 345
Utica, 145

Val di Chiana, 116
Val di Greve, 344
Val di Magra, 98, 175
Var, 304
Varro, 231
Vatican, 318
Vecchio, del, 342
Venedico Caccianemico, 72
Venice, 358
Venus, 244, 254
Vercelli, 113
Verde, 154, 312
Vergil, 7, 76, 94, 115, 126, 148, 153, 165, 168, 173, 174, 181, 194, 218, 225, 227, 228, 229, 236, 240, 249, 252, 259, 263, 346, 386
Vernaccian, 237
Verona, 62, 216
Veronica, 405
Verrucchio, 108
Veso, Monte, 65
Vicenza, 316
Victor, St, 330
Vitaliano, 68
Vulcan, 56

Wain, 46, 262
Wenceslas, 170
White, 98
William (II), 360
William (of Orange), 352
William the Marquis, 171
Wissant, 59

Xerxes, 254, 314

Zanche, Michel, 89, 134
Zeno, 20
Zeno, San, 216
Zephyr, 328
Zion, 156, 157
Zita, Santa, 84